The Guinness Book of

Cricket

FACTS AND FEATS

FOURTH EDITION

Bill Frindall

GUINNESS PUBLISHING

First published in 1983
Second edition 1987
Third edition 1991
Fourth edition 1996

Published in Great Britain by Guinness Publishing Ltd, 33 London Road, Enfield, Middlesex

Reprint 10 9 8 7 6 5 4 3 2 1 0

Text design and layout: Mitchell Associates

Cover design: Ad Vantage Studios

Front cover illustrations: Brian Lara, Lord's cricket ground

Printed and bound in Great Britain by
The Bath Press, Bath

'GUINNESS' is a registered trademark of
Guinness Publishing Ltd

British Library Cataloguing in Publication Data
Frindall, Bill 1939–
Cricket facts and feats. – 4th ed.
1. Cricket
I. Title II. Frindall, Bill 1939–.
Guinness cricket facts & feats
796.358

ISBN 0-85112-651-0

Contents

Contents

Preface and Acknowledgements

If one is lucky, perhaps once in a decade a cricketer will arrive on the international stage exhibiting a talent that is immeditely discernible as quite outstanding. For two such rarities to have emerged during the last three years is riches indeed. Brian Lara would probably have dominated most eras but his batting in 1994 was truly remarkable. A pocket-sized left-hander with the fastest pick-up and footwork in memory, he rewrote the major Test match and first-class batting records within a period of exactly 50 days. Not far behind the Trinidadian is the 'Wizard of Oz', Shane Warne, whose exploits have rescued Test cricket from the monotony of all-pace rollerball attacks and spawned a generation of embryo spinners throughout the world.

These contents have been revised to the start of the 1995–96 overseas season and include the 1995 English season which ended on 18 September. During the five years since our previous (third) edition the quantity of international cricket, already near saturation point, has been substantially increased by the reprieve of South Africa and the elevation of Zimbabwe to full ICC member status. In that period, the nine major cricket powers have played the staggering total of 153 Tests and 366 limited-overs internationals, carrying the overall tallies to 1303 Tests and 1001 internationals, an intriguing comparison considering that Test cricket began 94 years before its instant cousin. Clearly the International Cricket Council must regulate the amount of international cricket played, especially the endless succession of limited-overs tournaments played as mini world cups. Commercial greed is threatening the physical well-being of key players and can only devalue the product through overkill.

In Britain the Britannic Assurance county championship has completed its third season in

Bill Frindall

the entirely four-day format without achieving either of its main objectives of providing greater opportunities for spin bowlers and encouraging increased concentration spans for batsmen. Sadly the new format appears merely to have provided Parkinson's Law and done nothing to increase the entertainment factor of our most prestigious competition. Too often the pitches have been too poor or too good to produce a finish on the fourth day. It does not help that the matches are interrupted by a Sunday league thrash in grotesque clothing. Now that limited-overs internationals have been standardised at 50 overs per innings, it is clearly ludicrous that none of our three domestic one-day competitions (two more than deemed necessary by any of the other eight major boards incidentally) is of the requisite length.

Elsewhere the game has been revolutionised

by South Africa's introduction of the video camera to judge line decisions at international level and by Australia's introduction of floodlit cricket to the first-class scene. Importantly both Sri Lanka and Zimbabwe have established domestic first-class competitions at provincial first-class level, a vital basis for the game's development in those countries.

Again I want to emphasise that this is not just a catalogue of records. It is intended to be a rewarding read for those not besotted with statistics; hopefully providing as much interest and entertainment for readers with only the flimsiest interest in cricket as for the game's many *aficionados*.

The Names Index has been compiled as a major feature of this book and includes, where ascertainable, the birth – and death – dates and full names of every cricketer mentioned.

Unless specified otherwise, an asterisk (*) denotes either a 'not out' score or an unbroken partnership. Other symbols are explained where they appear.

I am delighted to have again had the editorial expertise of Beatrice Frei at the helm for this edition. In addition to my acknowledgements in the earlier volumes, sincere thanks are due to my wife, Debbie, and to Philip Bailey, Brian Hunt, Viv Isaacs, Rajesh Kumar, Richard Masters (TCCB), Mohandas Menon, Allan Miller, Harriet Monkhouse, Ken Piesse, Tariq Ali, John Ward and Wendy Wimbush.

BILL FRINDALL
Urchfont, Wiltshire

First Notches

First Notches

ORIGINS

The origins of cricket are obscure, unrecorded, and the source of much speculation. There are two major theories concerning the derivation of the word 'cricket'.

One concerns the Anglo-Saxon word cricce, meaning a crooked staff, ie a staff with a crook or with a club at one end. In the Saxon rendering of the 23rd Psalm, 'Thy staff' appears as 'cricc thin'. Developing this theory results in the supposed origins of the game being among shepherds hitting some appropriate object (a stone or pine cone perhaps) with their crooks and, at the same time, defending the wicket gate into the sheep fold.

The other theory traces the word 'criquet' to the Flemish or Dutch *krickstoel*, a piece of furniture on which one kneels in church. A low stool between 18 inches and 2 feet in length once generally called a 'cricket' in England, its profile is very similar to that of the long, low wicket in early cricket, or of the early stool in stool-ball. The word 'stool' is old Sussex dialect for a tree stump.

Other theories attribute the game's origins to club-ball, where the striker defends a hole in the ground, or to a game played in the churchyard.

EARLIEST REFERENCES

The first probable reference to cricket appears in the Wardrobe accounts for the 28th year of the reign of Edward I (1299–1300), published in 1787 by the London Society of Antiquaries, and first brought to notice by 'H.P.–T' (P.F. Thomas) in *Old English Cricket,* a collection of five pamphlets issued

Cricket in Marylebone Fields by Francis Hayman: the oldest surviving painting of a cricket match, c.1743 (Popperfoto)

The earliest known cricket photograph: Royal Artillery take on the Hunsdonbury Club in 1857 (Popperfoto)

between 1923 and 1929. Thomas's translation of the Latin reads:

'To Master John of Leek, Chaplain of Prince Edward, the King's son, for ready money disbursed for the said Prince's playing at Creag' and other sports, out of his and deputies' hands (was paid) at Westminster, on the 10th day of March (1300) the sum of 100 shillings. And to his Chamberlain Hugo, at Newenton, in the month of March 20 shillings. In all £6.'

The apostrophe after Creag is a shorthand method of showing the diminutive 'et'. 'Creaget', probably pronounced 'craiget', was almost certainly cricket; no alternative explanation has ever been offered. Prince Edward, the first Prince of Wales who was to become Edward II, was 16 years old in 1300. A Gascon youth, Piers Gaveston, was maintained at Court to provide company for the young prince. If Newenton was the village of Newenden in the Weald on the Kent/Sussex border of today, this document would show that Prince Edward and his friend were the first pair of known cricketers and that the Weald was its first known ground.

The first certain reference to cricket is contained in a document dated December 1478 and refers to **'criquet'** near St Omer, in what is now north-eastern France.

The earliest certain reference to cricket being played in England occurs in a document dated 16 January 1598, recording the evidence of John Derrick in a court case concerning a disputed piece of land in Guildford, Surrey. Then aged 59 and a coroner, Derrick attested that 'when he was a scholler in the free school of Guldeford, he and several of his fellowes did runne and play there at krickett and other plaies'. This means that cricket was being played there in the 1550s, just before the reign of Elizabeth I.

The earliest known dictionary to mention cricket was *A Worlde of Words*, compiled by Giovanni Florio, an Italian then living in England, and published in 1598. His Italian/English translation of *sgrillare* was 'to play cricket-a-wicket, to make merry'. In 1611, Randle Cotgrave's French English dictionary (the first such ever compiled) translated *crosse* as a 'crosier', or 'Bishop's staffe', also a 'cricket-staffe', or the 'crooked staffe wherewith boys play at cricket'.

The first recorded cricket match took place at Coxheath in Kent in 1646. This match also produced the first record of betting on cricket.

The earliest known reference to cricket being played abroad dates back to 1676 and is contained in the diary of a naval chaplain, Henry Teonge, who had visited Aleppo in what is now Syria:

'May 6, 1676. This morning early (as it is the custom all summer longe) at the least 40 of the English, with his worship the Consull, rod out of the cytty about 4 miles, to the Greene Platt, a fine vally by a river-syde, to recreate themselves. Where a princely tent was pitched; and we had several pastimes and sports, as duck-hunting, fishing, shooting, hand-ball, krickett, scrofilo . . .'

The first full description of a cricket match appeared in a Latin poem *In certamen pilae*, written by William Goldwin of Eton and King's College, Cambridge.

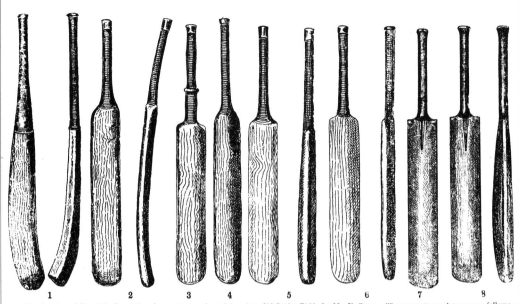

The drawings of Bats **1** to **6** are taken, by permission, from *Echoes from Old Cricket Fields*, by Mr. F. GALE. The approximate dates are as follow:— No. **1**, *1743*; No. **2**, weighing 5 lbs., *1771*; No. **3**, *1790*—this is a double-handed bat, and belonged to Robinson, a man with a crippled hand, who wore an iron strapped on to his wrist; No. **4**, marked on the back *1792*, and named " Little Joey," belonged to Ring of Dartford, an old Hambledon man, to whose style of play is attributed the origin of the law l-b-w; No. **5**, weighing about 2⅞ lbs., *1860*; No. **6**, marked on back with brass brads *1827*—belonged to John Bowyer, and weighed about 2⅝ lbs.; Nos. **7** and **8** are in my possession, and are of present date: they weigh 2 lbs. 5½ ozs., and illustrate the plan of splicing, No. **7** in addition showing the whale-bone. Figures **1, 2, 5, 6,** and **8,** show the front and edge of bat, and figures **3, 4,** and **7,** front only.

BATS—OLD STYLE AND THE NEW.

Tracing the evolution of the cricket bat from the mid 18th century (Popperfoto)

The first match between two counties took place on 29 June 1709 when Kent played Surrey at Dartford Brent.

The first great match of which the full score has survived was played between Kent and All-England on the Artillery Ground near Finsbury Square, London, on 18 June 1744.

The first cricket illustration was drawn by a Frenchman, Hubert d'Anville Bourguignon dit Gravelot (1699–1773) during his few years in England and was published on 7 May 1739 as *The Game of Cricket*. Depicting youngsters playing, it was one of a small collection of children's games and was re-issued in France 20 years later as *Le jeu de la crosse*.

The oldest surviving painting of a cricket match is *Cricket* in *Marylebone Fields* by Francis Hayman, R.A. (1708–76) and dates from *c* 1743. It was used for the illustration of the earliest printed version of the 1744 code of the Laws, on a handkerchief now in the MCC collection.

The earliest known cricket photographs were taken in 1857 by Roger Fenton at the Artillery Ground when the Royal Artillery played Hunsdonbury.

EVOLUTION OF MODERN CRICKET

THE BAT

The earliest bats were sticks and, probably, shepherds' crooks. These gave way to clubs and clubbed sticks before the introduction of the *batte*, with its long, thin shaft and curved thicker end not unlike a slightly straightened-out hockey stick. The clubbed design of these first bats was dictated by the type of bowling encountered, which was similar to that in the game of bowls – underarm and all along the ground.

By the early 18th century the batte had developed into a longer, heavier, curved version of the modern item; it had a handle and a blade but was carved out of a single piece of wood.

The oldest surviving cricket bat is inscribed 'J.C. 1729' – J.C. was John Chitty of Knaphill – and can be seen at The Oval.

There has never been any restriction on a bat's weight. Some used in the 1770s weighed as much as

5 pounds and many 19th-century players used 4-pound bats. The average weight of a modern bat is 2 pounds 5 ounces.

The bat used today consists of a willow blade with a cane handle (invented *c* 1853), layered with thin strips of rubber and bound with twine. This is covered by a tight rubber sheath – the grip. The 'V' shaped extension of the handle into the blade is the splice.

Until Thomas ('Shock' or 'Daddy') White of Reigate took guard with a bat wider than the wicket in 1771, there was no restriction on the implement's dimensions. Following White's inventiveness, the Hambledon Club, who were then the game's law-givers, limited the bat's width to 4½ inches. They constructed an iron gauge through which any suspect bat had to pass. White, incidentally, does not appear to have suffered any severe remorse as he lived actively until 1831 when he was 91.

The bat's length has been limited to 38 inches (96.5 cm) since 1835 and its maximum width is now 4¼ inches (10.8 cm).

THE BALL

Earliest cricket was played with stones, pieces of wood and probably sundry other available missiles. **The first 'manufactured' ball** was made by interlacing narrow strips of hide and was first mentioned in 1658.

The first six-seamed ball was made in 1775 by Dukes, a family firm at Penshurst in Kent, who presented it to the Prince of Wales (later King George IV).

The ball's colour is first mentioned in 1753 in *Sevenoke: A poem* which describes a match on the Sevenoaks Vine ground and refers to 'the crimson ball'. Probably by accident the colour at the opposite end of the spectrum from green was adopted, but this happens to be the perfect contrast as the human eye cannot focus the two colours simultaneously.

Balls are made of hand-stitched leather quarters dyed red, covering an interior of cork wound round with twine.

Dimensions have altered little. The 1744 code laid down merely that 'ye ball must weigh between 5 and 6 ounces'. The present weight of between 5½ and 5¾ ounces (155.9 and 163 g) was established in 1774. The circumference was established as between 9 and 9¼ inches in 1838. This was changed to the present measurements of between 8¹³/₁₆ and 9 inches (22.4 and 22.9 cm) in 1927, to legalize the smaller ball that had been used for some years without anyone noticing.

The oldest surviving cricket ball in the Lord's collection was used in the MCC v Norfolk match of 1820, when William Ward scored 278, the highest innings at Lord's until 1925.

THE STUMPS

Wickets in the early 17th century were up to 6 feet wide and often under 12 inches high. By 1700 they had narrowed to 2 feet wide and 1 foot high.

The third stump is believed to have been introduced in 1775 when Hambledon Players were engaged in a match in London. Not until 1785 did the third stump become mandatory.

By 1775 the wicket had narrowed to 6 inches and was 22 inches high. After being increased to 24 x 7 inches in 1798, an additional 2 inches was added to its height in 1819, and a further inch to both dimensions in 1823. No other tampering occurred until 1931. Then, in response to a general horror of high scores and drawn matches in the county championship, the wicket was enlarged by one inch in both directions. Although various experiments have taken place behind the scenes, including one involving a fourth stump, today's wickets are the same measurement as those of 1931, namely 28 inches (71.1 cm) high and 9 inches (22.86 cm) wide.

THE BAILS

The wicket in its early form carried only one bail, sometimes several feet long. The first mention of two bails for each wicket occurred in 1786 when an 'unofficial' version of the Laws was issued in Maidstone. Each bail must be 4⅜ inches (11.1 cm) long and, when in position on top of the stumps, must not project more than ½ inch (1.3 cm) above them.

THE PITCH

The first known measurement for the length of the pitch wicket-to-wicket is the 23 yards given in the 1727 Articles of Agreement between the second Duke of Richmond and Mr Brodrick of Peper Harow in Surrey

The 1744 code stipulates 22 yards (20.12 m), a distance which has remained steadfast for more than two centuries despite the vast and fundamental changes in the techniques of bowling and batting. It is also the length of the agricultural chain invented by Gunter in the early 17th century and derived from four rods, poles or perches.

THE LAWS

The first known Laws were issued in 1744 as a result of a meeting of 'the London Star and Garter' Club.

This was a full set of Laws and the ones under which Kent played All-England in the first match for which the full score has survived.

The earliest known documented playing regulations are to be found in a copy of the 1727 Articles of Agreement between the Duke of Richmond and Mr Brodrick. These were really instructions to the umpires and team managers, and they obviously were an attempt to clarify certain points of dispute arising from an earlier full code of Laws which has not been found.

The first 'Laws' of which any documentary evidence exists are two which have survived from the 17th century: a batsman could be out 'caught', and, if he was in danger of being caught, he could charge down the fielder attempting the catch.

In 1755 the Laws were revised by the 'Star and Garter' Club, some of whose members were to form (c 1782) the White Conduit Club, which was to merge with the new Marylebone Cricket Club in 1787.

The MCC holds the world copyright of the 'Laws of Cricket' and the Club's permission is required before they can be reprinted.

The latest revision was drafted by S.C. ('Billy') Griffith, Secretary of the MCC 1962–74, and was issued as a new code in 1980.

An early scorecard records the events of the Grand Match between 11 of England and 33 of Norfolk in 1797 (Allsport)

SCORING AND RECORDS

The earliest method of scoring did not involve paper and pen but the cutting of notches in wooden staves. Every tenth notch was cut larger than the previous nine to facilitate a tally at the end of the innings.

No doubt there were other ingenious methods. Certainly none could match the simplicity of an early West Indian method whereby leaves were put into a hat during the first innings and removed during the second. Either one run was required for victory when the hat was emptied or the winning margin of runs remained in it when the last wicket fell.

The first great match of which a full score survives was played on 18 June 1744 between Kent and All-England on the Artillery Ground, London. The score also survives of a less important match played a few days earlier.

The first known stroke-by-stroke score of a match was kept on 31 August 1769 when the Duke of Dorset's XI played Wrotham. It included the first known century, 107 by John Minshull who batted at number three. Soon afterwards, the Duke engaged Minshull as his gardener at 8 shillings a week.

The first recorded hundred partnership was scored in 1769: 128 for the first wicket by Thomas Sueter and George Leer for Hampshire against Surrey at Broadhalfpenny Down, Hambledon.

The first record of a bowler being credited with a catch off his own

bowling appeared in 1777. In the same year James Aylward scored 167 for Hampshire against England and batted on all three days. This was the highest score in an important match until 1820 and Hampshire's total of 403 was the first on record of 400.

The first recorded lbw dismissal is to be found in the scores of the match between Surrey and Thirteen of England at Moulsey Hurst on 12–15 August 1795. Batting at number three for England, the Hon John Tufton was lbw b Wells 3. Previous lbw dismissals had been recorded as 'bowled'.

The first evidence of a full bowling analysis being kept including maiden overs for the first time, is in the scores of the match between Yorkshire and Norfolk at Hyde Park, Sheffield, on 14–18 July 1834.

Wides were first recorded as such in 1827, three years before no-balls. Not until 1848 did the first leg-bye go on record. Wides (introduced in 1816) had been treated as byes, and no-balls as 'dead'.

The earliest known matchcard or scorecard was printed by the Sevenoaks Vine scorer for the match between Kent and Hampshire in 1776.

The telegraph scoreboard was introduced at Lord's in 1846, scorecards being sold there that season also for the first time.

Although scoreboards showing extended batting details had been used in Australia for many seasons before, the first board to give full bowling analyses as well did not appear until that designed by E.J. ('Ned') Gregory was brought into use in 1895. Gregory, the eldest of five brothers who played for New South Wales, played in the first-ever Test match and made the first duck in Test cricket. A useful right-handed all-rounder, he became curator of the Sydney Cricket Ground.

The standard technique of scoring has changed little over the years and is still used by most official scorers employed by first-class teams. A far more informative method is that invented in 1905 by W.H. Ferguson, the Australian scorer who recorded 208 Test matches and acted as scorer and baggage-master for Australia, England, South Africa, West Indies and New Zealand on 43 tours. 'Fergie's' lineal method involved vertical foolscap sheets with columns for each batsman and for each bowling end. Each line across the columns is one over, starting with a record of the time when it begins. All the action is noted in the column of the batsman facing the bowling, and various columns of totals are completed at the end of each over. From this system it is possible to tell who bowled each ball, at what time, from which end, to which batsman, and, with the aid of various symbols, exactly how it was dealt with. This is the system which radio and television scorers have used since the introduction of ball-by-

ball broadcasting in 1957.

The first radial scoring chart was devised in 1905 by Bill Ferguson while he was official scorer for Australia in England and on his first overseas tour.

The first cricket annual was published in 1791 by Samuel Britcher. Containing full scores of important and other matches for each season, Britcher's books of scores appeared regularly until 1805. Seasonal batting averages were not published until 1793.

BOWLING

Originally bowling in cricket was exactly the same as the bowling in bowls, with the ball rolled underarm along the ground. This method of bowling was unchallenged by experiment until the middle of the 18th century. Some time after 1744 bowlers began to pitch the ball and two new weapons, length and direction, had been added to their armoury. Before the advent of lob bowling the only variation possible had been in the degree of speed at which the ball travelled along the ground. Batsmen did not need to move their feet; they simply stood where they were, swung their long clubbed sticks and despatched the ball like golfers. The introduction of pitching compelled the batsman to play forward or back. It was arguably the most significant technical advance in the entire evolution of cricket.

One historian, G.B. Buckley, has suggested that during the 1744 match between Kent and England, the first match for which we have the complete scores, the ball was 'thrown' so that it described a low but airborne trajectory before bouncing. If so, then that match, already historically important, also marked the inception of length bowling at the highest playing level.

By 1773 length bowling had replaced true bowling. It soon led to further experiments. In the 1780s Thomas Walker of Hambledon tried out a form of round-arm delivery but was specifically warned against it. Gradually others tried to bowl it and in 1816 a Law was introduced to prohibit it:

'The ball must be bowled (not thrown or jerked), and be delivered underhand, with the hand below the elbow. But if the ball be jerked, or the arm extended from the body horizontally, and any part of the hand be uppermost, or the hand horizontally extended when the ball is delivered, the Umpire shall call "No Ball".'

Opponents of round-arm bowling feared that it would restrict scoring and lead to an imbalance in favour of the bowler. Statistics were to prove them right.

The first exponent of round-arm bowling was

Sussex play host to county neighbours Kent, pioneers of overarm bowling, at Brighton in 1849 (Allsport Historical Collection)

probably John Willes of Kent. He used to practise batting against the bowling of his sister, Christina. Because of her full skirt of the period she could only deliver the ball round-arm and Willes found it very difficult to play. When he opened the bowling round-arm for Kent against the MCC at Lord's on 15 July 1822, he became **the first bowler in the game's history to be no-balled for throwing.** *Bell's Life* describes him leaving the ground 'in high dudgeon' and his place had to be taken by another player.

By 1827 many bowlers had tried out the round arm method and the Sussex pair, William Lillywhite and James Broadbridge, had perfected it. Three experimental matches that season between Sussex and England, in which the effect on scoring was studied, led to the MCC authorizing round-arm bowling the following year. Bowlers were allowed to raise their hand level with their elbow. The change was incorporated into a revision of the Laws in 1835 but with 'shoulder' replacing 'elbow'.

Some were already experimenting with overarm bowling and it was frequently employed in matches when the umpires allowed. Edgar Willsher of Kent was **the first to be no-balled for bowling overarm,** by John Lillywhite at The Oval on 26 August 1862. Opening England's bowling against Surrey, he was called six times and the England team left the field causing play to be abandoned for the rest of the day.

Lillywhite refused to change his mind and was replaced as umpire for the final day. Thus reprieved, Willsher took 6 for 49.

Overarm bowling was legalized when an amendment to the Laws was passed on 10 June 1864. It did not lead to a wholesale overnight change in bowling actions. Most raised their arms to shoulder height. The 1878 Australians were **the first team to employ a specialist overarm attack** and another decade was to pass before the new style became prevalent.

The first underarm bowler to spin the ball deliberately was Lamborn who played just five seasons for Surrey and England (1777–82). No one knew his first name and he was always called 'The Little Farmer'. He invented the off-break by bowling for hours at a time against hurdles while tending his father's sheep. 'He was, it is believed, a Surrey man; but his christian name, native village, date of death, and age, could not be discovered. He was a regular country bumpkin, a very civil and inoffensive young fellow, but did not continue the game long, why is not recorded.' (*Scores and Biographies*)

The only other bowler known to have invented a new type of delivery was Bernard Bosanquet, the Middlesex and England all-rounder who introduced the 'googly' to the first-class game at Lord's in 1900. An off-break bowled with a leg-break action, it is known in Australia as the 'Bosie'.

OTHER IMPORTANT NOTCHES

Two Clubs have influenced the game more than any others: **Hambledon** and the **MCC**.

Formed in about 1767, **the Hambledon Club** with its ground on Broadhalfpenny Down, a strip of Hampshire heathland high above the village of Hambledon a mile away, was the centre of the cricketing world for more than two decades. Most of the Club's founders were old boys of Westminster School, influential gentlemen who were able to attract wealthy patrons to the game. The Hambledon Club became adept at promoting important matches and the great sides of the day, England, Sussex and Kent, were regular visitors. Frequently they were defeated by a team that was generally called Hampshire although it has been subsequently listed in some publications as Hambledon.

The Marylebone Club was formed in the late 18th century as an offshoot of a club at the Star and Garter tavern in Pall Mall, London, whose members frequented the White Conduit House and played cricket in the adjoining fields near Islington. Thomas Lord, a Thirsk-born Yorkshireman employed at the White Conduit Club as a bowler and general attendant, was persuaded to start a new private ground at what is now Dorset Square. It staged its first great match on 31 May-1 June 1787 when Middlesex defeated Essex. When the lease ended after the 1810 season, Lord had already moved his turf, so that 'the nobleman and Gentlemen of the MCC' should be able 'to play on the same footing as before', to a field at North Bank Regent's Park, on the St John's Wood Estate. In 1813 a third and final ground had to be found when Parliament decreed that the Regent's Canal would be cut through the middle of Lord's field. Now on its present site in St John's Wood, Lord's much-travelled turf staged its third great inaugural match on 22 June 1814 when the MCC beat Hertfordshire by an innings.

The present practice ground, 'The Nursery', was bought in the Club's centenary year, 1887. It had been the site of Henderson's Nursery Gardens and famous for its tulips and pineapples.

From its earliest days the MCC appears to have assumed, and have been conceded, lawmaking powers. The habitués of the Star and Garter tavern, who became known as the White Conduit Club, had revised the Laws in 1755 and 1774. When they formed the MCC the accepted powers of legislation were transferred to the new Club. Its membership, in terms of social status, patronage of the game and playing distinction, commanded universal and unrivalled prestige as the game's sole authority.

In 1903 the MCC became responsible for selection and administration of all overseas tours. Until the 1977–78 season, England teams overseas played under the MCC banner except during official Test matches.

In 1898 the MCC established The Board of Control at the request of the counties to administer Test cricket in England. In 1904 they were similarly invited to form an Advisory County Cricket Committee to provide an equivalent service for county cricket. In 1968 both bodies were replaced by the Test and County Cricket Board (TCCB) under the newly-constituted Cricket Council. The latter was formed as a democratic official body which the Government could recognize and thus grant financial aid to, for the game's development through the new Sports Council.

The Imperial Cricket Conference was founded at Lord's on 15 June 1909 by representatives of cricket in England, Australia and South Africa. Hosted and secretarially administered by the MCC until 1993, its membership was originally confined to the governing bodies of Test-playing countries within the British Commonwealth and met annually at Lord's to discuss current problems affecting the well-being of cricket.

The ICC has subsequently undergone two changes of title but has retained its original initials. On 15 June 1965 it became the **International Cricket Conference** and agreed to allow the election of countries from outside the Commonwealth. Associate members were admitted but were entitled to just one vote apiece on ICC resolutions whereas Foundation and Full Members were each granted two votes. On 12–13 July 1989 it was renamed the **International Cricket Council** and revised its voting procedures.

The ICC became an organization independent of the MCC on 7 July 1993, appointed its own administration (still housed at Lord's) and abolished the category of Foundation Member.

India, New Zealand and West Indies were elected Full members on 31 May 1926, to be joined by Pakistan (28 July 1952), Sri Lanka (21 July 1981) and Zimbabwe (8 July 1992). South Africa's membership lapsed when the Union left the Commonwealth in May 1961 but was elected as a Full member on 10 July 1991.

Associate membership, designed for countries (or areas) where cricket is firmly established and organized, was granted to Fiji and USA in 1965, Bermuda, Denmark, Holland, and East and Central Africa in 1966, Malaysia in 1967, Canada in 1968, Gibraltar and Hong Kong in 1969, Papua and New Guinea in 1973, Argentina, Israel and Singapore in

1974, West Africa in 1976, Bangladesh in 1977, Kenya in 1981, United Arab Emirates in 1990, Namibia in 1992, Ireland in 1993, Scotland in 1994 and Italy in 1995.

Affiliate membership, for countries or areas where ICC recognizes that cricket is played according to the Laws of Cricket, carries no voting rights. The twelve Affiliate members are Switzerland (1985), the Bahamas and France (1987), Nepal (1988), Japan (1989), Belgium and Germany (1991), Austria, Brunei and Spain (1992), and Greece and Vanuatu (1995).

The first overseas cricket tour was to have been undertaken in August 1789 by an English team to Paris. The Duke of Dorset, a great patron of cricket responsible for many matches at Hambledon and elsewhere, was Ambassador in Paris when the French Revolution began. He asked the Duke of Leeds, another cricket enthusiast who was then Foreign Secretary, for an assurance of goodwill to France from the British Government. The tour seems to have been arranged as a 'goodwill' visit. The project was abandoned when the team, arriving at Dover, were confronted by the sight of the Duke of Dorset fleeing from his post.

The first touring team actually to reach its objective overseas was the English expedition to Canada and the United States in the autumn of 1859. Organized by Fred Lillywhite, it was captained by George Parr, William Clarke's successor as leader of the All-England Eleven, and included John Wisden, founder of the rival United All-England Eleven. Six players from each of those professional Elevens constituted the 12-man touring team which left Liverpool on 7 September and arrived, via storms, icebergs, gales, fog and seasickness, in Quebec on 22 September. **The first match involving an overseas touring team** was played at Montreal on 24–27 September 1859 between 22 of Lower Canada and 11 of England, the tourists winning by eight wickets. Having won all its five matches, the team returned to England on 11 November after travelling approximately 7500 miles in slightly over two months. The expedition prompted the publication of the first 'tour book', *The English Cricketers' Trip to Canada and the United States in 1859* by Fred Lillywhite.

The first match between teams from two different countries was played between Toronto Cricket Club and St George's Cricket Club of New York in 1840, the latter winning by ten wickets.

Left, facing page: Commemorating the tour undertaken by an England party in 1859, this illustration shows the organiser, Fred Lillywhite, scoring in his tent (Popperfoto)

The first international match was played between the United States and Canada, involving players from the same two clubs who contested the 1840 encounter, in New York in 1844. It was played for a $1000 stake and won by Canada by 23 runs.

The first overseas team to visit England arrived from Australia in 1868 and played 47 matches (14 wins, 14 defeats, 19 draws) between 25 May and 17 October. The team, the first Australian sportsmen to play overseas, was organized, promoted, coached, managed and captained by Charles Lawrence, an all-rounder who, after occasional appearances for Surrey, Middlesex and the All-England Eleven, had been a member of **the first English expedition to Australia** in 1861–62. He had accepted an invitation to coach the newlyfounded Albert Club in Sydney and to play for New South Wales. The 13 Australians he brought to England in 1868, just four years after overarm bowling had been legalized, were all Aborigines. Their playing attire included white flannels and red Garibaldi shirts with blue sashes and neckties.

They gave many exhibitions of their native skills: dressed in possum skin they staged various field and track events (flat sprints, hurdling, high jumping, pole-vaulting, water bucket races), as well as demonstrating the art of throwing spears, boomerangs, and 'kangaroo rats' (a 2-foot handle with a knob on the end used for bringing down birds or small animals). Their native names and the nicknames under which they played were:

Arrahmunijarrimun	Peter
Ballrinjarrimin	Sundown
Bonnibarngeet	Tiger
Brimbunyah	Red Cap
Brippokei King	Cole
Bullchanach	Bullocky
Grongarrong	Mosquito
Jallachmurrimin	Jim Crow
Jungunjinanuke	Dick-a-Dick
Murrumgunarriman	Twopenny
Pripumuarraman	Charley Dumas
Unaarrimin	Mullagh
Zellanach	Cuzens

Only ten of the Aborigines completed the arduous tour. King Cole died of tuberculosis in Guy's Hospital, London, on 24 June, and Sundown and Jim Crow returned in August. Their departure left a tremendous workload for the survivors. Red Cap and Tiger played in all 47 matches, a record for any tour.

That historic first tour was commemorated in 1988 by a 28-match visit from the fledgling Aboriginal Cricket Association, an organization dedicated to gaining Australian Test selection for Aborigines.

ENGLAND'S LOST MAN

Of the 576 players to represent England in Test matches since 1877 there is only one for whom no known photograph exists: Reginald Wood. As his Test career involved just one match in which he scored 6 and 0 and was not invited to bowl, it is scarcely surprising that he has become the lost man of English cricket.

Chance played a vital role in his selection. Born in Cheshire in 1860 and educated at Charterhouse, he was a left-handed all-rounder whose medium-pace bowling had captured 95 wickets at 7.1 for the school in 1876. After appearing for Lancashire, as an amateur, in six matches spread over five seasons, he emigrated to Melbourne and played for Victoria against Alfred Shaw's England Eleven in November 1886. Wood happened to be in the right place when Shaw's meagre touring party was seriously depleted by their key all-rounder, Billy Barnes, damaging his

hand when a punch aimed for the Australian captain, Percy McDonnell, had connected with a wall. Wood was immediately co-opted into the visitors' team for three matches including the Second Test and a return match with Victoria, appearances which marked the pinnacle and end of his bizarre first-class career. He thus became the only player either to gain his initial selection for England straight from State cricket, or to play both for and against a State and a touring team in the same season.

Just eight days after his final first-class appearance, the ubiquitous Wood umpired a four-day match at the East Melbourne ground (where he just happened to be employed as coach) between Smokers and Non-Smokers, the latter scoring 803, then the highest total in all first-class cricket. The photograph below, kindly supplied by Ross Peacock, Librarian to the Melbourne Cricket Club, shows 22 players and umpire James ('Dimboola Jim') Phillips. It is just possible that Reg Wood is one of the unidentified shadowy background figures but perhaps we will never know.

The scoreboard shows the Non-Smokers' total of 803 as their opponents, the Smokers, join them for a photograph. Identified in the back row, left to right: Worrall, Bruce, Briggs, Lillywhite, Conway; seated at rear: Scotton, Shaw, Shrewsbury, Phillips, Houston, Cooper, Sherwin, Palmer, Boyle, Flowers; steps, next to front: Lewis, Read, Lohmann, Walters; front: Musgrove, Gunn, Bates, Browning (Melbourne Cricket Club)

Test Cricket

Test Cricket

Key to abbreviations

A	Australia
E	England
I	India
NZ	New Zealand
P	Pakistan
SA	South Africa
SL	Sri Lanka
WI	West Indies
Z	Zimbabwe
*	not out (unless otherwise stated)

Captains Kepler Wessels (South Africa, left) and Richie Richardson (West Indies) at the start of the historic match in 1992 which marked the South Africans' return to Test cricket (Allsport/Shaun Botterill)

RESULTS SUMMARY OF ALL TEST MATCHES
to 7 September 1995

	Opponents	Tests	Won by									Tied	Drawn
			E	A	SA	WI	NZ	I	P	SL	Z		
England	Australia	285	90	111	-	-	-	-	-	-	-	-	84
	South Africa	105	47	-	19	-	-	-	-	-	-	-	39
	West Indies	115	27	-	-	48	-	-	-	-	-	-	40
	New Zealand	75	34	-	-	-	4	-	-	-	-	-	37
	India	81	31	-	-	-	-	14	-	-	-	-	36
	Pakistan	52	14	-	-	-	-	-	7	-	-	-	31
	Sri Lanka	5	3	-	-	-	-	-	-	1	-	-	1
Australia	South Africa	59	-	31	13	-	-	-	-	-	-	-	15
	West Indies	81	-	32	-	27	-	-	-	-	-	1	21
	New Zealand	32	-	13	-	-	7	-	-	-	-	-	12
	India	50	-	24	-	-	-	8	-	-	-	1	17
	Pakistan	37	-	12	-	-	-	-	10	-	-	-	15
	Sri Lanka	7	-	4	-	-	-	-	-	0	-	-	3
South Africa	West Indies	1	-	-	0	1	-	-	-	-	-	-	-
	New Zealand	21	-	-	12	-	3	-	-	-	-	-	6
	India	4	-	-	1	-	-	0	-	-	-	-	3
	Sri Lanka	3	-	-	1	-	-	-	-	0	-	-	2
	Pakistan	1	-	-	1	-	-	-	0	-	-	-	-
West Indies	New Zealand	26	-	-	-	9	4	-	-	-	-	-	13
	India	65	-	-	-	27	-	7	-	-	-	-	31
	Pakistan	31	-	-	-	12	-	-	7	-	-	-	12
	Sri Lanka	1	-	-	-	0	-	-	-	0	-	-	1
New Zealand	India	32	-	-	-	-	6	12	-	-	-	-	14
	Pakistan	36	-	-	-	-	4	-	16	-	-	-	16
	Sri Lanka	13	-	-	-	-	4	-	-	2	-	-	7
	Zimbabwe	2	-	-	-	-	1	-	-	-	0	-	1
India	Pakistan	44	-	-	-	-	-	4	7	-	-	-	33
	Sri Lanka	14	-	-	-	-	-	7	-	1	-	-	6
	Zimbabwe	2	-	-	-	-	-	1	-	-	0	-	1
Pakistan	Sri Lanka	14	-	-	-	-	-	-	8	1	-	-	5
	Zimbabwe	6	-	-	-	-	-	-	4	-	1	-	1
Sri Lanka	Zimbabwe	3	-	-	-	-	-	-	-	0	0	-	3
		1303	246	227	47	124	33	53	59	5	1	2	506

	Tests	Won	Lost	Drawn	Tied	Toss won
England	718	246	204	268	-	355
Australia	551	227	155	167	2	274
South Africa	194	47	82	65	-	93
West Indies	320	124	77	118	1	167
New Zealand	237	33	98	106	-	121
India	292	53	97	141	1	146
Pakistan	221	59	49	113	-	111
Sri Lanka	60	5	27	28	-	30
Zimbabwe	13	1	6	6	-	6

THE FIRST TEST MATCH

This was **the first match played on level terms** (eleven-a-side) between an English touring side and a representative Australian team. It was not until Clarence Moody classified the early matches some fifteen years later in his *Australian Cricket and Cricketers*, that this encounter was given the accolade of 'Test' match. Moody's list was quoted by C.W. Alcock, instigator and organizer of the first Test match in England (1880) and a leading English authority of the day, in his weekly magazine *Cricket*. In 1895 J.N. Pentelow published his *England v Australia The Story of the Test Matches* with full scores and a commentary on each of the 43 Tests played between the two countries. This book of 180 small pages firmly established Moody's list and assured the 1877 contest a unique place in cricket history.

Neither team was fully representative. James Lillywhite's men were all professionals; their strength would have been increased by the inclusion of such amateurs as W.G. Grace whose 3669 runs in all matches during the 1876 season had included a little matter of 318 not out against Yorkshire. Dave Gregory's side was composed entirely of Sydney and Melbourne players, even though South Australia had recently thrashed Victoria by an innings and plenty. Almost five years were to pass before the first Adelaide cricketer, George Giffen, forced his way into the Australian team. Gregory was without three of his best bowlers, including 'The Demon' Spofforth who refused to play when his own wicket-keeper, Billy Murdoch, was not picked. Some of Lillywhite's side were still sea-sick after their return voyage from New Zealand when the match started and their wicket keeper, Ted Pooley, had been confiscated by the authorities during that interim tour. They were the fourth English team to visit Australia following those led by H.H. Stephenson (1861–62), George Parr (1863–64) and W.G. Grace (1873–74).

Play on the first day of Test cricket began at 1.05pm on a warm and sunny Thursday (15 March 1877), with a 34-year-old Nottinghamshire professional bowling the first ball to a 25-year-old Kentish man playing his tenth first-class innings. Charles Bannerman scored the first run off Alfred Shaw's second ball. Before lunch was taken from 2.00 until 2.40pm, Nat Thomson had become the first Test batsman to lose his wicket and Allen Hill the first bowler to capture one. Hill also held the first Test match catch.

Bannerman reached **the only first-class hundred of his career** in 160 minutes and had scored 126 out of Australia's 166 for 6 when play ended at 5.00pm. Resuming at 12.45pm on Friday, he advanced to 159 at lunch (2.00pm). Soon afterwards a rising ball from George Ulyett coincided with a damaged part of his right batting glove and badly split his second finger. Bannerman thus added the first 'retired hurt' to all his other unique achievements. He had offered no chance during his 4 hours 45 minutes at the crease and had hit 15 fours. Perhaps most notably he had scored his 165 runs out of a total of 240 for 7. His score represented 67 per cent of his side's eventual total and remains the **highest individual contribution to any Test innings**. No other Australian exceeded 20.

Shaw's match figures appear remarkable (89.3 overs, 50 maidens, 89 runs, 8 wickets), but it must be remembered that the over consisted of four balls. It is this analysis which lends most weight to Sir Donald Bradman's opinion 'that any reference to maiden overs has long since become anachronistic and serves no useful purpose'.

England, needing only 154 for victory when Australia's second innings had folded after Bannerman's early dismissal, fell to the left-arm slow bowling of Tom Kendall. **Australia won by 45 runs** on the Monday afternoon, 19 March 1877, a crowd of 3000 watching the final stages of their first victory against England in an eleven-a-side match.

One hundred years later this result and the victory margin were repeated exactly, and on the same ground.

Six of the team were from Sydney clubs, including the youngest player in the match, Tom Garrett, a right-arm medium-fast bowler and aggressive batsman. He was 18 years 232 days old when Test cricket began and remained its youngest participant for nearly 53 years, until Derek Sealy (17 years 122 days) was introduced into the West Indies team. Garrett outlived every other player in this match by more than ten years.

Billy Midwinter subsequently played four times for England before resuming his career for Australia. He is the only cricketer to have played both for and against Australia.

All but Southerton were then professionals for the counties of their birth. At 49 years 119 days, James Southerton remains **the oldest man ever to begin a Test career**.

A round-arm bowler of off-breaks who spun the ball considerably, he was also **the first Test cricketer to die** (16 June 1880).

AUSTRALIA v ENGLAND 1876–77 (1st Test)
Played at Melbourne Cricket Ground on 15, 16, 17, 19 March.
Toss: Australia.
Result: AUSTRALIA won by 45 runs.
Debuts: All.
Close of play scores: 1st day – Australia 166 for 6 (Bannerman 126, Blackham 3);
2nd day – England 109 for 4 (Jupp 54); 3rd day – Australia 83 for 9 (Kendall 5, Hodges 3).

AUSTRALIA

C. Bannerman	retired hurt	165		b Ulyett	4
N.F.D. Thomson	b Hill	1		c Emmett b Shaw	7
T.P. Horan	c Hill b Shaw	12		c Selby b Hill	20
D.W. Gregory*	run out	1	(9)	b Shaw	3
B.B. Cooper	b Southerton	15		b Shaw	3
W.E. Midwinter	c Ulyett b Southerton	5		c Southerton b Ulyett	17
E.J. Gregory	c Greenwood b Lillywhite	0		c Emmett b Ulyett	11
J.M. Blackham†	b Southerton	17		lbw b Shaw	6
T.W. Garrett	not out	18	(4)	c Emmett b Shaw	0
T. Kendall	c Southerton b Shaw	3		not out	17
J.R. Hodges	b Shaw	0		b Lillywhite	8
Extras	(B 4, LB 2, W 2)	8		(B 5, LB 3)	8
Total		**245**			**104**

ENGLAND

H. Jupp	lbw b Garrett	63	(3)	lbw b Midwinter	4
J. Selby†	c Cooper b Hodges	7	(5)	c Horan b Hodges	38
H.R.J. Charlwood	c Blackham b Midwinter	36	(4)	b Kendall	13
G. Ulyett	lbw b Thomson	10	(6)	b Kendall	24
A. Greenwood	c E.J. Gregory b Midwinter	1	(2)	c Midwinter b Kendall	5
T. Armitage	c Blackham b Midwinter	9	(8)	c Blackham b Kendall	3
A. Shaw	b Midwinter	10		st Blackham b Kendall	2
T. Emmett	b Midwinter	8	(9)	b Kendall	9
A. Hill	not out	35	(1)	c Thomson b Kendall	0
James Lillywhite*	c and b Kendall	10		b Hodges	4
J. Southerton	c Cooper b Garrett	6		not out	1
Extras	(LB 1)	1		(B 4, LB 1)	5
Total		**196**			**108**

ENGLAND	O	M	R	W	O	M	R	W
Shaw	55.3	34	51	3	34	16	38	5
Hill	23	10	42	1	14	6	18	1
Ulyett	25	12	36	0	19	7	39	3
Southerton	37	17	61	3				
Armitage	3	0	15	0				
Lillywhite	14	5	19	1	1	0	1	1
Emmett	12	7	13	0				

AUSTRALIA	O	M	R	W	O	M	R	W
Hodges	9	0	27	1	7	5	7	2
Garrett	18.1	10	22	2	2	0	9	0
Kendall	38	16	54	1	33.1	12	55	7
Midwinter	54	23	78	5	19	7	23	1
Thomson	17	10	14	1				
D.W. Gregory					5	1	9	0

FALL OF WICKETS

Wkt	A 1st	E 1st	A 2nd	E 2nd
1st	2	23	7	0
2nd	40	79	27	7
3rd	41	98	31	20
4th	118	109	31	22
5th	142	121	35	62
6th	143	135	58	68
7th	197	145	71	92
8th	243	145	75	93
9th	245	168	75	100
10th	–	196	104	108

Umpires: C.A. Reid and R.B. Terry.
* Captain.
† Wicket-keeper

THE FIRST TEST CRICKETERS

AUSTRALIA

	Born	Died
Bannerman, Charles (New South Wales)	Woolwich, England 23 July 1851	Surry Hills, Sydney 20 August 1930
Blackham, John McCarthy (Victoria)	North Fitzroy, Melbourne 11 May 1854	Melbourne 28 December 1932
Cooper, Bransby Beauchamp (Victoria)	Dacca, India 15 March 1844	Geelong, Victoria 7 August 1914
Garrett, Thomas William (New South Wales)	Wollongong, NSW 26 June 1858	Warrawee, Sydney 6 August 1943
Gregory, David William (New South Wales)	Fairy Meadow, NSW 15 April 1845	Turramurra, Sydney 4 August 1919
Gregory, Edward James (New South Wales)	Waverley, Sydney 29 May 1839	SCG, Sydney 22 April 1899
Hodges, John Robart (Victoria)	Knightsbridge, London 11 August 1855	Collingwood, Victoria 17 January 1933
Horan, Thomas Patrick (Victoria)	Midleton, Ireland 8 March 1854	Malvern, Melbourne 16 April 1916
Kendall, Thomas (Victoria)	Bedford, England 24 August 1851	Hobart, Tasmania 17 August 1924
Midwinter, William Evans (Victoria)	St Briavels, Glos., England 19 June 1851	Kew, Melbourne 3 December 1890
Thomson, Nathaniel Frampton Davis (New South Wales)	Surry Hills, Sydney 29 May 1839	Burwood, Sydney 2 September 1896

The 1878 Australian tourists in England, featuring many of the side which contested the first ever Test match in Melbourne the previous year. Back row, left to right: Blackam, Horan, Bailey, Conway (manager), A.C. Bannerman, C. Bannerman, Murdoch; seated: Spofforth, Allan, Gregory (captain), Midwinter, Garrett, Boyle (Allsport Historical Collection)

ENGLAND

	Born	Died
Armitage, Thomas (Yorkshire)	Walkley, Sheffield, Yorkshire 25 April 1848	Pullman, Chicago, USA 21 September 1922
Charlwood, Henry Rupert James (Sussex)	Horsham, Sussex 19 December 1846	Scarborough, Yorkshire 6 June 1888
Emmett, Thomas (Yorkshire)	Halifax, Yorkshire 3 September 1841	Leicester 30 June 1904
Greenwood, Andrew (Yorkshire)	Cowmes Lepton, Yorkshire 20 August 1847	Huddersfield, Yorkshire 12 February 1889
Hill, Allen (Yorkshire)	Kirkheaton, Yorkshire 14 November 1843	Leyland, Lancashire 29 August 1910
Jupp, Henry (Surrey)	Dorking, Surrey 19 November 1841	Bermondsey, London 8 April 1889
Lillywhite, James, Jr (Sussex)	Westhampnett, Sussex 23 February 1842	Westerton, Sussex 25 October 1929
Selby, John (Nottinghamshire)	Nottingham 1 July 1849	Nottingham 11 March 1894
Shaw, Alfred (Nottinghamshire)	Burton Joyce, Nottinghamshire 29 August 1842	Gedling, Nottinghamshire 16 January 1907
Southerton, James (Surrey)	Petworth, Sussex 16 November 1827	Mitcham, Surrey 16 June 1880
Ulyett, George (Yorkshire)	Pitsmoor, Sheffield, Yorkshire 21 October 1851	Pitsmoor, Yorkshire 18 June 1898

Alfred Shaw: eight wickets for England in the first ever Test match (Allsport)

TEAM RECORDS

The highest innings total in all Test cricket is 903 for 7 wickets declared by England against Australia on 20, 22 and 23 August 1938. Compiled on an over-prepared and lifeless Kennington Oval pitch in a timeless Test, it lasted 15 hours 17 minutes until tea on the third day. Len Hutton (364 in 13 hours 17 minutes), Maurice Leyland (187 in 6 hours 21 minutes in his final Test), and Joe Hardstaff (169 not out in 5 hours 26 minutes) were the main contributors.

HIGHEST INNINGS TOTALS

		Opponents	Venue	Series
England	903–7d	Australia	The Oval	1938
West Indies	790–3d	Pakistan	Kingston	1957–58
Australia	758–8d	West Indies	Kingston	1954–55
Pakistan	708	England	The Oval	1987
India	676–7	Sri Lanka	Kanpur	1986–87
New Zealand	671–4	Sri Lanka	Wellington	1990–91
South Africa	622–9d	Australia	Durban	1969–70
Sri Lanka	547–8d	Australia	Colombo	1992–93
Zimbabwe	544–4d	Pakistan	Harare	1994–95

The highest total by a side following-on, and the longest innings in all first-class cricket (16 hours 53 minutes) is Pakistan's 657 for 8 wickets declared against West Indies at Bridgetown on 20–23 January 1958 in the very first Test between those teams.

The highest second innings total in Test cricket is 671 for four wickets by New Zealand against Sri Lanka at the Basin Reserve, Wellington on 2–4 February 1991. Facing a daunting 323-run deficit on first innings, New Zealand forced a draw by surrendering only four wickets in 14 hours.

The only instance of both sides scoring 600 runs in an innings in 1303 Test matches to the end of the 1995 English season occurred at Manchester on 23–28 July 1964, England scoring 611 in reply to Australia's 656 for 8 declared.

There have been only eleven totals of over 400 runs in the fourth innings of Test matches. Two of those batting sides won (India at Port-of-Spain, Trinidad in 1975–76 and Australia at Leeds in 1948), four drew and the other five lost.

The highest aggregate of runs in a Test match is 1981 by South Africa (530 and 481) and England (316 and 654 for 5) in a timeless Test at Kingsmead, Durban in March 1939. The match began when the author was 3½ hours old and ended when rain stopped play with England only 42 runs away from victory some eleven days later when the touring side had to begin their two-day train journey to rejoin their ship, the *Athlone Castle*, at Cape Town. It remains **the longest first-class match** ever staged, with play taking place on nine days (March 3, 4, 6, 7, 8, 9, 10, 13 and 14 rain prevented play on 11 March). Time actually played amounted to 43 hours 16 minutes.

HIGHEST FOURTH INNINGS TOTALS

To Win	406–4	India v West Indies	Port-of-Spain	1975–76
To Tie	347	India v Australia	Madras	1986–87
To Draw	654–5	England v South Africa	Durban	1938–39
To Lose	445	India v Australia	Adelaide	1977–78

The longest match in England in terms of hours played is the drawn six-day Fourth Test between England and Australia at The Oval in 1975. Actual playing time, excluding 187 minutes lost and breaks between innings, totalled 32 hours 17 minutes. Two other six-day matches have been staged in England, both Test matches against Australia at The Oval. In 1930 Australia won at 3.50pm on the last day after rain had prevented play on the penultimate one. Forty-two years later Australia repeated their victory at 2.49pm on the sixth day.

The highest match aggregate by one side is 1121 by England who scored 849 and 272 for 9 declared against West Indies at Sabina Park, Kingston, Jamaica in April 1930.

LOWEST INNINGS TOTALS

		Opponents	Venue	Series
New Zealand	26	England	Auckland	1954–55
South Africa	30	England	Port Elizabeth	1895–96
	30	England	Birmingham	1924
Australia	36	England	Birmingham	1902
India	42	England	Lord's	1974
England	45	Australia	Sydney	1886–87
West Indies	53	Pakistan	Faisalabad	1986–87
Pakistan	62	Australia	Perth	1981–82
Sri Lanka	71	Pakistan	Kandy	1994–95
Zimbabwe	134	Pakistan	Karachi	1993–94

The lowest innings total in Test cricket is 26 by New Zealand at Eden Park, Auckland, on 28 March 1955. Playing the second of two Tests against Hutton's England team which had just retained the Ashes in Australia, New Zealand had contained the tourists to a first innings lead of 46. A crowd of 14 000 saw the home side reduced to 14 for 5 and eventually dismissed in 27 overs by Tyson (2 for 10), Statham (3 for 9), Appleyard (4 for 7) and Wardle (1 for 0). Opening batsman Bert Sutcliffe (11) achieved the only double-figure score of an innings which lasted 106 minutes either side of the tea interval on the third day. Appleyard took three wickets in four balls and narrowly missed the hat-trick. It was Hutton's final Test.

The lowest declared total is 32 for 7 wickets by Australia against England at Woolloongabba, Brisbane, on 4 December 1950. Caught on a 'sticky' wicket, Australia declared their innings when only 192 runs ahead, took six England second innings wickets for 30 runs before the close, and went on to win by 70 runs.

The shortest completed Test innings in terms of time was recorded by South Africa either at St George's Park in Port Elizabeth on 14 February 1896, or at Edgbaston, Birmingham, on 16 June 1924. On both occasions they were routed by England for totals of 30. Unfortunately, as contemporary match accounts loosely describe the length of both innings as being 'three-quarters of an hour', it is not possible to determine which instance was the shorter. Although the scorebook containing the 1924 match has survived to reveal that Arthur Gilligan (6 for 7) and Maurice Tate (4 for 12) in fact took 48 minutes to complete their destruction, no such record exists from which to measure the 1896 debacle exactly.

The shortest completed Test match was that played between Australia and South Africa on a vicious Melbourne 'sticky' on 12 and 15 February 1932. The total playing time in this Fifth Test amounted to 5 hours 53 minutes.

The shortest completed Test match in England was the Third of the 1888 series against Australia at Old Trafford, Manchester, on 30–31 August. The match ended before lunch, at 1.52pm on the second day, the total playing time being 6 hours 34 minutes. Australia's second innings of 70 lasted only 69 minutes and remains their shortest in all Test cricket.

The lowest aggregate of runs scored in a completed Test match is 234 by Australia (153) and South Africa (36 and 45) at Melbourne on 12 and 15 February 1932. South Africa's aggregate of 81 remains the lowest by any side losing all 20 wickets in a Test.

The greatest margin of victory in Test cricket was achieved by England at The Oval on 24 August 1938 when they defeated Australia by an innings and 579 runs on the fourth day. After amassing the record total of 903 for 7 in 15 hours 17 minutes before Hammond declared at tea on the third day, England dismissed Australia twice in 4¾ hours of play. With Fingleton and Bradman both injured and unable to bat, Australia scored 201 and 123.

The record margin of victory by runs alone was also achieved by England against Australia. On 5 December 1928 they won the first Test staged in Brisbane (and their only encounter at the Exhibition Ground) by 675 runs on the fifth day. After scoring 521, they bowled out Australia for 122, scored 342 for 8 before Chapman made the first declaration in a Test in Australia, and finally routed the home side for 66. After bowling 41 overs in the first innings, Jack Gregory damaged his knee so severely that he was unable to bat and never played cricket again.

The first Test match to result in a tie was played between Australia and West Indies at Woolloongabba, Brisbane, and ended on 14 December 1960. Australia, requiring 233 runs to win in 310 minutes, lost their last wicket to a run out off the seventh ball of the final over. After much confusion the scores were found to be level.

This rarest of results was emulated at the Chidambaram Stadium in Madras at 5.18pm on 22

Shane Warne (Australia, centre) holds his head as Pakistan snatch victory by one wicket at Karachi in 1994
(Allsport/Shaun Botterill)

September 1986, when, with the penultimate ball of the final over, Australia's off-spinner, Greg Matthews, claimed an lbw decision against India's last man, Maninder Singh.

Australia, who declared twice in the match and had gained a first innings lead of 177, set India 348 runs to win at the start of the final day. Sunil Gavaskar, playing in his 100th consecutive Test, contributed 90 to an impressive start of 158 for 1, but, having reached 331 for 6, they lost their last four wickets for 16 runs.

The narrowest victory by a team fielding last was achieved by West Indies when they beat Australia by a solitary run at the Adelaide Oval on 26 January 1993. This inappropriate Australia Day climax occurred when Craig McDermott, having added 40 for the tenth wicket with Tim May, thinly gloved a lifting ball from Courtney Walsh.

Seven Test matches have been won by a single wicket, one of them – between Australia and England at Melbourne in January 1908 – almost resulting in a tie. This was the first of 61 Test match appearances by Jack Hobbs who scored 83 and 28. When England's ninth wicket fell, 29 runs were still needed for victory. Sydney Barnes and Arthur Fielder, 'to the astonishment of everyone concerned' (*Wisden*), levelled the scores before risking a desperately quick run from a push to cover point. Gerry Hazlitt threw wildly at the stumps, missed, and delayed the first tie in Test cricket by almost 53 years. The most recent instance involved **the highest tenth-wicket partnership to win a Test,** Inzamam-ul-Haq (58*) and Mushtaq Ahmed (20*) adding 57 to bring Pakistan victory against Australia at Karachi's on 2 October 1994. The winning runs were boundary leg byes from a difficult stumping chance.

VICTORIES BY ONE WICKET

Victor	Opponents	Venue	Tenth Wicket Partnership	Series
England	Australia	The Oval	15*	1902
South Africa	England	Johannesburg	48*	1905–06
England	Australia	Melbourne	39*	1907–08
England	South Africa	Cape Town	5*	1922–23
Australia	West Indies	Melbourne	38*	1951–52
New Zealand	West Indies	Dunedin	4*	1979–80
Pakistan	Australia	Karachi	57*	1994–95

Only one of the 1303 Test matches played up to the end of the 1995 season has been won off the last possible ball. At Kingsmead in Durban on 20 December 1948, England's ninth-wicket pair, Alec Bedser and Cliff Gladwin, needed eight runs from the final eight-ball over from Lindsay Tuckett. Before Bedser brought the scores level off the sixth ball, all four results were possible. Gladwin missed the seventh ball. He also missed the last ball. It bounced off his thigh and the batsmen managed to scamper a leg bye.

England have provided the only two instances of a team winning a Test match after being forced to follow on. At Sydney in December 1894, England followed on 261 runs behind on first innings, scored 437 and dismissed Australia for 166 to win by ten runs. It was the first Test to go into a sixth day. In July 1981 at Headingley, Leeds, England were 135 for 7, after following on 227 runs behind on first innings, when Ian Botham was joined by Graham Dilley. They scored 117 in 80 minutes before Dilley was bowled for 56. Botham (149 not out) then added another 114 runs with the aid of Chris Old (29) and Bob Willis (2). On the fifth and final day, Australia, needing 130 runs to win, reached 56 for 1 before Willis (8 for 43) achieved the best analysis in a Test at Headingley and bowled England to victory by 18 runs against bookmakers' odds of 500–1.

The most runs scored in a single day of Test cricket is 588 by England (398) and India (190) on the second day (27 July) of the Manchester Test of 1936. That record aggregate was scored for the loss of six wickets at a rate of over 90 runs per hour in 6½ hours.

The highest number of runs by one team in a day is 503 scored by England on the second day of the Lord's Test against South Africa on 30 June 1924. When Arthur Gilligan declared the innings closed 66 minutes before stumps, Hobbs (whose 211 equalled the highest Test innings in England at that time), Sutcliffe, Woolley and Hendren had attained an average scoring rate of 93 runs per hour while losing only two wickets.

The fewest runs scored in a full day of Test cricket is 95. This bizarre record was established on the matting pitch of the National Stadium in Karachi on 11 October 1956, the first day of Test cricket between Pakistan and Australia. After a strenuous and unsuccessful tour of England's grass pitches, Australia's batsmen had been allowed no preliminary match practice in the different conditions. Shortly after tea they were all out for 80, the lowest total in Karachi Tests. It was compiled from 53.1 overs bowled by Fazal Mahmood (6 for 34) and Khan Mohammad (4 for 43). By the close Pakistan had reached 15 for 2 from 14.4 overs.

The least number of runs scored in a full day of Test cricket in England is 151 at Lord's on Saturday, 26 August 1978. England, resuming at 175 for 2, added 67 for 2 by lunch and were all out for 289 at 4.21pm when tea was taken. At the 6.30pm close, New Zealand had reached 37 for 7 off 25 overs. A total of 82.3 overs was bowled during this third day.

The highest number of wickets to fall in a day of Test cricket is 27 on 17 July 1888. The wicket of W.G. Grace, the champion cricketer of the day – some would argue of all time – featured twice in that incredible tally. The record was set on a farcically difficult mud pitch at Lord's on the second day of the First Test against Australia. At the start of play, England were 18 for 3 in reply to Australia's 116 all out. In under an hour they had lost their remaining seven wickets for 35 runs. Australia, at one stage 18 for 7, totalled 60 and set England 124 runs to win. By 4.25pm they had bowled out England for 62 and were being heartily cheered by thousands of spectators massed in front of the pavilion. Grace, the only England batsman to reach double figures in both innings, recorded the highest score of the match: 24. In just over three hours of actual play, 27 wickets had fallen for 157 runs.

Six weeks later those two teams set the record for losing the most wickets before lunch in a Test match. At Old Trafford, Manchester, on 31 August 1888, 18 wickets fell before lunch. Hot sun on a soft, wet pitch made batting conditions impossible. Australia, resuming at 32 for 2 in reply to England's 172, were all out for 81, followed on, and recovered from losing their first six wickets for seven runs to total 70. The match was completed at 1.55pm (before lunch on the second day) and remains the shortest Test match in which there was a result.

The only Test team to be dismissed twice in a day is India. At Old Trafford, Manchester, on 19 July 1952, they were bowled out by England for 58 and 82 in a total batting time of 3¾ hours, 22 wickets falling in the day.

Only nine uninterrupted days of Test cricket have failed to produce the fall of a wicket; five of them have occurred in the West Indies, one in Australia, one in India, one in Sri Lanka and one in England.

The only pair of batsmen to bat throughout two consecutive days of Test cricket are Gary Sobers (226) and Frank Worrell (197 not out) on 9 and 11 January 1960, the fourth and fifth days of the First Test between West Indies and England at Kensington Oval in Bridgetown, Barbados. The final hour of the fourth day was lost to rain and a rest day intervened. Their fourth-wicket partnership of 399 occupied 9 hours 39 minutes – the longest stand in Test cricket. The only Test match in which batsmen averaged

BATTING PARTNERSHIPS THAT HAVE SURVIVED A FULL DAY'S PLAY

Batsmen	Match	Day	Venue	Series
J.B. Hobbs, H. Sutcliffe	E v A	3rd	Melbourne	1924–25
D. St E. Atkinson, C.C. Depeiaza	WI v A	4th	Bridgetown	1954–55
M.H. ('Vinoo') Mankad, Pankaj Roy	I v NZ	1st	Madras	1955–56
C.C. Hunte, G. St A. Sobers	WI v P	3rd	Kingston	1957–58
G. St A. Sobers, F.M.M. Worrell	WI v E	5th	Bridgetown	1959–60
W.M. Lawry, R.B. Simpson	A v WI	1st	Bridgetown	1964–65
G.R. Viswanath, Yashpal Sharma	I v E	2nd	Madras	1981–82
A.P. Gurusinha, A. Ranatunga	SL v P	5th	Colombo (PSS)	1985–86
G.R. Marsh, M.A. Taylor	A v E	1st	Nottingham	1989

over 100 runs per wicket lost took place at Delhi in December 1955. In five days New Zealand (450 for 2d and 112 for 1) and India (531 for 7d) amassed 1093 runs for the loss of only ten wickets.

The most hundreds scored in a Test innings is five by Australia against West Indies at Kingston, Jamaica in June 1955. In reply to a total of 357, Australia compiled their highest total of 758 for 8 declared, with centuries from Colin McDonald (127), Neil Harvey (204), Keith Miller (109), Ron Archer (128) and Richie Benaud (121). Benaud reached his hundred in 78 minutes – the third-fastest in Tests.

The record number of fifties in a Test innings is seven by England (627 for 9d) against Australia at Manchester, in July 1934.

No country has won every Test in a six-match series, although Australia beat West Indies 5–1 in Australia in 1975–76 and were themselves beaten by England by a similar margin in 1978–79. There have been six instances of teams winning every Test in a five-match series, West Indies in England in 1984 being the only team to achieve this feat abroad: Australia beat England in 1920–21 and South Africa in 1931–32; England defeated India in 1959; West Indies beat India in 1961–62, and demolished England in successive series in 1984 and 1985–86.

West Indies hold the record for winning most consecutive Tests – they gained eleven successive victories between 4 April and 11 December 1984: three against Australia at home, five in England and another three in Australia.

The most successive victories against the same opponent is ten by West Indies against England in 1984 and 1985–86.

West Indies enjoyed a run of 27 matches without a defeat between January 1982 and December 1984. England were unbeaten in 26 matches between June 1968 and August 1971. At the other end of the scale, New Zealand failed to win any of their first 44 matches. Their first victory came on 13 March 1956 when they beat West Indies at Auckland by 190 runs 26 years after starting their first Test match, against

England at Christchurch on 10 January 1930.

Surprisingly, in view of their reputation for playing positive cricket, West Indies drew a record ten successive Tests between 1970–71 and 1972–73.

The most players to appear for one team during a single rubber is 30 for England in the 1921 five-match series. Whitewashed in the five Tests in Australia the previous winter, England lost the first three matches before drawing the last two. South Africa employed 20 players when they lost all three matches of their 1895–96 rubber against England.

Only three times has a team remained unchanged throughout a five-match series, England winning 3–2 in Australia in 1884–85, South Africa beating England 4–1 at home in 1905–06 and West Indies beating Australia 2–1 at home in 1990–91.

On only two occasions has an entire eleven bowled during a Test innings. The first was at The Oval in August 1884 when Australia scored the then monumental total of 551 off 311 four-ball overs. Declarations were not permitted until 1889. The tenth bowler called upon by Lord Harris was England's wicket-keeper, the Hon Alfred Lyttelton. His first spell with Walter Read behind the stumps was unsuccessful and Australia ended the first day at 363 for 2, with three batsmen scoring centuries. Lyttelton's lobs were not reintroduced until the total reached 532 for 6. This time Grace kept wicket and he held a good legside catch off the first ball of this second spell. Lyttelton, still wearing his pads, took the last four wickets for only eight runs in eight overs to finish with 4 for 19 – the best analysis in Test cricket by a player who began the innings as wicketkeeper.

The second instance occurred more than 95 years later on a perfect batting pitch at the Iqbal Stadium, Faisalabad in March 1980. Rain had washed out the first day and delayed the start of the second. By the time Australia's innings of 617 had ended, only 7 hours 15 minutes of play remained. Pakistan scored 382 for 2 in this time and only one of Greg Chappell's eleven bowlers, Geoff Dymock, took a wicket.

The most players to bowl in a Test match is 20, both South Africa and England calling upon ten in the drawn Third Test at Cape Town in January 1965.

There have been nine instances of all eleven batsmen reaching double figures in a Test innings. England, at Melbourne in January 1895, were the first to do so, whilst India's 524 for 9d, against New Zealand at Kanpur in November 1976, is **the highest total in Test cricket in which no batsman scored a century.**

Although there have been 16 totals of under 50 in Test matches, **only one completed innings has failed to produce a double figure score.** When South Africa were bowled out for 30 at Edgbaston, Birmingham, on 16 June 1924, their highest scorer was Herbie Taylor, their captain and opening batsman, who made seven. The main contribution came from 11 extras as Arthur Gilligan (6 for 7) and Maurice Tate (4 for 12) bowled unchanged. The Sussex pair took just 48 minutes and only 75 balls to complete the devastation.

EXTRAS TOP-SCORING IN A COMPLETED INNINGS

	Total	Highest Score	Extras	Opponents	Venue	Series
South Africa	58	13	17	England	Lord's	1912
South Africa	30	7	11	England	Birmingham	1924
New Zealand	97	19	20	England	Nottingham	1973
England	126	24	25	West Indies	Manchester	1976
England	227	33	46	Pakistan	Lord's	1982
Australia	200	29	36	West Indies	St John's	1983–84
England	315 †	47	59	West Indies	Port-of-Spain	1985–86
New Zealand	160	33	38	Pakistan	Lahore	1990–91
Australia	248	47	53	West Indies	Georgetown	1990–91
New Zealand	93	19	22	Pakistan	Hamilton	1992–93

† *The highest total in which no batsman had scored a fifty.*

BATTING RECORDS

The highest individual aggregate of runs in Test cricket is 11 174 (average 50.56) by Allan Border for Australia in 156 Tests (265 innings) between 29 December 1978 and 29 March 1994. He passed the previous record of 10 122 runs, scored for India in 214 innings by Sunil Gavaskar, at 1.51pm on 26 February 1993 at Lancaster Park, Christchurch, when he pulled a ball from Dipak Patel of New Zealand to the mid-wicket boundary to complete his 84th fifty in 240 innings.

Border also holds the world records for most matches (156), most innings (265), most scores of fifty or more (90), and has shared in most hundred partnerships (63).

Sunil Gavaskar, the previous holder of all those records, scored **most hundreds (34)**. He was also the first to appear in 100 consecutive Tests for his country.

Only one batsman has scored more than 4000 runs against one country: Don Bradman amassed 5028 runs (average 89.78) in 37 Tests for Australia against England between November 1928 and August 1948. **The highest aggregate for England against another country** is 3636 runs (average 54.26) by Jack Hobbs in 41 Tests against Australia between January 1908 and August 1930.

Allan Border: holder of several world records in Test cricket including the highest individual aggregate of runs
(Allsport/Joe Mann)

The **highest batting average in a Test career** involving more than five innings is 99.94 by Bradman for Australia. In 52 Tests he scored 6996 from 80 innings, ten of them undefeated. He averaged a century every 2.8 innings. He needed to score just four runs in his final Test innings on Saturday, 14 August 1948, in the Fifth Test at The Oval, to become the second (after Hammond) to score 7000 runs and the first to attain a career average of 100. Given a standing ovation by the crowd throughout his progress to the middle, Bradman was then saluted by three cheers from the England team. Shortly before six o'clock he took guard and safely negotiated the first ball, a leg-break from Eric Hollies. The next was pitched on a perfect length, a googly which spun past Bradman's forward defensive stroke and bowled him.

The **first batsman to score 1000 runs in Test cricket** was Arthur Shrewsbury of Nottinghamshire. He reached that landmark during the last of his three centuries for England, against Australia at Lord's on 17 July 1893.

Clem Hill, the Australian left-hander, was **the first to score both 2000 and 3000 runs in Tests.** He reached the 2000-mark against England on his home ground, the Adelaide Oval, on 15 January 1904. He completed his third thousand on the same ground almost exactly seven years later against South Africa.

Having exceeded Hill's final and record aggregate of 3412, Jack Hobbs went on to become **the first to reach both 4000** (at Lord's against Australia on 28 June 1926) **and 5000 runs** (on 14 March 1929 at Melbourne).

Wally Hammond continued this sequence by **taking the record beyond 6000** (against South Africa at Johannesburg on 24 December 1938) and, after an interval for Hitler, **past the 7000-mark** (on 19 August 1946 at The Oval against India).

Hammond's record of 7249 survived until 29 November 1970 when Colin Cowdrey overtook it at Brisbane. Then, against England at Kingston, Jamaica, on 20 February 1974, Gary Sobers became **the first to score 8000 runs in Test cricket.**

India's diminutive opening batsman Sunil Gavaskar was **the first to score both 9000 and 10 000 runs in Tests.** He reached the 9000-mark during his undefeated 166 against Australia at Adelaide on 17 December 1985. He became the first to notch five figures shortly after tea on 7 March 1987, against Pakistan at Ahmedabad's Gujarat Stadium and playing his penultimate Test. A jubilant crowd invasion halted play for more than 20 minutes.

The **only batsman to score 11 000 runs** is Australia's left-handed Allan Border. He achieved this feat during his innings of 84 against South Africa at

Adelaide at 1.57pm on 29 January 1994 in his 150th consecutive Test, his 90th in succession as captain and his final international match on home soil.

1000 RUNS IN FEWEST INNINGS

Runs	Batsman	Team	Innings
1000	H. Sutcliffe	England	12
	E. de C. Weekes	West Indies	12
2000	D.G. Bradman	Australia	22
3000	D.G. Bradman	Australia	33
4000	D.G. Bradman	Australia	48
5000	D.G. Bradman	Australia	56
6000	D.G. Bradman	Australia	68
7000	W.R. Hammond	England	131
8000	G. St A. Sobers	West Indies	157
9000	S.M. Gavaskar	India	192
10 000	S.M. Gavaskar	India	212
11 000	A.R. Border	Australia	259

The **highest aggregate of runs by a batsman in Test cricket during a calendar year** is 1710 (average 90.00) by Viv Richards in eleven matches for West Indies in 1976. His 19 innings were: 44, 2, 30, 101, 50 and 98 in Australia; 142, 130, 20, 177, 23 and 64 v India in the West Indies; 232, 63, 4, 135, 66, 38 and 291 in England.

The **only batsman to score 1000 runs in the year of his Test debut** is Mark Taylor of Australia with 1219 runs (average 64.15) in 1989.

Graham Gooch is the **only batsman to score 1000 runs in Test cricket during an English season** with 1058 runs in 11 innings against New Zealand and India in 1990. His 752 (average 125.33) in six innings against India established the **record for a three-match series.**

The **record individual aggregate in one rubber or series** is 974 (average 139.14) by Bradman in only seven innings during Australia's five-match series in England in 1930. His scores were: 8, 131, 254, 1, 334, 14 and 232. The only other batsman to exceed 900 runs in a series is Hammond who totalled 905 runs (average 113.12) for England in Australia in 1928–29.

The **most runs by a batsman playing in his first Test series** is 774 (average 154.80) by Sunil Gavaskar in four matches for India in the West Indies in 1971. His eight innings were: 65, 67 not out, 116, 64 not out, 1, 117 not out, 124 and 220. Surgery on a septic finger prevented his playing in the First Test.

The **highest individual aggregate in a Test match** is 456 runs by Graham Gooch with 333 and 123 for England against India at Lord's on 26–30 July 1990. Having recorded the **highest score in any cricket match at Lord's**, he went on to become **the first**

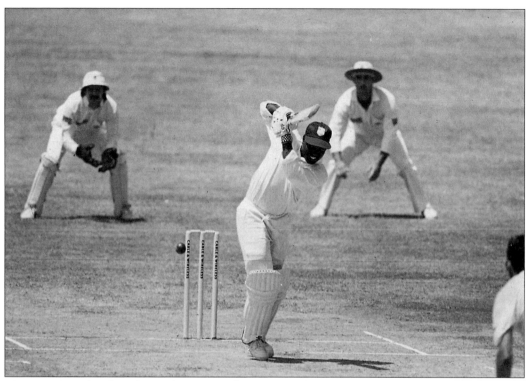

Brian Lara (West Indies) during his record Test innings of 375 against England in 1994 (Allsport/Ben Radford)

batsman to score a century and a triple century in any first-class match.

The highest individual Test innings is 375 by Brian Lara for West Indies at St John's Recreation Ground, Antigua, during the Fifth Test against England on 16–18 April 1994. Capitalizing on perfect batting conditions, the 24-year-old Trinidadian left-hander began his innings in the seventh over at 10.32 on the first morning and broke Sir Garfield Sobers's record with a pulled boundary in the 178th over at 11.46am on the third day. Sobers himself led the ensuing crowd invasion which lasted six minutes. His complete innings occupied 12 hours 48 minutes (536 balls) and produced 45 fours, 10 threes, 33 twos and 99 singles.

At 21 years 216 days, Sobers remains **the youngest to score a triple century in Test cricket**. His 365 not out for West Indies against Pakistan at Sabina Park, Kingston, Jamaica on 27 February to 1 March 1958 took only 10 hours 14 minutes but was scored against an attack reduced to two uninjured specialist bowlers on a small and fast outfield.

The most runs and only instance of over 300 in a day by one batsman is 309 by Bradman for Australia against England at Headingley, Leeds, on 11 July 1930. He scored 105 before lunch, 115 between lunch and tea, and 89 in the final session.

Bradman is alone in holding the record scores for two batting positions in Test matches. His innings of 270 at number seven against England at Melbourne in Jaunuary 1937 was an extraordinary performance by a player who was the established number three batsman and captaining his country for only the third time. Rain had produced a pitch on which 12 wickets fell in about three hours and, for the first time in Test cricket, each side had declared its first innings closed. The wicket was still a 'gluepot' when Australia had to begin their second innings but Bradman countered these conditions by sending his tailend batsmen in first. Australia were 97 for 5 when Bradman went to the wicket at 2.50pm on the following day to join his opening batsman, Jack Fingleton, who had been saved until number six. By the time 'The Don' was out two days later at 1.02pm, Australia were 549 for 9 and their lead 673. He had batted 7 hours 38 minutes, hit 22 fours, shared in what remains **the world record sixth-wicket partnership in Test cricket** of 346 with Fingleton, and recorded his highest innings against England in Australia. Throughout his innings Bradman was suffering from a severe chill. Two matches down in the series, Australia won this Test by 365 runs and went on to win the rubber 3–2.

The most runs added during one batsman's innings is 770 in 797 minutes by England against Australia at The Oval in August 1938 during Hutton's innings of 364. England eventually declared at 903 for 7.

The highest individual contribution to a completed Test match innings is 67 per cent by Charles Bannerman who on 15 and 16 March 1877 in the very first innings in Test cricket, scored 165 out of Australia's total of 245. As eight of those runs

were extras, Bannerman actually scored 69 per cent of the runs scored from the bat. Originally an Englishman, born in Woolwich 25 years earlier, he was playing his tenth first-class innings and seventh match. Having reached his only first-class hundred in 160 minutes, he was forced to retire hurt when a rising ball from George Ulyett split the second finger of his right hand through a damaged glove. He had batted chancelessly for 285 minutes, struck 15 fours, and established what is still **the highest score by an Australian in his first Test against England.**

MOST RUNS IN A TEST MATCH

456	G.A. Gooch (333, 123)	England v India	Lord's	1990
380	G.S. Chappell (247*, 133)	Australia v New Zealand	Wellington	1973–74
375	A. Sandham (325, 50)	England v West Indies	Kingston	1929–30
375	B.C. Lara (375)	West Indies v England	St John's	1993–94
365	G. St A. Sobers (365*)	West Indies v Pakistan	Kingston	1957–58
364	L. Hutton (364)	England v Australia	The Oval	1938
354	Hanif Mohammad (17, 337)	Pakistan v West Indies	Bridgetown	1957–58

How the record individual Test score has progressed since Charles Bannerman faced the first ball bowled, scored the first century and became the first batsman to retire hurt in Test cricket:

Score	Batsman	Minutes	Match	Venue	Series
165*	C. Bannerman	285	A v E	Melbourne	1876–77
211	W.L. Murdoch	485	A v E	The Oval	1884
287	R.E. Foster	419	E v A	Sydney	1903–04
325	A. Sandham	600	E v WI	Kingston	1929–30
334	D.G. Bradman	383	A v E	Leeds	1930
336*	W.R. Hammond	318	E v NZ	Auckland	1932–33
364	L. Hutton	797	E v A	The Oval	1938
365*	G. St A. Sobers	614	WI v P	Kingston	1957–58
375	B.C. Lara	768	WI v E	St John's	1993–94

HIGHEST INNINGS FOR EACH TEAM

For	Score	Batsman	Opponents	Venue	Series
England	364	L. Hutton	Australia	The Oval	1938
Australia	334	D.G. Bradman	England	Leeds	1930
South Africa	274	R.G. Pollock	Australia	Durban	1969–70
West Indies	375	B.C. Lara	England	St John's	1993–94
New Zealand	299	M.D. Crowe	Sri Lanka	Wellington	1990–91
India	236*	S.M. Gavaskar	West Indies	Madras	1983–84
Pakistan	337	Hanif Mohammad	West Indies	Bridgetown	1957–58
Sri Lanka	267	P.A. de Silva	New Zealand	Wellington	1990–91
Zimbabwe	266	D.L. Houghton	Sri Lanka	Bulawayo	1994–95

HIGHEST INNINGS FOR EACH BATTING POSITION

No.	Score	Batsman	Match	Venue	Series
1	364	L. Hutton	E v A	The Oval	1938
2	325	A. Sandham	E v WI	Kingston	1929-30
3	375	B.C. Lara	WI v E	St John's	1993–94
4	307	R.M. Cowper	A v E	Melbourne	1965–66
5	304	D.G. Bradman	A v E	Leeds	1934

No.	Score	Batsman	Match	Venue	Series
6	250	K.D. Walters	A v NZ	Christchurch	1976–77
7	270	D.G. Bradman	A v E	Melbourne	1936–37
8	209	Imtiaz Ahmed	P v NZ	Lahore	1955–56
9	173	I.D.S. Smith	NZ v I	Auckland	1989–90
10	117	W.W. Read	E v A	The Oval	1884
11	68*	R.O. Collinge	NZ v P	Auckland	1972–73

LONGEST INNINGS FOR EACH TEAM

	Minutes	Batsman (score)	Opponents	Venue	Series
England	797	L. Hutton (364)	Australia	The Oval	1938
Australia	762	R.B. Simpson (311)	England	Manchester	1964
South Africa	575	D.J. McGlew (105)	Australia	Durban	1957–58
West Indies	768	B.C. Lara (375)	England	St John's	1993–94
New Zealand	704	G.M. Turner (259)	West Indies	Georgetown	1971–72
India	708	S.M. Gavaskar (172)	England	Bangalore	1981–82
Pakistan	970	Hanif Mohammad (337)	West Indies	Bridgetown	1957–58
Sri Lanka	777	D.S.B.P. Kuruppu (201*)	New Zealand	Colombo (CCC)	1986–87
Zimbabwe	675	D.L. Houghton (266)	Sri Lanka	Bulawayo	1994–95

The only batsman to contribute over half his team's completed innings totals in a Test match is Jimmy Sinclair of South Africa. Playing against England at Newlands, Cape Town in April 1899, he scored 106 and 4 as South Africa were dismissed for 177 and 35 – scoring 51 per cent of his side's match aggregate. Massively-built, and a prodigious hitter who once struck a ball from Wilfred Rhodes so violently that it separated a cabby parked outside the Harrogate ground from his cab, Sinclair followed his century by taking six wickets in the first innings and three in the second. He was responsible for his country's first fifty (in the previous match) and first hundred, and was the first player to score a century and take six wickets in an innings of the same Test.

The longest individual innings in all first-class cricket lasted 999 minutes (16 hours 29 minutes) and was compiled by Hanif Mohammad for Pakistan against West Indies at Bridgetown, Barbados, on 20, 21, 22, 23 January 1958. Opening the innings an hour before tea on the third day, as Pakistan followed on 473 runs behind with three and a half days' play left, Hanif had scored 61 out of 161 for 1 at stumps. At the close of the fourth five-hour day he had made 161 out of 339 for 2, and he had progressed to 270 out of 525 for 3 by the end of the fifth. At tea on the sixth and final day he was 334 not out and just 30 runs short of the world record then held by Len Hutton (Sobers was to beat it two Tests later). Soon after the interval, Hanif tried to steer a single wide of slip to keep the strike, edged an outswinger from Denis Atkinson and was caught behind the wicket. He had scored 337 out of 626 for 6 when he was dismissed, 32 of that total being extras. Pakistan's eventual total of 657 for 8

declared remains the highest by any side after following on.

The most hundreds scored by one batsman in Test cricket is 34 in 214 innings by Sunil Gavaskar during 125 matches for India between 1971 and 1987.

MOST HUNDREDS FOR EACH TEAM

	100s	Batsman (innings)
England	22	W.R. Hammond (140), M.C. Cowdrey (188), G. Boycott (193)
Australia	29	D.G. Bradman (80)
South Africa	9	A.D. Nourse (62)
West Indies	26	G. St A. Sobers (160)
New Zealand	17	M.D. Crowe (128)
India	34	S.M. Gavaskar (214)
Pakistan	23	Javed Miandad (189)
Sri Lanka	7	P.A. de Silva (83)
Zimbabwe	3	D.L. Houghton (20)

The most hundreds in one series is five by Clyde Walcott for West Indies during their five-match home series against Australia between March and June 1955. He scored 108, 39, 126, 110, 8, 73, 15, 83, 155 and 110 to total 827 runs, average 82.70.

Another of the 'Three Ws', Everton Weekes, holds the Test record for scoring most hundreds in consecutive innings with five between March 1948 and January 1949. Starting his sequence with 141 against England at Kingston, Jamaica, he had to wait until November and the West Indies tour of India for his next innings – 128 at Delhi, one of four centuries in a total of 631. Weekes followed this with 194 at

Martin Crowe: record 17 centuries for New Zealand (Allsport)

Bombay, 162 and 101 at Calcutta, and 90 (run out from a magnificent piece of fielding by Nirode Chowdhury at point in the first of only two Test appearances) at Madras.

The first batsman to score a hundred in each innings of a Test match was Warren Bardsley when he scored 136 and 130 for Australia at The Oval in August 1909.

The record for scoring a hundred in each innings of a Test on most occasions is held by Sunil Gavaskar who has achieved this feat three times:

Scores		Opponents	Venue	Series
124	220	West Indies	Port-of-Spain	1970–71
111	137	Pakistan	Karachi	1978–79
107	182*	West Indies	Calcutta	1978–79

Lawrence Rowe of Jamaica is **the only batsman to score centuries in both innings of his first Test match.** Playing for West Indies against New Zealand on his home ground at Sabina Park, Kingston, in February 1972, the 23-year-old righthander scored 214 and 100 not out. **His aggregate of 314 is a record for any player in his first Test.** The only other batsman to exceed 300 on his debut was R.E. 'Tip' Foster who scored 287 and 19 for England against Australia at Sydney in December 1903.

The only batsman to score separate hundreds on successive days of a Test match is Vijay Hazare of India. Playing against Australia at Adelaide in 1948, he scored 108 of his first innings 116 on 26 January and 102 of his second innings 145 on 27 January.

Geoffrey Boycott achieved **the only instance in Test cricket of a batsman scoring 99 and a century.** In the Fifth Test between England and West Indies, played at Port-of-Spain, Trinidad, from 30 March to 5 April 1974, he scored 112 after being brilliantly caught off a leg glance in the first innings when the wicket-keeper, Deryck Murray, threw himself far to his left.

Bradman, who holds the record for **the most double centuries in a rubber** (three against England in 1930), is **the only batsman to score hundreds in six successive Test matches.** In terms of matches in which he actually batted, the sequence extended to eight. Commencing against England in January 1937, he scored 270 at Melbourne, 212 at Adelaide, and 169 at Melbourne, the last three Tests of a series that attracted 943 000 spectators, **an attendance aggregate that is still the largest for any rubber.** Continuing in England in 1938, Bradman scored 144 not out at Nottingham, 102 not out at Lord's, 103 at Leeds, but was unable to bat at The Oval after severely injuring his ankle while bowling during England's record innings of 903–7 declared. Resuming his war-interrupted career eight years later in November 1946, the world's greatest run-machine proved his appetite for large scores to be as rapacious as ever with innings of 187 at Brisbane and 234 at Sydney. In the Third Test at Melbourne Bradman failed at last, scoring a mere 79 and 49, dismissed by Norman Yardley on both occasions during the first drawn Test in Australia since March 1882.

The only batsman to score hundreds in each of his first three Tests is Mohammed Azharuddin for India against England in 1984–85. After celebrating his debut with 110 in the Third Test at Calcutta, he scored 48 and 105 at Madras followed by 122 and 54 not out at Kanpur.

The youngest player to score a hundred is Mushtaq Mohammad. The third of the Mohammad brethren to represent Pakistan was 17 years 82 days old when he scored 101 against India at Delhi on 12 February 1961. **The youngest to score a century for England** is Denis Compton; playing against Australia for the first time, he was 20 years 19 days old when he completed his innings of 102 at Nottingham on 11 June 1938.

Sachin Tendulkar is **the only batsman to score three Test hundreds before his 19th birthday, five before his 20th and seven before his 21st.**

Jack Hobbs, **the oldest man to score a hundred at Test level,** was 46 years 82 days old when he scored 142 on 8 March 1929 at Melbourne in his last Test in Australia.

The youngest to score a double century is Javed Miandad; he was 19 years 141 days old (unconfirmed) when he completed his innings of 206 for Pakistan against New Zealand at Karachi on 31 October 1976.

Gary Sobers was only 21 years 216 days old when he reached 300 during his world record 365 not out for West Indies against Pakistan at Kingston, Jamaica, on 1 March 1958, and established himself as **the youngest triple century-maker in Test cricket.**

It was his first three-figure score for West Indies.

The youngest to score a Test fifty is Sachin Tendulkar who was just 16 years 214 days when he made 59 for India against Pakistan at Faisalabad on 23–24 November 1989. Nine days earlier he had become **the youngest to make his Test debut for India.**

The first player to be dismissed for 99 in a Test was Clem Hill of Australia. Having been out at that score on 2 January 1902, he was out for 98 and 97 in the next match at Adelaide, and so became **the only player to be dismissed for three successive nineties in Tests.**

The fastest hundred in Test cricket was scored in 70 minutes (67 balls) by Jack Gregory for Australia against South Africa in Johannesburg on 12 November 1921. A right-arm fast bowler and spectacular left-handed batsman, Gregory was at his peak immediately after World War I. His introduction to Test cricket coincided with Australia gaining a record eight successive victories against England, Gregory's contribution being 40 wickets, 512 runs and 22 catches. In the 1921 rubber, his fearsome opening partnership with Ted McDonald had accounted for 46 wickets. Normally a late or middle-order batsman who seldom wore batting gloves, Gregory had opened the batting and scored 51 in the first Test of this three-match rubber played by Armstrong's team on their way home from England. He batted number four in this Second Test, joining Herbie Collins, his new captain, with the Old Wanderers scoreboard showing a total of 128 for 2. He reached his half-century in 35 minutes and maintained exactly the same rate for his second fifty. Surviving three dropped catches, he was eventually stumped off the slow left-arm bowling of Claude Carter for 119 – the higher of his two Test hundreds. The third-wicket partnership had added 209 runs in only 97 minutes. Although forced to follow on 207 runs in arrears, South Africa were able to draw the four-day match when Charlie Frank, in the middle of a three-match Test career, thwarted the efforts of Gregory, McDonald, Mailey and Hendry for 8 hours 38 minutes in an epic innings of 152.

The fastest recorded hundred in terms of balls received was scored off 56 balls (81 minutes) by Viv Richards on 15 April 1986. Captaining West Indies against England at St John's in his native Antigua, Richards reached his fifty off 34 balls in 46 minutes and declared after scoring 110 not out off 58 balls. His 20th Test hundred included 41 scoring strokes, 18 of them singles: 003612614102110 (28 at tea)

Sachin Tendulkar: India's youngest Test debutant, nine days later the youngest player ever to score a Test fifty (Allsport/Chris Cole)

041211120211100010162404411200664612021 04. This sensational display of controlled hitting enabled Richards to declare at 246 for 2, with a lead of 410 and with seven hours in which to dismiss England. West Indies duly concluded their task with 13.5 overs to spare, their 240-run victory completing their second consecutive series 'blackwash'.

The fastest hundred by an England batsman in Tests in terms of both minutes batted and balls faced is Gilbert Jessop's 75-minute, 76-ball onslaught against Australia at The Oval on 13 August 1902. Set 263 to win, England had lost five wickets for 48 on a rain-damaged pitch when 'The Croucher' began his innings at 1.10pm. Attacking the bowling from the start, he scored 22 off his first 12 balls, survived two chances, and was 29 not out at lunch after 20 minutes batting. After the interval he completed his fifty out of 70 added with the Hon F.S. Jackson in 43 minutes, and added four consecutive boundaries off the leftarm spin of Jack Saunders. At 3.02pm Jackson was out for 49, the partnership having added 109 in 67 minutes with Jessop's share being 83. Eight minutes later Jessop reached his hundred out of 135, having hit an all-run five, 16 fours, 2 threes, 4 twos and 17 singles off the bowling of Trumble (who bowled 33.5 overs unchanged throughout the innings from the pavilion end), Saunders, Noble and Armstrong. After hitting one more boundary, Jessop was out two minutes later having made 104 out of 139 in 77 minutes. England went on to snatch an historic victory in a 'crescendo of excitement' (*Wisden*) with their last pair of George Hirst (58 not out) and Wilfred Rhodes (6 not out) scoring the last 15 runs.

The most runs scored by a batsman for England before lunch on the first day is 98 by Charlie Barnett against Australia at Trent Bridge, Nottingham, on 10 June 1938. He reached 98 in the penultimate over before lunch but Hutton failed to score from the last six balls before the interval. The Gloucestershire right-hander off-drove the first ball of the afternoon session to the boundary, reaching his second Test hundred in two hours.

The most runs scored before lunch on any day of a Test match is 123 by Leslie Ames for England against South Africa at The Oval on 20 August 1935. Resuming his innings at 11am, on the last day of this three-day match, with his score 25, the Kent wicket-keeper was 148 not out when the innings was declared at lunch 2½ hours later.

Greg Chappell scored **the most recent century before lunch in Test cricket** when he took his overnight score from 76 to 176 in 96 minutes on the second day (20 March 1982) of Australia's Third Test against New Zealand at Christchurch.

The slowest Test hundred in terms of both minutes and balls faced took 9 hours 17 minutes and involved 420 balls, a dual record achieved by Mudassar Nazar for Pakistan against England at the Gaddafi Stadium, Lahore, on 14–15 December 1977. Opening the innings on a dead, mud pitch, he scored 52 in 330 minutes on the first day. Ten minutes after tea on the second day (25 minutes of play having been lost to a minor riot when he reached 99), he took his score to 100 out of 306 for 3. It remains **the slowest hundred in all first-class cricket**. His complete innings of 114 lasted 591 minutes.

The fastest double century in Tests was recorded by Don Bradman during his 334 for Australia against England at Headingley, Leeds, on 11 July 1930. He reached his 200 in 214 minutes, his century having taken 99 minutes.

Ian Botham reached his double century off only 220 balls (268 minutes) during his innings of 208 for England against India at The Oval on 8 and 9 July 1982 – **the fastest recorded 200 in Test cricket measured by balls faced**.

HUNDRED BEFORE LUNCH ON THE FIRST DAY

Batsman (final score)	Lunch Score	Match	Venue	Series
V.T. Trumper (104)	103*	A v E	Manchester	1902
C.G. Macartney (151)	112*	A v E	Leeds	1926
D.G. Bradman (334)	105*	A v E	Leeds	1930
Majid Khan (112)	108*	P v NZ	Karachi	1976–77

SLOWEST 50, 100, 200 AND 300 IN TESTS

Score	Min	Balls	Batsman (final score)	Match	Venue	Series
50:	357	350	T.E. Bailey (68)	E v A	Brisbane	1958–59
100:	557	420	Mudassar Nazar (114)	P v E	Lahore	1977–78
200:	777	548	D.S.B.P. Kuruppu (201*)	SL v NZ	Colombo (CCC)	1986–87
300:	858		Hanif Mohammad (337)	P v WI	Bridgetown	1957–58

Wally Hammond scored **the fastest triple century in Test cricket** when he reached 300 in 288 minutes for England against New Zealand at Auckland on 31 March–1 April 1933. His complete innings of 336 not out took 318 minutes and included **ten sixes, the most in any Test innings.**

The fastest fifty in Test cricket took only 28 minutes and was scored by Jack Brown for England during his 140 against Australia at Melbourne on 6 March 1895. A short, strongly-built Yorkshireman, Brown went on to reach his hundred in 95 minutes, the fastest in Test matches at that time. His third-wicket partnership of 210 with Albert Ward set a new Test record for any wicket and saw England within sight of victory in the last and decisive match of the series.

The fastest recorded fifty in terms of balls faced was scored by Kapil Dev during his innings of 73 for India in the Second Test against Pakistan at Karachi's National Stadium on 23 December 1982. Coming to the crease with India 70 for 5 on the first day, he completed his fifty off 30 balls in 50 minutes: 04414144164400000114000041011.

HIGHEST PARTNERSHIPS FOR EACH WICKET

Wkt	Runs	Batsmen (scores)	Match	Venue	Series
1st	413	M.H. Mankad (231), Pankaj Roy (173)	I v NZ	Madras	1955–56
2nd	451	W.H. Ponsford (266), D.G. Bradman (244)	A v E	The Oval	1934
3rd	467	A.H. Jones (186), M.D. Crowe (299)	NZ v SL	Wellington	1990–91
4th	411	P.B.H. May (285*), M.C. Cowdrey (154)	E v WI	Birmingham	1957
5th	405	S.G. Barnes (234), D.G. Bradman (234)	A v E	Sydney	1946–47
6th	346	J.H.W. Fingleton (136), D.G. Bradman (270)	A v E	Melbourne	1936–37
7th	347	D. St E. Atkinson (219), C.C. Depeiaza (122)	WI v A	Bridgetown	1954–55
8th	246	L.E.G. Ames (137), G.O.B. Allen (122)	E v NZ	Lord's	1931
9th	190	Asif Iqbal (146), Intikhab Alam (51)	P v E	The Oval	1967
10th	151	B.F. Hastings (110), R.O. Collinge (68*)	NZ v P	Auckland	1972–73

The highest partnership in Test cricket and the world first-class record for the third wicket added 467 runs in 548 minutes off 924 balls for New Zealand against Sri Lanka at Wellington's Basin Reserve on 3–4 February 1991. Led on first innings by 323 with 14 hours of play to survive, New Zealand were 148 for 2 when Martin Crowe (299) joined Andrew Jones (186). Crowe's score remains **the highest for New Zealand in Tests and the record for any match at the Basin Reserve**, while New Zealand's total of 671 for 4 is **the highest second innings total in Test cricket.**

HIGHEST PARTNERSHIPS FOR EACH COUNTRY

	Runs	Wkt	Batsmen (scores)	Opponents	Venue	Series
England	411	4th	P.B.H. May (285*), M.C. Cowdrey (154)	West Indies	Birmingham	1957
Australia	451	2nd	W.H. Ponsford (266), D.G. Bradman (244)	England	The Oval	1934
South Africa	341	3rd	E.J. Barlow (201), R.G. Pollock (175)	Australia	Adelaide	1963–64
West Indies	446	2nd	C.C. Hunte (260), G. St A. Sobers (365*)	Pakistan	Kingston	1957–58
New Zealand	467	3rd	A.H. Jones (186), M.D. Crowe (299)	Sri Lanka	Wellington	1990–91
India	413	1st	M.H. Mankad (231), Pankaj Roy (173)	New Zealand	Madras	1955–56
Pakistan	451	3rd	Mudassar Nazar (231), Javed Miandad (280*)	India	Hyderabad	1982–83
Sri Lanka	240*	4th	A.P. Gurusinha (116*), A. Ranatunga (135*)	Pakistan	Colombo	1985–86
Zimbabwe	269	4th	G.W. Flower (201*), A. Flower (156)	Pakistan	Harare	1994–95

The most boundaries in an individual Test innings – and the only instance of over 50 being struck – is 57 by John Edrich during his 310 not out for England against New Zealand at Headingley, Leeds, on 8–9 July 1965. He hit 5 sixes and 52 fours during an innings lasting 532 minutes. It remains the highest first-class score by an Englishman at Headingley.

The most boundaries off one over in Test cricket is six by Sandeep Patil for India in the Second Test against England at Manchester on 27 June 1982. Facing the bowling of Bob Willis, England's captain, Patil began the over with three successive fours, the third delivery being a no-ball. He failed to score off the next ball, a yorker, but hit fours off each of the last three balls. Patil thus equalled **the Test record for the most runs by one batsman off an over** (24), set by Andy Roberts for West Indies at Port-of-Spain, Trinidad, on 15 February 1981. Roberts, the first

Andy (left) and Grant Flower: record partnership for Zimbabwe of 269 against Pakistan (Allsport/Mike Hewitt)

Antiguan to represent West Indies, struck 46266 off the bowling of another England captain, Ian Botham, before taking a leg-bye off the last ball.

Botham subsequently exacted his revenge by equalling this record during his innings of 59 not out for England against New Zealand at The Oval on 25 August 1986. He savaged the medium-fast bowling of Derek Stirling for 464604.

During 1990 Ian Smith (New Zealand) and Kapil Dev (India) each equalled the record. Smith struck 244266 off an over from India's Atul Wassan at Eden Park, Auckland, on 22 February during his 136-ball innings of 173 (**the highest Test score by a number nine batsman**), while Kapil drove Eddie Hemmings for six off each of the last four balls of his 20th over at Lord's on 30 July. That spectacular onslaught enabled India to avoid following-on against England's record total of 653 for 4 declared and provided **the first instance in Test cricket of a batsman hitting four successive balls for six.**

Only five players have batted on each day of a five-day Test match, Kim Hughes doing so during the 1980 Centenary Test:

Batsman	Scores		Match	Venue	Series
M.L. Jaisimha	20*	74	I v A	Calcutta	1959-60
G. Boycott	107	80*	E v A	Nottingham	1977
K.J. Hughes	117	84	A v E	Lord's	1980
A.J. Lamb	23	110	E v WI	Lord's	1984
R.J. Shastri	111	7*	I v E	Calcutta	1984–5

The fewest runs scored by a batsman in an uninterrupted day of Test cricket is 49 by M.L. Jaisimha on 18 December 1960. Playing for India against Pakistan at Green Park, Kanpur, the Hyderabad all-rounder took his score from 5 to 54 in 330 minutes. After batting for 8 hours 20 minutes and spending nearly an hour in the nineties, he attempted to run a single from a push back to the bowler and was run out for 99.

The longest any batsman has taken to score his first run in a first-class innings is 97 minutes. Playing against Australia at Adelaide on 5–6 February 1947, Godfrey Evans joined Denis Compton (40*) with England's second innings total 255 for 8. He survived 20 balls that evening while Compton scored 19 runs off 60 deliveries. Next day Evans scored his first run off his 61st ball and enabled Compton to reach his second century of the match. When England were safe from defeat and Hammond declared, Evans had scored 10 not out off 98 balls, and Compton 63 of his 103 not out off 179 balls in a partnership of 85 in 133 minutes. Five years later Evans amassed 98 runs before lunch off India's bowlers in a Test at Lord's.

The record for being not out most times in a Test career is held, perhaps not surprisingly, by a late-order batsman, Bob Willis. In 128 innings between January 1971 and July 1984, the England fast bowler was not out 55 times.

Equally predictably, another tail-ender, Bhagwat Chandrasekhar, achieved the most pairs of ducks in Test Cricket. The Indian spin bowler was dismissed twice in a match without scoring on four occasions: by New Zealand at Wellington in February 1976, by England at Delhi in December 1976, and by Australia at Brisbane and Melbourne in the 1977–78 rubber.

The fastest pair in Test cricket was inflicted upon 'Ebbu' Ghazali of Pakistan by England at Old Trafford, Manchester, on 24 July 1954. Exactly two hours elapsed between the start of his first innings at 4.14pm and his second dismissal at 6.14pm.

Despite being out for nought six times in his first 73 innings, David Gower comfortably holds the record for the most consecutive Test innings without a duck. Between August 1982 and December 1990 he scored in each of his 119 innings.

The most innings before a first duck in Test cricket is 75 by Aravinda de Silva for Sri Lanka from August 1984 until October 1994.

Clyde Walcott was out for nought only once during his Test career. He played 74 innings for West Indies between January 1948 and March 1960, scoring 3798 runs (average 56.68) and making 15 centuries. His solitary duck occurred at Brisbane on 9 November 1951 when Ray Lindwall had him lbw in his first Test innings in Australia.

3000 RUNS IN TESTS

ENGLAND	M	I	Runs	Opponents A	SA	WI	NZ	I	P	SL
G.A. Gooch	118	215	8900	2632	139	2197	1148	1725	683	376
D.I. Gower	117	204	8231	3269	–	1149	1051	1391	1185	186
G. Boycott	108	193	8114	2945	373	2205	916	1084	591	–
M.C. Cowdrey	114	188	7624	2433	1021	1751	1133	653	633	–
W.R. Hammond	85	140	7249	2852	2188	639	1015	555	–	–
L. Hutton	79	138	6971	2428	1564	1661	777	522	19	–
K.F. Barrington	82	131	6806	2111	989	1042	594	1355	715	–
D.C.S. Compton	78	131	5807	1842	2205	592	510	205	453	–
J.B. Hobbs	61	102	5410	3636	1562	212	–	–	–	–
I.T. Botham	102	161	5200	1673	–	792	846	1201	647	41
J.H. Edrich	77	127	5138	2644	7	792	840	494	361	–
T.W. Graveney	79	123	4882	1075	234	1532	293	805	943	–
A.J. Lamb	79	139	4656	1138	–	1342	941	877	180	178
H. Sutcliffe	54	84	4555	2741	1336	206	250	22	–	–
P.B.H. May	66	106	4537	1566	906	986	603	356	120	–
E.R. Dexter	62	102	4502	1358	585	866	477	467	749	–
M.W. Gatting	79	138	4409	1661	–	258	435	1155	853	47
A.P.E. Knott	95	149	4389	1682	–	994	352	685	676	–
R.A. Smith	57	105	3982	1074	–	1333	485	507	314	269
M.A. Atherton	51	96	3812	1312	207	1077	630	426	145	15
D.L. Amiss	50	88	3612	305	–	1130	433	965	779	–
A.W. Greig	58	93	3599	1303	–	795	267	883	351	–
E.H. Hendren	51	83	3525	1740	876	909	–	–	–	–
F.E. Woolley	64	98	3283	1664	1354	–	235	30	–	–
K.W.R. Fletcher	59	96	3272	661	–	528	578	874	586	45
A.J. Stewart	48	87	3168	675	226	829	673	146	397	222

Graham Gooch (left) is congratulated by Australia's Allan Border after becoming England's all-time top run-scorer (Popperfoto)

						Opponents				
AUSTRALIA	M	I	Runs	E	SA	WI	NZ	I	P	SL
A.R. Border	156	265	11174	3548	298	2052	1500	1567	1666	543
D.C. Boon	101	181	7111	2237	433	1437	1187	1204	321	292
G.S. Chappell	87	151	7110	2619	–	1400	1076	368	1581	66
D.G. Bradman	52	80	6996	5028	806	447	–	715	–	–
R.N. Harvey	79	137	6149	2416	1625	1054	–	775	279	–
K.D. Walters	74	125	5357	1981	258	1196	901	756	265	–
I.M. Chappell	75	136	5345	2138	288	1545	486	536	352	–
W.M. Lawry	67	123	5234	2233	985	1035	–	892	89	–
M.A. Taylor	66	119	5005	1951	401	831	452	422	496	452
R.B. Simpson	62	111	4869	1405	980	1043	–	1125	316	–
I.R. Redpath	66	120	4737	1512	791	1247	413	475	299	–
S.R. Waugh	76	117	4440	1686	360	1020	695	85	307	287
K.J. Hughes	70	124	4415	1499	–	774	138	988	1016	–
R.W. Marsh	96	150	3633	1633	–	707	486	83	724	–
D.M. Jones	52	89	3631	1320	–	631	171	681	291	537
A.R. Morris	46	79	3533	2080	792	452	–	209	–	–
C. Hill	49	89	3412	2660	752	–	–	–	–	–
G.M. Wood	59	112	3374	1063	–	1077	393	287	550	4
V.T. Trumper	48	89	3163	2263	900	–	–	–	–	–
C.C. McDonald	47	83	3107	1043	786	880	–	224	174	–
A.L. Hassett	43	69	3073	1572	748	402	19	332	–	–
M.E. Waugh	48	77	3072	1172	349	947	240	83	220	61

SOUTH AFRICA	M	I	Runs	Opponents E	A	NZ				
B. Mitchell	42	80	**3471**	2732	573	166				

WEST INDIES	M	I	Runs	Opponents E	A	SA	NZ	I	P	SL
I.V.A. Richards	121	182	**8540**	2869	2266	–	387	1927	1091	–
G. St A. Sobers	93	160	**8032**	3214	1510	–	404	1920	984	–
C.G. Greenidge	108	185	**7558**	2318	1819	–	882	1678	861	–
C.H. Lloyd	110	175	**7515**	2120	2211	–	234	2344	606	–
D.L. Haynes	116	202	**7487**	2392	2233	81	843	990	928	20
R.B. Kanhai	79	137	**6227**	2267	1694	–	–	1693	573	–
R.B. Richardson	86	146	**5949**	1586	2175	46	512	871	708	51
E. de C. Weekes	48	81	**4455**	1313	714	–	478	1495	455	–
A.I. Kallicharran	66	109	**4399**	891	1325	–	365	1229	589	–
R.C. Fredericks	59	109	**4334**	1369	1069	–	537	767	592	–
F.M.M. Worrell	51	87	**3860**	1979	918	–	233	730	–	–
C.L. Walcott	44	74	**3798**	1391	914	–	199	909	385	–
D.J.L. Dujon	81	115	**3322**	798	1176	–	300	806	242	–
C.C. Hunte	44	78	**3245**	1005	927	–	–	670	643	–
H.A. Gomes	60	91	**3171**	801	1122	–	230	806	212	–
B.F. Butcher	44	78	**3104**	1373	810	–	216	572	133	–
B.C. Lara	31	52	**3048**	1563	774	81	149	198	265	18

*Vivian Richards: record total
of Test runs for West Indies
(Allsport/David Cannon)*

NEW ZEALAND	M	I	Runs	Opponents E	A	SA	WI	I	P	SL	Z
M.D. Crowe	74	128	**5394**	1421	1255	164	544	161	973	627	249
J.G. Wright	82	148	**5334**	1518	1277	–	535	804	576	624	–
B.E. Congdon	61	114	**3448**	1143	456	–	764	713	372	–	–
J.R. Reid	58	108	**3428**	953	–	914	212	691	658	–	–
R.J. Hadlee	86	134	**3124**	798	783	–	389	310	559	285	–

INDIA	M	I	Runs	E	A	SA	WI	NZ	P	SL	Z
					Opponents						
S.M. Gavaskar	125	214	10122	2483	1550	–	2749	651	2089	600	–
D.B. Vengsarkar	116	185	6868	1589	1304	–	1596	440	1284	655	–
G.R. Viswanath	91	155	6080	1880	1538	–	1455	585	611	11	–
Kapil Dev	131	184	5248	1355	687	201	1079	207	1054	588	76
M. Amarnath	69	113	4378	656	773	–	1076	407	1080	386	–
M. Azharuddin	65	94	4198	1236	431	120	476	519	627	738	51
R.J. Shastri	80	121	3830	1026	622	59	847	182	801	282	11
P.R. Umrigar	59	94	3631	770	227	–	1372	351	911	–	–
V.L. Manjrekar	55	92	3208	1181	377	–	569	507	574	–	–
C.G. Borde	55	97	3061	746	502	–	870	613	330	–	–

PAKISTAN	M	I	Runs	E	A	SA	WI	NZ	I	SL	Z
					Opponents						
Javed Miandad	124	189	8832	1329	1797	–	834	1919	2228	582	143
Zaheer Abbas	78	124	5062	1086	1411	–	259	428	1740	138	–
Salim Malik	84	124	4804	1201	914	100	456	805	719	502	107
Mudassar Nazar	76	116	4114	858	893	–	184	365	1431	383	–
Majid Khan	63	106	3931	751	915	–	821	936	445	63	–
Hanif Mohammad	55	97	3915	1039	548	–	736	622	970	–	–
Imran Khan	88	126	3807	500	862	–	775	308	1091	271	–
Mushtaq Mohammad	57	100	3643	1554	409	–	488	779	413	–	–
Asif Iqbal	58	99	3575	822	758	–	416	1113	466	–	–

SRI LANKA	M	I	Runs	E	A	SA	WI	NZ	I	P	Z
					Opponents						
A. Ranatunga	56	94	3134	322	499	250	31	598	654	623	157

ZIMBABWE

The leading scorer is D.L. Houghton with 912 runs in 13 Tests.

BOWLING RECORDS

At 10.34am on 8 February 1994, the opening day of India's Third Test against Sri Lanka at Ahmedabad's Gujarat Stadium, Kapil Dev had the left-handed Hashan Tillekeratne caught at short-leg in his eighth over to overhaul Sir Richard Hadlee's world record of 431 Test wickets. For 64 minutes most of India had been at a standstill monitoring his progress. Now the stadium erupted, his feat saluted by 432 balloons and a minute's ovation from a crowd of 6000.

Kapil played just one more Test, at Hamilton, New Zealand, the following month and extended his **world record for the most Test wickets** to 434 in 131 matches between 16 October 1978 and 23 March 1994. Surprisingly, in view of the slow, unresponsive nature of many of the pitches there, he took exactly half of those wickets in 65 Tests in India. He also holds **the world record for dismissing most batsmen for nought in Tests** (68).

The first bowler to take 100 wickets in Test matches was the Lancashire and England left-arm slow bowler, Johnny Briggs. He reached the landmark just before tea on the first day of the Fourth Test against Australia at Sydney on 1 February 1895 in his 25th match. Three days later, on the next day of actual play in the same match, the New South Wales fast-medium bowler, Charlie Turner, claimed his hundredth wicket in his 17th and last Test.

The fastest first hundred Test wickets in the terms of fewest matches played in and balls bowled was achieved by the Surrey and England medium-pace bowler, George Lohmann. He reached that aggregate at the Old Wanderers, Johannesburg, on 4 March 1896 in his 16th Test. At the end of that innings Lohmann had career totals of 3421 balls bowled and 1066 runs conceded; the next lowest in both categories was achieved by Briggs with 3514 and 1350 respectively. If measured by the least number of innings, then the fastest hundred wickets was achieved by 'Terror' Turner in only 30 innings.

In that respect he was two innings quicker than Lohmann although one match slower.

Measured in terms of time there is no such confusion. **The shortest period in which a bowler has attained an aggregate of 100 Test wickets** is one year 105 days. This record was achieved by Kapil Dev at Eden Gardens, Calcutta, in the Sixth Test against Pakistan on 31 January 1980. He had made his debut on 18 October 1978. In that short period India had played 25 Test matches, an extraordinary proliferation considering that their first 25 occupied a period of twenty years. Kapil Dev is also **the youngest bowler to take 100 wickets** at this level: 21 years 25 days. Two days later he established similar records by completing 1000 runs and the Test 'Double'.

All the preceding hundred wickets records refer to the first hundred dismissals of a bowler's Test career. **The fastest hundred wickets of all** was achieved by Sydney Barnes of Warwickshire, Staffordshire, Lancashire and England. Assessed by most of his contemporaries as the best bowler ever, Barnes took the last hundred of his 189 wickets in only eleven Tests (21 innings).

The first bowler to take 200 Test wickets was Australia's New Zealand-born leg-break bowler, Clarrie Grimmett. He reached that total on 17 February 1936 at the Old Wanderers, Johannesburg, in the penultimate Test of his career. **The first to take 200 wickets for England** was Alec Bedser on 26 June 1953 against Australia at Lord's.

The fastest first 200 wickets in terms of fewest matches and innings is that of Grimmett; he took 35 matches during which he bowled in 65 innings.

The youngest bowler to take 200 wickets is Kapil Dev; he was aged 24 years 68 days on 15 March 1983 when he celebrated his 50th Test by completing the 'double double' (v West Indies at Port-of-Spain).

Fred Trueman was **the first bowler to take 300 wickets in Test cricket.** He reached that total at The Oval in his 65th Test on 15 August 1964 when he had Neil Hawke of Australia caught at slip by Colin Cowdrey.

The fastest 300 wickets was achieved by Dennis Lillee in 56 Tests (108 innings), although Trueman completed his in 340 fewer balls.

Lillee also holds the record for **the most wickets against one country** with 167 wickets (average 21.00) in 29 Tests against England.

Although Kapil Dev, at the age of 28 years and one day, **is the youngest bowler to take 300 Test wickets,** he was appearing in his 83rd Test (v Sri Lanka at Cuttack on 7 January 1987).

The first bowler to take 400 Test wickets was Richard Hadlee on 4 February 1990 against India on his home ground at Lancaster Park, Christchurch. He reached this landmark at the age of 38 years 216 days after 80 Tests spread over 17 years and two days.

Richard Hadlee, the first bowler to 400 Test wickets, claims another victim against India (Allsport/Simon Bruty)

Kapil Dev equalled this feat on 3 February 1992 against Australia in Perth at the age of 33 years 28 days after 115 Tests occupying 13 years 110 days.

Hadlee, who appeared in two Tests in England after gaining a knighthood in the 1990 Birthday Honours, extended the record to 431 wickets in 86 Tests before retiring. His final wicket was captured with the last of his 21 918 deliveries.

Richard Hadlee also holds the Test record for **most instances of five or more wickets in an innings (36) and ten or more wickets in a match (9).**

300 WICKETS IN TEST CRICKET

		Wkts	Tests	Runs/Wkt	Balls	Balls/Wkt	5wI	10wM
Kapil Dev	India	434	131	29.64	27740	63.9	23	2
R.J. Hadlee	New Zealand	431	86	22.29	21918	50.8	36	9
I.T. Botham	England	383	102	28.40	21815	56.9	27	4
M.D. Marshall	West Indies	376	81	20.94	17584	46.7	22	4
Imran Khan	Pakistan	362	88	22.81	19458	53.7	23	6
D.K. Lillee	Australia	355	70	23.92	18467	52.0	23	7
R.G.D. Willis	England	325	90	25.20	17357	53.4	16	-
L.R. Gibbs	West Indies	309	79	29.09	27115	87.7	18	2
F.S. Trueman	England	307	67	21.57	15178	49.4	17	3
C.A. Walsh	West Indies	301	80	25.02	17093	56.7	11	2

The most wickets taken by one bowler in a calendar year is 85 (average 20.95) by Dennis Lillee in 13 Tests during 1981.

The lowest career bowling average by a bowler taking 25 or more Test wickets is 10.75 by George Lohmann, who took 112 wickets in 18 Tests for England between July 1886 and June 1896. The lowest in modern times is 15.02 by Mike Procter who, between January 1967 and March 1970, took 41 wickets in the last seven Tests played by South Africa.

The highest career bowling average is 294.00 by Roger Wijesuriya in four matches for Sri Lanka between 1982 and 1985. He bowled 586 balls, the most by any bowler taking only one wicket in Tests.

The highest wicket-taking rate in Test cricket was achieved by George Lohmann with a wicket every 34 balls (112 wickets in 3821 balls).

William Attewell of Nottinghamshire and England recorded the **most economical career figures in Test matches** by a bowler delivering at least 2000 balls. A medium pace bowler of exceptional accuracy, Attewell conceded just under 22 runs per 100 balls in taking 27 wickets in ten Tests between December 1884 and March 1892.

MOST WICKETS FOR EACH TEAM IN A SERIES

	Wickets	Bowler	Opponents	Venue	Tests	Series
England	49	S.F. Barnes	South Africa	SA	4	1913–14
Australia	44	C.V. Grimmett	South Africa	SA	5	1935–36
South Africa	37	H.J. Tayfield	England	SA	5	1956–57
West Indies	35	M.D. Marshall	England	E	5	1988
New Zealand	33	R.J. Hadlee	Australia	A	3	1985–86
India	35	B.S. Chandrasekhar	England	I	5	1972–73
Pakistan	40	Imran Khan	India	P	6	1982–83
Sri Lanka	20	R.J. Ratnayake	India	SL	3	1985–86
Zimbabwe	22	H.H. Streak	Pakistan	Z	3	1994–95

The highest number of wickets taken by one bowler in a series is 49 by Sydney Barnes for England in four Tests during the 1913–14 series on matting wickets in South Africa. Barnes took ten wickets in the First Test, established a Test record which stood until 1956 by taking 17 in the Second, claimed eight in the Third, and finished with 14 in the Fourth Test. That proved to be his final appearance for England. He declined to play in the Fifth Test following a difference of opinion concerning his wife's accommodation – much to the relief of the South Africans. His full figures were 222 overs (six-ball),

56 maidens, 536 runs, 49 wickets, average 10.93. In seven Tests against South Africa (the 1912 Triangular Tournament and the 1913–14 rubber), Barnes took 83 wickets (average 9.85), **the record against South Africa by a bowler from any country.** That tally included six instances of ten or more wickets in a match, and twelve of five or more in an innings.

The most wickets by one bowler in a series in England, and the only other instance of a bowler taking 45 or more wickets in one rubber, is 46 (average 9.60) by Jim Laker for England against Australia in the five-match series of 1956.

The lowest average recorded by any bowler taking 25 or more wickets in a series is 5.80 by George Lohmann when he claimed 35 South African wickets in the three-match rubber of 1895–96.

The record number of wickets to fall to one bowler in any first-class match is 19 taken by Jim Laker for England against Australia at Old Trafford, Manchester, on 27, 28, 30 and 31 July 1956. The Yorkshire-born, Surrey off-break bowler took 9 for 37 in 16.4 overs in the first innings and 10 for 53 in 51.2 overs in the second. Ten of his wickets were caught (including five by Alan Oakman at short leg), five were bowled, three lbw and one stumped. All 19 wickets were taken from the Stretford End although Laker frequently switched ends with Tony Lock. Perhaps the most astounding match statistic was Lock's bowling analysis. In 69 overs on a pitch favouring spin bowlers the Surrey left-arm bowler, then in his heyday, took only one wicket for 106 runs.

No other bowler has taken more than 17 wickets in any first-class match.

BEST MATCH ANALYSIS FOR EACH TEAM

For	Analysis	Bowler	Opponents	Venue	Series
England	19–90	J.C. Laker	Australia	Manchester	1956
Australia	16–137	R.A.L. Massie	England	Lord's	1972
South Africa	13–165	H.J. Tayfield	Australia	Melbourne	1952–53
West Indies	14–149	M.A. Holding	England	The Oval	1976
New Zealand	15–123	R.J. Hadlee	Australia	Brisbane	1985–86
India	16–136	N.D. Hirwani	West Indies	Madras	1987–88
Pakistan	14–116	Imran Khan	Sri Lanka	Lahore	1981–82
Sri Lanka	10–90	W.P.U.C.J. Vaas	New Zealand	Napier	1994–95
Zimbabwe	9–105	H.H. Streak	Pakistan	Harare	1994–95

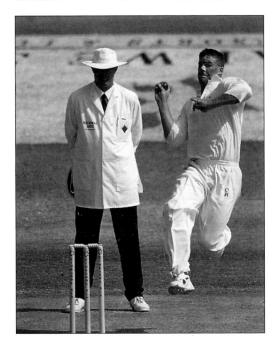

Heath Streak (Zimbabwe): 9–105 against Pakistan at Harare
(Allsport/Clive Mason)

The most runs conceded by one bowler in a Test match is 374 by 'Tommy' Scott for West Indies against England at Kingston, Jamaica, in April 1930. Scott bowled 105.2 overs and took nine wickets with his leg-breaks as England scored 849 and 272 for 9 declared in this Timeless Test. Arthur Mailey, the only other bowler to concede 300 runs in a Test match, was also a leg-spinner. Playing for Australia against England, he twice suffered this fate, taking 10 for 302 at Adelaide in January 1921 and 7 for 308 at Sydney in December 1924.

The highest number of balls bowled by one player in a Test is 774 by Sonny Ramadhin for West Indies against England at Edgbaston, Birmingham, in 1957 (30 May–4 June). Having taken 7 for 49 in the first innings as England were dismissed for 186, he was thwarted in the second by a record fourth-wicket stand of 411 by May and Cowdrey. England totalled 583 for 4 declared as Ramadhin bowled a record 98 overs to take 2 for 179. A finger-spinner who mesmerized batsmen by turning the ball either way without any obvious change of action, Ramadhin found himself treated as a straightforward off-break bowler and, after this traumatic experience, was never again so effective at Test level.

The best innings analysis in Test cricket – and the only instance of a bowler taking all ten wickets at that level – was recorded by Jim Laker at Old Trafford, Manchester, in 1956 when he took ten Australian second innings wickets for 53 runs. This historic performance was spread over five days including the rest day. Following on 375 behind, after Laker had devastated their first innings with a spell of eight wickets for seven runs in 22 balls to return a final analysis of 9 for 53, Australia lost their first wicket before stumps on the second day. Rain on the third day permitted only 45 minutes cricket during which Laker took his second wicket. Heavy rain fell on the Sunday rest day and allowed just an hour's play in two spells on the fourth day. Fierce winds compelled the use of heavy bails made from lignum vitae. They were not disturbed and Australia had still eight wickets intact when play began ten minutes late on the last day (31 July). They were still intact at lunch. Then the sun appeared, the ball began to turn more quickly and four wickets fell to Laker's off-spin before tea. England had 115 minutes in which to take the last four wickets and ensure retention of the Ashes. When Colin McDonald (89) was out to the second ball after tea, Australia's hopes of a draw vanished. He had batted on four different days for the only Australian score above 38 in the match. At 5.27pm Laker trapped wicket-keeper Len Maddocks lbw and England had won by an innings and 170 runs – or by 33 minutes. All Laker's wickets in both innings fell from the Stretford End. That night the heavy rain returned to cause the abandonment of the entire county cricket programme on the following day.

The most runs conceded by a bowler in one Test innings is 298 by 'Chuck' Fleetwood-Smith of Australia during England's record total of 903 for 7 declared at The Oval in August 1938. A left-arm, back-of-the-hand spin bowler whose natural ball was an off-break, Fleetwood-Smith sent down 87 overs in that innings for just one wicket. Only one England bowler had conceded over 200 runs in a Test innings and he was a Scotsman; fortunately Ian Peebles was also an extremely humorous man. He had the compensation of taking six wickets in the course of his 71 overs, while contributing 204 runs towards Australia's total of 695 (Bradman 232) at The Oval in August 1930.

DISMISSING ALL ELEVEN BATSMEN IN A MATCH

	Analysis	Match	Venue	Series
J.C. Laker	19–90	England v Australia	Manchester	1956
S. Venkataraghavan	12–152	India v New Zealand	Delhi	1964–65
G. Dymock	12–166	Australia v India	Kanpur	1979–80
Abdul Qadir	13–101	Pakistan v England	Lahore	1987–88
Waqar Younis	12–130	Pakistan v New Zealand	Faisalabad	1990–91

BEST INNINGS ANALYSIS FOR EACH TEAM

For	Analysis	Bowler	Opponents	Venue	Series
England	10–53	J.C. Laker	Australia	Manchester	1956
Australia	9–121	A.A. Mailey	England	Melbourne	1920–21
South Africa	9–113	H.J. Tayfield	England	Johannesburg	1956–57
West Indies	9–95	J.M. Noreiga	India	Port-of-Spain	1970–71
New Zealand	9–52	R.J. Hadlee	Australia	Brisbane	1985–86
India	9–69	J.M. Patel	Australia	Kanpur	1959–60

For	Analysis	Bowler	Opponents	Venue	Series
Pakistan	9–56	Abdul Qadir	England	Lahore	1987–88
Sri Lanka	8–83	J.R. Ratnayeke	Pakistan	Sialkot	1985–86
Zimbabwe	6–90	H.H. Streak	Pakistan	Harare	1994–95

WICKET WITH FIRST BALL IN TEST CRICKET

Bowler	Batsman	Match	Venue	Series
A. Coningham	A.C. MacLaren	A v E	Melbourne	1894–95
W.M. Bradley	F. Laver	E v A	Manchester	1899
E.G. Arnold	V.T. Trumper	E v A	Sydney	1903–04
G.G. Macaulay	G.A.L. Hearne	E v SA	Cape Town	1922–23
M.W. Tate	M.J. Susskind	E v SA	Birmingham	1924
M. Henderson	E.W. Dawson	NZ v E	Christchurch	1929–30
H.D. Smith	E. Paynter	NZ v E	Christchurch	1932–33
T.F. Johnson	W.W. Keeton	WI v E	The Oval	1939
R. Howorth	D.V. Dyer	E v SA	The Oval	1947
Intikhab Alam	C.C. McDonald	P v A	Karachi	1959–60
R.K. Illingworth	P.V. Simmons	E v WI	Nottingham	1991

Richard Illingworth (England): first bowler in over 30 years to take a wicket with his first ball in Test cricket (Allsport/Clive Mason)

The highest number of balls bowled in any first-class innings is 588 by Sonny Ramadhin for West Indies during England's second innings at Edgbaston, Birmingham, in June 1957. The 5ft 4in finger-spinner took 2 for 179 in 98 overs as Peter May (285 not out) and Colin Cowdrey (154) batted England to safety, adding 411 in England's highest-ever partnership. His total of 774 balls bowled in that match remains the Test record.

The most wickets taken by one bowler in a single day of Test cricket is 15 by Johnny Briggs for England against South Africa at Newlands, Cape Town, on 26 March 1889. The first English team to visit South Africa played only two eleven-a-side fixtures; this was the second, and both have come to be rated as full Test matches. South Africa, replying to England's total of 292, were bowled out by Briggs (left-arm slow) for 47 and 43. They were literally bowled out: six of his seven first innings wickets and all of his eight in the second were bowled. He gained all 15 wickets without the aid of a fieldsman, the other one being lbw. In the second innings **nine batsmen were bowled – the most in any Test innings**.

The most wickets to fall to one bowler in a day's Test cricket in England is 14 on 25 June 1934 at Lord's. Australia were caught on a drying pitch and bowled to their first defeat at Lord's since 1896 by the Yorkshire left-arm spinner, Hedley Verity.

There have been 22 hat-tricks in Test cricket, the first being achieved by 'The Demon' Spofforth for Australia against England at Melbourne on 2 January 1879 in only the third Test match played.

Two bowlers, both Australians, took two Test match hat-tricks. Hugh Trumble, a medium-pace off-spinner, took both of his against England at Melbourne, the first in January 1902 and the second in March 1904 in his final first-class match. Jimmy Matthews achieved **the unique feat of taking two hat-tricks in the same Test** – against South Africa at Old Trafford, Manchester, during the opening match of the 1912 Triangular Tournament. A right-arm leg-break bowler, he gained a hat-trick in each innings on the afternoon of 28 May, his only six wickets of the match and all taken without assistance from fieldsmen.

The most recent Test hat-trick was accomplished by Dominic Cork in his third Test, against West Indies at Old Trafford, Manchester on 30 July 1995. It was **the first Test match hat-trick to be achieved in the opening over of a day's play,** the first for England since 1957 and the first in England since 1960. Curiously, Cork's last victim, Carl Hooper, had also featured as the third dismissal in his hat-trick for Derbyshire against Kent the previous season.

The first bowler to take a hat-trick in his first Test was Maurice Allom, who took four wickets in five balls (W-WWW) during his eighth over for England, against New Zealand at Christchurch on his first day of Test cricket – 10 January 1930. There has

been only one subsequent instance of a bowler taking four Test wickets in five balls, Chris Old achieving this feat in his 19th over, for England against Pakistan at Edgbaston, Birmingham, on 1 June 1978. He took four wickets with successive legitimate balls but delivered a no-ball in the middle of the sequence, his over reading: WWnbWW1.

Only two bowlers have taken three wickets in a sequence of four balls on more than one occasion; both were Australians and in every instance their victims were England batsmen. On 29 August 1882, Spofforth became the first bowler to achieve this feat in the course of taking 7 for 44 at The Oval. His performance brought about England's first home defeat and led to the creation of the Ashes through a mock obituary notice in *The Times*. He repeated the feat at Sydney on 21 February 1885. The second Australian bowler was Dennis Lillee who took three wickets in four balls in the Manchester and Oval Tests of 1972.

Dominic Cork (England) shows off the man of the match award after his hat-trick against West Indies in 1995 (Allsport/Graham Chadwick)

100 WICKETS IN TESTS

ENGLAND	M	Wickets	A	SA	Opponents WI	NZ	I	P	SL
I.T. Botham	102	383	148	–	61	64	59	40	11
R.G.D. Willis	90	325	128	–	38	60	62	34	3
F.S. Trueman	67	307	79	27	86	40	53	22	–
D.L. Underwood	86	297	105	–	38	48	62	36	8
J.B. Statham	70	252	69	69	42	20	25	27	–
A.V. Bedser	51	236	104	54	11	13	44	10	–
J.A. Snow	49	202	83	4	72	20	16	7	–
J.C. Laker	46	193	79	32	51	21	8	2	–
S.F. Barnes	27	189	106	83	–	–	–	–	–
G.A.R. Lock	49	174	31	15	39	47	26	16	–
M.W. Tate	39	155	83	53	13	6	–	–	–
F.J. Titmus	53	153	47	27	15	28	27	9	–
J.E. Emburey	64	147	78	–	30	9	12	7	11
H. Verity	40	144	59	31	9	7	38	–	–
C.M. Old	46	143	40	–	18	21	43	21	–
A.W. Greig	58	141	44	–	36	20	27	14	–
P.A.J. DeFreitas	44	140	37	9	33	39	–	14	8
G.R. Dilley	41	138	41	–	36	24	17	20	–
T.E. Bailey	61	132	42	28	29	32	–	1	–
W. Rhodes	58	127	109	8	10	–	–	–	–
P.H. Edmonds	51	125	36	–	3	31	33	22	–
D.A. Allen	39	122	28	21	15	13	21	24	–
R. Illingworth	61	122	34	6	19	22	31	10	–
J. Briggs	33	118	97	21	–	–	–	–	–
D.E. Malcolm	34	116	36	10	30	17	10	13	–
G.G. Arnold	34	115	30	–	17	20	27	21	–
A.R.C. Fraser	29	115	42	7	43	7	16	–	–
G.A. Lohmann	18	112	77	35	–	–	–	–	–
D.V.P. Wright	34	108	48	37	11	8	4	–	–
J.H. Wardle	28	102	24	46	7	5	–	20	–
R. Peel	20	101	101	–	–	–	–	–	–
C. Blythe	19	100	41	59	–	–	–	–	–

AUSTRALIA	M	Wickets	E	SA	Opponents WI	NZ	I	P	SL
D.K. Lillee	70	355	167	–	55	38	21	71	3
C.J. McDermott	65	270	84	21	59	48	34	7	17
R. Benaud	63	248	83	52	42	–	52	19	–
G.D. McKenzie	60	246	96	41	47	–	47	15	–
R.R. Lindwall	61	228	114	31	41	2	36	4	–
C.V. Grimmett	37	216	106	77	33	–	–	–	–
M.G. Hughes	53	212	75	4	53	25	23	16	16
J.R. Thomson	51	200	100	–	62	6	22	10	–
A.K. Davidson	44	186	84	25	33	–	30	14	–
G.F. Lawson	46	180	97	–	39	10	–	33	1
S.K. Warne	38	176	61	33	25	35	1	18	3
T.M. Alderman	41	170	100	–	26	16	–	23	5
K.R. Miller	55	170	87	30	40	2	9	2	–
W.A. Johnston	40	160	75	44	25	–	16	–	–
W.J. O'Reilly	27	144	102	34	–	8	–	–	–
H. Trumble	32	141	141	–	–	–	–	–	–

AUSTRALIA	M	Wickets	Opponents E	SA	WI	NZ	I	P	SL
M.H.N. Walker	34	138	56	–	37	28	–	17	–
A.A. Mallett	38	132	50	6	16	19	28	13	–
B. Yardley	33	126	29	–	35	13	21	21	7
R.M. Hogg	38	123	56	–	22	10	15	19	1
M.A. Noble	42	121	115	6	–	–	–	–	–
B.A. Reid	27	113	47	–	12	16	24	14	–
I.W. Johnson	45	109	42	22	22	–	19	4	–
G. Giffen	31	103	103	–	–	–	–	–	–
A.N. Connolly	29	102	25	26	20	–	31	–	–
C.T.B. Turner	17	101	101	–	–	–	–	–	–

SOUTH AFRICA	M	Wickets	Opponents E	A	NZ
H.J. Tayfield	37	170	75	64	31
T.L. Goddard	41	123	63	53	7
P.M. Pollock	28	116	32	52	32
N.A.T. Adcock	26	104	57	14	33

WEST INDIES	M	Wickets	Opponents E	A	SA	NZ	I	P	SL
M.D. Marshall	81	376	127	87	–	36	76	50	–
L.R. Gibbs	79	309	100	103	–	11	63	32	–
C.A. Walsh	80	301	101	67	4	32	61	35	1
J. Garner	58	259	92	89	36	7	35		
C.E.L. Ambrose	59	258	117	90	8	5	5	30	3
M.A. Holding	60	249	96	76	–	16	61	–	–
G. St A. Sobers	93	235	102	51	–	19	59	4	–
A.M.E. Roberts	47	202	50	51	–	3	67	31	–
W.W. Hall	48	192	65	45	–	1	65	16	–
S. Ramadhin	43	158	80	22	–	32	15	9	–
A.L. Valentine	36	139	40	43	–	23	30	3	–
C.E.H. Croft	27	125	33	32	–	–	10	50	–
I.R. Bishop	24	110	48	23	–	–	16	23	–
V.A. Holder	40	109	33	28	–	12	31	5	–

NEW ZEALAND	M	Wickets	Opponents E	A	SA	WI	I	P	SL	Z
R.J. Hadlee	86	431	97	130	–	51	65	51	37	–
D.K. Morrison	41	143	23	37	8	8	20	27	20	–
B.L. Cairns	43	130	32	23	17	22	21	–	15	–
E.J. Chatfield	43	123	34	24	–	23	6	14	22	–
R.O. Collinge	35	116	48	17	–	–	23	28	–	–
B.R. Taylor	30	111	28	–	–	32	29	22	–	–
J.G. Bracewell	41	102	31	38	–	2	19	6	6	–
R.C. Motz	32	100	28	–	21	17	22	12	–	–

INDIA	M	Wickets	Opponents E	A	SA	WI	NZ	P	SL	Z
Kapil Dev	131	434	85	79	8	89	25	99	45	4
B.S. Bedi	67	266	85	56	–	62	57	6	–	–
B.S. Chandrasekhar	58	242	95	38	–	65	36	8	–	–
E.A.S. Prasanna	49	189	41	57	–	34	55	2	–	–

M.H. Mankad	44	**162**	54	23	–	36	12	37	–	–
S. Venkataraghavan	57	**156**	23	20	–	68	44	1	–	–
R.J. Shastri	80	**151**	30	26	2	37	20	24	11	1
S.P. Gupte	36	**149**	24	8	–	49	34	34	–	–
D.R. Doshi	33	**114**	36	38	–	–	5	27	8	–
K.D. Ghavri	39	**109**	19	32	–	36	5	17	–	–
N.S. Yadav	35	**102**	9	55	–	9	1	17	11	–

					Opponents				
PAKISTAN	**M**	**Wickets**	**E**	**A**	**SA**	**WI**	**NZ**	**P**	**SL**	**Z**
Imran Khan	88	**362**	47	64	–	80	31	94	46	–
Wasim Akram	61	**261**	39	26	4	47	55	31	35	24
Abdul Qadir	67	**236**	82	45	–	42	26	27	14	–
Waqar Younis	33	**190**	22	14	–	35	56	6	30	27
Sarfraz Nawaz	55	**177**	37	52	–	26	26	36	–	–
Iqbal Qasim	50	**171**	24	57	–	19	22	34	15	–
Fazal Mahmood	34	**139**	25	24	–	41	5	44	–	–
Intikhab Alam	47	**125**	49	9	–	8	54	5	–	–

SRI LANKA
The leading wicket-taker is R.J. Ratnayake with 73 wickets in 23 Tests.

ZIMBABWE
The leading wicket-taker is H.H. Streak with 43 wickets in 9 Tests.

Pakistan strike bowler Waqar Younis
(Popperfoto)

WICKET-KEEPING RECORDS

The most dismissals by a wicket-keeper in Test cricket is 355 by Rodney Marsh, who, between 27 November 1970 and 6 January 1984, held a record 343 catches and made 12 stumpings in 96 matches for Australia. Marsh gained the record on 18 July 1981 when he caught Botham in England's first innings of the Third Test at Headingley, Leeds, to overtake Alan Knott's total of 263 dismissals. Although Knott was recalled for the last two Tests of that series and held six more catches, he was unable to regain the record.

Marsh also holds **the record for taking most catches off one bowler**, 95 of his victims being caught off his fellow West Australian Dennis Lillee.

100 DISMISSALS IN TESTS

		Tests	Dis	Ct	St	Opponents E	A	SA	WI	NZ	I	P	SL	Z
R.W. Marsh	A	96	355	343	12	148	–	–	65	58	16	68	–	–
P.J.L. Dujon	WI	81	272	267††	5	84	86	–	–	20	60	22	–	–
A.P.E. Knott	E	95	269	250	19	–	105	–	43	26	54	41	–	–
I.A. Healy	A	73	248	231	17	89	–	12	55	34	19	28	11	–
Wasim Bari	P	81	228	201	27	54	66	–	21	32	55	–	–	–
T.G. Evans	E	91	219	173	46	–	76	59	37	28	12	7	–	–
S.M.H. Kirmani	I	88	198	160	38	42	41	–	36	28	–	50	1	–
D.L. Murray	WI	62	189	181	8	94	40	–	–	7	27	21	–	–
A.T.W. Grout	A	51	187	163	24	76	–	33	41	–	20	17	–	–
I.D.S. Smith	NZ	63	176	168	8	42	39	–	16	–	29	23	27	–
R.W. Taylor	E	57	174	167	7	–	57	–	–	45	40	29	3	–
J.H.B. Waite	SA	50	141	124	17	56	28	–	–	57	–	–	–	–
K.S. More	I	49	130	110	20	37	13	11	21	13	–	21	11	3
W.A.S. Oldfield	A	54	130	78	52	90	–	27	13	–	–	–	–	–
J.M. Parks	E	46	114	103†	11	–	21	30	31	22	9	1	–	–
R.C. Russell	E	39	108	99	9	–	28	–	39	16	12	7	6	–
Salim Yousuf	P	32	104	91	13	15	15	–	22	22	11	–	19	–

The most dismissals by a wicket-keeper for Sri Lanka and Zimbabwe are:

		Tests	Dis	Ct	St	E	A	SA	WI	NZ	I	P	SL	Z
S.A.R. Silva	SL	9	34	33	1	6	–	–	–	2	22	4	–	–
A. Flower	Z	13*	31	29	2	–	–	–	–	6	3	17	5	–

† Including 2 catches in 3 Tests when not keeping wicket.
†† Including 2 catches in 2 Tests when not keeping wicket.
* Including 4 Tests in which he did not keep wicket.

The highest aggregate of stumpings in a Test career was achieved by Bert Oldfield who made 52 stumpings in 54 matches for Australia between December 1920 and March 1937.

Oldfield became **the first to make 100 wicket-keeping dismissals at Test level** when he stumped Verity off Grimmett at Lord's on 23 June 1934 in his 41st match. His 28 stumpings off Grimmett's leg-breaks, googlies and top-spinners constitute the record off one bowler.

The first wicket-keeper to make 200 dismissals was Godfrey Evans when he caught 'Collie' Smith in West Indies' second innings at Headingley, Leeds on 27 July 1957 in his 80th Test.

The youngest player to keep wicket in a Test match was Hanif Mohammad. He was 17 years 300 days old when he played in Pakistan's first official Test, against India at Feroz Shah Kotla, Delhi, on 16 October 1952. A specialist opening batsman who later established the long-standing record first-class score of 499, Hanif conceded 28 byes in India's only innings and kept wicket in only the first three of his 55 Tests.

Another specialist batsman, Frank Woolley, became **the oldest player to keep wicket in a Test** when he deputized for the injured Ames in the Fifth Test against Australia at The Oval on 22 August 1934. Recalled after a break of two years to make the last international appearance by a pre-First World War Test player, Woolley was 47 years 87 days old when he conceded 37 byes – still **the record for a Test innings**.

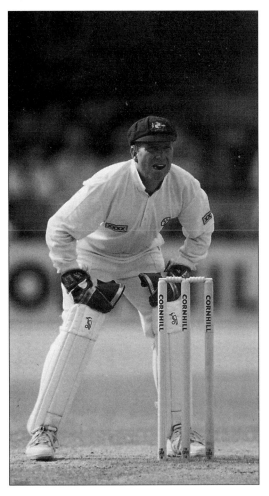

Ian Healy: 248 Test dismissals for Australia, the fourth highest total of all time (Popperfoto)

The most dismissals in a Test series is 28 – all caught by Rodney Marsh in five Tests against England in Australia in 1982–83. At Brisbane in the Second Test he set one Ashes record (six catches in an innings), equalled another (nine in a match), and became the first to hold 300 catches in Tests.

The most stumpings in a Test series is nine by Percy Sherwell in South Africa's five-match series in Australia in 1910–11, seven of them off the googly bowling of Reggie Schwarz.

The match record for wicket-keeping dismissals and catches is ten by Bob Taylor (including eight off Ian Botham's bowling), for England in the Golden Jubilee Test against India at the Wankhede Stadium, Bombay, in February 1980. In the first innings of

that match, Taylor equalled **the Test record for dismissals in an innings** – seven (all caught) by Wasim Bari for Pakistan against New Zealand at Auckland on 23 Feb 1979. This feat was emulated on 23–24 February 1991 by Ian Smith for New Zealand against Sri Lanka in the first Test to be staged in Hamilton.

The Test records for most stumpings in an innings and a match are five and six respectively by India's Kiran More against West Indies at Madras on 14–15 January 1988. All except one of his dismissals came off the leg-break and googly bowling of debutant Narendra Hirwani who took eight wickets in each innings.

The most dismissals in two successive Tests is 18 by Amal Silva for Sri Lanka against India in Colombo in August–September 1985. In the second match, at the Saravanamuttu Stadium, he became **the first wicket-keeper to score a hundred and make nine dismissals in the same Test.**

The highest innings total in which no byes were conceded is New Zealand's 671 for 4 wickets at the Basin Reserve, Wellington when Hashan Tillekeratne was Sri Lanka's wicket-keeper.

The highest total without byes in which all ten wickets fell is 652 by Pakistan against India at Iqbal Stadium, Faisalabad, on 4–7 January 1983. India's wicket-keeper was Syed Kirmani.

The record for conceding no byes in most consecutive Test matches is held by Denis Lindsay of South Africa. He accomplished this by not allowing a bye during four successive appearances against Australia in South Africa in February 1967 and February/March 1970. Australia totalled 1580 runs in the eight innings concerned. During those matches Lindsay held 17 catches and scored a century in a post-tea session.

W.G. Grace is believed to be the **only player to make a dismissal off his first ball as a wicket-keeper in Test cricket.** At The Oval on 12 August 1884, he deputized for the Hon Alfred Lyttelton and held a good legside catch off the latter's first lob of that spell. Lyttelton, the tenth of eleven England bowlers called upon by Lord Harris in Australia's innings of 551 (declarations were not permitted until 1889), took the last four wickets while still wearing his pads. He finished with 4 for 19 – **the best analysis in Test cricket by a player who began the innings as a wicket-keeper.**

The highest score by an appointed wicket-keeper in a Test match is 210 not out by Taslim Arif for Pakistan at the Iqbal Stadium, Faisalabad, on 10 and 11 March 1980. Opening the innings on the fourth day in reply to Australia's 617 all out, Taslim, playing in only his third Test, batted for 7¼ hours, hit 20 fours, and was on the field throughout the match.

FIELDING RECORDS

The most catches taken by a non-wicket-keeper in a Test career is 156 by Allan Border in 156 matches for Australia between December 1978 and March 1994. He gained the record in his 121st match, against Sri Lanka during the inaugural Test at Hobart. It was at the Bellerive Oval on 17 December 1989 that he held his 123rd catch (Rumesh Ratnayake at slip) to overtake the total which Greg Chappell had achieved in 87 matches for Australia between 1970 and 1984.

100 CATCHES IN TESTS

							Opponents					
		Tests	Ct	E	A	SA	WI	NZ	I	P	SL	Z
A.R. Border	A	156	156	57	–	5	19	31	14	22	8	–
G.S. Chappell	A	87	122	61	–	–	16	18	5	22	–	–
I.V.A. Richards	WI	121	122	29	24	–	–	7	39	23	–	–
I.T. Botham	E	102	120	–	61	–	15	14	14	14	2	–
M.C. Cowdrey	E	114	120	–	40	22	21	15	11	11	–	–
R.B. Simpson	A	62	110	30	–	27	29	–	21	3	–	–
W.R. Hammond	E	85	110	–	43	30	22	9	6	–	–	–
G. St A. Sobers	WI	93	109	40	27	–	–	11	27	4	–	–
S.M. Gavaskar	I	125	108	35	19	–	17	11	–	19	7	–
I.M. Chappell	A	75	105	31	–	11	24	16	17	6	–	–
G.A. Gooch	E	113	103	–	29	1	28	13	21	7	4	–

The records for South Africa, New Zealand, Pakistan, Sri Lanka and Zimbabwe are:

							Opponents					
		Tests	Ct	E	A	SA	WI	NZ	I	P	SL	Z
B Mitchell	SA	42	56	43	10	–	–	3	–	–	–	–
M.D. Crowe	NZ	74	70	19	10	7	12	–	1	16	4	1
Javed Miandad	P	124	93	22	10	–	12	20	18	–	11	–
H.P. Tillekeratne	SL	19 †	34	4	–	6	–	12	6	4	–	2
M.H. Dekker	Z	8	10	–	–	–	–	–	–	3	7	–

† *Excluding 11 Tests in which he made 32 dismissals as a wicket-keeper.*

The first fielder to hold 100 catches was Wally Hammond of England. He reached that landmark on 25 July 1939 against West Indies at Old Trafford, Manchester in his 76th match.

The fewest Tests to reach an aggregate of 100 catches is 54 by Bob Simpson of Australia between December 1957 and December 1977.

Both Chappell brothers, Ian and Greg, took their hundredth catch in their 69th Test.

The record number of catches taken by a fielder in one series is 15 by Australian Jack Gregory in the five-match home series of 1920–21 against England. Like many of cricket's most prolific catchers, Gregory was primarily a slip fieldsman.

The most catches held by a fielder in one Test match is seven by Greg Chappell for Australia against England at Perth in December 1974, by Yajurvindra Singh for India against England at Bangalore in January and February 1977 and by Hashan Tillekeratne for Sri Lanka against New Zealand at the Sinhalese Sports Club Ground,

Colombo in December 1992.

Yajurvindra Singh, playing in his first Test match, also equalled the record for **the most catches in an innings** set on 3 March 1936 at Kingsmead, Durban, by Vic Richardson of Australia. The Chappells' grandfather caught five of the last six South African wickets to fall for 21 runs in his final Test. This record was subsequently twice equalled for India, first by Mohammed Azharuddin against Pakistan at Karachi in November 1989 and secondly by Krish Srikkanth against Australia at Perth in February 1992.

One of the most famous and decisive catches in Test cricket was held by a substitute fielder, Sydney Copley, in the First Test between England and Australia at Trent Bridge, Nottingham, on 17 June 1930. Australia were 200 runs away from victory on that final afternoon of a four-day match. They had seven wickets in hand, including those of Bradman and McCabe who had added 77, when Stan McCabe slightly mistimed an on-drive. Copley, a 24-year-old member of the Nottinghamshire groundstaff who was fielding as substitute for Larwood, 'Made a lot of ground, took the ball at full-length and, although rolling over, retained possession' (*Wisden*). That catch turned the course of the innings and England went on to gain (by 93 runs) their only victory of the series. Eight days later Copley made the only first-class appearance of his career, against Oxford University; batting at number four he was dismissed for 4 and 3 by Ian Peebles.

RECORD ALL-ROUND PERFORMANCES

Test cricket's 'Double' – the scoring of 1000 runs allied to the taking of 100 wickets – has been achieved by 29 cricketers, the earliest instance being recorded in 1896. Not until 1963 did the first of six of those players achieve the 'Double Double' of 2000 runs and 200 wickets. Twenty-one years later the first instance of the 'Treble Double' (3000 runs and 300 wickets) was completed by Ian Botham.

THE TEST 'DOUBLE'

ENGLAND	Tests	Runs	Wkts	Tests for 'double'
T.E. Bailey	61	2290	132	47
I.T. Botham	102	5200	383	21
J.E. Emburey	64	1713	147	46
A.W. Greig	58	3599	141	37
R. Illingworth	61	1836	122	47
W. Rhodes	58	2325	127	44
M.W. Tate	39	1198	155	33
F.J. Titmus	53	1449	153	40
AUSTRALIA				
R. Benaud	63	2201	248	32
A.K. Davidson	44	1328	186	34
G. Giffen	31	1238	103	30
M.G. Hughes	53	1032	212	52
I.W. Johnson	45	1000	109	45
R.R. Lindwall	61	1502	228	38
K.R. Miller	55	2958	170	33
M.A. Noble	42	1997	121	27
SOUTH AFRICA				
T.R. Goddard	41	2516	123	36
WEST INDIES				
M.D. Marshall	81	1810	376	49
G. St A. Sobers	93	8032	235	48
NEW ZEALAND				
J.G. Bracewell	41	1001	102	41
R.J. Hadlee	86	3124	431	28
INDIA				
Kapil Dev	131	5248	434	25
M.H. Mankad	44	2109	162	23
R.J. Shastri	80	3830	151	44

PAKISTAN				
Abdul Qadir	67	1029	236	62
Imran Khan	88	3807	362	30
Intikhab Alam	47	1493	125	41
Sarfraz Nawaz	55	1045	177	55
Wasim Akram	61	1401	261	45

The Lion of Pakistan: Imran Khan completed the double in just 30 Tests, a record for his country (Allsport/Ben Radford)

The fewest Test matches in which a player has completed the 'double' is 21 by Ian Botham for England between 28 July 1977 and 30 August 1979. Botham holds similar records for the doubles of 1500 runs and 150 wickets (30 Tests), 2000 runs and 200 wickets (42 Tests) and 3000 runs and 300 wickets (72 Tests).

The fastest 'double' in terms of time was achieved by Kapil Dev for India in one year 107 days between 18 October 1978 and 2 February 1980. At 21 years 27 days, Kapil Dev is the youngest to score 1000 runs and take 100 wickets in a Test career.

The first player to complete the 'double' was George Giffen, the first South Australian to gain an Australian cap. Known as 'The W.G. Grace of Australia', he achieved this feat when he took his 100th wicket on 18 July 1896 against England at Old Trafford, Manchester, in his 30th match. No Englishman did the 'double' until 26 December 1913 when Wilfred Rhodes claimed his 100th wicket, at the Old Wanderers, Johannesburg.

Gary Sobers was the first player to score 1000 runs, take 100 wickets and hold 100 catches in Test cricket. In 93 matches between 30 March 1954 and 5 April 1974, he scored 8032 runs, took 235 wickets and held 109 catches. Ian Botham is the only other player to achieve this feat; in 97 matches between 1977 and 1989, he scored 5119 runs, took 376 wickets and held 112 catches.

300 RUNS AND 30 WICKETS IN A SERIES

	Tests	Runs	Wkts	Series	Venue	Season
G. Giffen	5	475	34	A v E	A	1894–95
R. Benaud	5	329	30	A v SA	SA	1957–58
I.T. Botham	6	399	34	E v A	E	1981

The only player to score 500 runs and take 25 wickets in a series is Aubrey Faulkner of South Africa. In five matches against England, between 1 January and 14 March 1910, he scored 545 runs (average 60.55) and took 29 wickets (average 21.89) with his variations of flight, pace and spin. One of the earliest exponents of the googly, Faulkner was a dependable right-handed batsman and versatile fieldsman whom many rate as South Africa's greatest all-rounder. One of the game's keenest analysts, he later settled in England and opened the first indoor cricket school (near Richmond-upon-Thames).

The first player to complete the 'double double' was Richie Benaud. He scored his 2000th run on 6 December 1963 against South Africa at Brisbane – in the last of his 28 matches as Australia's captain.

The first player to complete the 'treble double' was Ian Botham when he took his 300th wicket – against West Indies at The Oval on 9 August 1984 in his 72nd Test.

The first player to score a century and take ten or more wickets in the same Test match was Ian Botham. In the Golden Jubilee Test on 15–19 February 1980 at Bombay's newest Test arena, the Wankhede Stadium, Botham took 6 for 58, scored 114 and then routed India's second innings by taking 7 for 48. No other batsman scored fifty in the match. His unique performance hurried the game to a premature end, England winning by ten wickets a day and a half ahead of schedule. Botham's feat was emulated by Imran Khan at the Iqbal Stadium, Faisalabad, on 3–8 January 1983 when Pakistan's captain scored 117 and returned match figures of 11 for 180.

Alan Davidson is the only other cricketer to take ten wickets and score a total of 100 runs in a Test. In the famous tie with West Indies at Brisbane's 'Gabba' on 9–14 December 1960, the Australian left-hander scored 44 and 80, and recorded analyses of 5 for 135 and 6 for 87.

The only player to score a century and take five wickets in an innings of the same Test on more than two occasions is Ian Botham of Somerset and England. He achieved this feat five times during a span of 61 Tests within a six-year period of his Test career:

103	5–73	v New Zealand	Christchurch	1977–78
108	8–34	v Pakistan	Lord's	1978
114	6–58 7–48	v India	Bombay	1979–80
149*	6–95	v Australia	Leeds	1981
138	5–59	v New Zealand	Wellington	1983–84

The only wicket-keeper to score 3000 runs and make 300 dismissals in Test cricket is Rodney Marsh of Western Australia. He completed this treble on 20 March 1982 against New Zealand at Christchurch. Sixteen players have achieved the wicket-keeper's career 'double' of 1000 runs and 100 dismissals:

	Tests	Runs	Dismissals	Tests for 'Double'
England				
T.G. Evans	91	2439	219	42
A.P.E. Knott	95	4389	269	30
J.M. Parks	46	1962	114	41
R.C. Russell	39	1454	108	37
R.W. Taylor	57	1156	174	47
Australia				
I.A. Healy	73	2557	248	36
R.W. Marsh	96	3633	355	25
W.A.S. Oldfield	54	1427	130	41

	Tests	Runs	Dismissals	Tests for 'Double'
South Africa				
J.H.B. Waite	50	2405	141	36
West Indies				
P.J.L. Dujon	81	3322	272	30
D.L. Murray	62	1993	189	33
New Zealand				
I.D.S. Smith	63	1815	176	42
India				
S.M.H. Kirmani	88	2759	198	42
K.S. More	49	1285	130	39
Pakistan				
Salim Yousuf	32	1055	104	32
Wasim Bari	81	1366	228	53

Jack Russell (England): 37 Tests to achieve the wicket-keeper's double (Popperfoto)

The first wicket-keeper to score 1000 runs and make 100 dismissals was Bert Oldfield of Australia. He achieved that record on 23 June 1934 while playing against England at Lord's in his 41st Test.

The fewest Tests in which a wicket-keeper has reached this double landmark is 25 by Rodney Marsh of Australia, during the period from 27 November 1970 to 24 March 1974.

The youngest to complete the wicket-keeper's Test 'double' is Alan Knott. He was 25 years 120 days old when he made his 100th dismissal for England on 7 August 1971 during the Manchester Test against India.

The first wicket-keeper to make 25 dismissals and score 250 runs in a series was John Waite of South Africa. In five matches against New Zealand in South Africa during the 1961–62 season, he scored 263 runs and set a new series record (since beaten) by making 26 dismissals. This feat was emulated in 1993 by Australia's Ian Healy when he scored 296 runs and made 26 dismissals in England.

The most runs in a series by a wicket-keeper is 606, average 86.57, by Waite's successor, Denis Lindsay. Playing in five Tests against Australia in South Africa during the 1966–67 season, Lindsay scored 69, 182, 5, 81, 137, 131 and 1. In the First Test, his contribution to South Africa's first home victory against Australia was 251 runs and eight catches.

The only other wicket-keeper to score 500 runs in a series is 'Budhi' Kunderan of India, who achieved an aggregate of 525 at home against England in the 1963–64 season.

The first wicket-keeper to score a century and make five dismissals in an innings of the same Test was Denis Lindsay. Playing for South Africa against Australia at the New Wanderers in Johannesburg on 23–28 December 1966, he held six catches in the first innings and scored 182 runs in the second.

His achievement has been emulated twice: Ian Smith scored 113 not out and claimed five dismissals for New Zealand against England at Eden Park, Auckland, on 10–15 February 1984; and Amal Silva scored 111 and held five catches for Sri Lanka against India at Colombo's P. Saravanamuttu Stadium on 6–11 September 1985.

CAPTAINCY RECORDS

The youngest Test captain was the Nawab of Pataudi, jr (later Mansur Ali Khan). He was 21 years 77 days old when he first led India against West Indies at Bridgetown, Barbados, on 23 March 1962. He replaced Nari Contractor, whose skull had been fractured in the tourists' previous match, and went on to lead his country in 40 Tests.

The youngest England captain was Monty Bowden of Surrey. On the first tour of South Africa he led England in the Second Test at Newlands, Cape Town, in the absence of C. Aubrey Smith. Bowden, who was 23 years 144 days old when the match began on 25 March 1889, remained in South Africa and played for Transvaal in the inaugural Currie Cup Challenge Match. Later he travelled to Rhodesia with the Pioneer Column of Cecil Rhodes. After three years there he died in the glorified mud hut which served as Umtali Hospital. His body had to be protected from marauding lions by an armed guard before it was interred in a coffin made out of whisky cases.

The **oldest Test captain** was W.G. Grace who was 50 years 320 days of age at the end of his 13th match as captain of England. That Test, the first ever played at Trent Bridge, Nottingham, ended on 3 June 1899 and marked the end of Grace's international career. By coincidence, it also marked the England debut of Wilfred Rhodes who was destined to become the oldest man to play in a Test match.

The **second-oldest Test captain**, and the oldest of modern times, 'Gubby' Allen, was 45 years 245 days old when England's Fourth Test against West Indies ended at Kingston, Jamaica, on 1 April 1948.

The **record number of Test matches (and the longest unbroken sequence) as captain** is 93 by Allan Border who led Australia between 7 December 1984 and 29 March 1994.

Border also holds the captaincy records for **most defeats (22), most draws (38)** and for **winning most tosses (47)**.

The **most successful captains** in terms of the highest number of wins gained under their leadership, have been Clive Lloyd of West Indies (36 wins in 74 Tests), Allan Border of Australia (32 wins in 93 matches), Viv Richards of West Indies (27 wins in 50 matches), Greg Chappell of Australia (21 wins in 48 Tests), and Peter May of England (20 wins in 41 matches). Mike Brearley (18 wins in 31 matches) led England in 19 home Tests without a defeat (12 wins, 7 draws).

The **record for winning the toss most matches in succession** is nine by Colin Cowdrey for England (two v West Indies in 1959–60, all five v South Africa in 1960, and two v Australia in 1961).

The following captains have won every toss in a five-match series:

Captain	Series	Venue	Season
Hon F.S. Jackson	E v A	England	1905
M.A. Noble	A v E	England	1909
H.G. Deane	SA v E	South Africa	1927–28
J.D.C. Goddard	WI v I	India	1948–49
A.L. Hassett	A v E	England	1953
M.C. Cowdrey	E v SA	England	1960
Nawab of Pataudi, jr	I v E	India	1963–64
G. St A. Sobers	WI v E	England	1966
G. St A. Sobers	WI v NZ	West Indies	1971–72
C.H. Lloyd	WI v I	West Indies	1982–83

No captain has won every toss in a six-match series but four captains have won five out of six:

Captain	Series	Venue	Season
I.M. Chappell	A v E	Australia	1974–75
G.S. Chappell	A v WI	Australia	1975–76
G.N. Yallop	A v E	Australia	1978–79
K.W.R. Fletcher	E v I	India	1981–82

The **first captain to elect to field first on winning the toss in a Test match** was Percy McDonnell, the only Greek scholar to lead Australia. He was actually responsible for the first two instances of 'insertion'; both were against England at Sydney (January 1887 and February 1888), and both gambles resulted in defeat for Australia.

OTHER INDIVIDUAL RECORDS

The **record number of Test match appearances** is 156 by Allan Border for Australia between 29 December 1978 and 29 March 1994. Border also holds the record for **most consecutive Test appearances** –153 between 10 March 1979 and his final match, including a record unbroken sequence of 93 as captain.

Colin Cowdrey: won every toss as captain of England in the series against South Africa in 1960
(Hulton-Deutsch Collection)

MOST APPEARANCES FOR EACH TEAM

For	Total		E	A	SA	WI	NZ	I	P	SL	Z
						Opponents					
England	118	G.A. Gooch	–	42	3	26	15	19	10	3	–
Australia	156	A.R. Border	47	–	6	31	23	20	22	7	–
South Africa	50	J.H.B. Waite	21	14	–	–	15	–	–	–	–
West Indies	121	I.V.A. Richards	36	34	–	–	7	28	16	–	–
New Zealand	86	R.J. Hadlee	21	23	–	10	–	11	15	6	–
India	131	Kapil Dev	27	20	4	25	10	–	29	14	2
Pakistan	124	Javed Miandad	22	25	–	16	18	28	–	12	3
Sri Lanka	56	A. Ranatunga	4	7	3	1	11	14	13	–	3

The most appearances for Zimbabwe is 13 by A.D.R. Campbell, A. Flower, G.W. Flower and D.L. Houghton.

The youngest cricketer to play in a Test match is Mushtaq Mohammad, who was 15 years 124 days of age (unconfirmed) when he appeared for Pakistan against West Indies at Bagh-i-Jinnah, Lahore, on 26 March 1959. The youngest whose date of birth has been confirmed is Derek Sealy who was aged 17 years 122 days when he made his debut for West Indies against England at Bridgetown, Barbados, on 11 January 1930. **The youngest Englishman to play Test cricket** is Brian Close, who was 18 years 149 days old when he played against New Zealand at Old Trafford, Manchester, on 23 July 1949.

The oldest man to play in a Test match was Wilfred Rhodes of Yorkshire and England. When he ended the last of his 58 appearances on 12 April 1930, he was 52 years 165 days old.

The oldest man to make his first appearance at Test level was James Southerton, who was 49 years 119 days of age when he played for England against Australia on 15 March 1877 in the first Test of all.

Wilfred Rhodes also holds the record for **the longest Test career**, a period of 30 years 315 days elapsing between his debut at Trent Bridge, Nottingham, on 1 June 1899 and the end of his final match for England at Kingston, Jamaica, on 12 April 1930.

The longest interval between Test match appearances is 22 years 222 days by off-spin bowler John Traicos. After three appearances for South Africa in February–March 1970, in that country's last matches prior to expulsion from the ICC, he resumed his international career on 18 October 1992 in Zimbabwe's inaugural Test. The longest interval in appearances for England is 17 years 316 days by George Gunn of Nottinghamshire and England. After playing against Australia at Sydney in a match ending on 1 March 1912, he was not recalled until 11 January 1930 at the start of a four-match series in the West Indies during his 51st year.

The most matches missed between appearances is 104 by Younis Ahmed of Pakistan between November 1969 and February 1987.

The longest-lived Test cricketer was The Mackinnon of Mackinnon whose sole Test match appearance was for Lord Harris's team at Melbourne in January 1879. Francis Mackinnon, 35th Chief of the Clan, died at his Morayshire home (Drumduan in Forres) in 1947 at the age of 98 years 324 days. He played in 78 matches for Kent (1875–85) and was the Club's president in 1889.

Twelve cricketers have represented more than one team at Test level. The first to do so, and the only player to appear both for and against Australia, was Billy Midwinter. Born at St Briavels in the Forest of Dean, he emigrated to Australia, became a professional in Melbourne and played against England in the first-ever Test, taking 5 for 78 in the first innings. The first of cricket's international commuters, he played for Gloucestershire from 1877 until 1882, as well as appearing for Victoria. Touring Australia with Alfred Shaw's team, he opened the bowling for England in two of his four appearances in 1881–82 before resuming his Test career for Australia.

The record number of Test match appearances by an umpire is 63 (to the end of the 1995 season) by Harold ('Dickie') Bird. He first officiated in 1973 and remains **the only umpire to stand in 50 or more Tests.**

Harold 'Dickie' Bird: officiated in record number of Tests before retirement in 1996 (Popperfoto)

PLAYERS WHO HAVE REPRESENTED TWO COUNTRIES

Amir Elahi	India (1) 1947–48	Pakistan (5) 1952–53
J.J. Ferris	Australia (8) 1886–87 to 1890	England (1) 1891–92
S.C. Guillen	West Indies (5) 1951–52	New Zealand (3) 1955–56
Gul Mahomed	India (8) 1946 to 1952–53	Pakistan (1) 1956–57
F. Hearne	England (2) 1888–89	South Africa (4) 1891–92 to 1895–96
A.H. Kardar	India (3) 1946	Pakistan (23) 1952–53 to 1957–58
W.E. Midwinter	Australia (8) 1876–77 to 1886–87	England (4) 1881–82
F. Mitchell	England (2) 1898–99	South Africa (3) 1912
W.L. Murdoch	Australia (18) 1876–77 to 1890	England (1) 1891–92
Nawab of Pataudi, sr	England (3) 1932–33 to 1934	India (3) 1946
A.J. Traicos	South Africa (3) 1969–70	Zimbabwe (4) 1992–93
A.E. Trott	Australia (3) 1894–95	England (2) 1898–99
K.C. Wessels	Australia (24) 1982–83 to 1985–86	South Africa (16) 1991–92 to 1994
S.M.J. Woods	Australia (3) 1888	England (3) 1895–96

Kepler Wessels: represented Australia in 24 Tests before returning to captain his native South Africa (Popperfoto)

GROUND RECORDS

Official Test matches have been played on 74 different grounds, in 58 towns and cities, and within 14 countries (if one includes Bangladesh, seven Tests being staged at Dacca when it was within Pakistan).

The only city to have employed four grounds for Test cricket is Colombo. The P. Saravanamuttu Stadium (formerly the Colombo Oval), the Sinhalese Sports Club, the Colombo Cricket Club and the R. Premadasa (Khettarama) Stadium have collectively staged 17 of Sri Lanka's 27 home Tests. Eleven other centres have staged Test matches on more than one ground; Johannesburg and Bombay have used three, while London, Brisbane, Durban, Lucknow, Madras, Karachi, Lahore, Rawalpindi and Bulawayo have each employed two grounds.

The first Test match venue was the Melbourne Cricket Ground (MCG), frequently described as 'the paddock that grew'. Largely rebuilt as the main stadium for the 1956 Olympic Games, it has attracted crowds of over 120 000 for the grand finals of the Australian (Rules) football season. **The largest recorded attendance at any ground for a day of cricket** assembled at the MCG on 11 February 1961; numbering 90 800, it watched the second day's play in the Fifth Test between Australia and West Indies. The receipts for that day amounted to £A13 132 (£10 484 sterling).

The most Test matches staged on one ground is 93 by Lord's Cricket Ground in London which celebrated the Bicentenary of its first Great Match in 1987.

The greatest attendance at any cricket match is the estimated 394 000 for the Fourth Test between India and England at Eden Gardens, Calcutta, on 1–6 January 1982. **The largest recorded attendance** is 350 534 (receipts £30 124) for the Third Test between Australia and England at Melbourne on 1–7 January 1937. **The largest match attendance in England** is 159 000 for the Fourth Test between England and Australia at Headingley, Leeds, on 22–27 July 1948.

The record attendance for a Test series is 933 513 (receipts £87 963) for the five matches between Australia and England during the 1936–37 Australian season. The English record is 549 650 (receipts £200 428) for the series against Australia in 1953.

The world record for receipts from a cricket match is £2 209 321 from an attendance of 111 219 at the Second Test between England and West Indies at Lord's on 22–26 June 1995.

The Test series record for receipts is £8 293 637 from the six matches between England and West Indies in 1995. Played between 8 June and 28 August, they attracted a total attendance of 425 813.

Test Match Centres	Grounds	First Test Match Day	No of Tests
ENGLAND			(365)
Birmingham	Edgbaston	29.5.1902	31
Leeds	Headingley	29.6.1899	57
Lord's, London	Lord's Cricket Ground	21.7.1884	93
Manchester	Old Trafford	10.7.1884†	62
Nottingham	Trent Bridge	1.6.1899	43
Oval, London	Kennington Oval	6.9.1880	78
Sheffield	Bramall Lane	3.7.1902	1
† Rain prevented play until 11.7.1884.			
AUSTRALIA			(284)
Adelaide	Adelaide Oval	12.12.1884	53
Brisbane	Exhibition Ground (1928–29 to 1930–31)	30.11.1928	2
	Woolloongabba	27.11.1931	37
Hobart	Bellerive Oval	16.12.1989	2
Melbourne	Melbourne Cricket Ground	15.3.1877	87
Perth	Western Australia Cricket Association (WACA) Ground	11.12.1970	22
Sydney	Sydney Cricket Ground (No. 1)	17.2.1882	81
SOUTH AFRICA			(109)
Cape Town	Newlands	25.3.1889	27

Test Match Centres	Grounds	First Test Match Day	No of Tests
Durban	Lord's (1909–10 to 1921–22)	21.1.1910	4
	Kingsmead	18.1.1923	22
Johannesburg	Old Wanderers (1895–96 to 1938–39)	2.3.1896	22
	Ellis Park (1948–49 to 1953–54)	27.12.1948	6
	Wanderers (New)	24.12.1956	15
Port Elizabeth	St George's Park	12.3.1889	13
WEST INDIES			**(138)**
Bridgetown, Barbados	Kensington Oval	11.1.1930	31
Georgetown, Guyana	Bourda	21.2.1930	23
Kingston, Jamaica	Sabina Park	3.4.1930	31
Port-of-Spain, Trinidad	Queen's Park Oval	1.2.1930	44
St John's, Antigua	Recreation Ground	27.3.1981	9
NEW ZEALAND			**(115)**
Auckland	Eden Park	14.2.1930††	37
Christchurch	Lancaster Park	10.1.1930	33
Dunedin	Carisbrook	11.3.1955	9
Hamilton	Trust Bank (Seddon) Park	22.2.1991	3
Napier	McLean Park	16.2.1979	3
Wellington	Basin Reserve	24.1.1930	30

†† Rain prevented play until 17.2.1930.

INDIA			**(156)**
Ahmedabad	Gujarat Stadium	12.11.1983	3
Bangalore	Karnataka State Cricket Association Stadium (Chinnaswamy Stadium)	22.11.1974	10
Bombay	Gymkhana (1933–34 only)	15.12.1933	1
	Brabourne Stadium (1948–49 to 1972–73)	9.12.1948	17
	Wankhede Stadium	23.1.1975	15
Calcutta	Eden Gardens	5.1.1934	27
Chandigarh	Sector 16 Stadium	23.11.1990	1
Cuttack	Barabati Stadium	4.1.1987	1
Delhi	Feroz Shah Kotla	10.11.1948	23
Hyderabad (Deccan)	Fateh Maidan (Lal Bahadur Stadium)	19.11.1955	3
Jaipur	Sawai Mansingh Stadium	21.2.1987	1
Jullundur	Burlton Park	24.9.1983	1
Kanpur	Green Park (Modi Stadium)	12.1.1952	16
Lucknow	University Ground	23.10.1952	1
	K.D. 'Babu' Singh Stadium	18.1.1994	1
Madras	Chepauk (Chidambaram Stadium)	10.2.1934	21
	Corporation (Nehru) Stadium (1955–56 to 1964–65)	6.1.1956	9
Mohali	Punjab Cricket Association Stadium	10.12.1994	1
Nagpur	Vidarbha Cricket Assocation Ground	3.10.1969	4
PAKISTAN			**(100)**
Bahawalpur	Dring Stadium	15.1.1955	1
Dacca	Dacca Stadium	1.1.1955	7
Faisalabad	Iqbal Stadium	16.10.1978	16
Gujranwala	Municipal Stadium	20.12.1991	1
Hyderabad (Sind)	Niaz Stadium	16.3.1973	5
Karachi	National Stadium	26.2.1955	31
	Defence Stadium	1.12.1993	1

Test Match Centres	Grounds	First Test Match Day	No of Tests
Lahore	Lawrence Gardens (Bagh-i-Jinnah) (1954–55 to 1958–59)	29.1.1955	3
	Lahore (Gaddafi) Stadium	21.11.1959	27
Multan	Ibne-e-Qasim Bagh Stadium	30.12.1980	1
Peshawar	Services Ground	13.2.1955	1
Rawalpindi	Pindi Club Ground	27.3.1965	1
	Cricket Stadium	9.12.1993	2
Sialkot	Jinnah Stadium	27.10.1985	3
SRI LANKA			**(27)**
Colombo	P. Saravanamuttu Stadium (PSS)	17.2.1982	6
	Sinhalese Sports Club Ground (SSC)	16.3.1984	7
	Colombo Cricket Club Ground (CCC)	24.3.1984	3
	R. Premadasa (Khettarama) Stadium	28.8.1992	1
Kandy	Asgiriya Stadium	22.4.1983	6
Moratuwa	Tyronne Fernando Stadium	8.9.1992	4
ZIMBABWE			**(9)**
Bulawayo	Bulawayo Athletic Club	1.11.1992	1
	Queen's Sports Club	20.10.94	2
Harare	Harare Sports Club	18.10.1992	6

The 1890 and 1938 Tests at Manchester, the 1970–71 Third Test at Melbourne, the 1988–89 Test at Dunedin and the 1989–90 Test at Georgetown, all abandoned without a ball being bowled, plus the cancelled 1980–81 Second Test at Georgetown and 1994–95 Second Test at Colombo (SCC), are excluded from these figures.

RECORD TOTALS FOR EACH TEST MATCH CENTRE

Centre	Highest Total			Lowest Total (Completed Innings)		
England						
Birmingham	633–5d	England v India	1979	30	S. Africa v England	1924
Leeds	653–4d	Australia v England	1993	67	N. Zealand v England	1958
Lord's	729–6d	Australia v England	1930	42	India v England	1974
Manchester	656–8d	Australia v England	1964	58	India v England	1952
Nottingham	658–8d	England v Australia	1938	88	S. Africa v England	1960
Oval	903–7d	England v Australia	1938	44	Australia v England	1896
Sheffield	289	Australia v England	1902	145	England v Australia	1902
Australia						
Adelaide	674	Australia v India	1947–48	82	Australia v W. Indies	1951–52
Brisbane	645	Australia v England	1946–47	58	Australia v England	1936–37
				58	India v Australia	1947–48
Hobart	544–6d	Australia v Sri Lanka	1993–94	161	N. Zealand v Australia	1993–94
Melbourne	604	Australia v England	1936–37	36	S.Africa v Australia	1931–32
Perth	592–8d	England v Australia	1986–87	62	Pakistan v Australia	1981–82
Sydney	659–8d	Australia v England	1946–47	42	Australia v England	1887–88
South Africa						
Cape Town	559–9d	England v S. Africa	1938–39	35	S. Africa v England	1898–99
Durban	654–5	England v S. Africa	1938–39	75	Australia v S. Africa	1949–50
Johannesburg	620	S. Africa v Australia	1966–67	72	S. Africa v England	1956–57
Port Elizabeth	549–7d	Australia v S. Africa	1949–50	30	S. Africa v England	1895–96

Centre	Highest Total				Lowest Total (Completed Innings)		

West Indies

Bridgetown	668	Australia v W. Indies	1954–55		94	N. Zealand v W. Indies	1984–85
Georgetown	569	W. Indies v Australia	1990–91		109	W. Indies v Australia	1972–73
Kingston	849	England v W. Indies	1929–30		97*	India v W. Indies	1975–76
Port-of-Spain	681–8d	W. Indies v England	1953–54		46	England v W. Indies	1993–94
St John's	593–5d	W. Indies v England	1993–94		154	England v W. Indies	1989–90

New Zealand

Auckland	616–5d	Pakistan v N. Zealand	1988–89		26	N. Zealand v England	1954–55
Christchurch	580–9d	England v N. Zealand	1991–92		65	N. Zealand v England	1970–71
Dunedin	507–6d	Pakistan v N. Zealand	1972–73		74	N. Zealand v West Indies	1955–56
Hamilton	374–6d	N. Zealand v Sri Lanka	1990–91		93	N. Zealand v Pakistan	1992–93
Napier	402	N. Zealand v Pakistan	1978–79		109	N. Zealand v Sri Lanka	1994–95
Wellington	671–4	N. Zealand v Sri Lanka	1990–91		42	N. Zealand v Australia	1945–46

India

Ahmedabad	395	Pakistan v India	1986–87		103	India v W. Indies	1983–84
Bangalore	541–6d	India v Sri Lanka	1993–94		116	Pakistan v India	1986–87
Bombay	629–6d	W. Indies v India	1948–49		88	India v N. Zealand	1964–65
Calcutta	614–5d	W. Indies v India	1958–59		90	India v W. Indies	1983–84
Chandigarh	288	India v Sri Lanka	1990–91		82	Sri Lanka v India	1990–91
Cuttack	400	India v Sri Lanka	1986–87		142	Sri Lanka v India	1986–87
Delhi	644–8d	W. Indies v India	1958–59		75	India v W. Indies	1987–88
Hyderabad	498–4d	India v N. Zealand	1955–56		89	India v New Zealand	1969–70
Jaipur	465–8d	India v Pakistan	1986–87		341	Pakistan v India	1986–87
Jullundur	374	India v Pakistan	1983–84		337	Pakistan v India	1983–84
Kanpur	676–7	India v Sri Lanka	1986–87		105	Australia v India	1959–60
Lucknow	511	India v Sri Lanka	1993–94		106	India v Pakistan	1952–53
Madras	652–7d	England v India	1984–85		83	India v England	1976–77
Mohali	443	W. Indies v India	1994–95		114	India v W. Indies	1994–95
Nagpur	546–9d	India v West Indies	1994–95		109	India v N. Zealand	1969–70

Pakistan

Bahawalpur	312–9d	Pakistan v India	1954–55		235	India v Pakistan	1954–55
Dacca	439	England v Pakistan	1961–62		70	N. Zealand v Pakistan	1955–56
Faisalabad	674–6	Pakistan v India	1984–85		53	W. Indies v Pakistan	1986–87
Gujranwala	109–2	Pakistan v Sri Lanka	1991–92				
Hyderabad	581–3d	Pakistan v India	1982–83		189	India v Pakistan	1982–83
					189	N. Zealand v Pakistan	1984–85
Karachi	565–9d	Pakistan v N. Zealand	1976–77		80	Australia v Pakistan	1956–57
Lahore	699–5	Pakistan v India	1989–90		77	Pakistan v W. Indies	1986–87
Multan	249	W. Indies v Pakistan	1980–81		166	Pakistan v W. Indies	1980–81
Peshawar	245	India v Pakistan	1954–55		182	Pakistan v India	1954–55
Rawalpindi	537	Pakistan v Australia	1994–95		79	N. Zealand v Pakistan	1964–65
Sialkot	423–5d	Pakistan v Sri Lanka	1991–92		157	Sri Lanka v Pakistan	1985–86

Sri Lanka

Colombo:

(PSS)	446	India v Sri Lanka	1993–94		175	Sri Lanka v England	1981–82
(SSC)	547–8d	Sri Lanka v Australia	1992–93		102	Sri Lanka v N. Zealand	1992–93
(CCC)	459	N. Zealand v Sri Lanka	1983–84		132	Pakistan v Sri Lanka	1985–86
(KS)	296–6d	Australia v Sri Lanka	1992–93		247	Australia v Sri Lanka	1992–93
Kandy	514–4d	Australia v Sri Lanka	1982–83		71	Sri Lanka v Pakistan	1994–95
Moratuwa	337	Australia v Sri Lanka	1992–93		190	Sri Lanka v W. Indies	1993–94

Centre	Highest Total			Lowest Total (Completed Innings)			

Zimbabwe

Bulawayo	462–9d	Zimbabwe v Sri Lanka	1994–95	146	Zimbabwe v Pakistan	1994–95
Harare	544–4d	Zimbabwe v Pakistan	1994–95	137	Zimbabwe v N. Zealand	1992–93

* Five men were absent hurt. The second lowest total at Kingston is 103 by England in 1934–35.

HIGHEST INDIVIDUAL SCORE FOR EACH TEST CENTRE

England

Birmingham	285*	P.B.H. May	England v West Indies	1957
Leeds	334	D.G. Bradman	Australia v England	1930
Lord's	333	G.A. Gooch	England v India	1990
Manchester	311	R.B. Simpson	Australia v England	1964
Nottingham	278	D.C.S. Compton	England v Pakistan	1954
Oval	364	L. Hutton	England v Australia	1938
Sheffield	119	C. Hill	Australia v England	1902

Australia

Adelaide	299*	D.G. Bradman	Australia v South Africa	1931–32
Brisbane	226	D.G. Bradman	Australia v South Africa	1931–32
Hobart	168	M.J. Slater	Australia v New Zealand	1993–94
Melbourne	307	R.M. Cowper	Australia v England	1965–66
Perth	200	D.C. Boon	Australia v New Zealand	1989–90
Sydney	287	R.E. Foster	England v Australia	1903–04

Looking towards the Pavilion End at Lord's, the headquarters of cricket (Popperfoto)

South Africa

Cape Town	209	R.G. Pollock	South Africa v Australia	1966–67
Durban	274	R.G. Pollock	South Africa v Australia	1969–70
Johannesburg	231	A.D. Nourse	South Africa v Australia	1935–36
Port Elizabeth	167	A.L. Hassett	Australia v South Africa	1949–50

West Indies

Bridgetown	337	Hanif Mohammad	Pakistan v West Indies	1957–58
Georgetown	259	G.M. Turner	New Zealand v West Indies	1971–72
Kingston	365*	G. St A. Sobers	West Indies v Pakistan	1957–58
Port-of-Spain	220	S.M. Gavaskar	India v West Indies	1970–71
St John's	375	B.C. Lara	West Indies v England	1993–94

New Zealand

Auckland	336*	W.R. Hammond	England v New Zealand	1932–33
Christchurch	258	S.M. Nurse	West Indies v New Zealand	1968–69
Dunedin	201	Mushtaq Mohammad	Pakistan v New Zealand	1972–73
Hamilton	135	M.J. Greatbatch	New Zealand v Pakistan	1992–93
Napier	119*	Majid Khan	Pakistan v New Zealand	1978–79
Wellington	299	M.D. Crowe	New Zealand v Sri Lanka	1990–91

India

Ahmedabad	152	M. Azharuddin	India v Sri Lanka	1993–94
Bangalore	172	S.M.Gavaskar	India v England	1981–82
Bombay	242*	C.H. Lloyd	West Indies v India	1974–75
Calcutta	256	R.B. Kanhai	West Indies v India	1958–59
Chandigarh	88	R.J. Shastri	India v Sri Lanka	1990–91
Cuttack	166	D.B. Vengsarkar	India v Sri Lanka	1986–87
Delhi	230*	B. Sutcliffe	New Zealand v India	1955–56
Hyderabad	223	P.R. Umrigar	India v New Zealand	1955–56
Jaipur	125	R.J. Shastri	India v Pakistan	1986–87
Jullundur	201	A.D. Gaekwad	India v Pakistan	1983–84
Kanpur	250	S.F.A.F. Bacchus	West Indies v India	1978–79
Lucknow	142	S.R. Tendulkar	India v Sri Lanka	1993–94
Madras	236*	S.M. Gavaskar	India v West Indies	1983–84
Mohali	174*	J.C. Adams	West Indies v India	1994–95
Nagpur	179	S.R. Tendulkar	India v West Indies	1994–95

Pakistan

Bahawalpur	142	Hanif Mohammad	Pakistan v India	1954–55
Dacca	165	G. Pullar	England v Pakistan	1961–62
Faisalabad	235	G.S. Chappell	Australia v Pakistan	1979–80
Gujranwala	51*	Ramiz Raja	Pakistan v Sri Lanka	1991–92
Hyderabad	280*	Javed Miandad	Pakistan v India	1982–83
Karachi	211	Javed Miandad	Pakistan v Australia	1988–89
Lahore	235*	Zaheer Abbas	Pakistan v India	1978–79
Multan	120*	I.V.A. Richards	West Indies v Pakistan	1980–81
Peshawar	108	P.R. Umrigar	India v Pakistan	1954–55
Rawalpindi	237	Salim Malik	Pakistan v Australia	1994–95
Sialkot	101	Salim Malik	Pakistan v Sri Lanka	1991–92

Sri Lanka

Colombo (PSS)	151	R.S. Mahanama	Sri Lanka v India	1993–94
Colombo (SSC)	137	A.P. Gurusinha	Sri Lanka v Australia	1992–93
Colombo (CCC)	201*	D.S.B.P. Kuruppu	Sri Lanka v New Zealand	1986–87
Colombo (KS)	100*	D.M. Jones	Australia v Sri Lanka	1992–93

Kandy	143*	D.W. Hookes	Australia v Sri Lanka	1982–83
Moratuwa	153	R.S. Mahanama	Sri Lanka v New Zealand	1992–93

Zimbabwe

Bulawayo	266	D.L. Houghton	Zimbabwe v Sri Lanka	1994–95
Harare	201*	G.W. Flower	Zimbabwe v Pakistan	1994–95

BEST INNINGS BOWLING ANALYSIS FOR EACH TEST CENTRE

England

Birmingham	7–17	W. Rhodes	England v Australia	1902
Leeds	8–43	R.G.D. Willis	England v Australia	1981
Lord's	8–34	I.T. Botham	England v Pakistan	1978
Manchester	10–53	J.C. Laker	England v Australia	1956
Nottingham	8–107	B.J.T. Bosanquet	England v Australia	1905
Oval	9–57	D.E. Malcolm	England v South Africa	1994
Sheffield	6–49	S.F. Barnes	England v Australia	1902

Australia

Adelaide	8–43	A.E. Trott	Australia v England	1894–95
Brisbane	9–52	R.J. Hadlee	New Zealand v Australia	1985–86
Hobart	6–31	S.K. Warne	Australia v New Zealand	1993–94
Melbourne	9–86	Sarfraz Nawaz	Pakistan v Australia	1978–79
Perth	8–87	M.G. Hughes	Australia v West Indies	1988–89
Sydney	8–35	G.A. Lohmann	England v Australia	1886–87

South Africa

Cape Town	8–11	J. Briggs	England v South Africa	1888–89
Durban	8–69	H.J. Tayfield	South Africa v England	1956–57
Johannesburg	9–28	G.A. Lohmann	England v South Africa	1895–96
Port Elizabeth	8–7	G.A. Lohmann	England v South Africa	1895–96

West Indies

Bridgetown	8–38	L.R. Gibbs	West Indies v India	1961–62
Georgetown	7–44	I.W. Johnson	Australia v West Indies	1954–55
Kingston	7–34	T.E. Bailey	England v West Indies	1953–54
Port-of-Spain	9–95	J.M. Noreiga	West Indies v India	1970–71
St John's	6–54	C.A. Walsh	West Indies v Australia	1994–95

New Zealand

Auckland	8–76	E.A.S. Prasanna	India v New Zealand	1975–76
Christchurch	7–47	P.C.R. Tufnell	England v New Zealand	1991–92
Dunedin	7–52	Intikhab Alam	Pakistan v New Zealand	1972–73
Hamilton	5–22	Waqar Younis	Pakistan v New Zealand	1992–93
Napier	5–43	W.P.U.C.J. Vaas	Sri Lanka v New Zealand	1994–95
Wellington	7–23	R.J. Hadlee	New Zealand v India	1975–76

India

Ahmedabad	9–83	Kapil Dev	India v West Indies	1983–84
Bangalore	7–27	Maninder Singh	India v Pakistan	1986–87
Bombay	7–48	I.T. Botham	England v India	1979–80
Calcutta	7–49	Ghulam Ahmed	India v Australia	1956–57
Chandigarh	6–12	S.L.V. Raju	India v Sri Lanka	1990–91

Cuttack	5–85	J.R. Ratnayeke	Sri Lanka v India	1986–87
Delhi	8–52	M.H. Mankad	India v Pakistan	1952–53
Hyderabad	7–128	S.P. Gupte	India v New Zealand	1955–56
Jaipur	4–88	G. Sharma	India v Pakistan	1986–87
Jullundur	4–50	Wasim Raja	Pakistan v India	1983–84
Kanpur	9–69	J.M. Patel	India v Australia	1959–60
Lucknow	7–42	Fazal Mahmood	Pakistan v India	1952–53
Madras	8–55	M.H. Mankad	India v England	1951–52
Mohali	5–65	K.C.G. Benjamin	West Indies v India	1994–95
Nagpur	7–51	Maninder Singh	India v Sri Lanka	1986–87

Pakistan

Bahawalpur	6–74	P.R. Umrigar	India v Pakistan	1954–55
Dacca	6–21	Khan Mohammad	Pakistan v New Zealand	1955–56
Faisalabad	7–52	C. Pringle	New Zealand v Pakistan	1982–83
Gujranwala	1–27	G.P. Wickremasinghe	Sri Lanka v Pakistan	1991–92
Hyderabad	7–87	S.L. Boock	New Zealand v Pakistan	1984–85
Karachi	8–60	Imran Khan	Pakistan v India	1982–83
Lahore	9–56	Abdul Qadir	Pakistan v England	1987–88
Multan	5–62	Imran Khan	Pakistan v West Indies	1980–81
Peshawar	5–63	S.P. Gupte	India v Pakistan	1954–55
Rawalpindi	5–56	H.H. Streak	Zimbabwe v Pakistan	1993–94
Sialkot	8–83	J.R. Ratnayeke	Sri Lanka v Pakistan	1985–86

Sri Lanka

Colombo (PSS)	6–33	J.E. Emburey	England v Sri Lanka	1981–82
Colombo (SSC)	6–85	R.J. Ratnayake	Sri Lanka v India	1985–86
Colombo (CCC)	5–29	R.J. Hadlee	New Zealand v Sri Lanka	1983–84
Colombo (KS)	4–53	C.J. McDermott	Australia v Sri Lanka	1992–93
Kandy	6–34	Waqar Younis	Pakistan v Sri Lanka	1994–95
Moratuwa	5–69	A.A. Donald	South Africa v Sri Lanka	1993–94

Zimbabwe

Bulawayo	6–113	D.N. Patel	New Zealand v Zimbabwe	1992–93
Harare	7–116	K.R. Pushpakumara	Sri Lanka v Zimbabwe	1994–95

First-Class Cricket in Britain

First-Class Cricket in Britain

The term 'first-class match' was not officially defined until 19 May 1947 when the Imperial Cricket Conference agreed that 'a match of three or more days duration between two sides of eleven players officially adjudged first-class, shall be regarded as a first-class fixture. Matches in which either team has more than eleven players or which are scheduled for less than three days shall not be regarded as first-class. The governing body in each country shall decide the status of teams.'

This ICC definition did not have retrospective effect. Although the MCC had controlled the status of the counties since 1895, the classification of matches outside the County Championship had rested largely with the Cricket Reporting Agency. This agency compiled the first-class averages for the leading publications of the day but only occasionally consulted the MCC about the status of non-Championship fixtures. Prior to 1895 the ranking of matches had been virtually a lottery, with scant agreement even on the status of certain counties.

In 1973 cricket statisticians founded an association which now boasts a world-wide membership of nearly 1300 and its own headquarters opposite the Trent Bridge ground. The most important of its many publications is *The Guide to First-Class Matches Played in the British Isles 1864–1946*. Until the Association of Cricket Statisticians first published that guide in 1976, all compilers of cricket records had to decide on their own list of first-class matches.

In compiling this section, I have accepted the *Guide*'s classification of matches and have also only included matches played since the start of the 1864 season. Although 'Great Matches' can be traced back until 1709 when Kent played Surrey, no detailed score survives before that of the 1744 match between All-England and Kent and it was not until 1864 that **over-arm bowling was legalized** (10 June).

Cricket Curiosities
The first major match to be started on one ground and finished on another took place between London and Kent in August 1730. Begun 'at the end of Frog Lane, near Islington', it was finished on Kennington Common.

That year also marked the first appearance of W.G. Grace in important matches (he scored 170 and 56 not out for the South Wales club against the Gentlemen of Sussex shortly before his sixteenth birthday), and the first publication by John Wisden & Co of *The Cricketer's Almanack*.

TEAM RECORDS

The highest innings total in any first-class match in Britain is 903 for 7 declared by England against Australia at The Oval in 1938. Full details appear in the Test Cricket section.

The highest innings total in County cricket – and the second-highest in all first-class matches in the British Isles – is 887 by Yorkshire against Warwickshire at Edgbaston, Birmingham, on 7–8 May 1896. It occupied the whole of the first two days (10 hours 50 minutes) and was **the longest innings in County matches** until 15–18 July 1994 (when Lancashire batted 11 hours 18 minutes – 174.5 overs – against Derbyshire at Blackpool in scoring 589, **the highest total after following-on in Championship matches**). It was **the first time in any first-class match that four batsmen had scored hundreds in the same innings**: F.S. Jackson 117, E. Wainwright 126, R. Peel 210 not out, and Lord Hawke 166.

The highest second innings total in Britain is 703 for 9 declared by Cambridge University against Sussex at Hove on 20–21 June 1890. Cambridge began their second innings 91 runs behind at 12.25pm on the second day and declared after 90 minutes batting on the last morning, once the previous record first-class score (698 by Surrey in 1888) had been passed. The main contributors were F.G.J. Ford (191), C.P. Foley (117) and G. MacGregor (131), and the runs were scored at the rate of 74 per 100 balls.

Cambridge University also achieved **the highest fourth innings total in English first-class cricket** when they scored 507 for 7 on 26–27 June 1896 against MCC at Lord's. It remains **the world record total by a winning side in the fourth innings**. The main scorers were H.H. Marriott (146*) and N.F. Druce (146).

The highest fourth innings total in Britain without the loss of a wicket is 270 by Surrey against Kent at The Oval on 25 July 1900. With Surrey needing 346 runs for victory in only 170 minutes, Bobby Abel (120*) and William Brockwell (132*) made a remarkable attempt at the virtually impossible target.

The highest match aggregate in Britain is 1808 runs by Sussex (591 and 312 for 3 declared) and Essex (493 for 4 declared and 412 for 3) at Hove on 31 August–3 September 1993.

The highest Championship aggregate in a three-day match is 1641 by Glamorgan and Worcestershire at Abergavenny on 21–24 July 1990.

The lowest innings total in all first-class cricket is 12, the two instances being by Oxford University (batting one short) against the MCC at Cowley Marsh, Oxford, on 24 May 1877, and by Northamptonshire against Gloucestershire at Gloucester on 11 June 1907.

Played on a poor wicket during a memorably wet season, the Oxford match was completed in one day (12.35 to 6.30pm). Taking first innings and without their captain and future England cap, A.J. Webbe, Oxford were dismissed for just seven scoring strokes off 174 balls in two hours. Fred Morley's immaculate left-handed swing bowling claimed seven wickets for six runs. With another six wickets for eight runs in Oxford's second innings of 35, Morley returned, in terms of runs per wicket, the best match analysis in all first-class cricket: 13 wickets for 14 runs.

Northamptonshire were victims of some brilliant left-arm slow bowling on a drying pitch, George Dennett being virtually unplayable and taking eight wickets for only nine runs, including the hat-trick. After dismissing Gloucestershire for 88, Northants needed 136 to win and had lost seven wickets (all to Dennett, who took 15 for 21 in the day) for 40 runs when rain washed out the final day's play.

The lowest first-class match aggregate by one team in Britain is 42 by Northamptonshire who, with one man absent ill, were dismissed for 27 and 15 by Yorkshire at Northampton in 2 hours 15 minutes on 8 May 1908.

The lowest aggregate of runs by both sides in any completed first-class match is 105 by the MCC (33 – F.R. Spofforth 6 for 4 including the hat-trick – and 19) and the Australians (41 and 12 for 1) at Lord's on 27 May 1878. Starting at 12.03pm, the match was all over at 6.20pm.

The most wickets to fall in a single day's play in a first-class match is 39. This record was established at the Old Magdalen Ground in Oxford on 28 May 1880 when the MCC beat the University by one wicket. Because of rain the match did not begin until 11.30am on the second day. By the time it ended at 7pm, Oxford had been dismissed for 53 and 75 by the Nottinghamshire opening bowlers, Alfred Shaw (12 for 53) and Fred Morley (8 for 62), who operated unchanged throughout both innings. In September they were to contribute towards England's victory against Australia in the first Test match to be played in England. The MCC made 89 and 41 for 9, scraping home through an epic last-wicket partnership of 20 by their two successful bowlers.

The largest margin of victory in English first-class cricket is the innings and 579 runs by which England beat Australia at The Oval in August 1938. Excluding Test matches, the record is an innings and 517 runs by the Australians against Nottinghamshire at Trent Bridge, Nottingham, in June 1921. After amassing 675 (C.G. Macartney 345 in 235 minutes), the touring team bowled out Nottinghamshire for 58 and 100.

The largest margin of victory in a County Championship match is an innings and 485 runs by Surrey (698) against Sussex (114 and 99) at The Oval in August 1888.

The largest victory by a runs margin in English first-class cricket is 562 runs by Australia (701 and 327) against England at The Oval in August 1934.

The only instance of a side winning a first-class match in England without losing a wicket occurred at Old Trafford, Manchester, in July 1956 when Lancashire scored 166 for 0 declared and 66 for 0, beating Leicestershire (108 and 122) by ten wickets. Alan Wharton (87* and 33*) and Jack Dyson (75* and 31*) were the first pair of batsmen in all first-class cricket to monopolize totally their team's victory.

The most recent tied first-class match in England – there have been 33 such results since 1864 – occurred on 2 May 1993 at Trent Bridge, Nottingham. Worcestershire's captain, Tim Curtis, having top-scored in both innings with 43 and 113, set Nottinghamshire a target of 296 in 87 overs. Attempting a second run that would have gained victory off the last available ball, Andy Pick was run out by a return from the square-leg boundary. It was Nottinghamshire's first tie in first-class matches and Worcestershire's first since 1939.

The last first-class match to end on the first day was between Kent (187) and Worcestershire (25 and 61) at the Nevill Ground, Tunbridge Wells on 15 June 1960.

The fewest runs in a full day's play in first-class matches in Britain since 1837 is 134 by Glamorgan (134 for 3) against Hampshire at the United Services Officer's Ground, Portsmouth, on 5 June 1964. Glamorgan, 175 runs behind on first innings, batted throughout the final day – the second day had been lost to rain – scoring only 134 for 3 wickets off 95 overs.

Both Tim Curtis (Worcestershire, left) and Nottinghamshire's Andy Pick (above) starred in the most recent tied first-class match in England (Popperfoto & Allsport/Anton Want)

The most runs in any day of first-class cricket is 721 by the Australians against Essex at Southchurch Park, Southend-on-Sea, in 5 hours 48 minutes on 15 May 1948. Sid Barnes (79), Bill Brown (153), Don Bradman (187 in 125 minutes), Ron Hamence (46), Sam Loxton (120), and Ron Saggers (104*) took full advantage of a fast pitch and small ground to delight a packed Whit Saturday crowd. The total was scored at a rate of 120 runs per hour and 93 runs per 100 balls.

The most hundreds in an innings of a first-class match in Britain is four. There have been 18 instances, the most recent occurring at Northampton on 25–28 August 1995 when Northamptonshire, in response to Nottinghamshire's 527, amassed their record total of 781 for 7 declared (Alan Fordham 130, Allan Lamb 115, Russell Warren 154 and David Capel 114*) and went on to win the match by an innings and 97 runs.

The highest number of fifties in any first-class innings is eight by the Australians against Oxford and Cambridge Universities Past and Present at the United Services Ground, Portsmouth on 31 July, 1 and 2 August 1893. The main contributors to a total of 843 were, in batting order, J.J. Lyons (51), A.C. Bannerman (133), G.H.S. Trott (61), H. Graham (83), W. Bruce (191), H. Trumble (105), C.T.B. Turner (66) and W.F. Giffen (62). The innings, which lasted ten hours and was compiled at a rate of 69 runs per 100 balls, was then the highest in all first-class matches and remains the highest by any representative Australian team.

The only instance in all first-class cricket of all 22 players bowling in a match occurred at the Central Ground, Hastings, in September 1964 during a light-hearted festival match between A.E.R. Gilligan's XI and the Australians.

The only instance of ten different fielders holding catches during a first-class innings happened at Grace Road, Leicester, on 31 August 1967. The only Leicestershire player not to take a catch during Northamptonshire's first innings of 211, Jack Birkenshaw, compensated by capturing three wickets with his off-breaks.

Although there are now ten ways in which a batsman can lose his wicket, three of them occur very rarely and the tenth one ('timed out') was introduced in 1980 and has yet to claim its first victim at first-class level. The most recent instances of the three unusual dismissals in English first-class cricket are:

Handled the Ball	G.A. Gooch	England v Australia	Manchester 1993
Hit the Ball Twice	J.H. King	Leicestershire v Surrey	The Oval 1906
Obstructing the Field	Khalid Ibadulla	Warwickshire v Hampshire	Coventry 1963

The most extras conceded in an innings of a first-class match in Britain is 81, there being four instances in Championship matches, all in 1994 under an experimental rule which inflicted a penalty of two extras in addition to any runs scored or awarded.

BATTING RECORDS

The highest individual score in all first-class cricket is 501 not out by Brian Lara for Warwickshire against Durham at Edgbaston, Birmingham on 3 and 6 June 1994. He batted 7 hours 54 minutes, faced 427 balls and hit 10 sixes and 62 fours. In addition to becoming **the first to score 500 runs in a first-class innings**, he set the following world records: **first to score seven hundreds in eight innings; most runs in a day (390); most runs in an innings from strokes worth four or more (308).**

The highest score by an English batsman is 424 by Archie MacLaren for Lancashire against Somerset at Taunton on 15–16 July 1895. The same opposition and venue were involved when, aged 21 years 349 days, Graeme Hick, **the youngest to score 400 in a first-class innings in Britain**, made 405 not out for Worcestershire on 5–6 May 1988.

The highest score by a batsman in Britain making his first appearance in first-class cricket is 215 not out by Hubert Doggart for Cambridge University against Lancashire at Fenner's on 3 May 1948.

The highest score by a batsman appearing only once in English first-class cricket is 156 by 2nd Lt Michael Harbottle for the Army against Oxford University at the Royal Military College (Sandhurst)

The Edgbaston scoreboard tells the story of Brian Lara's record innings of 501 for Warwickshire (Allsport/Ben Radford)

Ground, Camberley, on 25 June 1938. A 21-year-old left-handed opening batsman from the Oxfordshire and Buckinghamshire Light Infantry, he scored another century (before lunch) a month later against the Royal Navy at Lord's but never played again at first-class level. His playing career with Dorset spanned 21 seasons (1936–56). Brigadier Harbottle became director of the Centre for Peacebuilding Studies and one of the 'Generals for Peace'.

The highest score by anyone carrying their bat through a completed first-class innings is 357 not out by Bobby Abel during Surrey's 811 against Somerset at The Oval on 29–30 May 1889. He batted just over 8½ hours, hitting a six, 7 fives, 38 fours, 11 threes, 23 twos and 85 singles.

The highest score by a number eleven batsman in all first-class cricket is 163 by Peter Smith for Essex against Derbyshire at Queen's Park, Chesterfield on 7 August 1947. Beginning his innings when Essex were 24 runs behind Derbyshire's first innings total of 223, he added 218 with Frank Vigar in what remains the record Essex partnership for the tenth wicket. Smith hit 3 sixes and 22 fours in an historic innings which paved the way for his team's victory by five wickets. The next highest score by a 'last man' is 126.

The record score in all first-class cricket by a batsman compelled by injury to bat with the aid of a runner is 181 by Gerald Crutchley. Playing for the Free Foresters against Cambridge University at Fenner's on 6–7 June 1919 he made the highest score of his career while 'suffering from lameness' (*Wisden*).

Although the score at which he became lame is not on record, Walter Hadow, a hard-hitting Oxford blue, scored 'the greater portion' of his 217 for Middlesex against the MCC and Ground at Lord's on 12–13 June 1871 with a runner.

The only batsman to score hundreds in each innings of a first-class match with the aid of a runner is Graeme Fowler of Lancashire at Southport on 29–30 July 1982. He strained a thigh muscle while fielding during Warwickshire's record fourth-wicket stand of 470 on the first day. Opening Lancashire's reply, he managed to score 26 before adding a further 100 runs with a runner. His scores of 126 and 128 not out enabled Lancashire to win an amazing match by ten wickets. When Fowler completed his second hundred, his runner had his hand shaken by a fielder and waved his bat to acknowledge the applause. A month later Fowler marked his Test debut with a fine innings of 86 which gained his selection for the imminent England tour of Australasia.

The only batsman to score double centuries in both innings of a first-class match is Arthur Fagg of

Graeme Fowler (Lancashire): hundred in each innings with the aid of a runner (Popperfoto)

Kent. Playing against Essex at Castle Park, Colchester, on 13–15 July 1938, the right-handed opener scored 244 in five hours and 202 not out in only 170 minutes. His second innings opening partnership of 283 with Peter Sunnucks remains the county record.

The only batsman to score two first-class hundreds on the same day is K.S. Ranjitsinhji who scored 100 and 125 not out on 22 August 1896. Playing for Sussex against Yorkshire at Hove, he began the day with his first innings overnight score at 0 not out.

The record for the most hundreds in consecutive first-class innings was set in 1901 by Charles Fry when he ended the season with six in succession. After scoring 106, 209, 149, 105 and 140 for Sussex, he hit 105 for the Rest of England against Yorkshire at Lord's. His final century was his thirteenth of the season, setting a record which stood until 1925. Don Bradman and Mike Procter subsequently equalled Fry's record run of six hundreds during seasons overseas.

The only batsman to score hundreds in each innings of successive first-class matches in Britain is Tom Hayward of Surrey. Within a period of six days during the first week of June 1906, he opened the innings with scores of 144 not out and 100 against Nottinghamshire at Trent Bridge, Nottingham, and 143 and 125 against Leicestershire at Aylestone Road, Leicester.

The only instance of a father and son each scoring hundreds in the same first-class innings occurred at Edgbaston, Birmingham, on 23–24 July 1931 when George Gunn and his son George Vernon Gunn scored 183 and 100 not out respectively for Nottinghamshire against Warwickshire. George Gunn, then aged 52, made only one more hundred before retiring from the first-class scene the following year. For his 26-year-old son it was the first of eleven hundreds during a career which ended in 1950 with an isolated emergency recall, eleven years after his retirement from the county game.

The most occasions that any batsman has scored a double century and a century in the same match is four by Zaheer Abbas for Gloucestershire. All eight innings were not out:

Scores		Opponents	Venue	Season
216*	156*	Surrey	The Oval	1976
230*	104*	Kent	Canterbury	1976
205*	108*	Sussex	Cheltenham	1977
215*	150*	Somerset	Bath	1981

The only batsman to score a century and a triple century in the same first-class match is Graham Gooch with 333 and 123 for England against India in the First Test at Lord's on 26–30 July 1990. Besides recording **the highest individual score in ANY match at Lord's**, he achieved a new **highest individual aggregate for any first-class match in Britain (456)**.

The first batsman to carry his bat through both innings of a first-class match and to score centuries on each occasion was Cecil Wood of Leicestershire. Playing against Yorkshire at Park Avenue, Bradford, in June 1911, he contributed 107 not out and 117 not out towards Leicestershire's totals of 309 and 296. He batted in all for 8 hours 40 minutes and in neither innings did he give a chance. His feat was emulated by Jimmy Cook when, batting for a total of 9 hours 5 minutes and hitting 31 fours, he scored 120 not out and 131 not out for Somerset (186 and 218) against Nottinghamshire at Trent Bridge, Nottingham, on 19–21 July 1989.

The record for the most fifties in consecutive first-class innings was set by Ernest Tyldesley with ten in succession between 26 June and 27 July 1926. It was equalled by Don Bradman during the 1947–48 Australian season and the 1948 tour of England and by Romesh Kaluwitharana for Galle and Western Province South during Sri Lanka's 1994–95 domestic season. Tyldesley's sequence of scores was as follows:

144	Lancashire v Warwickshire	Birmingham
69	Lancashire v Kent	Dover
144*	Lancashire v Kent	Dover
226	Lancashire v Sussex	Manchester
51	Lancashire v Surrey	The Oval
131	Lancashire v Surrey	The Oval
131	Players v Gentlemen	Lord's
106	Lancashire v Essex	Nelson
126	Lancashire v Somerset	Taunton
81	England v Australia	Manchester

The highest sequence of runs scored by any batsman before being dismissed in first-class matches in Britain is 645 by Graeme Hick for Worcestershire on 19–25 July 1990. After scoring 171* and 69* against Somerset at Worcester, he made 252* and 100* against Glamorgan at Abergavenny before being out for 53 against Derbyshire at Derby. He set this record during a sequence of 12 fifties in 13 consecutive innings, including seven in succession.

The fastest first-class fifty against genuine bowling was struck in 11 minutes by Jim Smith for

Graeme Hick: record 645 runs for Worcestershire between dismissals in 1990 (Popperfoto)

Middlesex against Gloucestershire at Bristol in 1938. His 12 scoring strokes included 6 sixes and 2 fours and he went on to reach 66 in 18 minutes.

Regrettably, Smith's record was technically surpassed in farcical circumstances by a fifty taking only 8 minutes (1.22 to 1.30pm), and scored off 13 balls by Clive Inman for Leicestershire against Nottinghamshire at Trent Bridge, Nottingham on 20 August 1965. With the home county giving away cheap runs to encourage an early declaration on the final day, the 29-year-old left-hander from Colombo was fed slow full tosses by Norman Hill, who was very much a non-bowler. After getting off the mark with a single from the last ball of an over from Brian Bolus, another very occasional bowler, Inman struck Hill's two overs for 50 runs (440064 and 466664) with pulls to and over the mid-wicket boundary.

The fastest first-class hundred against genuine bowling was scored in 35 minutes by Percy Fender for Surrey against Northamptonshire at Northampton on 26 August 1920. Surrey were 448 for 5 in reply to the home county's 306, when Fender joined Alan Peach with 29 minutes to go before tea on the second day. Dropped after making his first run, Fender scored 93 in the 29 minutes before tea and added his next ten runs in 6 minutes afterwards, reaching his century with a six. His first 50 took 19 minutes. The declaration came at 619 for 5 when Peach completed his 200, Fender having scored 113 not out during an unfinished partnership of 171 in 42 minutes. This represents a rate of 244 runs per hour and is the fastest partnership on record of more than 30 minutes duration. Fender's time would almost certainly have been even faster but for the tea interval occurring during his innings. After tea Peach had most of the strike so that he could reach his 200 before the closure. It was his maiden three-figure innings at first-class level.

Although it is generally acknowledged that the only fair and accurate method of assessing the scoring rate of an innings is by comparing the number of balls received, very few first-class innings have been recorded in this way. The 'lineal' scoring system, devised in 1905 by the renowned and much-travelled Australian scorer, Bill Ferguson, has only recently gained favour with the majority of scorers at first-class matches. Recording the number of balls faced by an individual batsman under the standard system of scoring is very much a hit and miss affair. From the official scorebook it is impossible to calculate the number of balls which Fender received during those 35 minutes. Scorebook research shows that it is likely to have been between 40 and 46.

Fender's world record has subsequently been equalled or bettered in contrived and bizarre circumstances when rubbish bowling and deliberate mis-fielding have provided the opposition with fast runs prior to a declaration on the last day. These mockeries have been relegated to footnotes in the record books and have no place here.

The fastest 150 in all first-class matches took Gilbert Jessop just 63 minutes. Playing for the Gentlemen of the South against the Players of the South in the Hastings Festival on 3 September 1907, `The Croucher' scored 191 out of 234 in 90 minutes, taking only 42 minutes to reach his century after being bowled for a duck in the first innings.

The fastest time for scoring a first-class double-century in Britain is exactly 2 hours and two instances have been recorded. Gilbert Jessop was responsible for the first. Playing for Gloucestershire against Sussex at Hove on 1 June 1903, he made 286 – his highest score – out of 355 in under three hours and with the aid of 41 fours. Jessop's record time was equalled 73 years later by Clive Lloyd when he scored 201 not out against Glamorgan at St Helen's, Swansea. On 9 August 1976, while captaining the West Indians, the Guyanese left-hander hit 7 sixes and 27 fours, reached his hundred in 80 minutes (including a break for drinks), and raced to his share of the record just 40 minutes later.

The fastest triple century in first-class cricket in Britain was scored by Charles Macartney for the Australians against Nottinghamshire at Trent Bridge, Nottingham, on 25 June 1921. After reaching his 300 in 205 minutes, he added another 45 in half an hour before falling lbw after hitting 4 sixes and 47 fours. His innings of 345 remains the highest for the Australians in all matches.

The first batsman to score a century before lunch on the first day of what was then described as an 'important' match was W.G. Grace. On 11 August 1869 at the St Lawrence Ground, Canterbury, he opened the MCC's innings against Kent and was 116 not out at lunch. His innings of 127 founded a total of 449 and victory by an innings.

The only batsman to score a pre-lunch hundred in both innings of any first-class match is Gilbert Jessop. Playing for Gloucestershire against Yorkshire at Park Avenue, Bradford, he scored 104 before lunch on the second day (24 July 1900), and 139, including 7 sixes off Wilfred Rhodes, during the same session on the third. Both his innings were begun and completed before lunch. Jessop was the most prolific scorer of hundreds in an hour or less with eleven instances between 1897 and 1913.

The highest number of runs scored in a pre-lunch session in English first-class cricket is 180 by K.S. Ranjitsinhji for Sussex against Surrey. At Hastings on 15 July 1902, the second day of a match which was to set a new record English aggregate of 1427 runs, 'Ranji' took his overnight score from 54 to 234 not out in 150 minutes. It was a chanceless piece of batting which included 39 fours.

The most runs scored from a single hit in any first-class match is ten by Samuel Wood (later Hill-Wood) of Derbyshire off a ball from C.J. Burnup (MCC) in the second innings at Lord's on 26 May 1900. This instance was recorded under the experimental 'net' system of scoring which the MCC tried out in their own club matches during the early part of that season. The boundary was enclosed with a net of between two and three feet in height with the object of making batsmen run all their hits. Three runs were scored if the ball went over the net and two runs were added to any completed if the net stopped the ball. The system put a premium on hits that just reached the netting but discounted full-blooded strokes, and the whole idea was abandoned after a few trials.

The most runs off any over without no-balls in all first-class cricket is 36, a record set by Garfield Sobers when he was batting for Nottinghamshire against Glamorgan at St Helen's, Swansea, on 31 August 1968. Coming to the wicket ten minutes before tea on the first day with the scoreboard showing 308 for 5, the Nottinghamshire and West Indies captain had scored 40 in 30 minutes when Malcolm Nash began his historic over. Normally a medium-fast swing bowler, the 23-year-old left-hander was experimenting with a slower style of delivery. Sobers struck the first four balls for giant sixes. His next stroke sent the ball soaring towards long-off but it was caught by Roger Davis just inside the boundary. After completing the catch, Davis fell and his shoulders crossed the line. Sobers was saved by an experimental clause added to Law 35 which decreed that: 'The Fieldsman must have no part of his body grounded outside the playing area in the act of making a catch and afterwards.' The umpires conferred with Davis before awarding a six and Sobers celebrated by striking the last delivery into the garden of The Cricketers pub. The ball was lost until a schoolboy recovered it the next day and it was duly presented to Sobers. As the crowd stood cheering, he closed the innings at 394 for 5. He had scored 76 not out in 35 minutes. As Tony Lewis, captain of Glamorgan, commented: 'It wasn't sheer slogging through strength, but scientific hitting with every movement working in harmony.'

Ravi Shastri equalled this world record in 1985 (see 'First-Class Cricket in India').

Mike Procter is the only other batsman to hit 6 successive sixes in first-class cricket. Captaining Gloucestershire against Somerset at Taunton on 27 August 1979, he struck sixes off the last two balls of Dennis Breakwell's second over. Procter's partner, Andy Stovold, then played out a maiden over from

Ian Botham, before the South African all-rounder hit sixes off the first four balls of the left-arm slow bowler's third over.

Until the law was amended in 1910, the ball usually had to be hit right out of the ground and not just over the boundary for six runs to be scored. Before that change the record was held by Charles Thornton with 9 sixes. Batting for Kent on the Common at Tunbridge Wells against Sussex on 13 July 1869, he had to strike the ball over the canvas surrounding the ground to gain six runs. In the words of one of the Sussex team, 'At least three of the hits would have gone away for eights (*if they had been run out*).'

The world records for most sixes in any first-class innings (16) and match (20) were set by

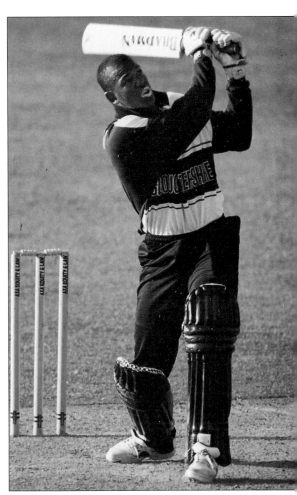

Big-hitting Gloucestershire batsman Andrew Symonds: set records for sixes in a first-class innings and match in 1995 (Allsport/Ben Radford)

Andrew Symonds for Gloucestershire against Glamorgan at Abergavenny in 1995. During his 254 not out on 24–25 August he broke the existing record of 15 by John Reid (set in New Zealand in 1962–63) before overhauling Jim Stewart's match record of 17 (Blackpool 1959) by striking four more during his second innings of 76 a day later.

The highest number of runs in any first-class innings from strokes worth four or more is 308 (10 sixes and 62 fours) by Brian Lara during his world record innings of 501 not out for Warwickshire against Durham at Edgbaston, Birmingham on 3 and 6 June 1994. The previous record was set by Percy Perrin of Essex against Derbyshire at Queen's Park, Chesterfield, on 18–19 July 1904. Batting first wicket down, he hit 68 fours in his score of 343 not out, made in 5¾ hours. **Besides containing the most fours on record in any first-class innings, his score remains the highest for Essex, the highest by any Englishman who was never selected for England, and the highest by any player on the losing side.**

The slowest fifty in English first-class cricket was recorded at Lord's on 15–16 August 1982 when Chris Tavaré, playing for England in the Second Test against Pakistan, took 350 minutes to reach his half-century. In that time he faced 236 balls, scoring off only 25 (3 fours, 5 threes, 7 twos and 10 singles), and playing out no fewer than 17 maiden overs. He batted 67 minutes before scoring and spent exactly an hour on 24, thus recording **the only first-class innings to include two runless periods of an hour or more.**

The slowest fifty in Championship matches was reached after 302 minutes by James Hall for Sussex against Surrey at The Oval on 28–29 July 1994. His innings of 85, which occupied 380 minutes (304 balls) and was the highest of the match, paved the way for an innings victory.

The slowest first-class hundred in Britain took Keith Fletcher 7 hours 38 minutes. Playing for England in the Third Test against Pakistan at The Oval in August 1974, he reached his fifth Test century off his 329th ball after hitting 7 fours, 5 threes, 10 twos and 39 singles.

The slowest hundred in Championship matches was recorded by Jason Gallian (118) after Lancashire had followed on 407 runs in arrears against Derbyshire at Blackpool. Spread over three days (15–18 July 1994), it was completed after 7 hours 33 minutes and contributed to **the highest total (589) by a team following on in Britain.**

The slowest double and triple centuries in first-class matches in Britain were recorded by Bob Simpson during his innings of 311 for Australia against England in the Fourth Test at Old Trafford, Manchester, in July 1964. He took 10 hours 8

Jason Gallian (Lancashire): slowest hundred in a Championship match (Allsport/Ben Radford)

minutes to reach 200, and 12 hours 33 minutes for his triple century. It was his maiden Test hundred and his 52nd innings for Australia.

The longest time any batsman has waited to score his first run during a first-class innings in Britain is 81 minutes. This bizarre record fell to a 19-year-old Law student from Pembroke College, Cambridge, at Lord's in July 1974 during the 130th University Match. Cambridge were 136 runs ahead of Oxford with three second innings wickets in hand, when Edward Jackson began his remarkable innings 66 minutes before the end of the second day's play. Next morning he battled on for a further 15 minutes before getting off the mark with a pull to the mid-wicket boundary off his 72nd ball. In the next over, after that one scoring stroke, he was caught at the wicket off the new ball. The match ended in a disappointing draw.

The longest period without adding to an individual score in a first-class match in Britain is 90 minutes by Graeme Fowler for Lancashire against Warwickshire at Edgbaston, Birmingham, on 20 April 1989. Opening the innings on a seaming pitch with uneven bounce, he remained on 39 for 20 overs.

The longest individual innings in English first-class cricket lasted 13 hours 17 minutes and was played by Len Hutton for England against Australia at The Oval on 20, 22 and 23 August 1938. He scored 160 in 355 minutes on the first day, and 140 in 307 minutes on the second, both days being interrupted by rain. Sixth out at 2.30pm on the third day after helping to add a world record 770 runs, Hutton had amassed the (then) record Test score of 364 by hitting 35 fours, 15 threes, 18 twos and 143 singles.

The world record for the highest percentage of runs by one batsman in any completed first-class innings was set by Glenn Turner on 30 June 1977. Opening the batting for Worcestershire against Glamorgan at St Helen's, Swansea, he carried his bat throughout the innings of 169 and took his overnight score of 39 to 141 not out. He thus contributed over 83 per cent of the total. The other batsmen managed only 14 scoring strokes between them and none reached double figures. Turner batted for 220 minutes and hit a six and 18 fours.

The lowest completed innings total to include an innings of 50 in first-class cricket is 66 by the Indians against Yorkshire at St George's Road, Harrogate, in July 1932. While his ten colleagues managed nine runs between them, Nazir Ali rattled up 52 in an hour, hitting 3 sixes and 5 fours.

The lowest total to include a first-class century is 143 by Nottinghamshire against Hampshire at Dean Park, Bournemouth, on 4 July 1981. Clive Rice, their captain, scored 105 not out on a well-grassed pitch and under heavy cloud. Coming to the wicket at 19 for 2, he struck a six, a five and 16 fours.

The lowest completed innings total to include a double century is 298 by Gloucestershire against Glamorgan at Newport on 8 August 1956. Starting his innings with the score 9 for 2, Tom Graveney scored 200 in 340 minutes, struck 3 sixes and 20 fours, and, unlike the batsmen monopolizing the previous two records, he finished on the winning side.

The highest number of runs scored in any season of first-class cricket is 3816 by Denis Compton of Middlesex and England in 1947. He averaged 90.85 runs per completed innings and set another world record by making 18 hundreds. He scored 2033 runs in Championship matches, 753 in five Tests against South Africa, and 1030 in other matches; altogether 1187 of his runs came off the South African attack. In addition the 29-year-old Compton took 73 first-class wickets, 57 of them in the County Championship. That same summer his 'terrible twin' Bill Edrich scored 3539 runs and took 67 wickets. Perhaps not surprisingly Middlesex were County Champions and England were comfortable winners of the rubber against South Africa.

The first batsman to score 2000 runs in first-class matches in a single season was W.G. Grace when he amassed 2739 runs in 1871. War years excepted, at least one batsman scored 2000 runs in every season from 1895 until 1973 inclusive, but no one attained that total in 1974, 1975, 1979, 1980 or 1987. The first to score 3000 runs in a season was K.S. Ranjitsinhji with 3159 in 1899.

The record for scoring 2000 runs in a season most times is 17 by Jack Hobbs of Surrey and England between 1907 and 1931.

The youngest batsman to score 2000 runs in a season is Graeme Hick of Worcestershire who was 20 years 112 days old when he reached that milestone during his final innings of the 1986 season.

The only batsman to score 2000 runs in a season without hitting a century is David Green. Playing for Lancashire in 1965, he scored 2037 runs (average 32.85). Although he reached 40 on 20 occasions, his highest score was only 85.

The record for scoring 1000 runs in an English first-class season most times is 28. It is shared by W.G. Grace of Gloucestershire and London County, between 1869 and 1902, and Frank Woolley of Kent who achieved the feat in 28 consecutive seasons from 1907 to 1938 inclusive.

The first batsman to score ten first-class hundreds in a season was W.G. Grace in 1871, and the record has progressed as follows: 12 – R. Abel (1900); 13 – C.B. Fry (1901); 16 – J.B.Hobbs (1925); 18 – D.C.S. Compton (1947). Not until 1978–79 did any batsman score ten centuries in an overseas season.

The first player to average over 100 runs per completed innings in an English season was Don Bradman (115.66 in 1938). On each of his four tours of Britain (1930, 1934, 1938 and 1948) he averaged over 80 (98.66, 84.16, 115.66 and 89.92), and on each tour he exceeded the average of the leading home batsman of that season.

The first English batsman to average over 100 in a home season and the only player to do so on more than one occasion is Geoffrey Boycott (see p. 82).

The highest aggregate of runs scored by a batsman in the season in which he made his initial appearance in first-class cricket is 1839 by Herbert Sutcliffe in 1919. Because of the First World War, he made his debut at the comparatively late age of 24.

The youngest player to score 1000 runs in his first season is Denis Compton who was 18 years 7 days old when he made his first-class debut, scoring 14 at number eleven against Sussex at Lord's in May 1936.

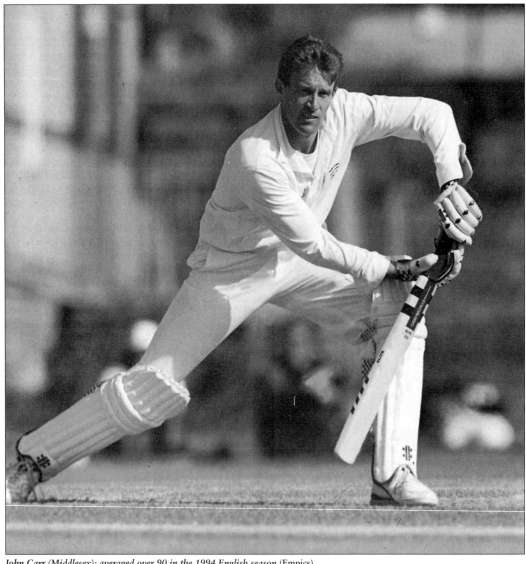

John Carr (Middlesex): averaged over 90 in the 1994 English season (Empics)

HIGHEST BATTING AVERAGES IN AN ENGLISH SEASON
(Qualification: 12 innings)

		Season	I	NO	Runs	Average
D.G. Bradman	Australians	1938	26	5	2429	115.66
G. Boycott	Yorkshire	1979	20	5	1538	102.53
W.A. Johnston	Australians	1953	17	16	102	102.00
G.A. Gooch	Essex	1990	30	3	2746	101.70
G. Boycott	Yorkshire	1971	30	5	2503	100.12
D.G. Bradman	Australians	1930	36	6	2960	98.66
H. Sutcliffe	Yorkshire	1931	42	11	3006	96.96
C.L. Hooper	West Indians	1991	25	9	1501	93.86

		Season	I	NO	Runs	Average
R.M. Poore	Hampshire	1899	21	4	1551	91.23
D.R. Jardine	Surrey	1927	14	3	1002	91.09
D.C.S. Compton	Middlesex	1947	50	8	3816	90.85
J.D. Carr	Middlesex	1994	27	10	1543	90.76
G.A. Hick	Worcestershire	1990	35	9	2347	90.26
G.M. Turner	Worcestershire	1982	16	3	1171	90.07

The highest partnerships for each wicket by English teams in first-class cricket in Britain have all been recorded in County Championship matches:

Wkt	Runs	Batsmen (scores)	Match	Venue	Season
1st	555	P. Holmes (224*), H. Sutcliffe (313)	Yorkshire v Essex	Leyton	1932
2nd	465 *	J.A. Jameson (240*), R.B. Kanhai (213*)	Warwicks v Gloucs	Birmingham	1974
3rd	424 *	W.J. Edrich (168*), D.C.S. Compton (252*)	Middlesex v Somerset	Lord's	1948
4th	470	A.I. Kallicharran (230*), G.W. Humpage (254)	Warwicks v Lancs	Southport	1982
5th	393	E.G. Arnold (200*), W.B. Burns (196)	Worcs v Warwicks	Birmingham	1909
6th	411	R.M. Poore (304), E.G. Wynyard (225)	Hampshire v Somerset	Taunton	1899
7th	344	K.S. Ranjitsinhji (230), W. Newham (153)	Sussex v Essex	Leyton	1902
8th	292	R. Peel (210*), Lord Hawke (166)	Yorkshire v Warwicks	Birmingham	1896
9th	283	J. Chapman (165), A. Warren (123)	Derbyshire v Warwicks	Blackwell	1910
10th	235	F.E. Woolley (185), A. Fielder (112*)	Kent v Worcestershire	Stourbridge	1909

With the exception of the sixth and tenth wickets, the English team records have not been improved upon by visiting teams from overseas.

Only three batsmen have scored 1000 runs in May, although five others have reached that aggregate before June with the aid of innings in April. W.G. Grace was the first to do so (1895); he was also the oldest (46 years 10 months), and he did so in the fewest innings, 10 (13, 103, 18, 25, 288, 52, 257, 73*, 18, 169). Wally Hammond achieved the highest May aggregate with 1042 in 1927, while Charles Hallows was the last to do so in 1928 and achieved the highest average for 1000 runs in May (125.00).

The five batsmen who scored 1000 runs before June have been Tom Hayward (1900), Don Bradman (1930 and 1938), Bill Edrich (1938, all scored at Lord's), Glenn Turner (1973) and Graeme Hick (1988).

The most first-class runs scored in April is 410 by Graeme Hick for MCC and Worcestershire in 1988.

The earliest date for scoring 1000 runs in a first-class season in Britain is 27 May and was recorded in 1938 by Don Bradman, captain of the Australian touring team.

The earliest dates for reaching both 2000 and 3000 runs in a season were achieved by Tom Hayward of Surrey in 1906. He scored his 2000th run on 5 July and completed his 3000 on 20 August. In 1937 Wally Hammond of Gloucestershire equalled the latter record.

The highest sixth-wicket partnership in Britain is 428 between M.A. Noble (284) and W.W. Armstrong (172*) for the Australians against Sussex at Hove in 1902.

The record tenth-wicket partnership is 249 between C.T. Sarwate (124*) and S.N. Banerjee (121) for the Indians against Surrey at The Oval in 1946. This stand provided the only instance of the last two batsmen in the order scoring centuries in the same innings.

The world record for the most consecutive runless innings in first-class matches is 12 by Mark Robinson, the Northamptonshire tail-ender, in 1990. After starting the season confidently with 1*, 0* and 1, he failed to score in any first-class innings between 4 May and 13 September: 0, 0*, 0*, 0*, 0*, 0*, 0, 0, 0, 0*, 0*, and 0. Happily he ended his barren run with a glorious 1* in his final innings of the Year of the Willow.

BOWLING RECORDS

The only bowler to take all ten wickets in a first-class innings on three occasions is A.P. 'Tich' Freeman of Kent:

O	M	R	W	Opponents	Venue	Season
42	9	131	10	Lancashire	Maidstone	1929
30.4	8	53	10	Essex	Southend	1930
36.1	9	79	10	Lancashire	Manchester	1931

The only bowler to take all ten wickets in a first-class innings twice in the same season is Jim Laker in

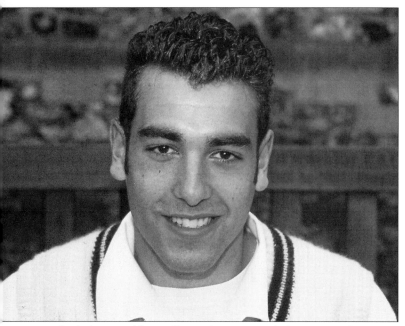

Richard Johnson (Middlesex): all ten wickets against Derbyshire in 1994 (Allsport)

1956. Both instances were achieved against the Australians: 10 for 88 for Surrey at The Oval on 16 May, in 46 overs bowled in 4¼ hours interrupted only by the lunch and tea intervals; and 10 for 53 for England in the Fourth Test at Old Trafford, Manchester, on 28, 30 and 31 July, in 51.2 overs. Only one other bowler, Edward Barratt for the Players in 1878, has taken all ten Australian wickets in an innings.

The least expensive ten wickets analysis in first-class cricket and the only instance to include a hat-trick, was achieved by Hedley Verity for Yorkshire at Headingley, Leeds, on 12 July 1932. At lunch on that last day, Nottinghamshire had scored 38 without loss after gaining a first innings lead of 71. After the interval they lost all ten wickets for the addition of only 29 runs, Verity ending the innings with a spell of seven wickets in 15 balls, including four in six balls. His full analysis read: 19.4–16–10–10.

The last bowler to take all ten wickets in a first-class innings in Britain was Richard Johnson, who took 10 for 45 for Middlesex against Derbyshire at Derby on 2 July 1994, the first instance in Britain for 30 years. At 19 years 185 days, he was the second-youngest after Imran Adil (18) – (see 'First-Class Cricket in Pakistan') to take all ten wickets in a first-class innings.

The only bowler to take 19 wickets in any first-class match is Jim Laker who took 9 for 37 and 10 for 53 for England against Australia in the Fourth

Test at Manchester in July 1956. His performance is fully described in the Test Cricket section.

The most outstanding match analysis in County cricket (and, Laker's 19 for 90 excepted, the most wickets for least runs in all first-class cricket), is 17 for 48 by Colin Blythe for Kent against Northamptonshire at Northampton on 1 June 1907. Rain had restricted play on the first two days to just three hours. Kent, 212 for 4 overnight, hastily took their total to 254 all out.

'Northamptonshire gave a deplorable display', according to *Wisden*, and lost their first seven wickets for four runs, two of them extras, with six of their first seven batsmen failing to score. Shortly after lunch they were all out for 60, Blythe taking all ten for 30 in 16 overs. Following on, they fared even worse and were dismissed in 75 minutes for 39, Blythe's left-arm spin claiming 7 for 18 in 15.1 overs. He bowled unchanged throughout both innings and became **the first player to take 17 wickets in a day**. Heavy rain fell almost immediately after Kent had completed this remarkable victory.

The most outstanding spell of wicket-taking in first-class cricket was recorded by Alonzo Drake for Yorkshire against Somerset at Weston-super-Mare on 28 August 1914. Bowling unchanged throughout both innings of the match with Major Booth for the second time that week, he took all ten second innings wickets in the space of 42 balls. A left-arm bowler of slow to medium pace, he took full advantage of a rain-affected, newly-laid pitch to become the first Yorkshire bowler to take all ten wickets in a first-class innings.

The most dramatic spell of wicket-taking in post-war first-class cricket was achieved by Pat Pocock's off-breaks in the closing minutes of the match between Sussex and Surrey at The Saffrons, Eastbourne on 15 August 1972 . Sussex, needing 205 for victory, were 187 for 1 with three of the 20 overs compulsory in the last hour still to be bowled. Geoffrey Greenidge (68*) and Roger Prideaux (92*) had so far added 160 runs in 107 minutes for the second wicket and a Sussex victory seemed assured. Pocock's analysis at this stage was 14–1–63–0. Then, at exactly six o'clock, he began his historic spell:

Ball	Striker	Result	Total	Runs required	Balls remaining
1	Greenidge	bowled	187–2	18	17
2	M.A. Buss	no run	187–2	18	16
3	M.A. Buss	bowled	187–3	18	15
4	J.M. Parks	2 runs	189–3	16	14
5	J.M. Parks	no run	189–3	16	13
6	J.M. Parks	ct by bowler	189–4	16	12

Prideaux (4,1) and Mike Griffith (0,0,6,0) took eleven runs off the penultimate over, bowled by Robin Jackman, and five runs were needed for victory when Pocock began the final over:

Ball	Striker	Result	Total	Runs required	Balls remaining
1	Prideaux	caught	200–5	5	5
2a	Griffith	caught	200–6	5	4
3b,c	J.D. Morley	stumped	200–7	5	3
4	J. Spencer	1 run	201–7	4	2
5d,e	A. Buss	bowled	201–8	4	1
6	U.C. Joshi	run out going for 2nd run	202–9	3	–

And so the match was left drawn. Five wickets fell in the final over – **a world record for any over in first-class cricket** – and eight wickets were lost in 18 balls for 15 runs in 20 minutes. The historic final over took ten minutes to bowl. At the end of it Pocock's analysis read 16–1–67–7 and he had equalled or broken three world records. The highlights of his performance were: a) Hat-trick – his second in first-class matches b) Four wickets in four balls – only the third instance by a Surrey bowler. c) **Six wickets in nine balls –world record.** d) **Seven wickets in eleven balls – world record.** e) **Five wickets in six balls – equalling world record.**

The only other bowler to take five wickets in six balls in English first-class cricket is Bill Copson who achieved this feat for Derbyshire against Warwickshire at Derby on 17 July 1937. Returning after a month's absence through injury, 'he maintained great speed and made the ball swing disconcertingly either way' (*Wisden*). Warwickshire were bowled out for 28, Copson returning figures of 8 for 11 in 8.2 overs – the best analysis of a first-class career which began sensationally in 1932 when he took the wicket of Andy Sandham with his very first ball.

The first recorded instance of a hat being given to a bowler for taking three wickets with consecutive balls occurred on 8 September 1858. Playing for the All-England Eleven against 22 of Hallam and Staveley at the Hyde Park Ground, Sheffield, H.H. Stephenson accomplished this feat in the second innings and was presented with a white hat. The terms 'to do a hat-trick' and 'to get a hat' evolved from this practice.

The only bowler to have hit the stumps with five successive balls in a first-class match is Charlie Parker of Gloucestershire. Bowling against County champions Yorkshire at Bristol in his own benefit match on 10 August 1922, he suffered the mortification of having the second dismissal nullified by a call of 'no ball'.

The only bowler to take two hat-tricks in the same innings of a first-class match in England is Albert Trott. He achieved this unique performance for Middlesex in his benefit match against Somerset at Lord's on 22 May 1907. After taking four wickets with four balls (one lbw and three bowled), he completed his county's victory by 166 runs with his second hat-trick (two caught and one bowled), finishing with figures of 7 for 20 in eight overs.

The only bowler to achieve a hat-trick with three stumpings in all first-class cricket is Charles Townsend of Gloucestershire. A 16-year old leg-spinner, he was playing against Somerset at Cheltenham on 15 August 1893, when he finished off their second innings with the aid of three successive stumpings by William Brain.

The only bowler to take a hat-trick entirely through lbw decisions on more than one occasion in first-class cricket is Mike Procter. Playing for Gloucestershire, he first achieved this unusual feat against Essex at Westcliff in 1972, and repeated it against Yorkshire at Cheltenham seven years later.

The record number of hat-tricks achieved by a bowler in first-class matches in Britain is six. Charlie Parker (left-arm spin) was the first to reach this total; all his instances were for Gloucestershire between 1922 and 1930, and, in 1924, he established another record by taking three hat-tricks in the same season.

The only other bowler to take six hat-tricks in Britain is Doug Wright; he claimed all his for Kent between 1937 and 1949 with his unique assortment of leg-breaks and googlies delivered at a bounding medium pace. Wright's last instance established the world record as it was his seventh in all first-class matches, the extra hat-trick being achieved for the MCC against Border at East London in January 1939.

TWO HAT-TRICKS IN THE SAME MATCH

Bowler	For	Opponents	Venue	Season
A. Shaw†	Nottinghamshire	Gloucestershire	Nottingham	1884
T.J. Matthews	Australia	South Africa	Manchester	1912
C.W.L. Parker	Gloucestershire	Middlesex	Bristol	1924
R.O. Jenkins	Worcestershire	Surrey	Worcester	1949

† Alfred Shaw also took three wickets in four balls, a combination of bowling feats never equalled within a single first-class match.

The only bowler to take a wicket with his first ball in BOTH innings of his maiden first-class match is Rudi Webster. A Barbadian fast bowler who was later to represent Warwickshire and Otago as well as his home Island, Webster played for Scotland against the MCC at Glenpark, Greenock, on 14–16 June 1961 while studying medicine at Edinburgh University. He bowled T.C. 'Dickie' Dodds of Essex with his first ball in the first innings, and repeated the feat against Arthur Phebey of Kent in the second. His first match analysis was 11 for 100.

The highest number of runs conceded by a bowler in a first-class innings in Britain is 298 by L.O. ('Chuck') Fleetwood-Smith of Australia, during 87 overs bowled in England's world record Test total of 903 for 7 declared at The Oval in August 1938. The most expensive analysis in County Championship matches is 6 for 231 by Charlie Parker for Gloucestershire against Somerset at Bristol in August 1923. He bowled 63 overs in the innings which was closed at 532 for 9.

The most runs conceded by a bowler in a first-class match in Britain is 331 by A.P. 'Tich' Freeman of Kent. Playing against the MCC at Folkestone in September 1934, he bowled 68 overs in the match, taking 6 for 199 and 2 for 132. The most runs conceded in a County Championship match is 306 by Johnny Briggs of Lancashire. In July 1897 he bowled 126 five-ball overs against Sussex at Old Trafford, Manchester, taking 2 for 174 and 2 for 132.

The most balls bowled in a first-class innings in Britain is 588 by Sonny Ramadhin for West Indies at Edgbaston in June 1957. After taking 7 for 49 in England's first innings, he was unable to break a partnership of 411 between May and Cowdrey and had figures of 2 for 179 from his record 98 overs. The most sent down by one bowler in a Championship match is 501 by Alfred Shaw for Sussex at Trent Bridge, Nottingham, in May 1895. Eighteen years after bowling the first ball in Test cricket, he contributed 100.1 five-ball overs and took 4 for 168 in Nottinghamshire's (then) record total of 726 all out.

The most balls bowled in a first-class match in Britain is 774 by Sonny Ramadhin for West Indies against England at Edgbaston in 1957. The record for a County Championship match is held by Johnny Briggs of Lancashire. He bowled 630 balls in taking 4 for 306 against Sussex at Old Trafford, Manchester, in July 1897.

The last instance of a pair of bowlers operating throughout both completed innings of a first-class match anywhere occurred in June 1967. Brian Crump (5 for 45 and 7 for 29) and Ray Bailey (5 for 64 and 3 for 31) bowled Northamptonshire to victory over Glamorgan by 132 runs in the first-class match at Sophia Gardens, Cardiff.

The most recent instance of a bowler taking a wicket with his first ball in first-class cricket in Britain occurred on 16 June 1990 in The Parks at Oxford when Australia's Under-19 captain, Jason Gallian, sharing the new ball on his first appearance for Lancashire, dismissed David Hagan of Oxford University with the seventh ball of the match.

The last player to bowl eight batsmen in an innings of a first-class match in Britain was G.O.B. 'Gubby' Allen. Playing for Middlesex against Lancashire at Lord's on 15 June 1929, he took all ten wickets for 40, hitting the stumps eight times and getting his remaining victims caught at the wicket and stumped respectively.

The only bowler to take 300 wickets in a first-class season is A.P. 'Tich' Freeman of Kent. One of the finest leg-break bowlers of all time, he took over 200 wickets in each of eight consecutive seasons from 1928 until 1935 inclusive. It was in the first year of that unique run that he took 304 wickets. Many of his victims were stumped by Les Ames and the two players formed a highly efficient partnership; Ames made over 100 dismissals in 1928, 1929 and 1932, and 47 per cent of his aggregate for those three seasons were stumpings.

MOST FIRST-CLASS WICKETS
IN A SEASON

Bowler	Season	Balls	Runs	Wkts	Avge
A.P. Freeman	1928	11 857	5489	304	18.05
A.P. Freeman	1933	12 234	4549	298	15.26
T. Richardson	1895	8451	4170	290	14.37
C.T.B. Turner	1888	9710	3307	283	11.68
A.P. Freeman	1931	9708	4307	276	15.60
A.P. Freeman	1930	11487	4632	275	16.84
T. Richardson	1897	8019	3945	273	14.45
A.P. Freeman	1929	10 025	4879	267	18.27
W. Rhodes	1900	9318	3606	261	13.81
J.T. Hearne	1896	10016	3670	257	14.28
A.P. Freeman	1932	9395	4149	253	16.39
W. Rhodes	1901	9390	3797	251	15.12

The last bowler to take 200 wickets in a first-class season was Tony Lock of Surrey in 1957 (212 wickets at 12.02 runs apiece).

The last bowler to take 150 wickets in a first-class season was another left-arm slow-medium bowler, Derek Underwood of Kent. In 1966 he captured 157 wickets at an average of 13.80 runs each.

The highest aggregate of first-class wickets in any season since 1966 is 134 by Malcolm Marshall in 22 matches for Hampshire in 1982.

The feat of taking 100 first-class wickets was achieved in every season from 1864 until 1971 inclusive, war years excepted. In 1972 the County Championship programme was reduced to 20 matches for each county and no bowler took 100 wickets in 1972 or 1976. Order was restored with the addition of two matches from 1977 until 1982 inclusive, and a further two from 1983 until 1988 when four-day matches were introduced. For five seasons when the programme involved 16 three-day and six four-day matches per county only four bowlers attained the hundred mark: Franklyn Stephenson and Kevin Cooper for Nottinghamshire in 1988, and Neil Foster and Waqar Younis in 1991. In three seasons of a 'pure' 17-match four-day schedule, only Anil Kumble, Northamptonshire's Indian leg-spinner, has reached the magic three figures with 105 wickets in 1995.

The record for taking 100 first-class wickets in a season most times is held by Wilfred Rhodes of Yorkshire. The greatest wicket-taker of all time (4184), this left-arm slow bowler, who played Test cricket at a later age than any other man, captured 100 or more wickets in a season 23 times between 1898 and 1929.

The highest number of consecutive seasons in which any bowler has taken 100 first-class wickets is 20. This incredible record of consistency was achieved by Derek Shackleton of Hampshire

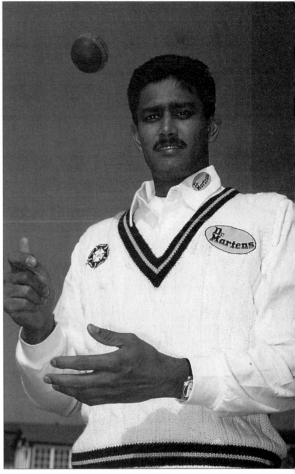

Anil Kumble: took over 100 wickets for Northamptonshire in 1995 (Popperfoto)

between 1949 and 1968 inclusive. Such was 'Shack's' skill and accuracy that his career average dropped as the years progressed.

The lowest recorded average by a bowler taking 100 wickets in a season is 8.54 runs per wicket by Alfred Shaw of Nottinghamshire when he took 186 wickets for 1589 runs in 1880.

The two most expensive instances of taking 100 first-class wickets in a season were recorded by Ray Smith of Essex. An all-rounder who could bowl either right-arm medium-pace or slow off-spin, he took 125 wickets (average 37.26) in 1947 and 102 (average 34.77) in 1950.

Only eleven bowlers have taken 100 wickets in the season in which they made their debut in first-class cricket. Wilfred Rhodes took most wickets in his first year (154). Derek Underwood was the last to do so and the youngest.

100 WICKETS IN DEBUT SEASON

Bowler	County	Age	Season	Wickets	Average
G.P. Harrison	Yorkshire	21	1883	100	13.26
A.W. Mold	Lancashire	25	1889	102	11.83
C.H.G. Bland	Sussex	24	1897	129	21.68
W. Rhodes	Yorkshire	20	1898	154	14.60
F. Barratt	Nottinghamshire	20	1914	115	21.80
A. Waddington	Yorkshire	26	1919	100	18.74
J.M. Gregory	Australians	23	1919	131	18.19
G.W. Brook	Worcestershire	41	1930	132	21.88
C. Cook	Gloucestershire	24	1946	133	18.62
D.B. Close	Yorkshire	18	1949	113	27.87
D.L. Underwood	Kent	17	1963	101	21.12

Jack Gregory did not play first-class cricket in Australia until the 1919–20 season.

The earliest date for taking 100 first-class wickets in a season is 12 June. Jack Hearne of Middlesex set the record in 1896, and Charlie Parker of Gloucestershire equalled it in 1931.

The earliest date for taking 200 first-class wickets in a season is 27 July, a record established by A.P. 'Tich' Freeman of Kent in 1928.

The only instance of a bowler taking 300 first-class wickets in a season was achieved by Freeman in 1928, that unique total being reached on 15 September.

The only instance in important matches of a player bowling ten batsmen in an innings was achieved by John Wisden at Lord's on 15 July 1850. Playing for the North against the South, the founder of the most famous *Cricketers' Almanack* bowled unchanged from the Pavilion End for the second time in the match. 'Without exaggeration, his balls turned in a yard from the off' (*Haygarth*).

The records for the most runs conceded and most balls bowled in a first-class season were, perhaps not surprisingly, set by the man who took most wickets: A.P. 'Tich' Freeman. In 1928 when he achieved his record haul of 304 wickets, he conceded 5489 runs – the only instance of any bowler conceding 5000 runs in a single summer. Five years later, when he took 298 wickets, he bowled 12 234 balls – the only instance of one man sending down 12 000 balls in one season.

The longest recorded distance for a bail to travel from the stumps after a batsman has been bowled is 67 yards 6 inches. This record occurred at Old Trafford, Manchester, on 29 June 1911 when Robert Burrows of Worcestershire bowled William Huddleston of Lancashire and one of the bails flew as far as the boundary.

WICKET-KEEPING RECORDS

The record number of wicket-keeping dismissals in any first-class innings in Britain is eight by David East of Essex on 27 July 1985 against Somerset at Taunton. He celebrated his 26th birthday by equalling Wally Grout's (then) world record (set at

Kent wicket-keeper Steve Marsh: equalled the record for dismissals in a first-class innings with 8 catches against Middlesex in 1991 (Allsport/John Gichigi)

Brisbane in 1960). East established a world record of his own by **catching the first eight batsmen dismissed in the innings.** The ninth wicket fell to a run out before Ian Botham closed the Somerset innings.

East's record was equalled by Kent's Steve Marsh (8 catches) against Middlesex at Lord's in 1991 and by Tim Zoehrer (6 catches, 2 stumpings) for the 1993 Australians against Surrey at The Oval.

The world record for the most stumpings in any first-class innings is six by Hugo Yarnold for Worcestershire against Scotland at Broughty Ferry, near Dundee, on 2 July 1951. His stumpings, made off the leg-breaks and googlies of 'Roly' Jenkins and the slow left-arm deliveries of Michael Bradley, were preceded by a catch to equal the current world record for most dismissals (then seven, set by E.J. 'Tiger' Smith in 1926).

The only wicket-keeper to accomplish a hat-trick of stumpings in a first-class match is William Brain of Gloucestershire. Keeping to the leg-breaks of Charles Townsend, then aged 16, at Cheltenham on 15 August 1893, he stumped Somerset's last three batsmen off successive balls in the second innings.

The only wicket-keepers to complete a hat-trick of catches in first-class cricket are George Dawkes of Derbyshire (off Les Jackson against Worcestershire at Kidderminster on 16 June 1958), and R.C. 'Jack' Russell of Gloucestershire (one off Courtney Walsh and two off David Lawrence, against Surrey at The Oval on 4 September 1986).

The most dismissals by a wicket-keeper in any first-class match is 12 by Ted Pooley for Surrey against Sussex at The Oval on 6–7 July 1868. His aggregate, comprising six dismissals in each innings and including one stumping in the first innings and three in the second, has been equalled twice in Australian Sheffield Shield matches.

The highest number of catches held in any first-class match is eleven, a world record established by Arnold Long, also for Surrey against Sussex, at Hove on 18–21 July 1964. His performance, which involved catching seven batsmen in the first innings (equalling the English record) and four in the second, has been emulated on three occasions by Australians, and in Britain by David Bairstow for Yorkshire against Derbyshire at Scarborough in 1982, by Warren Hegg for Lancashire against Derbyshire at Chesterfield in 1989, by Alec Stewart for Surrey against Leicestershire at

Leicester in 1989 and by Keith Piper for Warwickshire against Derbyshire at Chesterfield in 1994.

The record number of stumpings for any first-class match is nine by Fred Huish for Kent against Surrey at The Oval on 21–23 August 1911 during the benefit match for his opposite number in the Surrey team, Herbert Strudwick. In the first innings, he made four stumpings off Douglas Carr's leg-breaks, and in the second added another to three off Frank Woolley and one off Colin Blythe (both left-arm leg-spinners). He also held a second innings catch off Woolley, but even his unique performance could not deny Surrey victory by nine runs.

The most wicket-keeping dismissals in a first-class season is 128 (79 catches and 49 stumpings) by Leslie Ames of Kent in 34 matches in 1929 – a summer in which he also scored 1795 runs.

Keith Piper (Warwickshire): equalled the record for the number of catches in a first-class match in 1994 (Popperfoto)

Only seven wicket-keepers have made 100 dismissals in a first-class season, Leslie Ames accomplishing this feat three times:

		Year	Dis	Ct	St
F.H. Huish	Kent (2)	1911	101	62	39
		1913	102	69	33
G. Duckworth	Lancashire	1928	107	77	30
L.E.G. Ames	Kent (3)	1928	122	70	52
		1929	128	79	49
		1932	104	40	64
H. Yarnold	Worcestershire	1949	110	63	47
J.T. Murray	Middlesex (2)	1957	104	82	22
		1960	102	95	7
J.G. Binks	Yorkshire	1960	107	96	11
R. Booth	Worcestershire (2)	1960	101	85	16
		1964	100	91	9

The highest number of catches in any first-class season is 96 by Jimmy Binks of Yorkshire in 38 matches in 1960.

The most stumpings in a season is 64 by Leslie Ames in 1932, a summer in which he stumped almost twice as many batsmen as he caught. Ames, who also made 52 stumpings in 1928, is alone in making 50 stumpings in a season.

The highest innings in all first-class cricket in which no byes were conceded is 672 for 7 declared by Hampshire at Taunton on 20–21 July 1899. Equally remarkable is the fact that Somerset's wicket-keeper during this marathon was the 43-year-old Vicar of Martock, Rev Prebendary Archdale Palmer Wickham.

FIELDING RECORDS

All records in this section exclude performances by wicket-keepers.

The highest number of catches by one fielder in any first-class innings is seven. The record was set by Micky Stewart of Surrey during Northamptonshire's second innings, on 7 June 1957. Rain had enlivened the Northamptonshire pitch. Fielding very close to the wicket, Stewart held six catches at backward short-leg and one in the gully; three were off the bowling of Tony Lock, two off Jim Laker, and two off Alec Bedser.

Stewart's record was equalled at Trent Bridge, Nottingham, on 26 July 1966, when Tony Brown of Gloucestershire held seven catches during Nottinghamshire's second innings on another rain-affected pitch. After diving low to his right to intercept a drive off his own bowling, he caught three batsmen at backward short-leg, two at gully and one at second slip. Four catches came from lifting off-breaks bowled by David Allen. Before Brown made the first of his catches he could have claimed a simple skier that was left to the wicket-keeper.

Four other fielders – Bill Voce, Brian Sellers, Arthur Milton and Stuart Surridge – have taken seven catches in a single day of a first-class match but have done so in the course of both innings.

Playing for Kent at Folkestone on 6–7 July 1966, Alan Ealham caught five Gloucestershire batsmen off Derek Underwood's bowling whilst fielding in the same position topographically; four right-handers were caught at long-off and one left-hander was taken at long-on.

The record number of catches taken by a fielder in any first-class match is ten by Wally Hammond for Gloucestershire. Playing against Surrey at Cheltenham College on 16–17 August 1928, he held four catches in the first innings and six in the second. Eight were held at slip off the left-arm bowling of Charlie Parker. No other fielder has held more than eight catches in a first-class match. Hammond made his performance even more exceptional by scoring a century in each innings.

MOST CATCHES IN A DAY

Fielder	For	Opponents	Venue	Season
W. Voce	Nottinghamshire	Glamorgan	Pontypridd	1929
A.B. Sellers	Yorkshire	Essex	Leyton	1933
C.A. Milton	Gloucestershire	Sussex	Hove	1952
W.S. Surridge	South	North	Kingston upon Thames	1952
M.J. Stewart	Surrey	Northamptonshire	Northampton	1957
A.S. Brown	Gloucestershire	Nottinghamshire	Nottingham	1966

The highest number of catches by a fielder in a first-class season is 78 by Wally Hammond of Gloucestershire in 1928. Ten of them were held in one match.

Only six fielders have held more than 65 catches in a first-class season, John Tunnicliffe and Peter Walker exceeding this total twice:

		Year	Ct
J. Tunnicliffe	Yorkshire	1895	66
		1901	70
W.R. Hammond	Gloucestershire	1928	78
J.G. Langridge	Sussex	1955	69
M.J. Stewart	Surrey	1957	77
P.M. Walker	Glamorgan	1960	69
		1961	73
P.J. Sharpe	Yorkshire	1962	71

RECORD ALL-ROUND PERFORMANCES

The only cricketer to score a century and take all ten wickets in an innings in a first-class match in Britain since 1864 is W.G. Grace. Playing for the MCC against Oxford University in the Oxford Parks on 21 and 22 June 1886, 'The Champion' scored 104 in his only innings, before taking all ten Oxford second innings wickets for 49 runs in 36.2 four-ball overs.

The only player to score a hundred in each innings and take five wickets twice in any first-class match is George Hirst of Yorkshire. At Bath on 27, 28 and 29 August 1906, he scored 111 and 117 not out (during which he completed his 2000 runs for the season), and took 6 for 70 and 5 for 45.

The only players besides Hirst to score hundreds in each innings and take ten wickets in a first-class match are Bernard Bosanquet, originator of the googly (or 'bosie' as Australians call it) and Franklyn Stephenson. Playing for Middlesex against Sussex at Lord's in May 1905, Bosanquet scored 103 in 105 minutes, took 3 for 75, hit 100 not out in 75 minutes, and then applied the coup de grâce which secured victory by 324 runs when he bowled unchanged through the last innings to return figures of 8 for 53. Stephenson became the last player to complete the season's double (see below) when he rounded off Trent Bridge's 150th anniversary season on 14–17 September 1988 by scoring his first hundreds for Nottinghamshire and taking 11 wickets: 111 in 157 minutes, 117 in 137 minutes, 4 for 105 and 7 for 117. But even his prodigious feats could not deny Yorkshire victory by 127 runs.

Seven cricketers have scored a century and taken a hat-trick in the same first-class match in Britain, Mike Procter being the only one to do so twice. William Roller achieved a unique version of this record when he scored a double century and did the hat-trick for Surrey against Sussex in June 1885.

CENTURY AND HAT-TRICK IN THE SAME MATCH

Batsman	Score	For	Opponents	Venue	Season
G. Giffen	113	Australians	Lancashire	Manchester	1884
W.E. Roller	204	Surrey	Sussex	The Oval	1885
W.B. Burns	102*	Worcestershire	Gloucestershire	Worcester	1913
V.W.C. Jupp	102	Sussex	Essex	Colchester	1921
L.N. Constantine	107	West Indians	Northamptonshire	Northampton	1928
D.E. Davies	139	Glamorgan	Leicestershire	Leicester	1937
M.J. Procter	102	Gloucestershire	Essex	Westcliff	1972
M.J. Procter	122	Gloucestershire	Leicestershire	Bristol	1979

The double of 100 runs and 100 wickets in a first-class season was first achieved in 1874 by W.G. Grace when he scored 1664 runs and took 140 wickets. 'The Champion' repeated this performance in each of the next four seasons, but it was not until 1882 that another player, C.T. Studd, emulated him.

From 1895 until 1967 inclusive and war years excepted, the double of 1000 runs and 100 wickets was achieved at least once each season apart from 1951 and 1958. Only two players have completed the double since the Championship was reduced by four matches per county in 1969. Both instances were achieved by overseas players and for Nottinghamshire. In 1984 Richard Hadlee completed the first double for 17 years in his 21st match. Four seasons later, his successor, Franklyn Stephenson of Barbados, reached the target in his 22nd and final match of the season. Needing to score 210 runs against Yorkshire at Trent Bridge, he made 111 and 117; by also taking 11 wickets he became only the third player in history to score hundreds in each innings and take ten wickets in the same first-class match.

The fastest double was completed on 28 June 1906 by George Hirst of Yorkshire after 16 matches.

The youngest player to achieve the double, and the only one to do so in his first season of first-class cricket, was Brian Close of Yorkshire in 1949 at the age of 18.

Two players did this double for two counties: Vallance Jupp for Sussex (1920 and 1921) and Northamptonshire (eight times between 1925 and 1933); and Freddie Brown for Surrey (1932) and Northamptonshire (1949).

The record for scoring 1000 runs and taking 100 wickets in a season most times is held by Wilfred Rhodes of Yorkshire; he achieved this double 16 times between 1903 and 1926 inclusive.

The most consecutive seasons in which a player has done the double is eleven by George Hirst of Yorkshire from 1903 until 1913 inclusive. He achieved the double 14 times in all, a total second only to that of Rhodes.

The only player to do the double double of 2000 runs and 200 wickets in a first-class season is also George Hirst. In 1906, at the age of 35, he scored 2385 runs and took 208 wickets in 35 matches.

The only player to score 3000 runs and take 100 wickets in a season of first-class cricket is J.H. Parks (Jim Parks sr). In 1937, at the age of 34, he scored 3003 runs and took 101 wickets in 35 matches.

Only three cricketers have scored 1000 runs and taken 200 wickets in a first-class season, Maurice Tate achieving this unusual feat in three consecutive years:

	Season	M	Runs	Wkts
A.E. Trott	1899	32	1175	239
A.E. Trott	1900	36	1337	211
A.S. Kennedy	1922	34	1129	205
M.W. Tate	1923	36	1168	219
M.W. Tate	1924	36	1419	205
M.W. Tate	1925	35	1290	228

Only two wicket-keepers have scored 1000 runs and made 100 dismissals in first-class matches during a season, Leslie Ames achieving the feat on three occasions:

	Season	M	Runs	Dsmls
L.E.G. Ames	1928	37	1919	122
L.E.G. Ames	1929	34	1795	128
L.E.G. Ames	1932	36	2482	104
J.T. Murray	1957	33	1025	104

The first all-rounder to complete the treble of 1000 runs, 100 wickets and 50 catches was Percy Fender of Surrey in 1921, when he did the first of his six doubles. In 34 matches he scored 1152 runs, took 134 wickets and held 52 catches. Forty years later Peter Walker of Glamorgan equalled this feat with 1347 runs, 101 wickets and 73 catches in 35 matches.

OTHER INDIVIDUAL RECORDS

Wilfred Rhodes, the Yorkshire and England all-rounder whose career extended from 1898 until 1930, holds the world record for **the most first-class match appearances** (1107) and the record for **the most appearances for one county** (881).

The oldest man to play in a first-class match in England since 1864 was George Robert Canning, the 4th Lord Harris (1851–1932). When he ended his final appearance for Kent on 4 July 1911, against All India at Catford, he had reached the age of 60 years 151 days. In his final first-class innings his lordship scored 36, the second-highest contribution in Kent's first innings total of 318, and shared in the highest partnership of the match, adding 98 runs for the sixth wicket in under an hour. His last act at first-class level was to abet the tourists' defeat by taking 1 for 34 in ten overs in the second innings. Thirty-one years earlier Lord Harris had led England against Australia at The Oval in the first Test match to be staged in England.

The youngest to appear in English first-class cricket was Charles Robertson Young (1852–) when he played for Hampshire against Kent at Gravesend on 13 June 1867 at the age of 15 years 131 days. Batting at number nine, he scored 20 not out and was promoted to open the second innings. Although he was out for 8, he later had the satisfaction of taking 1 for 12 in eight overs in his first spell at first-class level. Young was born in Indiaat Dharwar near Bombay and his date of birth has been confirmed at the India Office as 2 February 1852. His father, David Young, was an Assistant Superintendent Revenue Surveyor for Southern Marathee County. No record of C.R. Young's death has so far been traced. His last appearance for Hampshire occurred in 1890 but to date no further mention of him has been found. He is not included in the death registers at St Catherine's House nor is there any record of him in the Probate Registry. Possibly he died abroad during or after a coaching assignment.

The second-youngest first-class cricketer was George Frederick Grace. A younger brother of Dr W.G. Grace, 'G.F.' made his first-class debut on 21 May 1866 for the Gentlemen of England against Oxford University, at Oxford, when aged 15 years 159 days.

The second-youngest player to appear for a first-class county was Charles Edgar Winter who was 15 years 288 days old when he appeared for Somerset against Hampshire at Southampton on 24 July 1882. By coincidence, Charles Young was playing for the opposition.

The longest-lived English first-class cricketer on record was Edward Apsey English who played in 18 matches for Hampshire from 1898 to 1901 inclusive. Born at Dorking in Surrey on 1 January 1864, he died at Tiverton in Devon on 8 September 1966 at the age of 102 years 250 days. He held the world record for longevity amongst first-class cricketers from April 1966 (when he outlived the 102 years 102 days of John Wheatley, an Australian who moved to Christchurch and represented Canterbury for many seasons) until August 1986 when Rupert de Smidt (Western Province) died after extending the record by a mere four days.

The only other British Isles first-class cricketer known to have reached his century of years was George Richard Uniake Harman (101 years 191 days). Born at Crosshaven, Co. Cork on 6 June 1874, he died at Torpoint, Cornwall, on 14 December 1975. Although his only first-class appearance was for Dublin University in 1895, he did represent Ireland at rugby union. His brother, William Ronayne Harman, played first-class cricket for Ireland and lived to the age of 93.

THE COUNTY CHAMPIONSHIP

Inter-county cricket has existed since the early 18th century. The earliest match on record took place on 29 June 1709 when Kent played Surrey at Dartford Brent. The origins of the County Championship, and the identity of the champions prior to the competition being officially constituted in 1890, are subjects which have provoked considerable argument and controversy.

The concept of a county championship seems to have resulted from a sports journalist or wealthy patron of the game attempting to promote interest in certain inter-county matches in the same way that bare-knuckle prize-fights were publicized. Although it is possible to prepare a list of champions from 1826 by researching contemporary publications, it would be ludicrous to include them with the winners of the modern championship. In several of those early and pre-Victorian seasons only two county matches were played, and only four of the 17 county clubs of today were founded before 1863. Reference to county champions were very scattered and most usually found in newspapers local to the county claiming the title.

After 1864, the year in which overarm bowling

was legalized and as many as 24 county matches were staged, references to a champion county become more frequent. There was still scant agreement among contemporary cricket publications concerning the title-holders. Frequently the title was left undecided as there was no generally accepted method of determining the holder. Although the 'least matches lost' method existed, it was not consistently applied. The playing quality of a team seems to have been as important as its results. Although rules governing playing qualifications were agreed by the counties in 1873, it was not until 1888 that an unofficial points system was introduced.

On 10 December 1889 a private meeting of the representatives of Gloucestershire, Kent, Lancashire, Middlesex, Nottinghamshire, Surrey, Sussex and Yorkshire took place at Lord's and agreed a method of deciding the championship. Only from 1890 was the competition officially constituted and the title awarded by the counties themselves. Only from that date can any authorized list of county champions commence.

From 1969 onwards, Championship regulations awarded priority of final place for any counties finishing equal on points to the side with most wins.

The **earliest date for winning the title** is 12 August (1912) – by Kent, when they beat Gloucestershire by an innings in two days at Cheltenham.

The **record number of successive titles** is seven by Surrey from 1952 to 1958 inclusive. Their playing record during that period was: played 195, won 121, lost 28, drew 46.

The **highest number of victories in a season** is 25 by Yorkshire in 1923. They lost only one of their 32 matches, Nottinghamshire winning by three runs at Headingley, gained first innings lead in four of their six drawn games, and obtained 133 points out of a possible maximum of 155.

The **longest unbeaten run in Championship matches** was achieved by Yorkshire when, after losing to Surrey at The Oval on 26 August 1924, they avoided defeat until Warwickshire beat them at Hull on 24 May 1927. During that period they played 70 matches, winning 41, drawing 28 and having one abandoned.

The **most defeats in a season** is 20, an unfortunate record set by Glamorgan in 1925, when they won only one of their 26 matches, and equalled by Nottinghamshire in 1961 when they won four of their 28 games.

The **longest run of Championship matches without a victory** was endured by Northampton-shire. It lasted from their win against Somerset at Taunton on 14 May 1935 until 29 May 1939, when they inflicted an innings defeat upon a startled

Leicestershire in two days at Northampton. During that barren period they lost 61 of their 99 matches. Northamptonshire supporters had to wait until 16 July 1946 for their next victory, a lengthy innings from the Third Reich intervening, and thus were able to celebrate just one solitary success in a period of more than eleven years.

Six counties have remained unbeaten throughout a season of County Championship cricket, Yorkshire achieving this feat on five occasions:

NO DEFEATS IN A SEASON

	Season	Played	Won	Drew	Position
Yorkshire	1900	28	16	12	1st
Lancashire	1904	26	16	10	1st
Nottinghamshire	1907	19	15	4	1st
Yorkshire	1908	28	16	12	1st
Yorkshire	1925	32	21	11	1st
Yorkshire	1926	31	14	17	2nd
Lancashire	1928	30	15	15	1st
Yorkshire	1928	26	8	18	4th
Lancashire	1930	28	10	18	1st
Glamorgan	1969	24	11	13	1st
Warwickshire	1972	20	9	11	1st
Hampshire	1973	20	10	10	1st
Lancashire	1974	20	5	15	8th

There have been only ten instances of a side gaining an outright result in every match during a season. The outstanding instance was achieved by Surrey under the captaincy of Stuart Surridge in 1955. Leicestershire's record in 1910 excludes their match against Yorkshire which, restricted to two days because of the funeral of King Edward VII, was not counted (along with five others) in the Championship. In 1911, matches in which no result on first innings was achieved were not counted, Northamptonshire's fixture against Yorkshire at Dewsbury being the lone instance.

NO DRAWN MATCHES IN A SEASON

	Season	Played	Won	Lost	Tied	Position
Sussex	1890	12	1	11	–	8th
Surrey	1894	16	13	2	1	1st
Leicestershire	1910	17	6	11	–	10th
Northamptonshire	1911	17	8	9	–	10th
Somerset	1914	19	3	16	–	15th
Derbyshire	1920	17	–	17	–	16th
Gloucestershire	1921	24	12	12	–	7th
Surrey	1955	28	23	5	–	1st
Essex	1995	17	8	9	–	5th
Durham	1995	17	4	13	–	17th

Eight counties have failed to win a single match during an entire season, Derbyshire suffering this misfortune on four occasions. With the exception of Nottinghamshire, who finished in 16th place in 1967, all the counties concerned finished last in the Championship table.

NO VICTORIES IN A SEASON

	Season	Played	Drew	Lost
Derbyshire	1897	16	7	9
Hampshire	1900	22	6	16
Derbyshire	1901	20	7	13
Somerset	1910	18	3	15
Derbyshire	1920	17	–	17
Derbyshire	1924	24	11	13
Worcestershire	1928	30	11	19
Northamptonshire	1936	24	15	9
Northamptonshire	1937	24	8	16
Northamptonshire	1938	24	7	17
Nottinghamshire	1967	28	24	4
Glamorgan	1979	21	11	10
Warwickshire	1982	22	14	8

The highest number of drawn matches involving one county during a Championship season is 24 by Nottinghamshire in 1967 when they failed to win any of their 28 fixtures.

The most appearances in County Championship matches is 762 by Wilfred Rhodes for Yorkshire from 1898 until 1930 inclusive.

The highest number of consecutive appearances is 423 by Ken Suttle for Sussex between 18 August 1954 and 28 July 1969, including one match abandoned without a ball being bowled.

The oldest player to appear in a Championship match is the Rev Reginald Moss, who was 57 years 89 days old when he made his only appearance for Worcestershire on 23–26 May 1925 against Gloucestershire at Worcester. He had previously represented Oxford University and Lancashire.

The leading run-scorer in Championship matches is Philip Mead of Hampshire, who made 665 appearances in the period 1906–36. He holds the records for the most runs in a career (46 268), most runs in a season (2843 in 1928), most hundreds (132), most times 1000 runs in a season (26), and most times 2000 runs in a season (9). Wally Hammond holds the records for the most double centuries (22) and the most hundreds in a season (13 in 1938).

The leading wicket-taker in Championship matches is A.P. 'Tich' Freeman of Kent. He established the records for most wickets in a career (3151 during the period 1914–36), most wickets in a season (252 in 1933), most instances of ten or more wickets in a match (123), most times ten or more wickets in a season (15 – equalling the record set by Tom Richardson of Surrey), and most times 200 wickets in a season (6). Until 1968, when Derek Shackleton surpassed it with his 18th and final instance, Freeman also shared (with Wilfred Rhodes) the record for taking 100 wickets in a season most times.

The two most successful all-rounders in the history of the County Championship are Yorkshire's 'great twin brethren' from the Golden Age of cricket, George Herbert Hirst and Wilfred Rhodes. Both batted right-handed and bowled left, and both scored over 20 000 runs and took more than 2000 wickets in Championship matches – a double achieved by no other player. Hirst, who played from 1891 until 1921 inclusive, scored 27 318 runs and took 2096 wickets, achieving the double of 1000 runs and 100 wickets in a season eight times. Rhodes (1898–1930) scored 26 874 runs, took 3118 wickets and did the double seven times.

The wicket-keeping records are more widely distributed. Until 1980, Herbert Strudwick (1902–27) held the career record for most catches (964) and until 1982, that for most dismissals (1132). In those seasons Bob Taylor established new records, having started his career with Derbyshire in 1961. When he retired from county cricket at the end of the 1984 season, Taylor had made 1222 dismissals, including 1087 catches, in 480 Championship matches.

The only instances of 100 dismissals in a season were achieved by Leslie Ames, who made 102 in 1929 and 100 in 1928. Ames is also alone in making 50 stumpings in a season of Championship cricket – 52 in 1932. His career total of stumpings fell just two short of the record of 315 established by his Kent predecessor, Fred Huish (1895–1914).

The most catches in a season is 88 by Roy Booth for Worcestershire in 1964.

The highest career aggregate of catches in Championship matches by a fielder other than a wicket-keeper is 710 by Frank Woolley for Kent in 707 matches between 1906 and 1938 inclusive.

The most catches by a non-wicket-keeper during a season of Championship matches is 66 by John Langridge for Sussex in 1959. Like Woolley, Langridge was an outstanding slip fielder.

THE COUNTY CHAMPIONSHIP FINAL POSITIONS SINCE 1890

	Derby	Dur	Essex	Glam	Glos	Hants	Kent	Lancs	Leics	Middx	Nor	Notts	Som	Sur	Sus	War	Wor	Yor
1890	–	–	–	–	6	–	3	2	–	7	–	5	–	1	8	–	–	3
1891	–	–	–	–	9	–	5	2	–	3	–	4	5	1	7	–	–	8
1892	–	–	–	–	7	–	7	4	–	5	–	2	3	1	9	–	–	6
1893	–	–	–	–	9	–	4	2	–	3	–	6	8	5	7	–	–	1
1894	–	–	–	–	9	–	4	4	–	3	–	7	6	1	8	–	–	2
1895	5	–	9	–	4	10	14	2	12	6	–	12	8	1	11	6	–	3
1896	7	–	5	–	10	8	9	2	13	3	–	6	11	4	14	12	–	1
1897	14	–	3	–	5	9	12	1	13	8	–	10	11	2	6	7	–	4
1898	9	–	5	–	3	12	7	6	13	2	–	8	13	4	9	9	–	1
1899	15	–	6	–	9	10	8	4	13	2	–	10	13	1	5	7	12	3
1900	13	–	10	–	7	15	3	2	14	7	–	5	11	7	3	6	12	1
1901	15	–	10	–	14	7	7	3	12	2	–	9	12	6	4	5	11	1
1902	10	–	13	–	14	15	7	5	11	12	–	3	7	4	2	6	9	1
1903	12	–	8	–	13	14	8	4	14	1	–	5	10	11	2	7	6	3
1904	10	–	14	–	9	15	3	1	7	4	–	5	12	11	6	7	13	2
1905	14	–	12	–	8	16	6	2	5	11	13	10	15	4	3	7	8	1
1906	16	–	7	–	9	8	1	4	15	11	11	5	11	3	10	6	14	2
1907	16	–	7	–	10	12	8	6	11	5	15	1	14	4	13	9	2	2
1908	14	–	11	–	10	9	2	7	13	4	15	8	16	3	5	12	6	1
1909	15	–	14	–	16	8	1	2	13	6	7	10	11	5	4	12	8	3
1910	15	–	11	–	12	6	1	4	10	3	9	5	16	2	7	14	13	8
1911	14	–	6	–	12	11	2	4	15	3	10	8	16	5	13	1	9	7
1912	12	–	15	–	11	6	3	4	13	5	2	8	14	7	10	9	16	1
1913	13	–	15	–	9	10	1	8	14	6	4	5	16	3	7	11	12	2
1914	12	–	8	–	16	5	3	11	13	2	9	10	15	1	6	7	14	4
1919	9	–	14	–	8	7	2	5	9	13	12	3	5	4	11	15	–	1
1920	16	–	9	–	8	11	5	2	13	1	14	7	10	3	6	12	15	4
1921	12	–	15	17	7	6	4	5	11	1	13	8	10	2	9	16	14	3
1922	11	–	8	16	13	6	4	5	14	7	15	2	10	3	9	12	17	1
1923	10	–	13	16	11	7	5	3	14	8	17	2	9	4	6	12	15	1
1924	17	–	15	13	6	12	5	4	11	2	16	6	8	3	10	9	14	1
1925	14	–	7	17	10	9	5	3	12	6	11	4	15	2	13	8	16	1
1926	11	–	9	8	15	7	3	1	13	6	16	4	14	5	10	12	17	2
1927	5	–	8	15	12	13	4	1	7	9	16	2	14	6	10	11	17	3
1928	10	–	16	15	5	12	2	1	9	8	13	3	14	6	7	11	17	4
1929	7	–	12	17	4	11	8	2	9	6	13	1	15	10	4	14	16	2
1930	9	–	6	11	2	13	5	1	12	16	17	4	13	8	7	15	10	3
1931	7	–	10	15	2	12	3	6	16	11	17	5	13	8	4	9	14	1
1932	10	–	14	15	13	8	3	6	12	10	16	4	7	5	2	9	17	1
1933	6	–	4	16	10	14	3	5	17	12	13	8	11	9	2	7	15	1
1934	3	–	8	13	7	14	5	1	12	10	17	9	15	11	2	4	16	5
1935	2	–	9	13	15	16	10	4	6	3	17	5	14	11	7	8	12	1
1936	1	–	9	16	4	10	8	11	15	2	17	5	7	6	14	13	12	3
1937	3	–	6	7	4	14	12	9	16	2	17	10	13	8	5	11	15	1
1938	5	–	6	16	10	14	9	4	15	2	17	12	7	3	8	13	11	1
1939	9	–	4	13	3	15	5	6	17	2	16	12	14	8	10	11	7	1
1946	15	–	8	6	5	10	6	3	11	2	16	13	4	11	17	14	8	1
1947	5	–	11	9	2	16	4	3	14	1	17	11	11	6	9	15	7	7
1948	6	–	13	1	8	9	15	5	11	3	17	14	12	2	16	7	10	4
1949	15	–	9	8	7	16	13	11	17	1	6	11	9	5	13	4	3	1
1950	5	–	17	11	7	12	9	1	16	14	10	15	7	1	13	4	6	3
1951	11	–	8	5	12	9	16	3	15	7	13	17	14	6	10	1	4	2
1952	4	–	10	7	9	12	15	3	6	5	8	16	17	1	13	10	14	2

Warwickshire skipper Dermot Reeve lifts the Britannic Assurance County Championship trophy in 1995 (Allsport)

	Derby	Dur	Essex	Glam	Glos	Hants	Kent	Lancs	Leics	Middx	Nor	Notts	Som	Sur	Sus	War	Wor	Yor
1953	6	–	12	10	6	14	16	3	3	5	11	8	17	1	2	9	15	12
1954	3	–	15	4	13	14	11	10	16	7	7	5	17	1	9	6	11	2
1955	8	–	14	16	12	3	13	9	6	5	7	11	17	1	4	9	15	2
1956	12	–	11	13	3	6	16	2	17	5	4	8	15	1	9	14	9	7
1957	4	–	5	9	12	13	14	6	17	7	2	15	8	1	9	11	16	3
1958	5	–	6	15	14	2	8	7	12	10	4	17	3	1	13	16	9	11
1959	7	–	9	6	2	8	13	5	16	10	11	17	12	3	15	4	14	1
1960	5	–	6	11	8	12	10	2	17	3	9	16	14	7	4	15	13	1
1961	7	–	6	14	5	1	11	13	9	3	16	17	10	15	8	12	4	2
1962	7	–	9	14	4	10	11	16	17	13	8	15	6	5	12	3	2	1
1963	17	–	12	2	8	10	13	15	16	6	7	9	3	11	4	4	14	1
1964	12	–	10	11	17	12	7	14	16	6	3	15	8	4	9	2	1	5
1965	9	–	15	3	10	12	5	13	14	6	2	17	7	8	16	11	1	4
1966	9	–	16	14	15	11	4	12	8	12	5	17	3	7	10	6	2	1
1967	6	–	15	14	17	12	2	11	3	7	9	16	8	4	13	10	5	1
1968	8	–	14	3	16	5	2	6	9	10	13	4	12	15	17	11	7	1
1969	16	–	6	1	2	5	10	15	14	11	9	8	17	3	7	4	12	13
1970	7	–	12	2	17	10	1	3	15	16	14	11	13	5	9	7	6	4
1971	17	–	10	16	8	9	4	3	5	6	14	12	7	1	11	2	15	13
1972	17	–	5	13	3	9	2	15	6	8	4	14	11	12	16	1	7	10
1973	16	–	8	11	5	1	4	12	9	13	3	17	10	2	15	7	6	14
1974	17	–	12	16	14	2	10	8	4	6	3	15	5	7	13	9	1	11
1975	15	–	7	9	16	3	5	4	1	11	8	13	12	6	17	14	10	2
1976	15	–	6	17	3	12	14	16	4	1	2	13	7	9	10	5	11	8
1977	7	–	6	14	3	11	1	16	5	1	9	17	4	14	8	10	13	12

	Derby	Dur	Essex	Glam	Glos	Hants	Kent	Lancs	Leics	Middx	Nor	Notts	Som	Sur	Sus	War	Wor	Yor
1978	14	–	2	13	10	8	1	12	6	3	17	7	5	16	9	11	15	4
1979	16	–	1	17	10	12	5	13	6	14	11	9	8	3	4	15	2	7
1980	9	–	8	13	7	17	16	15	9	1	12	3	5	2	4	14	11	6
1981	12	–	5	14	13	7	9	16	8	4	15	1	3	6	2	17	11	10
1982	11	–	7	16	15	3	13	12	2	1	9	4	6	5	8	17	14	10
1983	9	–	1	15	12	3	7	12	4	2	6	14	10	8	11	5	16	17
1984	12	–	1	13	17	15	5	16	4	3	11	2	7	8	6	9	10	14
1985	13	–	4	12	3	2	9	14	16	1	10	8	17	6	7	15	5	11
1986	11	–	1	17	2	6	8	15	7	12	9	4	16	3	14	12	5	10
1987	6	–	12	13	10	5	14	2	3	16	7	1	11	4	17	15	9	8
1988	14	–	3	17	10	15	2	9	8	7	12	5	11	4	16	6	1	13
1989	6	–	2	17	9	6	15	4	13	3	5	11	14	12	10	8	1	16
1990	12	–	2	8	13	3	16	6	7	1	11	13	15	9	17	5	4	10
1991	3	–	1	12	13	9	6	8	16	15	10	4	17	5	11	2	6	14
1992	5	18	1	14	10	15	2	12	8	11	3	4	9	13	7	6	17	16
1993	15	18	11	3	17	13	8	13	9	1	4	7	5	6	10	16	2	12
1994	17	16	6	18	12	13	9	10	2	4	5	3	11	7	8	1	15	13
1995	14	17	5	16	6	13	18	4	7	2	3	11	9	12	15	1	10	8

COUNTY FIRST-CLASS RECORDS

DERBYSHIRE

Badge	Rose and Crown
Colours	Chocolate, Amber and Pale Blue
Foundation	4 November 1870 at The Guildhall, Derby
Headquarters	County Cricket Ground, Nottingham Road, Derby, DE2 6DA
Champions	(1) 1936

DERBYSHIRE RECORDS IN ALL FIRST-CLASS CRICKET

MATCH RECORDS

For Derbyshire	Record	Holder(s)	Opponents	Venue	Season
Highest Total	645		Hampshire	Derby	1898
Lowest Total	16		Nottinghamshire	Nottingham	1879
Highest Score	274	G.A. Davidson	Lancashire	Manchester	1896
Highest Partnership	349	C.S. Elliot, J.D. Eggar	Nottinghamshire	Nottingham	1947
Best Bowling – Innings	10–40	W. Bestwick	Glamorgan	Cardiff	1921
– Match	17–103	W. Mycroft	Hampshire	Southampton	1876
Most Dismissals – Innings	7	R.W. Taylor (7c)	Glamorgan	Derby	1966
	7	R.W. Taylor (7c)	Yorkshire	Chesterfield	1975
– Match	10	H. Elliott (8c,2s)	Lancashire	Manchester	1935
	10	R.W. Taylor (10c)	Hampshire	Chesterfield	1963

Against Derbyshire	Record	Holder(s)	Opponents	Venue	Season
Highest Total	662		Yorkshire	Chesterfield	1898
Lowest Total	23		Hampshire	Burton upon Trent	1958
Highest Score	343 *	P.A. Perrin	Essex	Chesterfield	1904
Highest Partnership	554	J.T. Brown, J. Tunnicliffe	Yorkshire	Chesterfield	1898
Best Bowling – Innings	10–45	R.L. Johnson	Middlesex	Derby	1994
– Match	16–101	G. Giffen	Australians	Derby	1886

Long-serving skipper Kim Barnett led Derbyshire to victory in the 1993 Benson & Hedges Cup (Popperfoto)

SEASON RECORDS

Most Runs	2165	D.B. Carr	1959
Most Hundreds	8	P.N. Kirsten	1982
Most Wickets	168	T.B. Mitchell	1935
Most Wicket-Keeping Dismissals	90	H. Elliott (69c, 21s)	1935
Most Catches (non WK)	49	M.H. Page	1967

CAREER RECORDS

Most Appearances	540	D.C. Morgan	1950–69
Most Runs	20 516	D. Smith	1927–52
Most Hundreds	46	K.J. Barnett	1979–95
Most Times 1000 Runs in a Season	12	D. Smith (1931–50)	1927–52
	12	K.J. Barnett (1983–95)	1979–95
Most Wickets	1670	H.L. Jackson	1947–63
Most Hat-Tricks	4	A.E.G. Rhodes (1947–51)	1937–54
Most Times 100 Wickets in a Season	12	C. Gladwin (1946–58)	1939–58
Most Wicket-Keeping Dismissals	1304	R.W. Taylor (1157c, 147s)	1961–84
Most Catches (non WK)	563	D.C. Morgan	1950–69

DURHAM

Badge	Coat of Arms of the County of Durham
Colours	Navy Blue, Yellow and Maroon
Foundation	10 May 1882
Headquarters	County Ground, Riverside, Chester-le-Street, Co Durham, DH3 3QR
Champions	No instance

DURHAM RECORDS IN ALL FIRST-CLASS CRICKET

MATCH RECORDS

For Durham	Record	Holder(s)	Opponents	Venue	Season
Highest Total	625–6d		Derbyshire	Chesterfield	1994
Lowest Total	83		Lancashire	Manchester	1993
Highest Score	204	J.E. Morris	Warwickshire	Birmingham	1994
Highest Partnership	222	P.W.G. Parker, J.D. Glendenen	Oxford U.	Oxford	1992
Best Bowling– Innings	8–118	A. Walker	Essex	Chelmsford	1995
– Match	14–177	A. Walker	Essex	Chelmsford	1995
Most Dismissals – Innings	5	C.W. Scott (5c)	Sussex	Hove	1994
	5	C.W. Scott (3c, 2s)	Kent	Canterbury	1994
– Match	7	C.W. Scott (7c)	Warwickshire	Darlington	1993

Against Durham	Record	Holder(s)	Opponents	Venue	Season
Highest Total	810–4d		Warwickshire	Birmingham	1994
Lowest Total	73		Oxford U.	Oxford	1994
Highest Score	501*	B.C. Lara	Warwickshire	Birmingham	1994
Highest Partnership	322*	B.C. Lara, K.J. Piper	Warwickshire	Birmingham	1994
Best Bowling – Innings	8–69	A.R. Caddick	Somerset	Chester-le-Street	1995
– Match	12–68	J.N.B. Bovill	Hampshire	Stockton	1995
Most Dismissals – Innings	7	S.A. Marsh (6c, 1s)	Kent	Canterbury	1994
– Match	9	S.A. Marsh (8c, 1s)	Kent	Canterbury	1994

SEASON RECORDS

Most Runs	1536	W. Larkins	1992
Most Hundreds	4	D.M. Jones	1992
	4	W. Larkins	1992
	4	J.E. Morris	1994
Most Wickets	74	S.J.E. Brown	1994
Most Wicket-Keeping Dismissals	56	C.W. Scott (54c, 2s)	1994
Most Catches (non WK)	24	W. Larkins	1993

CAREER RECORDS

Most Appearances	72	S.J.E. Brown	1992–95
Most Runs	4278	W. Larkins	1992–95
Most Hundreds	10	W. Larkins	1992–95
Most Times 1000 Runs in a Season	2	W. Larkins (1992–93)	1992–95
	2	J.E. Morris (1994–95)	1994–95
Most Wickets	236	S.J.E. Brown	1992–95
Most Hat-Tricks	–		
Most Times 100 Wickets in a Season	–		
Most Wicket-Keeping Dismissals	134	C.W. Scott (126c, 8s)	1992–95
Most Catches (non WK)	62	W. Larkins	1992–95

Wayne Larkins: recruited by Durham from Northampton to anchor the team in its first County Championship season, now the county's leading scorer (Popperfoto)

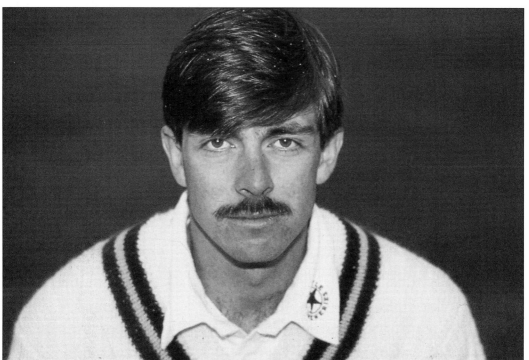

Simon Brown: leading wicket-taker for Durham in first-class matches (Allsport/Gary M. Prior)

ESSEX

Badge	Three Seaxes above Scroll bearing 'Essex'
Colours	Blue, Gold and Red
Foundation	14 January 1876 at The Shire Hall, Chelmsford
Headquarters	County Ground, New Writtle Street, Chelmsford, CM2 0PG
Champions	(6) 1979, 1983, 1984, 1986, 1991, 1992

ESSEX RECORDS IN ALL FIRST-CLASS CRICKET

MATCH RECORDS

For Essex	Record	Holder(s)	Opponents	Venue	Season
Highest Total	761–6d		Leicestershire	Chelmsford	1990
Lowest Total	30		Yorkshire	Leyton	1901
Highest Score	343*	P.A. Perrin	Derbyshire	Chesterfield	1904
Highest Partnership	403	G.A. Gooch, P.J. Prichard	Leicestershire	Chelmsford	1990
Best Bowling – Innings	10–32	H. Pickett	Leicestershire	Leyton	1895
– Match	17–119	W. Mead	Hampshire	Southampton	1895
Most Dismissals – Innings	8	D.E. East (8c)	Somerset	Taunton	1985
– Match	9	K.L. Gibson (7c, 2s)	Derbyshire	Leyton	1911
	9	D.E. East	Sussex	Hove	1983

Against Essex	Record	Holder(s)	Opponents	Venue	Season
Highest Total	803–4d		Kent	Brentwood	1934
Lowest Total	14		Surrey	Chelmsford	1983
Highest Score	332	W.H. Ashdown	Kent	Brentwood	1934
Highest Partnership	555	P. Holmes, H. Sutcliffe	Yorkshire	Leyton	1932
Best Bowling – Innings	10–40	E.G. Dennett	Gloucestershire	Bristol	1906
– Match	17–56	C.W.L. Parker	Gloucestershire	Gloucester	1925

SEASON RECORDS

Most Runs	2559	G.A. Gooch	1984
Most Hundreds	9	J. O'Connor	1929, 1934
	9	D.J. Insole	1955
Most Wickets	172	T.P.B. Smith	1947
Most Wicket-Keeping Dismissals	89	B. Taylor (79c, 10s)	1962
Most Catches (non WK)	40	K.W.R. Fletcher	1966

CAREER RECORDS

Most Appearances	575	K.W.R. Fletcher	1962–88
Most Runs	29 434	K.W.R. Fletcher	1962–88
Most Hundreds	86	G.A. Gooch	1973–95
Most Times 1000 Runs in a Season	19	K.W.R. Fletcher (1963–84)	1962–88
Most Wickets	1610	T.P.B. Smith	1929–51
Most Hat-Tricks	2	J.W.H.T. Douglas (1905–23)	1901–28
Most Times 100 Wickets in a Season	11	M.S. Nichols (1926–39)	1924–39
Most Wicket-Keeping Dismissals	1231	B. Taylor (1040c, 191s)	1949–73
Most Catches (non WK)	519	K.W.R. Fletcher	1962–88

Keith Fletcher: set records for most appearances and runs in a distinguished Essex career (Popperfoto)

GLAMORGAN

Badge	Gold Daffodil
Colours	Blue and Gold
Foundation	6 July 1888 at Cardiff
Headquarters	Sophia Gardens, Cardiff, CF1 9XR
Champions	(2) 1948, 1969

GLAMORGAN RECORDS IN ALL FIRST-CLASS CRICKET

MATCH RECORDS

For Glamorgan	Record	Holder(s)	Opponents	Venue	Season
Highest Total	587–8d		Derbyshire	Cardiff	1951
Lowest Total	22		Lancashire	Liverpool	1924
Highest Score	287*	D.E. Davies	Gloucestershire	Newport	1939
Highest Partnership	425*	A. Dale, I.V.A. Richards	Middlesex	Cardiff	1993
Best Bowling – Innings	10–51	J. Mercer	Worcestershire	Worcester	1936
– Match	17–212	J.C. Clay	Worcestershire	Swansea	1937
Most Dismissals – Innings	7	E.W. Jones (6c, 1s)	Cambridge U.	Cambridge	1970
	7	C.P. Metson (7c)	Derbyshire	Chesterfield	1991
– Match	9	C.P. Metson (9c)	Worcestershire	Worcester	1993
	9	C.P. Metson (9c)	Surrey	The Oval	1995

Against Glamorgan	Record	Holder(s)	Opponents	Venue	Season
Highest Total	657–7d		Warwickshire	Birmingham	1994
Lowest Total	33		Leicestershire	Ebbw Vale	1965
Highest Score	313*	S.J. Cook	Somerset	Cardiff	1990
Highest Partnership	344	A. Sandham, R.J. Gregory	Surrey	The Oval	1937
Best Bowling – Innings	10–18	G. Geary	Leicestershire	Pontypridd	1929
– Match	16–96	G. Geary	Leicestershire	Pontypridd	1929

SEASON RECORDS

Most Runs	2276	H. Morris		1990
Most Hundreds	10	H. Morris		1990
Most Wickets	176	J.C. Clay		1937
Most Wicket-Keeping Dismissals	94	E.W. Jones (85c, 9s)		1970
Most Catches (non WK)	67	P.M. Walker		1961

CAREER RECORDS

Most Appearances	647	D.J. Shepherd	1950–72
Most Runs	34 056	A. Jones	1957–83
Most Hundreds	52	A. Jones	1957–83
Most Times 1000 Runs in a Season	23	A. Jones (1961–83)	1957–83
Most Wickets	2174	D.J. Shepherd	1950–72
Most Hat-Tricks	1	(8 bowlers)	1926–69
Most Times 100 Wickets in a Season	12	D.J. Shepherd (1952–70)	1950–72
Most Wicket-Keeping Dismissals	933*	E.W. Jones (840c, 93s)	1961–83
Most Catches (non WK)	656	P.M. Walker	1955–72

* Including 21 catches as a fielder.

Wicket-keeper Colin Metson: county record nine catches in a match twice in the 1990s (Popperfoto)

GLOUCESTERSHIRE

Badge	Coat of Arms of the City and County of Bristol
Colours	Blue, Gold, Brown, Silver, Green and Red
Foundation	1871 (between 14 March and mid-May)
Headquarters	Phoenix County Ground, Nevil Road, Bristol, BS7 9EJ
Champions	No instance since 1890

GLOUCESTERSHIRE RECORDS IN ALL FIRST-CLASS CRICKET

MATCH RECORDS

For Gloucestershire	Record	Holder(s)	Opponents	Venue	Season
Highest Total	653–6d		Glamorgan	Bristol	1928
Lowest Total	17		Australians	Cheltenham	1896
Highest Score	318*	W.G. Grace	Yorkshire	Cheltenham	1876
Highest Partnership	395	D.M. Young, R.B. Nicholls	Oxford U.	Oxford	1962
Best Bowling – Innings	10–40	E.G. Dennett	Essex	Bristol	1906
– Match	17–56	C.W.L. Parker	Essex	Gloucester	1925
Most Dismissals – Innings	6	H. Smith (3c, 3s)	Sussex	Bristol	1923
	6	A.E. Wilson (6c)	Hampshire	Portsmouth	1953
	6	B.J. Meyer (6c)	Somerset	Taunton	1962
– Match	10	A.E. Wilson (10c)	Hampshire	Portsmouth	1953

Against Gloucestershire	Record	Holder(s)	Opponents	Venue	Season
Highest Total	774–7d		Australians	Bristol	1948
Lowest Total	12		Northamptonshire	Gloucester	1907
Highest Score	296	A.O. Jones	Nottinghamshire	Nottingham	1903
Highest Partnership	465*	J.A. Jameson, R.B. Kanhai	Warwickshire	Birmingham	1974
Best Bowling – Innings	10–66	A.A. Mailey	Australians	Cheltenham	1921
	10–66	K. Smales	Nottinghamshire	Stroud	1956
– Match	15–87	A.J. Conway	Worcestershire	Moreton-in-Marsh	1914

SEASON RECORDS

Most Runs	2860	W.R. Hammond		1933
Most Hundreds	13	W.R. Hammond		1938
Most Wickets	222	T.W.J. Goddard		1937
	222	T.W.J. Goddard		1947
Most Wicket-Keeping	75	J.H. Board (52c, 23s)		1895
Dismissals	75	B.J. Meyer (59c, 16s)		1964
Most Catches (non WK)	62	W.R. Hammond		1928

CAREER RECORDS

Most Appearances	602	C.W.L. Parker	1903–35
Most Runs	33 664	W.R. Hammond	1920–51
Most Hundreds	113	W.R. Hammond	1920–51
Most Times 1000 Runs in a Season	17	W.R. Hammond (1923–46)	1920–51
Most Wickets	3170	C.W.L. Parker	1903–35
Most Hat-Tricks	6†	C.W.L. Parker (1922–30)	1903–35
Most Times 100 Wickets in a Season	16	C.W.L. Parker (1920–35)	1903–35
	16	T.W.J. Goddard (1929–50)	1922–52
Most Wicket-Keeping Dismissals	1016	J.H. Board (699c, 317s)	1891–1914
Most Catches (non WK)	719	C.A. Milton	1948–74

† Including two hat-tricks in the same match.

Gloucestershire's favourite son, W.G. Grace: still holds the record for the highest ever score for the county (Allsport)

HAMPSHIRE

Badge	Tudor Rose and Crown
Colours	Blue, Gold and White
Foundation	12 August 1863 in Southampton
Headquarters	County Cricket Ground, Northlands Road, Southampton, SO15 2UE
Champions	(2) 1961, 1973

HAMPSHIRE RECORDS IN ALL FIRST-CLASS CRICKET

MATCH RECORDS

For Hampshire	Record	Holder(s)	Opponents	Venue	Season
Highest Total	672–7d		Somerset	Taunton	1899
Lowest Total	15		Warwickshire	Birmingham	1922
Highest Score	316	R.H. Moore	Warwickshire	Bournemouth	1937
Highest Partnership	411	R.M. Poore, E.G. Wynyard	Somerset	Taunton	1899
Best Bowling – Innings	9–25	R.M.H. Cottam	Lancashire	Manchester	1965
– Match	16–88	J.A. Newman	Somerset	Weston-s-Mare	1927
Most Dismissals – Innings	6	Seven instances by G. Ubsdell, B.S.V. Timms, G.R. Stephenson, R.J. Parks (3) and A.N. Aymes			
– Match	10	R.J. Parks (10c)	Derbyshire	Portsmouth	1981
	10	A.N. Aymes (10c)	Oxford U.	Oxford	1989

Against Hampshire	Record	Holder(s)	Opponents	Venue	Season
Highest Total	742		Surrey	The Oval	1909
Lowest Total	23		Yorkshire	Middlesbrough	1965
Highest Score	302*	P. Holmes	Yorkshire	Portsmouth	1920
Highest Partnership	379	R. Abel, W. Brockwell	Surrey	The Oval	1897
Best Bowling – Innings	10–46	W. Hickton	Lancashire	Manchester	1870
– Match	17–103	W. Mycroft	Derbyshire	Southampton	1876

SEASON RECORDS

Most Runs	2854	C.P. Mead		1928
Most Hundreds	12	C.P. Mead		1928
Most Wickets	190	A.S. Kennedy		1922
Most Wicket-Keeping Dismissals	83	L. Harrison (76c, 7s)		1959
Most Catches (non WK)	56	P.J. Sainsbury		1957

CAREER RECORDS

Most Appearances	700	C.P. Mead	1905–36
Most Runs	48 892	C.P. Mead	1905–36
Most Hundreds	138	C.P. Mead	1905–36
Most Times 1000 Runs in a Season	27	C.P. Mead (1906–36)	1905–36
Most Wickets	2669	D. Shackleton	1948–69
Most Hat-Tricks	3	A.S. Kennedy (1920–24)	1907–36
Most Times 100 Wickets in a Season	19	D. Shackleton (1949–68)	1948–69
Most Wicket-Keeping Dismissals	700	R.J. Parks (630c, 70s)	1980–92
Most Catches (non WK)	629	C.P. Mead	1905–36

Bobby Parks: finished his Hampshire career in 1992 with a record 700 dismissals behind the stumps (Allsport/Howard Boylan)

KENT

Badge	White Horse on a Red Ground
Colours	Maroon and White
Foundation	1 March 1859 in Maidstone (substantially reorganized 6 Dec 1870)
Headquarters	St Lawrence Ground, Canterbury, CT1 3NZ
Champions	(6) 1906, 1909, 1910, 1913, 1970, 1978
Joint Champions	(1) 1977

KENT RECORDS IN ALL FIRST-CLASS CRICKET

MATCH RECORDS

For Kent	Record	Holder(s)	Opponents	Venue	Season
Highest Total	803–4d		Essex	Brentwood	1934
Lowest Total	18		Sussex	Gravesend	1867
Highest Score	332	W.H. Ashdown	Essex	Brentwood	1934
Highest Partnership	366	S.G. Hinks, N.R. Taylor	Middlesex	Canterbury	1990
Best Bowling – Innings	10–30	C. Blythe	Northamptonshire	Northampton	1907
– Match	17–48	C. Blythe	Northamptonshire	Northampton	1907
Most Dismissals –Innings	8 (8c)	S.A. Marsh	Middlesex	Lord's	1991
– Match	10	F.H. Huish (1c, 9s)	Surrey	The Oval	1911
	10	J.C. Hubble (9c, 1s)	Gloucestershire	Cheltenham	1923

Against Kent	Record	Holder(s)	Opponents	Venue	Season
Highest Total	676		Australians	Canterbury	1921
Lowest Total	16		Warwickshire	Tonbridge	1913
Highest Score	344	W.G.Grace	MCC	Canterbury	1876
Highest Partnership	413	D.J. Bicknell, D.M. Ward	Surrey	Canterbury	1990
Best Bowling – Innings	10–48	C.H.G. Bland	Sussex	Tonbridge	1899
– Match	17–106	T.W.J. Goddard	Gloucestershire	Bristol	1939

SEASON RECORDS

Most Runs	2894	F.E. Woolley	1928
Most Hundreds	10	F.E. Woolley	1928
	10	F.E. Woolley	1934
Most Wickets	262	A.P. Freeman	1933
Most Wicket-Keeping Dismissals	116	L.E.G. Ames (71c, 45s)	1929
Most Catches (non WK)	48	C.J. Tavaré	1978

CAREER RECORDS

Most Appearances	764	F.E. Woolley	1906–38
Most Runs	47 868	F.E. Woolley	1906–38
Most Hundreds	122	F.E. Woolley	1906–38
Most Times 1000 Runs in a Season	27	F.E. Woolley (1907–38)	1906–38
Most Wickets	3340	A.P. Freeman	1914–36
Most Hat-Tricks	6	D.V.P. Wright (1937–49)	1932–57
Most Times 100 Wickets in a Season	17	A.P. Freeman (1920–36)	1914–36
Most Wicket-Keeping Dismissals	1253	F.H. Huish (901c, 352s)	1895–1914
Most Catches (non WK)	773	F.E. Woolley	1906–38

Frank Woolley: clean sweep of the season and career batting records for Kent (Popperfoto)

LANCASHIRE

Badge	Red Rose
Colours	Red, Green and Blue
Foundation	12 January 1864 in Manchester
Headquarters	Old Trafford, Manchester, M16 0PX
Champions	(7) 1897, 1904, 1926, 1927, 1928, 1930, 1934
Joint Champions	(1) 1950

LANCASHIRE RECORDS IN ALL FIRST-CLASS CRICKET

MATCH RECORDS

For Lancashire	Record	Holder(s)	Opponents	Venue	Season
Highest Total	863		Surrey	The Oval	1990
Lowest Total	25		Derbyshire	Manchester	1871
Highest Score	424	A.C. MacLaren	Somerset	Taunton	1895
Highest Partnership	371	F.B. Watson, G.E. Tyldesley	Surrey	Manchester	1928
Best Bowling – Innings	10–46	W. Hickton	Hampshire	Manchester	1870
– Match	17–91	H. Dean	Yorkshire	Liverpool	1913
Most Dismissals – Innings	7	W. Farrimond (6c, 1s)	Kent	Manchester	1930
	7	W.K. Hegg (7c)	Derbyshire	Chesterfield	1989
– Match	11	W.K. Hegg (11c)	Derbyshire	Chesterfield	1989

Against Lancashire	Record	Holder(s)	Opponents	Venue	Season
Highest Total	707–9d		Surrey	The Oval	1990
Lowest Total	22		Glamorgan	Liverpool	1924
Highest Score	315*	T.W. Hayward	Surrey	The Oval	1898
Highest Partnership	470	A.I. Kallicharran, G.W. Humpage	Warwickshire	Southport	1982
Best Bowling – Innings	10–40	G.O.B. Allen	Middlesex	Lord's	1929
– Match	16–65	G. Giffen	Australians	Manchester	1886

SEASON RECORDS

Most Runs	2633	J.T. Tyldesley		1901
Most Hundreds	11	C. Hallows		1928
Most Wickets	198	E.A. McDonald		1925
Most Wicket-Keeping Dismissals	97	G. Duckworth (69c, 28s)		1928
Most Catches (non WK)	63	K.J. Grieves		1950

CAREER RECORDS

Most Appearances	573	G.E. Tyldesley	1909–36
Most Runs	34 222	G.E. Tyldesley	1909–36
Most Hundreds	90	G.E. Tyldesley	1909–36
Most Times 1000 Runs in a Season	19	J.T. Tyldesley (1897–1919)	1895–1923
Most Wickets	1816	J.B. Statham	1950–68
Most Hat-Tricks	3	R.G. Barlow (1879–86)	1871–91
	3	E.A. McDonald (1925–30)	1924–31
Most Times 100 Wickets in a Season	11	J. Briggs (1887–1900)	1879–1900
Most Wicket-Keeping Dismissals	922	G. Duckworth (634c, 288s)	1923–38
Most Catches (non WK)	555	K.J. Grieves	1949–64

Warren Hegg: entered the county record books with seven catches in an innings (11 in the match) against Derbyshire in 1989
(Allsport/Chris Cole)

LEICESTERSHIRE

Badge	Gold Running Fox on Green Ground
Colours	Dark Green and Scarlet
Foundation	25 March 1879 at Leicester
Headquarters	County Ground, Grace Road, Leicester, LE2 8AD
Champions	(1) 1975

LEICESTERSHIRE RECORDS IN ALL FIRST-CLASS CRICKET

MATCH RECORDS

For Leicestershire	Record	Holder(s)	Opponents	Venue	Season
Highest Total	701–4d		Worcestershire	Worcester	1906
Lowest Total	25		Kent	Leicester	1912
Highest Score	252*	S. Coe	Northamptonshire	Leicester	1914
Highest Partnership	390	B. Dudleston, J.F. Steele	Derbyshire	Leicester	1979
Best Bowling – Innings	10–18	G. Geary	Glamorgan	Pontypridd	1929
– Match	16–96	G. Geary	Glamorgan	Pontypridd	1929
Most Dismissals – Innings	6	Five instances by P. Corrall (2), R.W. Tolchard (2) and P.A. Nixon			
– Match	10	P. Corrall (7c, 3s)	Sussex	Hove	1936

Against Leicestershire	Record	Holder(s)	Opponents	Venue	Season
Highest Total	761–6d		Essex	Chelmsford	1990
Lowest Total	24		Glamorgan	Leicester	1971
	24	Oxford U.		Oxford	1985
Highest Score	341	G.H. Hirst	Yorkshire	Leicester	1905
Highest Partnership	403	G.A. Gooch, P.J. Prichard	Essex	Chelmsford	1990
Best Bowling – Innings	10–32	H. Pickett	Essex	Leyton	1895
– Match	16–102	C. Blythe	Kent	Leicester	1909

SEASON RECORDS

Most Runs	2446	L.G. Berry		1937
Most Hundreds	7	L.G. Berry		1937
	7	W. Watson		1959
	7	B.F. Davison		1982
Most Wickets	170	J.E. Walsh		1948
Most Wicket-Keeping Dismissals	85	J. Firth (60c, 25s)		1952
Most Catches (non WK)	56	M.R. Hallam		1961

CAREER RECORDS

Most Appearances	628	W.E. Astill	1906–39
Most Runs	30143	L.G. Berry	1924–51
Most Hundreds	45	L.G. Berry	1924–51
Most Times 1000 Runs in a Season	18	L.G. Berry (1925–50)	1924–51
Most Wickets	2130	W.E. Astill	1906–39
Most Hat-Tricks	2	T. Jayes, J.H. King, V.E. Jackson, J. Birkenshaw, P.B. Clift	
Most Times 100 Wickets in a Season	9	G. Geary (1914–36)	1912–38
Most Wicket-Keeping Dismissals	903†	R.W. Tolchard (794c, 109s)	1965–83
Most Catches (non WK)	427	M.R. Hallam	1950–70

† Including 16 catches taken as a fielder

George Geary: best innings and match analysis for Leicestershire (Colorsport)

MIDDLESEX

Badge	Three Seaxes
Colours	Blue
Foundation	2 February 1864 at the London Tavern, Bishopsgate
Headquarters	Lord's Cricket Ground, London, NW8 8QN
Champions	(10) 1903, 1920, 1921, 1947, 1976, 1980, 1982, 1985, 1990, 1993
Joint Champions	(2) 1949, 1977

MIDDLESEX RECORDS IN ALL FIRST-CLASS CRICKET

MATCH RECORDS

For Middlesex	Record	Holder(s)	Opponents	Venue	Season
Highest Total	642–3d		Hampshire	Southampton	1923
Lowest Total	20		MCC	Lord's	1864
Highest Score	331*	J.D.B. Robertson	Worcestershire	Worcester	1949
Highest Partnership	424*	W.J. Edrich,			
		D.C.S. Compton	Somerset	Lord's	1948
Best Bowling – Innings	10–40	G.O.B. Allen	Lancashire	Lord's	1929
– Match	16–114	G. Burton	Yorkshire	Sheffield	1888
	16–114	J.T. Hearne	Lancashire	Manchester	1898
Most Dismissals – Innings	7	W.F.F. Price (7c)	Yorkshire	Lord's	1937
– Match	9	M. Turner (6c,3s)	Nottinghamshire	Prince's	1875
	9	J.T. Murray (8c, 1s)	Hampshire	Lord's	1965

Against Middlesex	Record	Holder(s)	Opponents	Venue	Season
Highest Total	665		West Indians	Lord's	1939
Lowest Total	31		Gloucestershire	Bristol	1924
Highest Score	316*	J.B. Hobbs	Surrey	Lord's	1926
Highest Partnership	490	E.H. Bowley,			
		J.G. Langridge	Sussex	Hove	1933
Best Bowling – Innings	9–38	R.C. Robertson-Glasgow	Somerset	Lord's	1924
– Match	16–109	C.W.L. Parker	Gloucestershire	Cheltenham	1930

SEASON RECORDS

Most Runs	2669	E.H. Hendren	1923
Most Hundreds	13	D.C.S. Compton	1947
Most Wickets	158	F.J. Titmus	1955
Most Wicket-Keeping			
Dismissals	99	J.T. Murray (92c, 7s)	1960
Most Catches (non WK)	46	P.H. Parfitt	1960
	46	P.H. Parfitt	1966

CAREER RECORDS

Most Appearances	642	F.J. Titmus	1949–82
Most Runs	40 302	E.H. Hendren	1907–37
Most Hundreds	119	E.H. Hendren	1907–37
Most Times 1000 Runs			
in a Season	20	E.H. Hendren (1913–37)	1907–37
Most Wickets	2361	F.J. Titmus	1949–82
Most Hat-Tricks	4	F.A. Tarrant (1907–11)	1904–14
Most Times 100 Wickets			
in a Season	11	F.J. Titmus (1953–71)	1949–82
Most Wicket-Keeping			
Dismissals	1223	J.T. Murray (1024c, 199s)	1952–75
Most Catches (non WK)	561	E.H. Hendren	1907–37

E.H. 'Patsy' Hendren: all-round sportsman who played football for Brentford (pictured left in their colours), Queen's Park Rangers, Manchester City and Coventry City as well as scoring over 40,000 runs for Middlesex (Popperfoto)

NORTHAMPTONSHIRE

Badge	Tudor Rose
Colours	Maroon
Foundation	31 July 1878
Headquarters	County Ground, Wantage Road, Northampton, NN1 4TJ
Champions	No instance

NORTHAMPTONSHIRE RECORDS IN ALL FIRST-CLASS CRICKET

MATCH RECORDS

For Northamptonshire	Record	Holder(s)	Opponents	Venue	Season
Highest Total	781–7d		Nottinghamshire	Northampton	1995
Lowest Total	12		Gloucestershire	Gloucester	1907
Highest Score	300	R. Subba Row	Surrey	The Oval	1958
Highest Partnership	393	A. Fordham, A.J. Lamb	Yorkshire	Leeds	1990
Best Bowling – Innings	10–127	V.W.C. Jupp	Kent	Tunbridge Wells	1932
– Match	15–31	G.E. Tribe	Yorkshire	Northampton	1958
Most Dismissals – Innings	7	K.V. Andrew (7c)	Lancashire	Manchester	1962
– Match	10	L.A. Johnson (10c)	Sussex	Worthing	1963
	10	L.A. Johnson (8c, 2s)	Warwickshire	Birmingham	1965

Against Northamptonshire	Record	Holder(s)	Opponents	Venue	Season
Highest Total	670–9d		Sussex	Hove	1921
Lowest Total	33		Lancashire	Northampton	1977
Highest Score	333	K.S. Duleepsinhji	Sussex	Hove	1930
Highest Partnership	385	E.H. Bowley, M.W. Tate	Sussex	Hove	1921
Best Bowling – Innings	10–30	C.Blythe	Kent	Northampton	1907
– Match	17–48	C. Blythe	Kent	Northampton	1907

SEASON RECORDS

Most Runs	2198	D. Brookes		1952
Most Hundreds	8	R.A. Haywood		1921
Most Wickets	175	G.E. Tribe		1955
Most Wicket-Keeping Dismissals	90	K.V. Andrew (84c, 6s)		1962
Most Catches (non WK)	43	C. Milburn		1964

CAREER RECORDS

Most Appearances	492	D. Brookes	1934–59
Most Runs	28 980	D. Brookes	1934–59
Most Hundreds	67	D. Brookes	1934–59
Most Times 1000 Runs in a Season	17	D. Brookes (1937–59)	1934–59
Most Wickets	1097	E.W. Clark	1922–47
Most Hat-Tricks	2	S.G. Smith, V.W.C. Jupp, M.R. Dilley	
Most Times 100 Wickets in a Season	8	G.E. Tribe (1952–59)	1951–59
Most Wicket-Keeping Dismissals	810	K.V. Andrew (653c, 157s)	1953–66
Most Catches (non WK)	469	D.S. Steele	1963–84

Northamptonshire skipper Allan Lamb, pictured with the NatWest Trophy in 1992 (Popperfoto)

NOTTINGHAMSHIRE

Badge	Badge of City of Nottingham
Colours	Green and Gold
Foundation	March/April 1841
	(substantially reorganized 11 December 1866)
Headquarters	Trent Bridge, Nottingham, NG2 6AG
Champions	(4) 1907, 1929, 1981, 1987

NOTTINGHAMSHIRE RECORDS IN ALL FIRST-CLASS CRICKET

MATCH RECORDS

For Nottinghamshire	Record	Holder(s)	Opponents	Venue	Season
Highest Total	739–7d		Leicestershire	Nottingham	1903
Lowest Total	13		Yorkshire	Nottingham	1901
Highest Score	312*	W.W. Keeton	Middlesex	The Oval	1939
Highest Partnership	398	W. Gunn, A. Shrewsbury	Sussex	Nottingham	1890
Best Bowling – Innings	10–66	K. Smales	Gloucestershire	Stroud	1956
– Match	17–89	F.C. Matthews	Northamptonshire	Nottingham	1923
Most Dismissals – Innings	6	Ten instances by T.W. Oates (2), B. Lilley, E.A. Meads (2), G. Millman and B.N. French (4)			
– Match	10	T.W. Oates (9c, 1s)	Middlesex	Nottingham	1906
	10	B.N. French (7c, 3s)	Oxford U.	Oxford	1984
	10	C.W. Scott (10c)	Derbyshire	Derby	1988

Against Nottinghamshire	Record	Holder(s)	Opponents	Venue	Season
Highest Total	781–7d		Northamptonshire	Northampton	1995
Lowest Total	16		Derbyshire	Nottingham	1879
	16		Surrey	The Oval	1880
Highest Score	345	C.G. Macartney	Australians	Nottingham	1921
Highest Partnership	402	R.B. Kanhai, K. Ibadulla	Warwickshire	Nottingham	1968
Best Bowling – Innings	10–10	H. Verity	Yorkshire	Leeds	1932
– Match	17–89	W.G. Grace	Gloucestershire	Cheltenham	1877

SEASON RECORDS

Most Runs	2620	W.W. Whysall			1929
Most Hundreds	9	W.W. Whysall			1928
	9	M.J. Harris			1971
	9	B.C. Broad			1990
Most Wickets	181	B. Dooland			1954
Most Wicket-Keeping Dismissals	87	B.N. French (76c,11s)			1984
Most Catches (non WK)	44	W.W. Whysall			1929

CAREER RECORDS

Most Appearances	583	G.Gunn		1902–32
Most Runs	31 592	G. Gunn		1902–32
Most Hundreds	65	J. Hardstaff, jr		1930–35
Most Times 1000 Runs in a Season	20	G. Gunn (1905–31)		1902–32
Most Wickets	1653	T.G. Wass		1896–1920
Most Hat-Tricks	3†	A. Shaw (1875–84)		1864–97
	3	H.J. Butler (1937–39)		1933–54
Most Times 100 Wickets in a Season	10	T.G. Wass (1900–12)		1896–1920
Most Wicket-Keeping Dismissals	957	T.W. Oates (733c, 224s)		1897–1925
Most Catches (non WK)	466	A.O. Jones		1892–1914

† Including two in the same match

Bruce French: six dismissals in an innings on four occasions for Nottinghamshire (Popperfoto)

SOMERSET

Badge	Somerset Dragon
Colours	Black, White and Maroon
Foundation	18 August 1875 at Sidmouth, Devon
Headquarters	County Ground, St James Street, Taunton, TA1 1JT
Champions	No instance

SOMERSET RECORDS IN ALL FIRST-CLASS CRICKET

MATCH RECORDS

For Somerset	Record	Holder(s)	Opponents	Venue	Season
Highest Total	675–9d		Hampshire	Bath	1924
Lowest Total	25		Gloucestershire	Bristol	1947
Highest Score	322	I.V.A. Richards	Warwickshire	Taunton	1985
Highest Partnership	346	H.T. Hewett,			
		L.C.H. Palairet	Yorkshire	Taunton	1892
Best Bowling – Innings	10–49	E.J. Tyler	Surrey	Taunton	1895
– Match	16–83	J.C. White	Worcestershire	Bath	1919
Most Dismissals – Innings	6	H.W. Stephenson (5c, 1s)	Glamorgan	Bath	1962
	6	G. Clayton (6c)	Worcestershire	Kidderminster	1965
	6	D.J.S. Taylor (6c)	Sussex	Taunton	1981
	6	D.J.S. Taylor (6c)	Hampshire	Bath	1982
	6	R.J. Turner (6c)	West Indians	Taunton	1995
– Match	9	A.E. Newton (6c, 3s)	Middlesex	Lord's	1901
	9	H.W. Stephenson (8c, 1s)	Yorkshire	Taunton	1963

Against Somerset	Record	Holder(s)	Opponents	Venue	Season
Highest Total	811		Surrey	The Oval	1899
Lowest Total	22		Gloucestershire	Bristol	1920
Highest Score	424	A.C. MacLaren	Lancashire	Taunton	1895
Highest Partnership	424*	W.J. Edrich,			
		D.C.S. Compton	Middlesex	Lord's	1948
Best Bowling – Innings	10–35	A. Drake	Yorkshire	Weston-s-Mare	1914
– Match	17–137	W. Brearley	Lancashire	Manchester	1905

SEASON RECORDS

Most Runs	2761	W.E. Alley		1961
Most Hundreds	11	S.J. Cook		1991
Most Wickets	169	A.W. Wellard		1938
Most Wicket-Keeping Dismissals	86	H.W. Stephenson (50c, 36s)		1954
Most Catches (non WK)	42	R.T. Virgin		1966

CAREER RECORDS

Most Appearances	504	B.A. Langford	1953–74
Most Runs	21 142	H. Gimblett	1935–54
Most Hundreds	49	H. Gimblett	1935–54
Most Times 1000 Runs in a Season	12	H. Gimblett (1936–53)	1935–54
Most Wickets	2166	J.C. White	1909–37
Most Hat-Tricks	2	E. Robson (1898–1902)	1895–1923
Most Times 100 Wickets in a Season	14	J.C. White (1919–32)	1909–37
Most Wicket-Keeping Dismissals	1007	H.W. Stephenson (698c, 309s)	1948–64
Most Catches (non WK)	381	J.C. White	1909–37

Robert Turner: equalled the county record for dismissals in an innings in 1995 (Allsport/Ben Radford)

SURREY

Badge	Prince of Wales' Feathers
Colours	Chocolate
Foundation	22 August 1845 at The Horns, Kennington
Headquarters	The Oval, Kennington, London, SE11 5SS
Champions	(15) 1890, 1891, 1892, 1894, 1895, 1899, 1914, 1952, 1953, 1954, 1955, 1956, 1957, 1958, 1971
Joint Champions	(1) 1950

SURREY RECORDS IN ALL FIRST-CLASS CRICKET

MATCH RECORDS

For Surrey	Record	Holder(s)	Opponents	Venue	Season
Highest Total	811		Somerset	The Oval	1899
Lowest Total	14		Essex	Chelmsford	1983
Highest Score	357*	R. Abel	Somerset	The Oval	1899
Highest Partnership	448	R. Abel, T.W. Hayward	Yorkshire	The Oval	1899
Best Bowling – Innings	10–43	T. Rushby	Somerset	Taunton	1921
– Match	16–83	G.A.R. Lock	Kent	Blackheath	1956
Most Dismissals – Innings	7	A. Long (7c)	Sussex	Hove	1964
– Match	12	E. Pooley (8c, 4s)	Sussex	The Oval	1868

Against Surrey	Record	Holder(s)	Opponents	Venue	Season
Highest Total	863		Lancashire	The Oval	1990
Lowest Total	16		MCC	Lord's	1872
Highest Score	366	N.H. Fairbrother	Lancashire	The Oval	1990
Highest Partnership	377*	N.F. Horner, K. Ibadulla	Warwickshire	The Oval	1960
Best Bowling – Innings	10–28	W.P. Howell	Australians	The Oval	1899
– Match	15–57	W.P. Howell	Australians	The Oval	1899

SEASON RECORDS

				Season
Most Runs	3246	T.W. Hayward		1906
Most Hundreds	13	T.W. Hayward		1906
	13	J.B. Hobbs		1925
Most Wickets	252	T. Richardson		1895
Most Wicket-Keeping Dismissals	90	A. Long (73c, 17s)		1962
Most Catches (non WK)	77	M.J. Stewart		1957

CAREER RECORDS

Most Appearances	598	J.B. Hobbs		1905–34
Most Runs	43 554	J.B. Hobbs		1905–34
Most Hundreds	144	J.B. Hobbs		1905–34
Most Times 1000 Runs in a Season	24	J.B. Hobbs (1905–33)		1905–34
Most Wickets	1775	T. Richardson		1892–1904
Most Hat-Tricks	4	T. Richardson (1893–98)		1892–1904
Most Times 100 Wickets in a Season	10	T. Richardson (1893–1903)		1892–1904
Most Wicket-Keeping Dismissals	1223	H. Strudwick (1040c, 183s)		1902–27
Most Catches (non WK)	604	M.J. Stewart		1954–72

'The Master', Jack Hobbs: 1000 runs in a season 24 times (Allsport Historical Collection)

SUSSEX

Badge	County Arms of Six Martlets
Colours	Dark Blue, Light Blue and Gold
Foundation	1 March 1839
Headquarters	County Ground, Eaton Road, Hove, BN3 3AN
Champions	No instance

SUSSEX RECORDS IN ALL FIRST-CLASS CRICKET

MATCH RECORDS

For Sussex	Record	Holder(s)	Opponents	Venue	Season
Highest Total	705–8d		Surrey	Hastings	1902
Lowest Total	19		Nottinghamshire	Hove	1873
Highest Score	333	K.S. Duleepsinhji	Northamptonshire	Hove	1930
Highest Partnership	490	E.H. Bowley, J.G. Langridge	Middlesex	Hove	1933
Best Bowling – Innings	10–48	C.H.G. Bland	Kent	Tonbridge	1899
– Match	17–106	G.R. Cox	Warwickshire	Horsham	1926
Most Dismissals – Innings	6	Nine instances by H.R. Butt (3), A.A. Shaw, R.T. Webb (2), J.M. Parks, M.G. Griffith and H. Phillips			
– Match	10	H. Phillips (5c, 5s)	Surrey	The Oval	1872

Against Sussex	Record	Holder(s)	Opponents	Venue	Season
Highest Total	726		Nottinghamshire	Nottingham	1895
Lowest Total	18		Kent	Gravesend	1867
Highest Score	322	E. Paynter	Lancashire	Hove	1937
Highest Partnership	428	W.W. Armstrong, M.A. Noble	Australians	Hove	1902
Best Bowling – Innings	9–11	A.P. Freeman	Kent	Hove	1922
– Match	17–67	A.P. Freeman	Kent	Hove	1922

SEASON RECORDS

Most Runs	2850	J.G. Langridge	1949
Most Hundreds	12	J.G. Langridge	1949
Most Wickets	198	M.W. Tate	1925
Most Wicket-Keeping Dismissals	95	G.B. Street (69c, 26s)	1923
Most Catches (non WK)	69	J.G. Langridge	1959

CAREER RECORDS

Most Appearances	622	J. Langridge	1924–53
Most Runs	34 152	J.G. Langridge	1928–55
Most Hundreds	76	J.G. Langridge	1928–55
Most Times 1000 Runs in a Season	20	J. Langridge (1927–52)	1924–53
Most Wickets	2211	M.W. Tate	1912–37
Most Hat-Tricks	3	W.A. Humphreys, sr (1880–85)	1871–96
	3	V.W.C. Jupp (1911–21)	1909–21
Most Times 100 Wickets in a Season	13	M.W.Tate (1922–35)	1912–37
Most Wicket-Keeping Dismissals	1176	H.R. Butt (911c, 265s)	1890–1912
Most Catches (non WK)	779	J.G. Langridge	1928–55

The Langridge brothers, John (left) and James: fine servants of Sussex who hold eight individual county records between them
(Hulton-Deutsch Collection)

WARWICKSHIRE

Badge	Bear and Ragged Staff
Colours	Dark Blue, Gold and Silver
Foundation	8 April 1882 at the Queen's Hotel, Coventry (substantially reorganized 19 January 1884)
Headquarters	County Ground, Edgbaston, Birmingham, B5 7QU
Champions	(5) 1911, 1951, 1972, 1994, 1995

WARWICKSHIRE RECORDS IN ALL FIRST-CLASS CRICKET

MATCH RECORDS

For Warwickshire	Record	Holder(s)	Opponents	Venue	Season
Highest Total	810–4d		Durham	Birmingham	1994
Lowest Total	16		Kent	Tonbridge	1913
Highest Score	501*	B.C. Lara	Durham	Birmingham	1994
Highest Partnership	470	A.I. Kallicharran, G.W. Humpage	Lancashire	Southport	1982
Best Bowling – Innings	10–41	J.D. Bannister	Comb Services	Birmingham	1959
– Match	15–76	S. Hargreave	Surrey	The Oval	1903
Most Dismissals – Innings	7	E.J. Smith (4c , 3s)	Derbyshire	Birmingham	1926
	7	K.J. Piper (7c)	Essex	Birmingham	1994
	7	K.J. Piper (6c, 1s)	Derbyshire	Chesterfield	1994
– Match	11	K.J. Piper (10c, 1s)	Derbyshire	Chesterfield	1994

Against Warwickshire	Record	Holder(s)	Opponents	Venue	Season
Highest Total	887		Yorkshire	Birmingham	1896
Lowest Total	15		Hampshire	Birmingham	1922
Highest Score	322	I.V.A. Richards	Somerset	Taunton	1985
Highest Partnership	393	E.G. Arnold, W.B. Burns	Worcestershire	Birmingham	1909
Best Bowling – Innings	10–36	H. Verity	Yorkshire	Leeds	1931
– Match	17–92	A.P. Freeman	Kent	Folkestone	1932

SEASON RECORDS

Most Runs	2417	M.J.K. Smith	1959
Most Hundreds	9	A.I. Kallicharran	1984
	9	B.C. Lara	1994
Most Wickets	180	W.E. Hollies	1946
Most Wicket-Keeping Dismissals	80	G.W. Humpage (76c, 4s)	1985
Most Catches (non WK)	52	M.J.K. Smith	1961

CAREER RECORDS

Most Appearances	665	W.G. Quaife	1894–1928
Most Runs	35 146	D.L. Amiss	1960–87
Most Hundreds	78	D.L. Amiss	1960–87
Most Times 1000 Runs in a Season	20	W.G. Quaife (1898–1926)	1894–1928
	20	D.L. Amiss (1965–87)	1960–87
Most Wickets	2201	W.E. Hollies	1932–57
Most Hat-Tricks	3	T.L. Pritchard (1948–51)	1946–55
Most Times 100 Wickets in a Season	14	W.E. Hollies (1935–57)	1932–57
Most Wicket-Keeping Dismissals	800	E.J. Smith (662c, 138s)	1904–30
Most Catches (non WK)	422	M.J.K. Smith	1956–75

Dennis Amiss: totalled over 35,000 runs for Warwickshire (Allsport/Adrian Murrell)

WORCESTERSHIRE

Badge	Shield Argent a Fess between three Pears Sable
Colours	Dark Green and Black
Foundation	11 March 1865 at the Star Hotel, Worcester
Headquarters	County Ground, New Road, Worcester, WR2 4QQ
Champions	(5) 1964, 1965, 1974, 1988, 1989

WORCESTERSHIRE RECORDS IN ALL FIRST-CLASS CRICKET

MATCH RECORDS

For Worcestershire	Record	Holder(s)	Opponents	Venue	Season
Highest Total	670–7d		Somerset	Worcester	1995
Lowest Total	24		Yorkshire	Huddersfield	1903
Highest Score	405*	G.A. Hick	Somerset	Taunton	1988
Highest Partnership	393	E.G. Arnold, W.B. Burns	Warwickshire	Birmingham	1909
Best Bowling – Innings	9–23	C.F. Root	Lancashire	Worcester	1931
– Match	15–87	A.J. Conway	Gloucestershire	Moreton-in-Marsh	1914
Most Dismissals – Innings	7	H. Yarnold (1c, 6s)	Scotland	Dundee	1951
– Match	9	H. Yarnold (5c, 4s)	Hampshire	Worcester	1949
	9	S.J. Rhodes (9c)	Sussex	Kidderminster	1988

Against Worcestershire	Record	Holder(s)	Opponents	Venue	Season
Highest Total	701–4d		Leicestershire	Worcester	1906
Lowest Total	30		Hampshire	Worcester	1903
Highest Score	331*	J.D.B. Robertson	Middlesex	Worcester	1949
Highest Partnership	380	C.J.B. Wood, H. Whitehead	Leicestershire	Worcester	1906
Best Bowling – Innings	10–51	J. Mercer	Glamorgan	Worcester	1936
– Match	17–212	J.C. Clay	Glamorgan	Swansea	1937

SEASON RECORDS

Most Runs	2654	H.H.I. Gibbons		1934
Most Hundreds	10	G.M. Turner		1970
	10	G.A. Hick		1988
Most Wickets	207	C.F. Root		1925
Most Wicket-Keeping Dismissals	110	H. Yarnold (63c, 47s)		1949
Most Catches (non WK)	65	D.W. Richardson		1958

CAREER RECORDS

Most Appearances	589	D. Kenyon	1946–67
Most Runs	33 490	D. Kenyon	1946–67
Most Hundreds	72	G.M. Turner	1967–82
Most Times 1000 Runs in a Season	19	D. Kenyon (1947–67)	1946–67
Most Wickets	2143	R.T.D. Perks	1930–55
Most Hat-Tricks	3	G.A. Wilson (1900–05)	1899–1906
	3†	R.O. Jenkins (1948–49)	1938–58
	3	J.A. Flavell (1951–63)	1949–67
Most Times 100 Wickets in a Season	15	R.T.D. Perks (1934–55)	1930–55
Most Wicket-Keeping Dismissals	1015	R. Booth (868c, 147s)	1946–70
Most Catches (non WK)	412	D.W. Richardson	1952–67

† Including two in one match

The Worcestershire squad which secured consecutive County Championships at the end of the 1980s (Allsport/Gray Mortimore)

YORKSHIRE

Badge	White Rose
Colours	Dark Blue, Light Blue and Gold
Foundation	8 January 1863 at the Adelphi Hotel, Sheffield
Headquarters	Headingley Cricket Ground, Leeds, LS6 3BU
Champions	(29) 1893, 1896, 1898, 1900, 1901, 1902, 1905, 1908, 1912, 1919, 1922, 1923, 1924, 1925, 1931, 1932, 1933, 1935, 1937, 1938, 1939, 1946, 1959, 1960, 1962, 1963, 1966, 1967, 1968
Joint Champions	(1) 1949

YORKSHIRE RECORDS IN ALL FIRST-CLASS CRICKET

MATCH RECORDS

For Yorkshire	Record	Holder(s)	Opponents	Venue	Season
Highest Total	887		Warwickshire	Birmingham	1896
Lowest Total	23		Hampshire	Middlesbrough	1965
Highest Score	341	G.H. Hirst	Leicestershire	Leicester	1905
Highest Partnership	555	P. Holmes, H. Sutcliffe	Essex	Leyton	1932
Best Bowling – Innings	10–10	H. Verity	Nottinghamshire	Leeds	1932
– Match	17–91	H. Verity	Essex	Leyton	1933
Most Dismissals – Innings	7	D.L. Bairstow (7c)	Derbyshire	Scarborough	1982
– Match	11	D.L. Bairstow (11c)	Derbyshire	Scarborough	1982

Against Yorkshire	Record	Holder(s)	Opponents	Venue	Season
Highest Total	630		Somerset	Leeds	1901
Lowest Total	13		Nottinghamshire	Nottingham	1901
Highest Score	318*	W.G. Grace	Gloucestershire	Cheltenham	1876
Highest Partnership	448	R. Abel, T.W. Hayward	Surrey	The Oval	1899
Best Bowling – Innings	10–37	C.V. Grimmett	Australians	Sheffield	1930
– Match	17–91	H. Dean	Lancashire	Liverpool	1913

SEASON RECORDS

Most Runs	2883	H.Sutcliffe		1932
Most Hundreds	12	H.Sutcliffe		1932
Most Wickets	240	W. Rhodes		1900
Most Wicket-Keeping Dismissals	107	J.G. Binks (96c, 11s)		1960
Most Catches (non WK)	70	J. Tunnicliffe		1901
	70	P.J. Sharpe		1962

CAREER RECORDS

Most Appearances	883	W. Rhodes	1898–1930
Most Runs	38 558	H. Sutcliffe	1919–45
Most Hundreds	112	H. Sutcliffe	1919–45
Most Times 1000 Runs in a Season	21	H. Sutcliffe (1919–39)	1919–45
Most Wickets	3598	W. Rhodes	1898–1930
Most Hat-Tricks	4	G.G. Macaulay (1923–33)	1920–35
	4	F.S. Trueman (1951–63)	1949–68
Most Times 100 Wickets in a Season	22	W. Rhodes (1898–1929)	1898–1930
Most Wicket-Keeping Dismissals	1186	D. Hunter (863c, 323s)	1888–1909
Most Catches (non WK)	665	J. Tunnicliffe	1891–1907

Geoffrey Boycott: prolific Yorkshire batsman (Allsport/Adrian Murrell)

GENTLEMEN v PLAYERS MATCHES

This series of matches between amateurs and professionals began in 1806 and ended when amateur status in first-class cricket was abolished after the 1962 season.

The Lord's match between these two sides was the high point of the English season before Test matches became annual events. Teams for that fixture were selected by the MCC and an invitation to play was regarded as one of the game's highest honours, with the match itself effectively assuming the status of a Test trial. Until 1952, when Len Hutton was appointed as England's first professional captain of modern times, the captaincy of the Players was the greatest honour available to a professional cricketer. It was bestowed upon Jack Hobbs a record 22 times.

The first two matches were played at Thomas Lord's first ground in Dorset Fields (now Dorset Square) and both were won by the Gentlemen. Before the next encounter in 1819, Lord had moved his turf twice and it had come to rest in its present home in St John's Wood. The matches became very popular and additional fixtures at The Oval (1857–1934) and at the Scarborough Festival (1885–1962) became annual events. In 1919 Jack Hobbs scored a hundred in each of the three fixtures. Other matches under this title were occasionally staged at various grounds in Kent and Sussex, as well as at Prince's in London.

After the final match in 1962, the Players had won 68 of the 137 matches played on Lord's grounds, the Gentlemen had won 41, and 28 had been drawn.

The highest total in the fixtures was 651 for 7 declared by the Players at The Oval in 1934. The highest by the Gentlemen was 578 at The Oval in 1934. The best at Lord's was 579 by the Players in 1926.

Jack Hobbs played the highest individual innings in the series when he scored 266 not out for the Players at Scarborough in 1925. The record for the Gentlemen and the highest for either side in matches at Lord's was 232 not out by Charles Fry in 1903. During that innings Fry shared with Archie MacLaren the highest partnership for any wicket by either side in all these matches: 309 unbroken for the third wicket.

The best bowling analysis in these matches was 10 for 37 by Alex Kennedy for the Players at The Oval in 1927. His figures improved upon those of Arthur Fielder, who took 10 for 90 for the Players at Lord's in 1906 – the only other instance of a bowler

taking all ten wickets in this series. The best performance for the Gentlemen was 9 for 46 by Jack Stephenson at Lord's in 1936.

There were three instances of the match double of 100 runs and ten wickets in these contests and they were all accomplished by W.G. Grace for the Gentlemen:

134*		6–50	4–31	Lord's	1868
23	110	3–61	7–58	Prince's	1874
7	152	7–64	5–61	Lord's	1875

W.G. Grace dominated these matches from 1865 until he made the last of his record total of 85 appearances in 1906. The next highest number of appearances was 49 by Jack Hobbs for the Players between 1907 and 1934.

Six cricketers appeared for both sides in these matches:

	Gentlemen	Players
R. Daft	1858	1860–1879
E.J. Diver	1884	1886–1899
W.J. Edrich	1947–1957	1938
W.R. Hammond	1938–1946	1923–1937
J.H. Parsons	1929–1931	1914–1927
P.E. Richardson	1955–1958	1959

Wally Hammond achieved a unique double when he captained both sides to victory at Lord's in successive years – the Players in 1937 and the Gentlemen in 1938.

Ian Peebles, who was to play for England before appearing in county cricket, made his first-class debut for the Gentlemen against the Players at The Oval on 6 July 1927. The first of his 923 first-class wickets was Andrew Sandham – the first wicket to fall in the match and clean bowled by the 19-year-old leg-spinner from Aberdeen.

Cricket Curiosities
Surrey and England fast bowler Maurice Allom played tenor and baritone saxophone in a jazz band at The Savoy in 1927. He appeared regularly in a band formed from Cambridge undergraduates by Red Elizalde. A recording of them at Hayes in Middlesex on 22 June 1927 still survives. Allom made his England debut in New Zealand's first Test match, at Lancaster Park, Christchurch, on 10 January 1930, and took four wickets - including a hat-trick - in five balls.

UNIVERSITY CRICKET

The University Match between Cambridge and Oxford is the oldest surviving 'important' or 'great' fixture, having first been played in 1827. Apart from wartime intervals it has been staged annually since 1838.

Although the first encounter took place at Lord's, the fixture did not become established there until 1851. Five of the early matches were played in the Oxford area: 1829, 1846 and 1848 at Magdalen College; 1843 at Bullingdon Green; and 1850 at Cowley Marsh.

After the 1995 match, Cambridge had 55 wins, Oxford 48, and 47 of the 150 official contests had been drawn. The 1988 match suffered the singular fate of being abandoned without a ball being bowled. The most successive victories by either side is five by Cambridge from 1839 to 1843.

The most historic finish occurred in 1870 in Cobden's Match. With Oxford needing only three runs for victory and with three wickets in hand, Frank Cobden took a hat-trick and so snatched an extraordinary win for Cambridge. Although he appeared for Shropshire and Hertfordshire, Cobden, who was born in Nottinghamshire, never played for a first-class county.

Oxford holds the records for the highest and lowest totals in this series of matches – 503 in 1900 and 32 in 1878. The respective records for Cambridge are 432 for 9 declared in 1936 and 39 in 1858.

The highest of 47 hundreds for Oxford – and the record score in these matches – is 238 not out by the Nawab of Pataudi (sr) in 1931. The highest of 53 Cambridge hundreds is 211 by Gamini Goonesena in 1957, his seventh-wicket partnership of 289 with Geoffrey Cook being the highest for any wicket by either side in University Matches.

The only batsman to score a hundred in each innings of the University Match is Robin Boyd-Moss, who scored 139 and 124 in 1983. Having scored 100 the previous year, he also became the only player to score hundreds in three successive innings of this fixture. His aggregate of 489 is a record for these matches.

The only other batsman to score three centuries in these matches is M.J.K. (Mike) Smith of Oxford. The eventual captain of Warwickshire and England scored 201 not out in 1954, 104 in 1955 and 117 in 1956.

The best innings and match bowling analyses were achieved in the 1871 match by Samuel Butler for Oxford. A tall (6ft 2in), right-handed bowler whose pace was genuinely fast, he took all ten first innings wickets for 38 runs and a further 5 for 57 when Cambridge followed on. Butler, who became a barrister and settled in Somerset, was chosen for the

Gentlemen against the Players that season on the strength of his unique performance. The previous year he had been the first of Cobden's hat-trick victims. Ironically, the winning hit for Oxford in 1871 was made off Cobden's bowling.

The best innings and match analyses for Cambridge were achieved in 1878 by Allan Steel, later to lead England to victory in all three Tests of the 1886 series against Australia. An extremely accurate right-arm slow bowler who could spin the ball either way, he took 8 for 62 and, in Oxford's record and catastrophic total of 32, 5 for 11 in 20.1 four-ball overs. Three weeks later Steel played a major role in his University's historic two-day defeat of the Australians at Lord's.

The first player to do the match double (100 runs and ten wickets) in a University Match was an Australian Rhodes scholar. In 1910 Philip Le Couteur scored 160 of Oxford's total of 315 before taking 6 for 20 and 5 for 46. Cambridge, 76 and 113, lost by an innings and 126 runs – at that time their worst defeat by Oxford. Le Couteur, a right-handed batsman and deceptive leg-break bowler, took 8 for 99 in the second Cambridge innings the following year and made six appearances for the Gentlemen against the Players. After Oxford, he studied psychology at Bonn University before returning home to lecture in philosophy and play a few matches for Victoria.

The only Englishman to achieve the University Match double is Giles Toogood in 1985. Then a trainee doctor at the John Radcliffe Hospital in Headington, Oxford, he scored 149 (emulating M.J.K. Smith's feat of scoring hundreds for Oxford in successive years) and, bowling brisk-medium seamers from a lively run-up, returned match figures of 10 for 93. His first innings analysis of 8 for 52 doubled his aggregate of wickets for the season; three earlier years of off-spin had claimed only three victims at 73.66 runs apiece.

Blues are awarded for appearances in the University Match and, since the 1860s, these have been restricted to four per player. Not until 1976 did anyone gain blues from both universities. After representing Oxford in the 1975 match at the end of the fourth and final year of his Classics course at Worcester College, David Jarrett moved to St Catharine's College, Cambridge, for a one-year Certificate of Education course and appeared for Cambridge in 1976. He remains the only player to represent different universities in successive years at Lord's, although Stephen Wookey appeared for Cambridge in 1975 and 1976 and for Oxford in 1978, and Gajanand Pathmanathan gained four blues for Oxford (1975–76–77–78) before representing Cambridge in 1983.

First-Class Cricket in Australia

First-Class Cricket in Australia

The status of matches in Australia was first defined in 1908, when the Associations of New South Wales, South Australia and Victoria agreed that all international matches, all matches between English and other representative and interstate teams, all interstate matches and matches against New Zealand, and all matches of a representative character played on even terms and comprising first-class players, including Australia against The Rest of Australia, should be ranked as first-class.

This definition did not have retrospective effect. The term 'first-class match' was rarely used in Australia until the 1890s, major fixtures being described as 'important', 'representative' or 'inter-colonial'. In 1977, the Association of Cricket Statisticians produced their *Guide to First-Class Matches Played in Australia*, and their decisions regarding the status of doubtful matches played before 1908 have been respected in compiling these records.

The first inter-colonial match (and the first match in Australia to be ranked as first-class by the ACS) was played in February 1851 between Van Dieman's Land (Tasmania) and Port Philip District (Victoria) at Launceston. Its status has always been the subject of much argument but both teams were properly representative of their colonies, with the home team being drawn from clubs throughout the island and the Victorians able to choose from a host of immigrants attracted initially by the region's farming potential. The discovery of gold in Bathurst on 15 February 1851 was to give Victoria's selectors a considerably wider range of choice.

The first reference to cricket in Australia occurred in 1803 and described the game being played regularly in Sydney, although the first clubs there were not established until 1826.

The first match between two mainland colonies did not take place until March 1856 when New South Wales (76 and 16 for 7) beat Victoria (63 and 28) by three wickets on the Melbourne Cricket Club's new ground at Richmond Paddock – the Paddock that was to grow into the Melbourne Cricket Ground (MCG) of today. There can be no dispute about the status of this match. Traditionalists who disagree with the ACS *Guide* regard it as the start of first-class cricket in Australia, and it is the first overseas match to have its full scores published in *Scores and Biographies*.

TEAM RECORDS

The world record total in all first-class cricket is 1107 by Victoria against New South Wales at Melbourne on 27–28 December 1926. It was based on a first-wicket partnership of 375 runs (still the record for that wicket in Sheffield Shield matches), made in 3¼ hours by Bill Woodfull (133) and Bill Ponsford (352 including 36 fours). H.S.T.L. 'Stork' Hendry (100) and Jack Ryder (295 in just over four hours and including 6 sixes and 33 fours) were the other century-makers in an innings which lasted 10½ hours. It exceeded their previous record of 1059 (the only other four-figure total in first-class cricket), against Tasmania on the same ground in February 1923. A month later New South Wales avenged this massive defeat by dismissing Victoria for 35 and gaining an innings victory.

The highest second innings total in all first-class cricket is 770 by New South Wales against South Australia at the Adelaide Oval in January 1921 (Warren Bardsley 235, Johnny Taylor 180, Charles Kelleway 103 not out). South Australia's bowlers had conceded 724 runs in Victoria's second innings a few weeks earlier, their opponents' scores in Sheffield Shield matches that season being 639, 310, 724, 802, 304 and 770. Declarations were not permitted in that competition until the 1926–27 season and none occurred until the season after that.

The highest fourth innings total in Australia is 572 by New South Wales in December 1907 at Sydney. Even that effort, the highest innings of a match which produced 1716 runs in five days plus three balls, could not save them from a 20-runs defeat by South Australia.

The record match aggregate in Australia is 1929 by New South Wales (642 and 593) and South Australia (475 and 219) at Sydney in January 1926. South Australia, defeated by 541 runs, had to begin this eight-day epic immediately after an overnight rail journey following a six-day match that had ended in Melbourne the previous day.

The lowest innings total in first-class matches in Australia is 15 by Victoria against the MCC at Melbourne on 9 February 1904. Batting one man short on a sticky wicket, the State side, unequal to the wiles of Wilfred Rhodes (5 for 6) and Ted Arnold (4 for 8), were dismissed in ¾ hour (12.1 six-ball overs).

The lowest total in a Sheffield Shield match is 27 by South Australia against New South Wales at Sydney on 18 November 1955. Although overnight rain had caused moisture to condense on plastic covers and fall on the pitch, it was the late swing and pace variations of Keith Miller's bowling that produced this dramatic collapse. Supported by Pat Crawford (3 for 14), Miller took 7 for 12 in 7.3 eight-ball overs – the best analysis in the Sheffield Shield in terms of most wickets for least runs.

The two greatest margins of victory in Australian first-class cricket were obtained by Victoria as a result of their two record innings totals of over 1000 runs at Melbourne. In February 1923 they beat Tasmania by an innings and 666 runs after scoring 1059, and in December 1926 they defeated New South Wales by an innings and 656 runs after amassing 1107.

The largest victory by a runs margin in all first-class cricket occurred in January 1930 when New South Wales (235 and 761 for 8 declared) defeated Queensland (227 and 84) by 685 runs at Sydney. After ending the first innings only eight runs in arrears, the visiting State found themselves faced by Don Bradman in his most brilliant and insatiable form. His gentle cameo of 452 not out left them with the task of scoring 770 to win. The fast right-arm bowling of Sam Everett (6 for 23) ensured their record defeat.

Although no batsmen have been given out in Australian first-class cricket for hitting the ball twice or obstructing the field, there have been five instances of dismissals for handling the ball (see table).

Cricket Curiosities

When James Lillywhite's touring professionals challenged 22 of Goulburn in December 1876, play was disrupted when the field was invaded by six hares and two young kangaroos. A few weeks later the Englishmen were to play a representative Australian team on level terms for the first time in a game which subsequently became recognized as the first-ever Test match.

BATTING RECORDS

The highest individual innings in first-class matches in Australia is 452 not out by Donald George Bradman for New South Wales against Queensland at Sydney on 4 and 6 January 1930. Opening the batting and being dismissed for 3, the lowest score of the NSW first innings of 235, Bradman began his record innings on the second day with his side 22 for 1 and 30 runs ahead. He batted 415 minutes, hit 49 fours and took his score from 205 to 310 before lunch on the third day. 'Displaying a wider range of strokes than usual, Bradman batted without a trace of error during his long stay' (*Wisden*). His innings exceeded the previous highest first-class score of 437 by Bill Ponsford made two years earlier, and remained the world record until Hanif Mohammad (499) surpassed it in Pakistan almost exactly 29 years later. Bradman's match aggregate of 455 is the record for Australian first-class cricket.

The highest score by a batsman in Australia making his first appearance in first-class cricket is 232 not out by Sam Loxton at Melbourne on 19–20 December 1946. Taking full advantage of an opportunity created by five of his fellow Victorians being absent on Test duty, the 25-year-old right-hander batted for 390 minutes against Queensland's attack, hitting a six and 22 fours. When he had made 183 he concussed himself with the bat when attempting a hook. He managed to complete his innings and to take the first Queensland wicket before seeking medical treatment.

The world record for the highest score by a batsman who appeared in only one first-class match is 207 by Norman Callaway for New South Wales, at Sydney on 19–20 February 1915. A 19-year-old right-hander, he went to the wicket with the score at 17 for 3. His fifth-wicket partnership of 256 with Charles Macartney, his captain, was the basis of Queensland's defeat by an innings in two days. Two years later Callaway was killed in action in France.

The only number eleven batsman to score a century in Australian first-class cricket is Thomas Hastings. A wicket-keeper, he played 15 times for Victoria from 1887 until 1908 and achieved a career batting average of 11.91.

GIVEN OUT FOR HANDLING THE BALL

Batsman	For	Opponents	Venue	Season
W.H. Scotton	Smokers	Non-Smokers	East Melbourne	1886–87
E. Jones	South Australia	Victoria	Melbourne	1894–95
P.J.P. Burge	Queensland	New South Wales	Sydney	1958–59
A.M.J. Hilditch	Australia	Pakistan	Perth	1978–79
R.B. Gartrell	Tasmania	Victoria	Melbourne	1986–87

Mike Veletta (left): longest innings ever played in Australia (Allsport)

Playing against South Australia at Melbourne in January 1903, Hastings came to the wicket when Victoria were 261 for 9. His partnership with Mathew Ellis (118) took the total to 472, fell just 19 runs short of the world record for the tenth wicket at that time, and was largely responsible for his State's victory by 179 runs.

The longest innings played in Australia produced 262 runs and took Mike Veletta 12 hours 46 minutes on 21–23 March 1987 during the Sheffield Shield Final at Perth. Then the fourth-longest innings in all first-class cricket and the highest score for Western Australia, it drew the match against Victoria and ensured that, as table leaders, his state would win the title.

The only batsman to see over 800 runs scored during his innings in Australian first-class cricket is Bill Ponsford. Playing only his fourth first-class innings for Victoria, against Tasmania at Melbourne in February 1923, he scored 429 in 7 hours 57 minutes, hit 42 fours, and saw the total progress from 200 for 3 to 1001 for 8. There has been only one higher aggregate of runs during an individual innings, 811 being added during Bobby Abel's 357 not out for Surrey against Somerset in 1899. Ponsford is alone in making two scores in excess of

400 in first-class cricket, his later one being 437 against Queensland at Melbourne in December 1927; both scores were world records at the time.

The only batsman to score six hundreds in successive first-class innings in Australia is Don Bradman in the 1938–39 season. After scoring 118 for his own team against K.E. Rigg's XI at Melbourne, he made five consecutive Sheffield Shield centuries for South Australia (143 v New South Wales and 225 v Queensland at Adelaide, 107 v Victoria at Melbourne, 186 v Queensland at Brisbane, and 135 not out v New South Wales at Sydney). This sequence equalled the world record established by C.B. Fry in 1901 and was itself equalled by M.J. Procter in South Africa in 1970–71.

Ken Barrington achieved a unique feat when he exceeded 50 in each of the ten first-class innings he played at the Adelaide Oval for England and the MCC. His scores were 104, 52, 52*, 63 and 132* on the 1962–63 tour, and 69, 51, 63, 60 and 102 in 1965–66.

The first batsman to score a century in each innings of his first first-class match, and the only Australian to do so, was Arthur Morris, playing for New South Wales at Sydney in December 1940. Opening the innings, the 18-year-old left-hander scored 148 and 111 against the Queensland bowling.

The only Australian to score a hundred in each innings of successive first-class matches was another left-hander, David Hookes. Batting on his home ground at Adelaide, he scored 185 and 105 against Queensland on 11–14 February 1977 in a match which ended in a tie, and then made 135 and 156 against New South Wales on 18–21 February.

Archie Jackson was only 18 years 125 days old when he completed the second of his two hundreds (131 and 122) for New South Wales against South Australia at Sydney in January 1928.

The fastest recorded authentic first-class hundred in terms of fewest balls faced was scored by David Hookes on 25 October 1982. Captaining South Australia against Victoria at the Adelaide Oval, he reached his century off only 34 balls and in 43 minutes (**also the fastest hundred in Australian first-class cricket in terms of time**). Hitting 18 fours and three sixes, Hookes went to 102 (out of 120 for no wicket) in 8.4 overs. Twelve minutes later he was out caught for 107 – scored off 40 balls. He had made 137 in the first innings.

The most runs off one over in Australian first-class cricket is 32. Playing for Arthur Morris's XI against Lindsay Hassett's XI in the latter's Testimonial Match at Melbourne in January 1954, Ian Craig (3--66066) and Keith Carmody (-41-----) achieved the record off an eight-ball over from the off-break bowler, Ian Johnson. Together they added 50 in eight minutes, Craig scoring 106 and Carmody 66 before both fell to Johnson (4 for 182 in 18 overs). Hassett celebrated the occasion by scoring a century.

The most runs by one batsman off a first-class over in Australia, and the record in Sheffield Shield matches, is 29 by David Hookes of South Australia at Adelaide on 4 February 1977. During his first three-figure innings the left-hander struck 4 sixes, a four, and a single (60660641) from an over of leg-breaks from Victoria's Colin Thwaites. His innings of 163 was made out of a total of 290 all out, to which the next highest contribution was 24.

The highest number of boundaries hit during an individual first-class innings in Australia is 55 by C.W. (Charles) Gregory. Playing for New South Wales against Queensland at Brisbane in November 1906, Gregory opened the innings and scored 383 – then the record score in Australian first-class cricket – in 5¾ hours, 220 of his runs coming from boundaries. 'His play was disfigured by three chances, but when he gave the first of them he had scored 282' (*Wisden*). This match was played before Queensland were admitted to the Sheffield Shield competition in 1926.

The most runs during an individual first-class innings in Australia from scoring strokes worth four

or more is 224 by Geoff Marsh (355 not out) for Western Australia against South Australia in Perth on 15–16 December 1989. Opening the innings after his team had been put in on a plumb pitch, he registered his state's first triple hundred, shared in a Sheffield Shield record first-wicket partnership of 431, and hit 2 sixes and 53 fours (two of them all-run).

Two notable world first-class records for slow scoring were set in Australia, both during Test matches involving England. At Adelaide on 5–6 February 1947, Godfrey Evans batted for 97 minutes before scoring his first runs from his 61st ball – his innings is described in detail in the Test Cricket section. The other record was achieved by Trevor Bailey at Brisbane on 8–9 December 1958, during the first Test match to be televised in Australia, when he took 357 minutes to reach his 50. In spite of several determined attempts in recent Test matches, 'Barnacle's' innings has survived as **the slowest half-century in all first-class cricket**. His complete innings of 68 endured for 458 minutes at a rate of under nine runs an hour, and he scored off only 40 of the 425

Geoff Marsh (Western Australia): triple hundred against South Australia in 1989 (Allsport/Adrian Murrell)

balls he received: 4 fours, 3 threes, 10 twos and 23 singles. Years later, when confronted by this dismal survey, Bailey commented gleefully: 'Yes, and I ran out Tom Graveney too!'

The only Australian to score a first-class hundred without hitting a boundary is Paul Hibbert of Victoria. A left-handed opening batsman, Hibbert scored exactly 100 out of 233 for 7 against the Indian spinners at Melbourne on 11 November 1977. He batted for 327 minutes without being able to penetrate an astutely-placed field which was aided by damp turf. When India batted, Chetan Chauhan hit only two boundaries in his innings of 157 off 436 balls in 516 minutes.

Only seven Australian batsmen have scored 1000 runs in a home season when there were no matches against a touring team, Bill Ponsford achieving this feat in successive seasons (see below).

1000 RUNS IN A SEASON IN INTER-STATE MATCHES

	For	Season	I	NO	HS	Runs	Average	100
S.G. Barnes	NSW	1940–41	14	0	185	1050	75.00	6
D.G. Bradman	NSW	1933–34	11	2	253	1192	132.44	5
	SA	1939–40	15	3	267	1475	122.91	5
W.A. Brown	Q	1938–39	11	1	215	1057	105.70	3
A.F. Kippax	NSW	1926–27	13	1	217*	1039	86.58	5
A.R. Morris	NSW	1948–49	17	1	177	1069	66.81	6
N.C. O'Neill	NSW	1957–58	14	2	233	1005	83.75	4
W.H. Ponsford	V	1926–27	10	0	352	1229	122.90	6
	V	1927–28	8	0	437	1217	152.12	4

Ponsford's average of 152.12 in 1927–28 is the highest by any batsman scoring 1000 runs in an Australian season.

(NSW – New South Wales; Q – Queensland; SA – South Australia; V – Victoria)
Only two batsmen have scored 1000 runs in first-class matches against a team touring Australia, Don Bradman accomplishing this feat twice – against H.B. 'Jock' Cameron's South Africans and Lala Amarnath's Indians – and Ian Chappell doing so against the West Indies team captained by Garfield Sobers.

1000 RUNS IN A SEASON AGAINST A TOURING TEAM

	Season	I	NO	HS	Runs	Average	100
D.G. Bradman	1931–32	8	1	299*	1190	170.00	6
D.G. Bradman	1947–48	10	2	201	1081	135.12	6
I.M. Chappell	1968–69	12	1	188*	1062	96.54	5

The youngest batsman to score 1000 first-class runs in an Australian season is Darren Lehmann (South Australia) who, on 9 March 1990 when aged 20 years 32 days, beat the existing record set by Doug Walters in 1965–66 by 25 days.

The first to score 1000 runs in his debut season of first-class cricket in Australia was Matthew Hayden, whose 1028 runs in 21 innings for Queensland in 1991–92 included a chanceless 149 against South Australia in his very first innings and when aged 20 years 3 days.

The highest aggregate of runs by one batsman in an Australian first-class season is 1690, average 93.88, by Don Bradman in 1928–29 – his first full season and the one in which he began his Test career. He exceeded 1000 runs in a home season on 12 occasions, twice as many as any other batsman, and is alone in scoring 1500 runs more than twice. Bradman also scored over 2000 runs on each of his four tours of England.

The record number of first-class centuries by one batsman during an Australian season is eight in only 12

Matthew Hayden: 1000 runs in debut season
(Allsport/Ben Radford)

innings by Don Bradman in 1947–48. Six of those hundreds were scored against the Indian team captained by Lala Amarnath, including four in the five-match Test series, one for South Australia in his only Sheffield Shield match of the summer, and one for his Australian team against Western Australia before leaving for the 1948 tour of England.

HIGHEST PARTNERSHIPS IN AUSTRALIAN FIRST-CLASS CRICKET

Wkt	Runs	Batsmen (scores)	Match	Venue	Season
1st	456	W.H. Ponsford (248), E.R. Mayne (209)	Victoria v Queensland	Melbourne	1923–24
2nd	378	L.A. Marks (185), K.D. Walters (253)	NSW v South Australia	Adelaide	1964–65
3rd	390*	J.M. Wiener (221*), J.K. Moss (200*)	Victoria v W. Australia	Melbourne†	1981–82
4th	462*	D.W. Hookes (306*), W.B. Phillips (213*)	South Australia v Tasmania	Adelaide	1986–87
5th	464*	M.E. Waugh (229*), S.R. Waugh (216*)	NSW v W. Australia	Perth	1990–91
6th	346	J.H.W. Fingleton (136), D.G. Bradman (270)	Australia v England	Melbourne	1936–37
7th	335	C.W. Andrews (253), E.C. Bensted (155)	Queensland v NSW	Sydney	1934–35
8th	270	V.T. Trumper (138), E.P. Barbour (146)	NSW v Victoria	Sydney	1912–13
9th	232	C. Hill (365*), E. Walkley (53)	South Australia v NSW	Adelaide	1900–01
10th	307	A.F. Kippax (260*), J.E.H. Hooker (62)	NSW v Victoria	Melbourne	1928–29

† Junction Oval, St Kilda

The Waugh brothers, Steve (left) and Mark, celebrate another fine partnership (Allsport/Shaun Botterill)

The highest partnerships in Australia for the fifth and tenth wickets are world records for those wickets in all first-class cricket, the last wicket stand of 307 between Alan Kippax and Hal Hooker being probably the most remarkable in the entire history of cricket. It began at 11.50 on Christmas morning in 1928 at the Melbourne Cricket Ground. New South Wales were 113 for 9 in reply to Victoria's first innings total of 376. Their captain, Kippax, was 22 not out and, having failed in the first two Tests of that summer's series against England, he was under some pressure from the crowd. He cannot have dreamt that the 6ft 2in number eleven batsman, playing in only his sixth first-class match, about to join him in the middle would still be batting with him 24 hours later. John Edward Halford Hooker, then aged 30, was an extremely accurate, fast-medium, right-arm bowler whose stock ball was the late inswinger. Although he had won batting awards at grade level with the Mosman Club, he was a natural tail-ender by first-class standards. His main assets were a calm temperament and a good defence cultivated by observing Jack Hobbs. Kippax was a year older. Known as 'Mr Elegant', he was an extremely graceful player who had to date made three of his 22 appearances for Australia. Together they took the score to 170 at lunch (Kippax 60*, Hooker 18*). In the next session they managed to negotiate the second new ball and add 100 runs. Of those, Hooker contributed 14 while Kippax made 85. After tea the crowd, which had built up as news of this gallant partnership spread, switched their allegiance and cheered every run. The pair continued to thwart the Victorian attack which included four current or future Test bowlers, and were still there at stumps: New South Wales 367 for 9 (Kippax 221*, Hooker 51*). Just ten runs were needed for the vital first innings lead. Kippax accomplished it in the second over next day. Hooker then hit two successive boundaries off Ted a'Beckett. Attempting a third, he was caught high and one-handed by Jack Ryder at mid-off. It was 12.40pm on Boxing Day. New South Wales had made 420. Kippax, after a masterly exhibition in which he paraded his full range of strokes including many delightful late-cuts and leg-glances, was left 260 not out (387 minutes, 30 fours) – the last of his six double-centuries in Shield matches. Hooker, close to exhaustion after the longest innings of his life, finished with 62 including 3 fours. For 304 minutes he had resisted an extremely strong attack without giving a chance. His abiding memory though was of a very annoyed Kippax racing down the pitch to reprimand him: 'You fool! You threw it away! Why didn't you get a hundred?'

The Waugh twins' unbroken fifth-wicket partnership of 464 provided **the first instance of brothers each scoring a double-hundred in the same first-class innings.** Compiled on 20–21 December 1990, it included 20 runs awarded for no-balls under ACB playing conditions instead of just 7 which would have been gained under the Laws of Cricket.

Cricket Curiosities
During School cricket practice at Cowell, South Australia, during the 1967-68 season, Tony Wiseman saw a 3ft 6in poisonous snake slithering up the pitch towards him as the bowler delivered the ball. He allowed the ball to pass as he left his crease to kill the snake with his bat. Surprised not to hear an appeal for a stumping, he turned round to find that the wicket-keeper had vanished.

BOWLING RECORDS

The last bowler to take all ten wickets in a first-class innings in Australia was Ian Brayshaw at Perth on 21–22 October 1967. Swinging the ball at a little above medium pace, he returned figures of 10 for 44 as Victoria were dismissed for 152 in reply to Western Australia's 161. This historic performance led to victory by 136 runs. A consistent all-rounder, Brayshaw was unlucky not to gain representative honours. He retired from playing in 1978 and became a much-respected cricket writer and broadcaster.

ALL TEN WICKETS IN AN INNINGS

Bowler	O	M	R	W	Match	Venue	Season
G. Giffen	26	10	66	10	Australian XI v Rest	Sydney	1883–84
T.W. Wall	12.4	2	36	10	South Australia v NSW	Sydney	1932–33
P.J. Allan	15.6	3	61	10	Queensland v Victoria	Melbourne	1965–66
I.J. Brayshaw	17.6	4	44	10	Western Australia v Victoria	Perth	1967–68

The only bowler to take 17 wickets in a first-class match in Australia is George Giffen. South Australia's first Test cricketer, he was a highly talented all-rounder who bowled very accurately at slow-medium pace. Against Victoria at Adelaide in March 1886 he recorded match figures of 17 for 201 in 116.2 four-ball overs. After taking 9 for 91 (278 balls) in Victoria's first innings of 187, he had figures of 8 for 110 (188 balls) as they scored 219 in their second. Giffen completed a notable match double by scoring 20 and 82.

The most outstanding analysis in all first-class cricket in terms of most wickets for fewest runs was returned by Gideon Elliott when he took 9 for 2 against Tasmania. Playing for Victoria at Launceston on 26 February 1858, this 30-year-old right-arm fast bowler achieved these figures in an opening spell lasting 76 balls. Tasmania reached a first innings total of 33 thanks to 14 extras; no batsman contributed more than five runs.

The only Australian to take four wickets with consecutive balls in a first-class match in Australia is Halford Hooker of New South Wales. He performed this feat against Victoria at Sydney in January 1929 – just a month after sharing in a world record tenth-wicket partnership of 307 against them in Melbourne in his previous first-class match. After ending the Victorian first innings by dismissing their three specialist bowlers in a hat-trick, he bowled their opening batsman with his first ball of the second innings. Three of his victims were clean bowled and he caught the fourth himself. His analyses were 6 for 42 and 2 for 94. Hooker's all-round performances in the two key matches against Victoria made sure that New South Wales regained the Sheffield Shield from them.

The only other instance of a bowler taking four wickets with consecutive balls in Australian first-class cricket was accomplished by George Ulyett for Lord Harris's English XI on 10 February 1879. Rain followed by bright sun made the Association Ground pitch at Sydney absolutely unplayable and New South Wales lost their last five wickets for no runs in the second innings.

No pair of opening bowlers has bowled unchanged throughout both innings of a completed first-class match in Australia since 24–25 February 1888. On that occasion George Lohmann (9 for 67) and Johnny Briggs (11 for 58) accomplished this feat for Arthur Shrewsbury's XI against an Australian XI at Sydney. The last instance in Sheffield Shield cricket occurred on 9–10 February 1883 when Harry Boyle (8 for 46) and G.E. 'Joey' Palmer (9 for 61) bowled unchanged for Victoria during their innings defeat of New South Wales at Sydney.

The world record for the most runs conceded by one bowler during a first-class innings was established at Melbourne in December 1926 by Arthur Mailey. In the course of Victoria's world record total of 1107, the New South Wales legbreak bowler conceded 362 runs while taking four wickets in the course of 64 eight-ball overs.

The highest number of runs conceded by one bowler during a first-class match in Australia is 394 by Clarrie Grimmett. At Sydney on 8–16 January 1926, in an eight-day match against New South Wales, the South Australian leg-break bowler took 4 for 192 and 6 for 202. He bowled 106 eight-ball overs as the home State contributed totals of 642 and 593 towards the national match aggregate record of 1929 runs.

The most balls bowled during a first-class innings in Australia is 522 by George Giffen for South Australia against A.E. Stoddart's XI at Adelaide on 29 March–1 April 1895. During the English team's first innings of 609, Giffen bowled 87 six-ball overs and took 5 for 309. The highest number of balls bowled in a match in Australia is 848 by Clarrie Grimmett for South Australia against New South Wales at Sydney in January 1926 (see previous item).

The most first-class wickets taken by one bowler during an Australian season is 106 by Charlie Turner of New South Wales in 1887–88. Bowling fast-medium right-arm, with a chest-on action, he captured his wickets at a rate of one every 40 balls and at a cost of 13.59 runs apiece. Turner remains the only bowler to take 100 wickets in a season in Australia. His 283 wickets in England in 1888 is comfortably the world record by any bowler on tour.

WICKET-KEEPING RECORDS

The most dismissals by a wicket-keeper in any first-class innings in Australia is eight by A.T.W. 'Wally' Grout of Queensland. Returning from the Australians' long tour of Pakistan and India, Grout achieved his (then world) record at Brisbane on 15 February 1960 by catching eight Western Australia batsmen in the first innings.

The world record of 12 dismissals in a first-class match was established in 1868 by Ted Pooley of Surrey. It has been equalled on only two occasions, both of them in Australia. Don Tallon (Queensland) held nine catches and made three stumpings against New South Wales at Sydney on 2–4 January 1939. His performance was emulated exactly by Brian Taber (New South Wales) against South Australia at

Adelaide on 13–17 December 1968.

The highest number of catches taken in a first-class match is eleven. The record was set by Arnold Long for Surrey in 1964 and equalled by Rodney Marsh against Victoria at Perth on 15–17 November 1975 and by Tim Nielson for South Australia against Western Australia at Perth on 15–16 March 1991.

The Australian records for the most dismissals in a season and in a career are held by Rodney Marsh with 67 (63 ct, 4 st) in 1975–76 and an aggregate of 869 (803 ct, 66 st) from 1968–69 to 1983–84.

The world record for keeping wicket without conceding a bye while the highest number of first-class runs are scored was gained by Darren Berry of South Australia on 10 December 1989 – his 20th birthday – when he exceeded the 2132 runs set by Keith Andrew of Northamptonshire in 1965. Berry extended the record to 2446 runs before conceding his first bye in his ninth innings.

FIELDING RECORDS

These records exclude performances by wicket-keepers.

The only fielder to hold six catches in an innings of a first-class match in Australia is James Sheppard of Queensland. He accomplished this record at Brisbane's Exhibition Ground on 7 November 1914 during the first innings of New South Wales. Five of his catches were taken off the fast-medium left-arm bowling of Jack McAndrew.

Although the world record number of catches by a fielder in a first-class match is ten (by Wally Hammond in 1928), there has been no instance in Australia of more than seven being held. Three fielders have achieved this total, Greg Chappell setting a world Test record with his performance (see table below).

The Australian records for the most catches in the field in a season and in a career are held respectively by Ian Chappell (South Australia) with 27 in 1968–69 and by Bob Simpson (NSW and WA) with 383 between 1952–53 and 1977–78.

Cricket Curiosities
On 23 February 1976 the South Australian team went on strike. Captained by Ian Chappell and currently leading the Sheffield Shield they were angered by the selectors' decision to replace their twelfth man from the previous match with an all-rounder fresh to first-class cricket. When the selectors, chaired by Phil Ridings, threatened to select an entirely new team for the last two matches of the season, the strike, which had lasted for 18 hours, was called off.

Ian Chappell: record for most catches in a season, 27 for South Australia in 1968-69 (Allsport)

SEVEN CATCHES IN A MATCH

Fielder	For	Opponents	Venue	Season
J.A. Atkinson	Tasmania	Victoria	Melbourne	1928–29
E.W. Freeman	South Australia	Western Australia	Adelaide	1971–72
G.S. Chappell	Australia	England	Perth	1974–75

RECORD ALL-ROUND PERFORMANCES

The only player to score a double century and take 16 wickets in any first-class match is George Giffen of South Australia. Known as the 'W.G. Grace of Australia' he accomplished this unique double against Victoria at Adelaide on 7–11 November 1891. Batting at number three, he scored 271 in seven hours to take his aggregate against Victoria in his last seven innings to 921 runs. Giffen then completed the visitors' defeat by an innings and 164 runs when he took 9 for 96 and 7 for 70.

The last player to score a century and take ten wickets in a first-class match in Australia was Joe Scuderi (22) for South Australia against New South Wales at Adelaide Oval on 20–23 December 1991. A right-handed middle-order batsman and fast-medium bowler from north Queensland, he scored 110 (including 99 in a post-tea session) and took 7 for 79 and 3 for 86 from the marathon total of 64.1 overs.

The only player to score 1000 runs and take 50 wickets in an Australian first-class season is Garfield Sobers. The West Indies all-rounder achieved this remarkable feat twice, in 1962–63 and 1963–64 – his second and third seasons with South Australia.

OTHER INDIVIDUAL RECORDS

The youngest player to appear in first-class cricket in Australia was Leonard Junor of Victoria. A right-handed batsman, he was 15 years 266 days of age when he made his debut against Western Australia at Melbourne on 18 January 1930.

The oldest player to appear in first-class cricket in Australia whose date of birth has been confirmed was George Moore of New South Wales. A right-handed round-arm bowler, he was born in Ampthill, Bedfordshire, on 8 April 1820 and ended his three-match career, against Victoria on the Albert Ground at Sydney, on 8 March 1873 when he was 52 years 334 days old. Thirteen years later, his grandson and future captain of Australia, Charles Macartney, was born.

John Marshall of Tasmania, said to have been born in 1795, could have been in his 60th year when he played the last of his three matches in March 1854. Captain of Van Diemen's Land in the first match on Australian soil to be ranked as first-class, his date of birth is unconfirmed.

THE SHEFFIELD SHIELD

Although the first inter-colonial match took place in February 1851 when Tasmania received Victoria at Launceston, no regular competition existed when the Third Earl of Sheffield brought a team captained by W.G. Grace to Australia in 1891–92. This visit was so enthusiastically received that the Earl donated 150 guineas for the advancement of cricket in the colonies. The newly-formed Australian Cricket Council invested the money in a shield measuring 46 inches by 30 inches and bearing the Sheffield and Australian coats of arms.

The annual domestic championship was instituted the following season, with only the three leading cricket colonies, New South Wales, Victoria and South Australia, taking part. Queensland were admitted to the competition in 1926–27, from which season all matches were played on a time basis instead of to a finish. Western Australia were admitted on an experimental basis in 1947–48, playing the other states once only. Although they won the Shield in their first season, they were not admitted to full membership until 1956–57. Tasmania were admitted on a similar experimental basis in 1977–78 and, until 1982–83, played each state only once in a season.

Since 1982–83 the competition has culminated in a final between the first two teams in the Shield table.

SHEFFIELD SHIELD HOLDERS

1892–93 Victoria
1893–94 South Australia
1894–95 Victoria
1895–96 New South Wales
1896–97 New South Wales
1897–98 Victoria
1898–99 Victoria
1899–1900 New Sth Wales
1900–01 Victoria
1901–02 New South Wales
1902–03 New South Wales
1903–04 New South Wales
1904–05 New South Wales
1905–06 New South Wales
1906–07 New South Wales
1907–08 Victoria
1908–09 New South Wales
1909–10 South Australia
1910–11 New South Wales
1911–12 New South Wales
1912–13 South Australia
1913–14 New South Wales
1914–15 Victoria

1919–20 New South Wales
1920–21 New South Wales
1921–22 Victoria
1922–23 New South Wales
1923–24 Victoria
1924–25 Victoria
1925–26 New South Wales
1926–27 South Australia
1927–28 Victoria
1928–29 New South Wales
1929–30 Victoria
1930–31 Victoria
1931–32 New South Wales
1932–33 New South Wales
1933–34 Victoria
1934–35 Victoria
1935–36 South Australia
1936–37 Victoria
1937–38 New South Wales
1938–39 South Australia
1939–40 New South Wales
1946–47 Victoria
1947–48 Western Australia
1948–49 New South Wales
1949–50 New South Wales
1950–51 Victoria
1951–52 New South Wales
1952–53 South Australia
1953–54 New South Wales
1954–55 New South Wales
1955–56 New South Wales
1956–57 New South Wales
1957–58 New South Wales
1958–59 New South Wales
1959–60 New South Wales

1960–61 New South Wales
1961–62 New South Wales
1962–63 Victoria
1963–64 South Australia
1964–65 New South Wales
1966–67 Victoria
1967–68 Western Australia
1968–69 South Australia
1969–70 Victoria
1970–71 South Australia
1971–72 Western Australia
1972–73 Western Australia
1973–74 Victoria
1974–75 Western Australia
1975–76 South Australia
1976–77 Western Australia
1977–78 Western Australia
1978–79 Victoria
1979–80 Victoria
1980–81 Western Australia
1981–82 South Australia
1982–83 New South Wales
1983–84 Western Australia
1984–85 New South Wales
1985–86 New South Wales
1986–87 Western Australia
1987–88 Western Australia
1988–89 Western Australia
1989–90 New South Wales
1990–91 Victoria
1991–92 Western Australia
1992–93 New South Wales
1993–94 New South Wales
1994–95 Queensland

RESULTS SUMMARY 1892–93 TO 1994–95

	First Match	P	W	L	D	T	% won
New South Wales	1892–93	619	277	162	179	1	44.7
Victoria	1892–93	609	228	171	209	1	37.4
Western Australia	1947–48	383	128	109	146	–	33.4
South Australia	1892–93	609	174	268	166	1	28.6
Queensland	1926–27	496	122	183	190	1	24.6
Tasmania	1977–78	156	19	55	82	–	12.2
		1436	948	948	486	2	66.0

Matches abandoned without a ball bowled are excluded.

Wins:

42 – New South Wales; 25 – Victoria; 13 – Western Australia; 12 – South Australia;
1 – Queensland; 0 – Tasmania.

First-Class Cricket
in South Africa

First-Class Cricket in South Africa

British soldiers introduced cricket to South Africa, quite probably during the early period of the Napoleonic Wars when garrison troops first occupied the Cape (1795–1802). The first reference to cricket appeared in 1806, in *The Cape Town Gazette and African Advertiser*.

The first club was founded on 15 January 1843 when the Port Elizabeth Cricket Club was formed. Another 46 years were to pass before their ground at St George's Park saw the start of first-class and Test cricket in the Union.

The first tour of South Africa by a team of first-class cricketers took place in 1888 and was arranged by Major R.G. Warton. He had been attached to the Army General Staff in Cape Town and was a member of the Western Province Cricket club, whose ground at Newlands, at the foot of Table Mountain, was opened on 1 January 1888. Captained by C.A. Smith of Sussex ('Round-the-Corner' Smith, so named because of his bowling run-up, who was to become Sir Aubrey Smith and earn fame in Hollywood), and managed by Major Warton, the English team was only of county strength. Nevertheless, it won 13 of its 19 matches, all but two of which were played against sides of more than eleven players. Those two matches marked the start of first-class cricket in South Africa and were subsequently elevated to Test match status.

South African first-class cricket began at St George's Park in Port Elizabeth on 12 March 1889 and ended just before 3.30pm on the following day with England winning by eight wickets. The match was played on matting which produced an individual highest score of 46 (by Bobby Abel). Aubrey Smith became the only player to captain England on his only appearance in Test cricket.

TEAM RECORDS

The highest total in South African first-class cricket is 676 by the MCC against Griqualand West at Kimberley on 19–21 November 1938. Amassed under a 'baking sun', it was based on an opening stand of 263 in 156 minutes by Len Hutton (149) and Bill Edrich (109). Eddie Paynter (158) and

Norman Yardley (142) followed up with a fifth-wicket partnership of 107 in only 39 minutes. Hedley Verity was able to exploit a wearing pitch when the home team batted; his analyses of 7 for 22 and 4 for 44 saw the Englishmen to victory by an innings and 289 runs.

The highest total in Currie Cup matches is 664 for 6 declared by Natal against Western Province at Kingsmead, Durban, in March 1937. Its main contributors were I.J. ('Jack') Siedle (207) and Dudley Nourse (240); their partnership of 223 remains Natal's record for the third wicket.

The world record total for the fourth innings of a first-class match is 654 for 5 by England, when they required 696 runs to beat South Africa in the famous timeless Test at Durban in March 1939. That match produced the record aggregate of runs in South Africa with 1981 being scored for the loss of 35 wickets during 43 hours 16 minutes of play spread over a 12-day period.

The two lowest totals in South African first-class cricket and the world record lowest match aggregate by one team occurred at the Jan Smuts Ground, East London, on 19 and 21 December 1959. Border were dismissed by Natal for 16 and 18 in 23 and 26 six-ball overs respectively. Although the pitch was badly affected by rain during their first innings, it had returned to normal for their second. No Border player reached double figures in either innings; Niel During (9) made their highest score and it included their only boundary of the match.

Three first-class matches have been tied in South Africa. The first instance would have been regarded as a draw under present-day laws. Before 1948 a match was considered to be tied if the scores were level after the fourth innings, even if the side batting last had wickets in hand. The match at Ramblers, Bloemfontein, on 11–13 March 1926, between Orange Free State (100 and 349) and Eastern Province (225 and 224 for 8 wickets) ended with the scores level but with the last innings unfinished. In 1985–86 Eastern Province B tied successive matches – against Boland at Port Elizabeth's Albany Sports Club Ground on 13 January and against Natal B at Pietermaritzburg on 9 February.

The most runs by one side in a single day of first-class cricket in South Africa is 618 for 4 wickets declared by South Africa against The Rest of South Africa at the Wanderers, Johannesburg, on 2

October 1964. The total was scored off 114 six-ball overs and included 7 sixes and 84 fours. Openers Eddie Barlow (33) and Trevor Goddard (71) paved the way for Tony Pithey (110 in 223 minutes) and Graeme Pollock (123 in 105 minutes). The record was broken during an explosive and unbroken partnership of 267 in 99 minutes between Colin Bland (151 not out) and Denis Lindsay (107 not out).

The only instance of all eleven players bowling during a first-class innings in South Africa occurred at Kimberley on 3–4 January 1890. During Kimberley's innings of 445 the entire Natal team shared 116 overs.

UNUSUAL DISMISSALS IN SOUTH AFRICAN FIRST-CLASS CRICKET

Handled the ball

W.R. Endean (3)	South Africa v England (The first instance in Test cricket)	Cape Town	1956–57
R.G. Pollock (66)	Eastern Prov v Western Prov	Cape Town	1973–74
C.I. Dey (20)	Northern Transvaal v OFS	Bloemfontein	1973–74
D.K. Pearse (2)	Natal v Western Province	Cape Town	1978–79
M.J. Davis (0)	Northern Transvaal B v OFS B	Bloemfontein	1991–92

Christopher Dey's instance is unique as he was the non-striker. Backing up he collided with a fielder, fell with the ball under him and, while lying on the ground, threw the ball away.

Hit the ball twice

P.S. Wimble (0)	Transvaal v Griqualand West	Kimberley	1892–93

Obstructing the field

T. Quirk (10)	Northern Transvaal v Border	East London	1978–79

BATTING RECORDS

The highest individual score in South African first-class cricket is 337 not out by Daryll Cullinan for Transvaal against Northern Transvaal at the Wanderers, Johannesburg, on 23–25 October 1993. Commencing his innings when Transvaal were 23 for 3 in reply to the visitors' 517 for 8 declared and confronted by an attack including two Test match opening bowlers, the 26-year-old right-hander batted 10 hours 56 minutes, faced 528 balls, hit 3 sixes and 40 fours, and guided his team to first-innings points.

The first triple century in South African first-class cricket was scored by A.W. ('Dave') Nourse for Natal against Transvaal at Johannesburg in April 1920. His innings of 304 not out enabled Natal (532 for 8 declared) to win by an innings.

The world record for the fastest first-class triple century was established at Benoni on 3–4 December 1948. Playing for the MCC against North-Eastern Transvaal, Denis Compton produced possibly the most amazing exhibition of sustained brilliance and unorthodoxy ever seen at first-class level. He scored exactly 300 out of a third-wicket partnership of 399 with Reg Simpson (130 not out), his innings and that stand lasting only 181 minutes. He scored 120 in the last 91 minutes of the day and the remaining 180 in the first 90 minutes of the second morning before being caught on the boundary. His three centuries took 66, 78 and 37 minutes respectively. *Wisden* reports: 'Often he walked down the pitch before the bowler released the ball and mixed orthodoxy with a bewildering assortment of unclassified strokes which went from the middle of the bat at lightning speed. He whipped balls pitched outside his off stump to the mid wicket boundary and he stepped away in order to cut leg-breaks pitched outside the wicket.' His hits included 5 sixes and 42 fours – 198 of his runs coming in boundaries. Compton's own description of his innings, given 30 years later, was typically vague but he claimed to have progressed from his century to about 190 whilst enjoying a few experimental strokes, and from 200 to 290 while trying to get out!

The highest maiden hundred in South African first-class cricket is 261 not out by Stephen Steyn for Western Province against Border at Cape Town in December 1929. Although he was a member of the South African team which toured Australia in 1930–31, Steyn (nicknamed 'Stodgy') never played in a Test match.

The highest score on debut in first-class cricket in South Africa is 240 by Eric Marx when he opened the innings for Transvaal against Griqualand West at the (Old) Wanderers, Johannesburg, in December 1920. His innings, which included a six and 30 fours, lasted only 220 minutes.

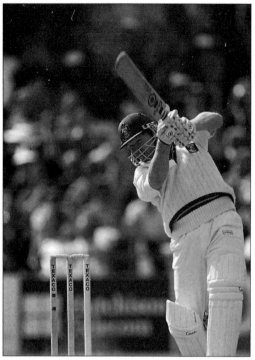

Daryll Cullinan: youngest century-maker (Popperfoto)

The record for scoring the most runs before being dismissed in first-class cricket was established by Raymond Watson-Smith of Border in November 1969. After scoring 183 not out in his first match, against Orange Free State at Bloemfontein batting at number seven, he made 125 not out in 145 minutes against Griqualand West at East London. He was stumped for 2 in his next innings and thus scored 310 runs before being dismissed in first-class cricket.

Peter May's first four innings in South Africa were hundreds; captaining the MCC on their 1956–57 tour, he scored 162 against Western Province at Cape Town, 118 against Eastern Province at Port Elizabeth, 124 not out against Rhodesia at Bulawayo, and 206 against Rhodesia at Salisbury. He scored another hundred two matches later (107 v Natal at Durban) before having the worst Test series of his career (6, 14, 8, 15, 2, 2, 61, 0, 24 and 21).

The youngest player to score a century in South African first-class cricket is Daryll Cullinan. He was 16 years 304 days old and still studying at Queens College, Queenstown, when he scored 106 not out for Border v Natal B at East London on 2 January 1984.

South African first-class cricket's youngest double century-maker is Graeme Pollock. He was 19 years 19 days old when he scored 209 not out for an Eastern Province Invitation XI against the Cavaliers, a touring side composed mainly of England and Australian Test cricketers, at Port Elizabeth on 18 March 1963.

The record for the most consecutive first-class hundreds was equalled in 1970–71 by Mike Procter of Rhodesia. The 24-year-old all-rounder accomplished his record in six different matches played between 21 November 1970 and 7 March 1971. His scores were: 119 against Natal 'B' at Bulawayo, 129 against Transvaal 'B' at Salisbury, 107 against Orange Free State at Bloemfontein, 174 against North-Eastern Transvaal at Pretoria, 106 against Griqualand West at Kimberley, and 254 in a friendly match against Western Province at Salisbury. Playing for the Rest of South Africa against Transvaal at Cape Town in his next innings, he struck his wicket in hitting a boundary and was out for 22. His performance equalled the world record set by Charles Fry in 1901 and emulated by Don Bradman in 1938–39.

The highest aggregate of runs by a South African in a home season is 1285 by Barry Richards of Natal in 1973–74. In 1969–70 Richards established the record number of first-class hundreds in a South African season. His total of six was equalled by Mike Procter in 1970–71 and by Peter Kirsten for Western Province and South African Universities in 1976–77.

The records for the most hundreds in South African first-class cricket and in Currie Cup matches are both held by Graeme Pollock. In a career spanning nearly 27 years, this supremely elegant left-hander scored 43 hundreds in South Africa, 36 of them in Currie Cup matches. In all first-class cricket he scored 64 centuries, including seven in his 23 Test matches. He was also the first South African to score a hundred in each innings of a first-class match on more than one occasion.

The fastest hundred in South African first-class cricket was scored in 53 minutes by M.G. Francis for Orange Free State against Griqualand West at Bloemfontein on 3 January 1928. His innings of 115 not out in 66 minutes carried his side to victory by seven wickets.

The fastest double century in first-class matches in South Africa was scored by Denis Compton in 144 minutes for the MCC against North-Eastern Transvaal at Benoni in December 1948. He went on to achieve the fastest triple century in all first-class cricket, reaching his 300 in 181 minutes.

The world record number of runs in a pre-lunch session of a first-class match was established at Ellis Park, Johannesburg, on 17 December 1954. Opening the Transvaal innings against Orange Free State on the first morning, Russell Endean scored 197 not out in three hours before the lunch interval. Afterwards he took his total to 235, made in 228 minutes and including 2 sixes and 34 fours. Four days earlier he had taken 88 minutes to score 16 against Natal at Durban.

The most runs off one over of authentic bowling in South African first-class cricket is 32 by Ian Redpath for the Australians against Orange Free State at Ramblers, Bloemfontein, on 19 March 1970. Not associated with aggressive strokeplay, Redpath launched a tremendous onslaught on the medium-pace bowling of Neil Rosendorff after reaching his hundred in 168 minutes. His next 51 runs came from 15 scoring strokes in 12 minutes, including 666644 off one Rosendorff over.

The slowest fifty and hundred in South African first-class cricket were both recorded by D.J. ('Jackie') McGlew during the 1957–58 series against Australia. He took 9 hours 5 minutes to reach his hundred when he scored 105 in the Third Test at Durban. In the second innings of the next Test at Johannesburg McGlew took 5 hours 13 minutes to reach 50, before progressing to 70 in 6 hours.

South Africa's slowest double century took Philip Amm (214) the first 10 hours 54 minutes of the Currie Cup Final against Transvaal at St George's Park, Port Elizabeth, on 10–11 March 1989. His marathon effort provided the lynchpin for victory by an innings and Eastern Province's first title in the trophy's 99-year history.

The longest 'duck' in South African first-class cricket was recorded at the Pietermaritzburg Oval on 20 January 1980 by Vincent Hogg. Playing for Zimbabwe-Rhodesia B against Natal B in the Castle Bowl competition, he survived for 87 minutes without scoring while his last-wicket partner and captain, Edward Parker (76*), increased the total by 64 runs.

BOWLING RECORDS

The first bowler to take all ten wickets in a first-class innings in South Africa was A.E.E. (Bert) Vogler. Playing for Eastern Province at the (Old) Wanderers Ground, Johannesburg, on 28 December 1906, he bowled unchanged throughout both innings and took 16 Griqualand West wickets in the day, including 10 for 26 in 12 six-ball overs in the second. A right-arm bowler of leg-breaks, googlies, top-spinners and flighted yorkers, he toured England in 1907 as one of South Africa's 'googly quartet' and was rated by England's captain, R.E. Foster, as 'the best bowler in the world'. Vogler's match analysis of 16 for 38 is the best by a South African in domestic first-class matches.

Steve Jefferies, a left-arm fast-medium swing bowler who took 10 for 59 for Western Province against Orange Free State at Newlands, Cape Town on 27–28 December 1987, is the only other bowler to emulate Vogler's feat in South Africa.

The two instances of a bowler taking 17 wickets in a first-class match in South Africa were both achieved by overseas players. Bill Howell, a bee farmer from New South Wales, took 17 for 54 against Western Province, including four wickets in five balls for the Australians at Cape Town on matting on 5–6 November 1902. Bowling medium-pace off-breaks throughout both innings, he took 8 for 31 and 9 for 23. On a similar pitch at Johannesburg in December 1913, Sydney Barnes of England took 8 for 56 and 9 for 103 in the Second Test. In four matches he set the world record for any series by taking 49 wickets.

HIGHEST PARTNERSHIPS IN SOUTH AFRICAN FIRST-CLASS CRICKET

Wicket	Runs	Batsmen (scores)	Match	Venue	Season
1st	424	J.F.W. Nicolson (252*), I.J. Siedle (174)	Natal v Orange Free State	Bloemfontein	1926–27
2nd	415	A.D. Jadeja (254*), S.V. Manjrekar (186)	Indians v Bowl XI	Springs	1992–93
3rd	399	R.T. Simpson (130*), D.C.S. Compton (300)	MCC v NE Transvaal	Benoni	1948–49
4th	342	E.A.B. Rowan (195), P.J.M. Gibb (203)	Transvaal v NE Transvaal	Johannesburg	1952–53
5th	355	A.J. Lamb (294), J.J. Strydom (107)	OFS v Eastern Province	Bloemfontein	1987–88
6th	259	S.A. Jones (209*), O. Henry (125)	Boland v Border	East London	1987–88
7th	299	B. Mitchell (159), A. Melville (153)	Transvaal v Griqualand W	Kimberley	1946–47
8th	222	S.S.L. Steyn (261*), D.P.B. Morkel (114)	Western Province v Border	Cape Town	1929–30
9th	221†	N.V. Lindsay (160*), G.R. McCubbin (97)	Transvaal v Rhodesia	Bulawayo	1922–23
10th	174	H.R. Lance (168), D. Mackay-Coghill (57*)	Transvaal v Natal	Johannesburg	1965–66

† The record in South Africa is:

| | 217 | A.W. Nourse (112*), B.C. Cooley (113) | Natal v Western Province | Johannesburg | 1906–07 |

No bowler has taken four wickets with consecutive balls or five wickets in six balls in South Africa since 28 February 1938 when W.A. Henderson accomplished both feats. Playing in a Currie Cup match for North Eastern Transvaal, he took seven Orange Free State second innings wickets and conceded only four runs from 75 balls.

The only player to take three hat-tricks in South African first-class cricket is Bob Crisp. A right-arm fast bowler, he achieved all three instances in Currie Cup matches for Western Province, and established a unique world record by twice taking four wickets with consecutive balls. His first two hat-tricks were taken during the 1931–32 season on the Wanderers' back ground in Johannesburg, against Griqualand West on 24 December 1931 when his analysis of 8 for 31 included four wickets in consecutive balls, and against Transvaal on 1 January 1932 when he took his four wickets in the space of five balls. Crisp's final hat-trick was part of another four-in-four sequence, against Natal at Durban on 3 March 1934 when he recorded the best analysis of his career: 9 for 64. Crisp, who was awarded the DSO and MC during wartime service as a tank commander, is the only Test cricketer to climb Mount Kilimanjaro twice.

The last pair of opening bowlers to operate unchanged throughout both innings of a completed first-class match in South Africa accomplished this feat in March 1938 in the final match of that season's Currie Cup programme. Norman Gordon (4 for 21 and 5 for 29) and F.J. Wickham (5 for 13 and 5 for 31) shared Transvaal's attack as Eastern Province were bowled out for 36 and 62 in a total of 29.7 eight-ball overs on a rain-affected Port Elizabeth pitch.

The world record number of balls by one bowler without conceding a run was established in the Third Test at Kingsmead, Durban, on 25–26 January 1957 by Hugh Tayfield. Undoubtedly South Africa's most outstanding off-break bowler, he bowled 16 consecutive maiden eight-ball overs in England's first innings, delivering a total of 137 balls without conceding a run.

Only two bowlers have taken 100 first-class wickets in a season in South Africa – Sydney Barnes took 104 wickets (average 10.74) in only 12 matches on matting during MCC's 1913–14 tour, and Richie Benaud established the national record by taking 106 wickets (average 19.39) in 18 matches on the Australians' 1957–58 tour.

The record number of wickets by a South African bowler in a home season is 75 (average 14.92) by Vintcent van der Bijl in 1981–82. A tall (6ft 7in), strong (17 stone), right-arm fast-medium bowler, his late swing and extra bounce played a major role in gaining Middlesex both the Championship and the Gillette Cup in 1980 – his solitary season in English cricket. With 682 wickets, average 16.77, he holds **the record career aggregate of first-class wickets taken in South Africa**.

WICKET-KEEPING RECORDS

The most dismissals in a first-class innings in South Africa is seven, a record shared by seven wicket-keepers (see table below). In successive Currie Cup matches at the Jan Smuts Ground, East London, in the 1959–60 season, the record was set by Malcolm Smith of Natal and then equalled by Noel Kirsten of Border.

The most wicket-keeping dismissals in a first-class match in South Africa is eleven by Ian Healy for the Australians against Northern Transvaal at Centurion Park, Verwoerdburg on 13–14 February 1994. He held five catches in each innings and added a stumping in the second.

The most stumpings in a first-class match in South Africa is seven by W.W. ('Billy') Wade of Natal at Kingsmead, Durban, on 21–24 November 1947. Playing against Griqualand West in a Currie Cup match, Wade scored 71 and made eight dismissals, his seven stumpings all coming off the leg-break bowling of V.I. (Ian) Smith, who had match figures of 11 for 119.

Roland Pearce of Natal enjoyed the most successful debut by a wicket-keeper/batsman in first-class cricket. Playing for Natal against Western Province at Kingsmead, Durban, on 30 November–2 December 1956, he made eight dismissals in the match and scored 95 in his only innings – after sharing in an opening partnership of 163, he was caught on the boundary.

SEVEN DISMISSALS IN AN INNINGS IN SOUTH AFRICA

	Ct	St	Match	Venue	Season
N. Kirsten	6	1	Border v Rhodesia	East London	1959–60
M.S. Smith	7	0	Natal v Border	East London	1959–60
R.J. East	6	1	OFS v Western Province B	Cape Town	1984–85
D.J. Richardson	7	0	Eastern Province v OFS	Bloemfontein	1988–89
P.J.L. Radley	7	0	OFS v Western Province	Cape Town	1990–91
P. Kirsten	7	0	Griqualand W v W Transvaal	Potchefstroom	1993–94
H.M. de Vos	7	0	W Transvaal v E Transvaal	Potchefstroom	1993–94

The most wicket-keeping dismissals in a South African season is 65 (57 catches and eight stumpings) by Ray Jennings in 1982–83. No other wicket-keeper has made 50 dismissals in a season, a total which Jennings also surpassed in 1984–85 with 49 catches and six stumpings.

FIELDING RECORDS

The most catches taken in the field in South Africa is five. This tally is shared by seven fielders (see table), notably Victor Richardson of Australia who set the current Test match record at Durban on 3 March 1936. Cyril White's performance includes a unique hat-trick of slip catches from successive balls bowled by R. Beesly, and Alan Jordaan's was achieved on his debut in first-class cricket.

FIVE CATCHES IN AN INNINGS

	Match	Venue	Season
A.D. Nourse	Natal v Border	Durban	1933–34
V.Y. Richardson	Australia v South Africa	Durban	1935–36
C.D. White	Border v Griqualand West	Queenstown	1946–47
P.H. Parfitt	MCC v SA Universities	Pietermaritzburg	1964–65
A.H. Jordaan	Northern Transvaal v Border	East London	1972–73
A. Barrow	Transvaal B v Northern Transvaal B	Pietersburg	1982–83
P.J.R. Steyn	Griqualand West v Western Province B	Kimberley	1985–86

SEVEN CATCHES IN A MATCH

	Match	Venue	Season
S.P. de Vigne	NE Transvaal v Orange Free State	Benoni	1950–51
A. Barrow	Transvaal B v Northern Transvaal B	Pietersburg	1982–83
C.B. Lambert	Northern Transvaal v Boland	Paarl	1994–95

RECORD ALL-ROUND PERFORMANCES

The first to accomplish the match double of 100 runs and ten wickets in a first-class match in South Africa was Albert Trott in February 1899. Playing for Lord Hawke's English Team against Transvaal at Johannesburg, he took 7 for 74 and scored 101 not out before completing the tourists' victory by an innings and 203 runs with 4 for 66 in the second innings.

The only player to achieve the match double twice in successive first-class matches is Xenophon Constantine Balaskas. Born in Kimberley of Greek parents, 'Bally' was a right-arm legbreak bowler and middle-order batsman. Both his doubles were inflicted upon Griqualand West's Currie Cup opponents in home matches at Kimberley, and both were major contributions towards innings victories. He scored 132 and had match figures of 11 for 130 against Eastern Province on 14–15 February 1930. A week later, against Western Province, he scored 101 of his team's record total of 603 and took 12 for 235.

500 RUNS AND 50 WICKETS IN A SOUTH AFRICAN SEASON

		Season	Runs	Wickets
A.E.E. Vogler	Eastern Province	1906–07	505	55
P.N.F. Mansell	Rhodesia	1951–52	571	52
J.R. Reid	New Zealanders	1953–54	1012	51
R. Benaud	Australians	1957–58	817	106
A.K. Davidson	Australians	1957–58	813	72
M.J. Procter	Rhodesia	1971–72	695	52
M.J. Procter	Rhodesia	1972–73	870	60

Mike Procter: twice achieved the double of 500 runs and 50 wickets in a South African season (Hulton-Deutsch)

THE CURRIE CUP (now CASTLE CUP)

South Africa's main domestic first-class competition was created as a direct result of Major R.G. Warton's team making the first English tour of the Union in 1888. Sir Donald Currie, head of the Castle Mail Packets Company whose ship brought Warton's team to South Africa, donated a trophy as a Challenge Cup to be awarded to the team which excelled most against the pioneer tourists.

The Currie Cup was first presented to Kimberley (later to be renamed Griqualand West). In subsequent seasons it was competed for by the provinces, first on a challenge basis and later as the trophy awarded to the winners of a full inter-provincial tournament. Transvaal won the first Currie Cup match when they defeated the original holders on 5–8 April 1890, but Kimberley regained it from them the following season. From November 1892 it became the feature of South Africa's main domestic competition, in succession to the 'Champion Bat' tournament which had been held five times between 1876 and 1891.

By 1946–47 the number of teams competing for the trophy had risen to nine, and the tournament was divided into two sections from 1951–52. Until

1966–67 the Currie Cup competition was not held during seasons when an overseas touring team visited the Union, occasional friendly matches being played between the provinces instead.

Since 1972–73 the competition has been sponsored by South African Breweries. After periods as the 'South African Breweries Cup' (1972–73 to 1975–76 and 1979–80), this premier competition became the 'Castle Currie Cup' (1976–77 to 1978–79 and 1983–84 to 1990–91) and is currently the 'Castle Cup'.

Rhodesia, who joined the competition in March 1905 and played as Zimbabwe-Rhodesia in 1979–80, were withdrawn from all South African cricket by the newly independent Zimbabwe government in 1980.

CURRIE CUP/CASTLE CUP WINNERS

1889–90 Transvaal
1890–91 Kimberley
1892–93 Western Province
1893–94 Western Province
1894–95 Transvaal
1896–97 Western Province
1897–98 Western Province
1902–03 Transvaal
1903–04 Transvaal
1904–05 Transvaal
1906–07 Transvaal
1908–09 Western Province
1910–11 Natal
1912–13 Natal
1920–21 Western Province
1921–22 Natal/Transvaal/Western Province
1923–24 Transvaal
1925–26 Transvaal
1926–27 Transvaal
1929–30 Transvaal
1931–32 Western Province
1933–34 Natal
1934–35 Transvaal
1936–37 Natal
1937–38 Natal/Transvaal
1946–47 Natal
1947–48 Natal

1950–51 Transvaal
1951–52 Natal
1952–53 Western Province
1954–55 Natal
1955–56 Western Province
1958–59 Transvaal
1959–60 Natal
1960–61 Natal
1962–63 Natal
1963–64 Natal
1965–66 Natal/Transvaal
1966–67 Natal
1967–68 Natal
1968–69 Transvaal
1969–70 Transvaal/Western Province
1970–71 Transvaal
1971–72 Transvaal
1972–73 Transvaal
1973–74 Natal
1974–75 Western Province
1975–76 Natal
1976–77 Natal
1977–78 Western Province
1978–79 Transvaal
1979–80 Transvaal
1980–81 Natal
1981–82 Western Province
1982–83 Transvaal
1983–84 Transvaal
1984–85 Transvaal
1985–86 Western Province
1986–87 Transvaal
1987–88 Transvaal
1988–89 Eastern Province
1989–90 Eastern Province/Western Province
1990–91 Western Province
1991–92 Eastern Province
1992–93 Orange Free State
1993–94 Orange Free State
1994–95 Natal

Outright wins: 24 – Transvaal; 19 – Natal; 14 – Western Province; 2 Eastern Province, Orange Free State; 1 – Kimberley (now Griqualand West).

Shared titles: 4 – Transvaal; 3 – Natal, Western Province; 1 – Eastern Province.

THE B SECTION COMPETITION (now UCB BOWL)

In 1951–52 the Currie Cup teams were divided into two sections (A: Eastern Province, Natal, Transvaal and Western Province; B: Border, Griqualand West, North-Eastern Transvaal, Orange Free State and Rhodesia) and a system of promotion and relegation instituted. In 1959–60 Transvaal became the first province to enter a second team into the B Section competion and it finished joint champions in its first season. Provinces with teams in both Sections were excluded from promotion and relegation.

The B Section was renamed the Castle Bowl in 1977–78, after the trophy presented by South African Breweries, and became the UCB (United Cricket Board) Bowl in 1991–92. The Bowl competition was extended in 1993–94 to include B teams from all the Castle Cup provinces, as well as Griqualand West, Eastern Transvaal and Western Transvaal, the teams being divided into two sections with the winners contesting a final.

B SECTION/UCB BOWL WINNERS

1951–52 Orange Free State
1952–53 Transvaal
1954–55 Eastern Province
1955–56 Rhodesia
1958–59 Border
1959–60 Eastern Province/Transvaal B
1962–63 Transvaal B
1963–64 Rhodesia
1965–66 N-Eastern Transvaal
1966–67 N-Eastern Transvaal
1967–68 Rhodesia
1968–69 Western Province
1969–70 Transvaal B
1970–71 Rhodesia
1971–72 Northern Transvaal
1972–73 Transvaal B
1973–74 Natal B
1974–75 Transvaal B
1975–76 Orange Free State
1976–77 Transvaal B
1977–78 Northern Transvaal
1978–79 Northern Transvaal
1979–80 Natal B
1980–81 Western Province B
1981–82 Boland
1982–83 Western Province B
1983–84 Western Province B
1984–85 Transvaal B
1985–86 Boland
1986–87 Transvaal B
1987–88 Boland
1988–89 Border
1989–90 Border/Western Province B
1990–91 Border/Western Province B
1991–92 Eastern Transvaal
1992–93 Boland
1993–94 Transvaal B/Western Province B
1994–95 Natal B

First-Class Cricket
in West Indies

First-Class Cricket in West Indies

The first inter-colonial match was played between Barbados, the traditional centre of West Indian cricket, and Demerara (now part of Guyana) on 15–16 February 1865 on the Garrison Savannah in Bridgetown.

The first West Indian team to play overseas toured North America in 1886. The 13-match programme was described in the first West Indian cricket book, published the following year in Georgetown.

The first touring team to visit the West Indies arrived from America in 1887. They dismissed West Indies for 19 in the only international match played.

The first inter-colonial tournament was held on 1–10 September 1891 at Wanderers Bay Pasture, Barbados, when the home team successfully challenged Demerara and Trinidad. From 1893 the colonies competed for a cup. Although Jamaica first played against Demerara and Barbados in 1896, they played only eleven regional matches before 1946 and the development of cricket there owed much to the visits of English teams. It was not until October 1956 that the four colonies contested a quadrangular tournament on the same ground (Bourda in Georgetown, British Guiana). Five years later the tournament became pentangular with the introduction of a combined team from the Leeward and Windward Islands.

The first sponsored regional tournament was instituted in January 1966 and resulted in Barbados becoming the first holders of 'The Shell Shield for Caribbean Regional Cricket'. The competition was held annually apart from in 1967–68 when the MCC were touring. At first the Leeward and Windward Islands participated as a joint Combined Islands team. For the Shield's second and third seasons they joined the four main territories as separate sides; it was not until 1969–70 that they competed as full members and played for points. They reverted to the Combined Islands format until 1981–82 when they again divided into two teams.

In 1988 the Jamaican-based company of Desnoes and Geddes, manufacturers of Red Stripe lager, became the regional tournament's new sponsors and renamed it the **Red Stripe Cup**. Appropriately, the new trophy remained in Jamaica until the end of its third season when the Leewards gained their first senior regional championship.

SHELL SHIELD HOLDERS

1965–66 Barbados
1966–67 Barbados
1968–69 Jamaica
1969–70 Trinidad
1970–71 Trinidad
1971–72 Barbados
1972–73 Guyana
1973–74 Barbados
1974–75 Guyana
1975–76 Trinidad/Barbados
1976–77 Barbados
1977–78 Barbados
1978–79 Barbados
1979–80 Barbados
1980–81 Combined Islands
1981–82 Barbados
1982–83 Guyana
1983–84 Barbados
1984–85 Trinidad
1985–86 Barbados
1986–87 Guyana
Shield wins: 11 – Barbados; 4 – Guyana; 3 – Trinidad; 1 – Combined Islands, Jamaica
Shared titles: 1 – Barbados, Trinidad

RED STRIPE CUP HOLDERS

1987–88 Jamaica
1988–89 Jamaica
1989–90 Leeward Islands
1990–91 Barbados
1991–92 Jamaica
1992–93 Guyana
1993–94 Leeward Islands
1994–95 Barbados

Cricket Curiosities
Seymour Nurse (West Indies) had the misfortune to be caught at deep fine-leg from a hit that rebounded off the head of a fielder at backward short-leg when he was batting against Australia in the Second Test at Melbourne in December 1968.

TEAM RECORDS

The highest innings total in any first-class match in the West Indies is 849 by England against West Indies at Sabina Park, Kingston, Jamaica, on 3–5 April 1930. It remained the highest total in Test cricket until August 1938, when England reached 903 for 8 declared against Australia at The Oval, and included the first triple century at Test level – 325 (out of 720 for 5 in ten hours) by Andrew Sandham. It also included an innings of 8 not out by Wilfred Rhodes who was to be 52 years 165 days of age and the oldest Test cricketer when the nine-day 'timeless' match was declared a draw after rain had prevented play on the last two days.

The highest total in West Indian domestic first-class matches is 753 by Barbados against Jamaica at Kensington Oval, Bridgetown, Barbados, on 17–22 January 1952.

The lowest total and the lowest match aggregate in West Indies first-class cricket were both inflicted upon colonies visiting Barbados in Bridgetown. Trinidad were dismissed on a rain-affected pitch for 16, in 69 minutes, on 20 July 1942, Derek Sealy taking 8 for 8, including four wickets in seven balls. Only three Trinidad batsmen got off the mark. In the first inter-colonial match ever played, on 15–16 February 1865, Demerara were bowled out for 22 and 38 by a brace of Smiths (F.B. and A.E.) who operated unchanged throughout both innings. Of the 18 wickets which fell to their bowling, 15 were bowled and three were caught – by the two Smiths! Just to ensure that their name would be firmly etched on the records of this match, F.B. Smith, the Barbados captain, became the first player to carry his bat through a first-class innings in the West Indies and the first to score a fifty (50 not out).

The largest variation in a side's totals in all first-class cricket is 551 runs. This extraordinary margin of difference has occurred on three occasions, the first two at Kensington Oval, Bridgetown, and the third at Chelmsford:

Barbados   175 & 726–7d v Trinidad   1926–27
Pakistan   106 & 657–8d v West Indies 1957–58
Middlesex   83 & 634–7d v Essex   1983

The only first-class match in the Caribbean to result in a tie took place at Kingston, Jamaica, on 3–5 April 1911. The first official MCC team to tour the West Indies dismissed Jamaica for 173 and 227 after scoring 269 and 131.

The world record for conceding most extras in a first-class innings under the Laws of Cricket (as opposed to experimental rules) was set at Bourda, Georgetown, British Guiana, in 1909. William Shepherd's Eleven conceded 74 extras (54 byes, 16 leg-byes, 1 wide and 3 no balls) in Demerara's total of 529 – the highest innings in West Indian first-class cricket at that time.

The only batsman to be dismissed for hitting the ball twice in West Indies first-class cricket is Alfred Binns of Jamaica. This unique instance occurred in the match against British Guiana at Georgetown on 16 October 1956, with the batsman's score on 151 – a slightly rapacious act by a player with that total on the board. The next highest score by any batsman being dismissed for falling foul of the three more obscure laws is 73.

The only batsman to be given out in West Indies first-class cricket for handling the ball is George Linton. Batting for Barbados against the Windward Islands at Kensington Oval, Bridgetown, on 17 January 1986, he played a defensive deadbat stroke to a lifting delivery from Desmond Collymore, and innocently picked up the ball to return it to the bowler.

So far no batsman has been dismissed for obstructing the field in the Caribbean.

BATTING RECORDS

The highest individual score in West Indies first-class cricket and the world record Test score is 375 by Brian Lara. Playing for West Indies against England in the Fifth Test at the Recreation Ground in St John's, Antigua, on 16–18 April 1994, he batted for 12 hours 48 minutes and hit 45 fours.

Lara eclipsed the record of 365 not out set by Garfield Sobers on 27 February–1 March 1958 against Pakistan at Sabina Park, Kingston, Jamaica. Sobers was then aged 21 years 216 days and remains the youngest to score a triple hundred in Test cricket.

The highest individual innings in West Indies domestic cricket is 324 by Jeffrey Stollmeyer, for Trinidad against British Guiana at Queen's Park Oval, Port-of-Spain in March 1947.

The longest innings in all first-class cricket is Hanif Mohammad's 337 which lasted 16 hours 39 minutes on 20–23 January 1958 at Kensington Oval, Bridgetown, Barbados, after Pakistan had been asked to follow on 473 runs behind.

Two generations of great West Indian batsmen: Sir Garfield Sobers (left) and Brian Lara pictured in 1994 (Popperfoto)

HIGHEST PARTNERSHIPS IN WEST INDIES FIRST-CLASS CRICKET

Wkt	Runs	Batsmen (scores)	Match	Venue	Season
1st	390	G.L. Wight (262*), G.L. Gibbs (216)	British Guiana v Barbados	Georgetown	1951–52
2nd	446	C.C. Hunte (260), G. St A. Sobers (365*)	West Indies v Pakistan	Kingston	1957–58
3rd	434	J.B. Stollmeyer (324), G.E. Gomez (190)	Trinidad v British Guiana	Port-of-Spain	1946–47
4th	574*	C.L. Walcott (314*), F.M.M. Worrell (255*)	Barbados v Trinidad	Port-of-Spain	1945–46
5th	327	P. Holmes (244), W.E. Astill (156)	MCC v Jamaica	Kingston	1925–26
6th	487*	G.A. Headley (344*), C.C. Passailaigue (261*)	Jamaica v Lord Tennyson's XI	Kingston	1931–32
7th	347	D.St E. Atkinson (219), C.C. Depeiaza (122)	West Indies v Australia	Bridgetown	1954–55
8th	255	E.A.V. Williams (131*), E.A. Martindale (134)	Barbados v Trinidad	Bridgetown	1935–36
9th	168	L.G. Crawley (85), F.B. Watson (103*)	MCC v Jamaica	Kingston	1925–26
10th	167	A.W.F. Somerset (53*), W.C. Smith (126)	MCC v Barbados	Bridgetown	1912–13

The partnership for the sixth wicket is a world first-class record.

William Smith (Surrey and MCC) is **the only player to score a first-class century batting at number eleven in the West Indies.**

BOWLING RECORDS

The only bowler to take *all* ten wickets in a first-class innings in the West Indies is the English off-spinner, Eddie Hemmings. Playing for an International XI against a West Indies Invitation XI at Sabina Park, Kingston, on 26–27 September 1982, he took 10 for 175 in 49.3 overs. It remains the most expensive ten-wickets analysis in all first-class cricket and the Invitation team's total of 419 is the highest in which any bowler has taken all ten wickets.

The best innings analysis in West Indies first-class cricket was achieved in a twelve-a-side match by Delmont Cameron St Clair 'Fitz' Hinds. Playing for A.B. St Hill's XII against Trinidad at Queen's Park Oval, Port-of-Spain on 10 January 1901, Hinds, a 20-year-old Barbadian, took 10 for 36 in 19.1 overs, bowling unchanged throughout the innings during the first of his 12 first-class appearances.

The best Test match innings analysis by a West Indies bowler is 9 for 95 by Jack Noreiga, against India at Port-of-Spain, Trinidad, in March 1971, in the second of his four international appearances. A 34-year-old off-spin bowler, Noreiga replaced a temporarily out-of-form Lance Gibbs and exploited a helpful pitch on his home ground to become the only West Indian to take nine wickets in a Test innings.

The best match analysis in first-class cricket in the West Indies is 16 for 58 by E.M. ('Toddles') Dowson for R.A. Bennett's XI against Jamaica at Kingston on 8–9 February 1902. No more than five feet tall, Dowson bowled left-arm leg-breaks extremely slowly. Aged 21 when he took part in this all-amateur mission, he was mid-way through his 4-year career with Cambridge University and Surrey.

The best match analysis in West Indian domestic cricket is 15 for 101 by Derek Parry for Combined Islands against Jamaica at Sabina Park, Kingston on 21–24 March 1980. An off-break bowler with the ability to turn the ball sharply on good pitches, Parry took 6 for 25 and 9 for 76 to establish innings and match record analyses for Shell Shield matches.

Cricket Curiosities
For nearly four decades virtually every cricket reference book credited R.L. Hunte with a Test match appearance for West Indies against England at Port-of-Spain, Trinidad, in February 1930. It was E.A.C. (Errol) Hunte who actually played, the second of his three Test appearances. The error was caused by a copy typist mishearing 'Erroll' as 'R.L.' and it resulted in Hunte having his career record separated under the two sets of initials in many publications.

WICKET-KEEPING RECORDS

The record number of dismissals in a first-class match in the Caribbean is nine by Michael Findlay for the Combined Islands against Guyana at Rose Hall, Berbice, Guyana, on 28 February–3 March 1974. He held four catches in the first innings and three in the second, as well as stumping one batsman in each innings.

SIX WICKET-KEEPING DISMISSALS IN AN INNINGS

	Ct	St Match		Venue	Season
A.P. Binns	3	3	Jamaica v British Guiana	Georgetown	1952–53
R.A. Pinnock	4	2	Jamaica v Trinidad	Port-of-Spain	1969–70
T.M. Findlay	3	3	Windward Is v Leeward Is	Roseau, Dominica	1971–72
M.C. Worrell	6	0	Barbados v Leeward Is	Bridgetown	1984–85
T.R.O. Payne	5	1	Barbados v England XI	Bridgetown	1985–86
M.V. Simon	6	0	Leeward Is v Jamaica	St John's	1986–87
L.L. Harris	5	1	Leeward Is v Trinidad	Pointe-à-Pierre	1987–88
R.D. Jacobs (2)	6	0	Leeward Is v Barbados	Bridgetown	1991–92
	5	1	Leeward Is v Jamaica	Kingston	1993–94

FIELDING RECORDS

FIVE CATCHES IN AN INNINGS

	Match	Venue	Season
T.N.M. Pierce	Barbados v Trinidad	Bridgetown	1942–43
O.M. Durity (2)	Trinidad v Guyana	Georgetown	1970–71
	South Trinidad v East Trinidad	Pointe-à-Pierre	1971–72
G.S. Camacho	Demerara v Berbice	Georgetown	1971–72
I.V.A. Richards	Leeward Islands v Barbados	Basseterre	1981–82
R.C. Haynes	Jamaica v Barbados	Bridgetown	1991–92
T.O. Powell	Jamaica v Trinidad	Port-of-Spain	1993–94

The record number of catches taken in the field in a first-class match in the West Indies is seven by Tom Pierce for Barbados against Trinidad at Kensington Oval, Bridgetown, on 18–21 July 1942.

First-Class Cricket in New Zealand

First-Class Cricket in New Zealand

The first fully recorded cricket match in New Zealand took place at Nelson in March 1844 between Nelson and the Surveyors of the Land Company. However, there are references to the game being played before New Zealand became a British crown colony under the Treaty of Waitangi on 6 February 1840.

The first inter-provincial match was a one-day game played between Wellington and Auckland at Wellington in March 1860.

The first match in New Zealand to be recognized as first-class by the Association of Cricket Statisticians was played at South Dunedin Recreation Ground on 27–29 January 1864. Otago (78 and 74) beat Canterbury (34 and 42) by 76 runs after being put in to bat. The highest individual score was 25 not out and the opening bowlers for Otago bowled unchanged throughout the match. This match was arranged as part of a cricket carnival in Dunedin which coincided with the arrival from Australia of George Parr's All-England XI, the first overseas team to visit New Zealand.

The first overseas tour by a team from New Zealand took place in the 1878–79 season when Canterbury visited Victoria and Tasmania.

TEAM RECORDS

The highest innings total in a first-class match in New Zealand is 752 for 8 declared by New South Wales against Otago at Carisbrook, Dunedin on 15–18 February 1924.

The highest total in an inter-provincial match is 693 for 9 declared by Auckland against Canterbury at Eden Park, Auckland on 5–9 January 1940.

The lowest total in New Zealand first-class cricket is 13 by Auckland against Canterbury at The Domain, Auckland on 28–31 December 1877.

The lowest innings total in all Test cricket was recorded at Eden Park, Auckland when New Zealand were dismissed for 26 by England on 28 March 1955.

Three first-class matches in New Zealand have resulted in a tie. The first instance occurred at Basin Reserve, Wellington on 17–18 March 1874 when the home side scored 63 and 118, and dismissed Nelson for 111(!) and 70. The second tie resulted when England (296 for 6 declared and 104) dismissed Central Districts (139 and 188) with the last possible ball of the match, at Pukekura Park, New Plymouth, on 1–3 February 1978. Hero of the dramatic finish was England's fast bowler Bob Willis, captaining an England XI for the first time. With the scores level, Willis bowled topscorer Terry Horne (40) leg stump. The Basin Reserve was again the scene of a tied match on 24 January 1989 when Canterbury, set 268 to win in 60 overs by Wellington, lost their last wicket to a run out when attempting a second leg-bye off the final possible ball.

BATTING RECORDS

The highest individual first-class score in New Zealand – is 385 by Bert Sutcliffe for Otago against Canterbury in a Plunket Shield match at Lancaster Park, Christchurch, on 26–27 December 1952. Opening the innings in reply to Canterbury's total of 309, Sutcliffe batted for 461 minutes, hit 46 fours and 3 sixes, and was ninth out when the total reached 500. The last wicket fell without addition to that score. Canterbury were dismissed for 98 and lost by an innings and 93 runs. His innings remained the highest by a left-handed batsman until Brian Lara scored 501 not out in 1994, a feat commemorated by a plaque which was unveiled at Lancaster Park on 1 March 1986. Sutcliffe also registered scores of 355, 275 and 264 for Otago and can still claim four of the eight highest innings by New Zealanders in domestic cricket, all of them occurring in Plunket Shield matches. In a career spanning the years 1941 to 1966, Sutcliffe achieved the record total of 26 first-class centuries in New Zealand.

The highest aggregate of runs by a batsman in one season is 1676, average 93.11, by Martin Crowe in 21 innings for Central Districts and New Zealand in 1986–87. In Shell Trophy matches alone he amassed a record 1348 runs. He also scored the most hundreds in a first-class season in New Zealand (8).

The first batsman to hit 15 sixes in a first-class innings was John Reid during his innings of 296 in a

Plunket Shield match for Wellington on 14–15 January 1963. Playing against Northern Districts on his home ground at Basin Reserve, the Wellington and New Zealand captain batted for only 220 minutes. Not out without scoring overnight, he raced to 174 in 142 minutes before lunch. His first 50 took 67 minutes and included no sixes. The times in minutes for his subsequent fifties, with the number of six-hits in brackets, were: 32 (3), 35 (3), 33 (0), and 28 (4). His last 46 runs came in 25 minutes and included 5 sixes. He also hit 35 fours and so scored 230 of his runs in boundaries. Reid contributed 70 per cent of his side's total of 422, the next highest contribution being 24. Reid's record was surpassed in 1995 when Andrew Symonds hit 16 sixes in his 254 not out for Gloucestershire against Glamorgan at Abergavenny.

HIGHEST PARTNERSHIPS IN NEW ZEALAND FIRST-CLASS CRICKET

Wkt	Runs	Batsmen (scores)	Match	Venue	Season
1st	373	B. Sutcliffe (275), L. Watt (96)	Otago v Auckland	Auckland	1950–51
2nd	317	R.T. Hart (167*), P.S. Briasco (157)	Central Districts v Canterbury	New Plymouth	1983–84
3rd	467	A.H. Jones (186), M.D. Crowe (299)	New Zealand v Sri Lanka	Wellington	1990–91
4th	350	Mushtaq Mohammad (201), Asif Iqbal (175)	Pakistan v New Zealand	Dunedin	1972–73
5th	341	G.R. Larsen (161), E.B. McSweeney (205*)	Wellington v Central Districts	Levin	1987–88
6th	269	V.T. Trumper (172), C. Hill (129)	Australians v New Zealand XI	Wellington	1904–05
7th	265	J.L. Powell (164), N. Dorreen (105*)	Canterbury v Otago	Christchurch	1929–30
8th	433	A. Sims (184*), V.T. Trumper (293)	Australians v Canterbury	Christchurch	1913–14
9th	239	H.B. Cave (118), I.B. Leggat (142*)	Central Districts v Otago	Dunedin	1952–53
10th	184	R.C. Blunt (338*), W. Hawksworth (21)	Otago v Canterbury	Christchurch	1931–32

The partnerships for the third and eighth wickets are world first-class records.

BOWLING RECORDS

The only bowler to take all ten wickets in a first-class innings in New Zealand is A.E. Moss of Canterbury. Playing against Wellington at Christchurch on 27–28 December 1889, Moss returned an analysis of 21.3–10–28–10 in a total of 71. He is the only bowler to take all ten wickets in an innings in his first first-class match.

The best match analysis in New Zealand first-class cricket is 15 for 60 by Sydney Callaway for Canterbury against Hawke's Bay at Napier on 14–15 January 1904. His full analyses were 23.3–10–33–8 and 17–7–27–7. An Australian who settled and eventually died in Christchurch, Callaway is the only bowler to take 15 wickets in a first-class match in New Zealand on two occasions. He had previously taken 15 for 175 for New South Wales against New Zealand at Christchurch in December 1895.

The only bowler to take four first-class wickets in four balls in New Zealand is Alec Downes of Otago. He achieved this feat against Auckland at Dunedin in 1893–94.

The record number of wickets by any bowler in a season in New Zealand is 66, average 16.48, in 1977–78 by Stephen Boock in 13 matches for Canterbury (9), South Island (1) and New Zealand (3 v England).

WICKET-KEEPING RECORDS

SEVEN DISMISSALS IN AN INNINGS

	Ct	St	Match	Venue	Season
R.M. Schofield	7	0	Central Districts v Wellington	Wellington	1964–65
Wasim Bari	7	0	Pakistan v New Zealand	Auckland	1978–79
B.A. Young	7	0	Northern Districts v Canterbury	Christchurch	1986–87
I.D.S. Smith	7	0	New Zealand v Sri Lanka	Hamilton	1990–91

NINE DISMISSALS IN A MATCH

			Match	Venue	Season
R.M. Schofield	9	0	Central Districts v Wellington	Wellington	1964–65
R.H. Vance	9	0	Wellington v Otago	Wellington	1977–78
E.B. McSweeney	8	1	Wellington v Otago	Lower Hutt	1983–84
B.A. Young	9	0	Northern Districts v Canterbury	Christchurch	1986–87
L.K. Germon	9	0	Canterbury v Northern Districts	Christchurch	1992–93
Rashid Latif	9	0	Pakistan v New Zealand	Auckland	1993–94

FIELDING RECORDS

FIVE CATCHES IN AN INNINGS

	Match	Venue	Season
N.T. Williams	Auckland v Hawke's Bay	Napier	1894–95
J.R. Lamason (2)	Wellington v Otago	Dunedin	1937–38
	North Island Army v South Island Army	Wellington	1942–43
J.T. Ikin	MCC v Auckland	Auckland	1946–47
J.F.M. Morrison	Wellington v Northern Districts	Wellington	1980–81
G.K. MacDonald	Canterbury v Pakistanis	Christchurch	1984–85
J.J. Crowe	Auckland v Canterbury	Auckland	1988–89

John Morrison's five second-innings catches in the instance above gave him the New Zealand first-class match record of seven.

THE PLUNKET SHIELD

During the 1906–07 season Lord Plunket, Governor General of New Zealand, gave a shield for a competition among the first-class provinces. The New Zealand Cricket Council, which had been formed in Christchurch on 27 December 1894, awarded the Plunket Shield to Canterbury as the association with the best record in 1906–07.

Until the 1921–22 season the Shield was contested on a challenge basis by the provinces of Auckland, Wellington, Canterbury and Otago, the players being recruited almost entirely from the cities of Auckland, Wellington, Christchurch and Dunedin respectively. There were 32 challenges during the first phase of this competition, Canterbury winning 16, Auckland 14 and Wellington 2.

Ian Smith: seven catches in an innings for New Zealand
(Popperfoto)

From 1921 until 1975, when Shell Oil began their sponsorship of New Zealand inter-provincial cricket, the Shield was contested on a league basis. Two new associations were formed in this period: Central Districts (the minor provinces of Taranaki, Wanganui, Hawke's Bay, Manawatu, Wairarapa, Nelson and Marlborough) competed from 1950–51; Northern Districts (Northland, Waikato, Bay of Plenty and Poverty Bay) were admitted in 1956–57.

PLUNKET SHIELD HOLDERS UNDER THE LEAGUE SYSTEM

1921–22 Auckland
1922–23 Canterbury
1923–24 Wellington
1924–25 Otago
1925–26 Wellington
1926–27 Auckland
1927–28 Wellington
1928–29 Auckland
1929–30 Wellington

1930–31 Canterbury
1931–32 Wellington
1932–33 Otago
1933–34 Auckland
1934–35 Canterbury
1935–36 Wellington
1936–37 Auckland
1937–38 Auckland
1938–39 Auckland
1939–40 Auckland
1945–46 Canterbury
1946–47 Auckland
1947–48 Otago
1948–49 Canterbury
1949–50 Wellington
1950–51 Otago
1951–52 Canterbury
1952–53 Otago
1953–54 Central Districts
1954–55 Wellington
1955–56 Canterbury
1956–57 Wellington
1957–58 Otago
1958–59 Auckland
1959–60 Canterbury
1960–61 Wellington
1961–62 Wellington
1962–63 Northern Districts
1963–64 Auckland
1964–65 Canterbury
1965–66 Wellington
1966–67 Central Districts
1967–68 Central Districts
1968–69 Auckland
1969–70 Otago
1970–71 Central Districts
1971–72 Otago
1972–73 Wellington
1973–74 Wellington
1974–75 Otago

Cricket Curiosities
J.G. ('Jock') Sutherland carried his bat through an innings of 21 for Wakatu CC against Waimea College but did not manage to score a run. The innings, played in October 1976 at Victory Square in Nelson, New Zealand, lasted 54 minutes.

THE SHELL TROPHY

A league-cup competition, sponsored by Shell Oil and with two separate trophies, replaced the Plunket Shield in 1975–76. Besides the financial advantages, this change increased the amount of first-class cricket and, in its first four seasons, had the added attraction of culminating in a final. From 1979–80, the two-trophy competition was abandoned and the single league system reintroduced. The Shell Cup, awarded initially to the winners of the first part of the season's programme, was won by Canterbury twice and by Northern Districts and Otago once each.

SHELL TROPHY HOLDERS

1975–76 Canterbury
1976–77 Otago
1977–78 Auckland
1978–79 Otago
1979–80 Northern Districts
1980–81 Auckland
1981–82 Wellington
1982–83 Wellington
1983–84 Canterbury
1984–85 Wellington
1985–86 Otago
1986–87 Central Districts
1987–88 Otago
1988–89 Auckland
1989–90 Wellington
1990–91 Auckland
1991–92 Central Districts/Northern Districts
1992–93 Northern Districts
1993–94 Canterbury
1994–95 Auckland

First-Class Cricket
in India

First-Class Cricket in India

The earliest reference to cricket being played on Indian soil dates back to 1721. This was an impromptu game among sailors from an East India Company trading ship at Cambay in the western region. Cricket matches were soon commonplace in Calcutta, usually between Army teams and the settlers of the East India Company.

The first club to be formed was the Calcutta Cricket Club. Dating from at least 1792 and with its membership restricted to Europeans, it was established on the site of the present Test match stadium at Eden Gardens, where in January 1982 the largest attendance at any cricket match, an estimated 394 000, watched the Fourth Test between India and England.

The first book of cricket scores known outside Britain was published in India in 1854 – *Calcutta Cricket Club Matches 1844–54*.

The Indians, notably the Parsees, began playing cricket in Bombay in the late 18th century, forming the Orient Club in 1848. In 1877 they beat a Europeans team and, in 1886, undertook the first tour from the subcontinent, to England.

The first known tour by an English team to India took place in 1889–90. Led by G.F. Vernon of Middlesex and including Lord Hawke, the all-amateur side lost only one match – to the Parsees of Bombay who dismissed them for 97 and 61.

The first match in India to be recognized as first-class by the Association of Cricket Statisticians was played between the Europeans and Parsees at Bombay's Gymkhana Ground on 26–27 August 1892.

India's first centralized cricket administration, the Board of Control for Cricket in India, was formed in 1928. Four years later came the inaugural Test match against England at Lord's.

TEAM RECORDS

The highest total in first-class cricket in India is 944 for 6 declared by Hyderabad against Andhra in a south zone Ranji Trophy match at the Gymkhana Grounds in Secunderabad on 9–11 January 1994. This total, the fourth highest in all first-class cricket, occupied 211 overs in 13 hours 27 minutes and included the first instance of three batsmen scoring double hundreds in the same innings: Maruti Sridhar (366), Vivek Jaisimha (211) and Noel David (207*). Sridhar's contribution (11 hours 39 minutes, 523 balls, 5 sixes and 37 fours), was the third-highest by an Indian and set the world record for the most runs added during one batsman's innings in all first-class matches: 850 (surpassing the 811 scored during Bobby Abel's 357 not out for Surrey in 1889).

The world record for the most individual hundreds in a first-class innings is six by Holkar in their 912 for 8 declared against Mysore in a Ranji Trophy semi-final at Indore on 2–4 March 1948: K.V. Bhandarkar (142), C.T. Sarwate (101), M.M. Jagdale (164), C.K. Nayudu (101), B.B. Nimbalkar (172), and R. Pratap Singh (100).

The lowest first-class innings total in India is 21 by the Muslims against the Europeans at Poona during the Quadrangular Tournament of 1915–16.

BATTING RECORDS

The highest individual innings in Indian first-class cricket is 443 not out by B.B. Nimbalkar for Maharashtra against Kathiawar at Poona on 16–18 December 1948. A 29-year-old right-handed batsman, Bhausahib Nimbalkar batted for 8 hours 14 minutes, hit a six and 49 fours, and shared in a second-wicket partnership of 455 with K.V. Bhandarkar which remained the world record until 1974. He is the only batsman to score 400 in a first-class innings and not to be selected for Test cricket. Maharashtra had reached 826 for 4 at lunch on the third day, with Nimbalkar just nine runs short of Bradman's record score (452 not out), when Kathiawar (238) refused to return to the field and thus conceded this Ranji Trophy match. His score is the fourth-highest in all first-class cricket.

Maharashtra were involved in another record batting feat, also at Poona, in that season's Ranji Trophy championship when they played Bombay in the semi-final on 5–11 March 1949. That match produced the unique record of three batsmen scoring a century in each innings: U.M. Merchant (143 and

156) and D.G. Phadkar (131 and 160) for Bombay, and M.R. Rege (133 and 100) for Maharashtra. Played over seven days, the match established **the world record aggregate of runs for all first-class cricket**: 2376 at an average of 64.2 runs per wicket.

The only instance of two batsmen scoring triple centuries in the same first-class innings took place at Panjim on 20–22 January 1989 when Woorkeri Raman (313 in 575 minutes) and Arjan Kripal Singh (302* in 560 minutes) shared a sixth-wicket partnership of 356 for Tamil Nadu against Goa.

The highest number of runs scored by any batsman in all first-class cricket between one dismissal and the next is 709 by K.C. Ibrahim of Bombay.

He achieved this record sequence in 1947–48 with scores of 218*, 36*, 234*, 77* and 144.

The world record partnership for any wicket in all first-class cricket was established in the final of the Ranji Trophy tournament at Baroda played on 7–11 March 1947. Baroda had scored 91 for 3 in reply to Holkar's 337, when Gul Mahomed joined Vijay Hazare in a partnership of 577 made in 533 minutes. It ended with Gul Mahomed's dismissal for an audacious 319, but Hazare went on to score 288 in 628 minutes. Holkar used nine bowlers during the record stand and, after eventually dismissing Baroda for 784, were themselves bowled out for 173 to lose by an innings and 409 runs.

Mohammed Azharuddin, of India and Hyderabad (Popperfoto)

HIGHEST PARTNERSHIPS IN INDIAN FIRST-CLASS CRICKET

Wkt	Runs	Batsmen (scores)	Match	Venue	Season
1st	464	R. Sehgal (216), R. Lamba (312)	Delhi v Himachal Pradesh	Delhi	1994–95
2nd	475	Zahir Alam (257), L.S. Rajput (239)	Assam v Tripura	Gauhati	1991–92
3rd	410*	R.S. Modi (156*), L. Amarnath (262)	India in England v Rest	Calcutta	1946–47
4th	577	V.S. Hazare (288), Gul Mahomed (319)	Baroda v Holkar	Baroda	1946–47
5th	360	U.M. Merchant (217), M.N. Raiji (170)	Bombay v Hyderabad	Bombay	1947–48
6th	371	V.M. Merchant (359*), R.S. Modi (168)	Bombay v Maharashtra	Bombay	1943–44
7th	460	Bhupinder Singh jr (297), P. Dharmani (202*)	Punjab v Delhi	Delhi	1994–95
8th	236	C.T. Sarwate (235), R.P. Singh (88)	Holkar v Delhi	Delhi	1949–50
9th	245	V.S. Hazare (316*), N.D. Nagarwalla (98)	Maharashtra v Baroda	Poona	1939–40
10th	233	A.K. Sharma (259*), Maninder Singh (78)	Delhi v Bombay	Bombay	1991–92

The partnerships for the second, fourth and seventh wickets are world first-class records.

BOWLING RECORDS

The best innings analysis in first-class cricket in India is 10 for 20 by P.M. Chatterjee for Bengal against Assam in a Ranji Trophy match at Jorhat in January 1957. Aged 29, Premansu Chatterjee, a versatile left-arm bowler who could swing a new ball at medium pace or spin leg-breaks, was responsible for dismissing Assam for 54. Bengal's handy lead of 451 was soon converted into an innings victory, but they were to lose their 'drawn' semi-final on the spin of a coin. Only two bowlers, Hedley Verity and George Geary, have taken ten wickets more cheaply.

The record match analysis in Indian first-class cricket is 16 for 99 by Anil Kumble for Karnataka at Tellicherry on 16–17 January 1995. His leg-breaks and top-spinners returned analyses of 8 for 58 and 8 for 41 as Kerala were dismissed for 124 and 109 in a south zone Ranji Trophy match.

The best match analysis in Indian domestic first-class cricket is 16 for 154 by Pradeep Sunderam at Jodhpur on 17–19 November 1985. Opening the Rajasthan attack aganst Vidarbha on a matting pitch, he bowled unchanged throughout the first innings to take 10 for 78 in 22 overs. A 25-year-old right-arm medium-fast bowler, he was only the third Indian to take all ten wickets in a first-class innings: he emulated the feats of P.M. Chatterjee (above) and S.P. Gupte (10 for 78 for Bombay v Pakistan Services and Bahawalpur at Bombay in 1954–55). Sunderam, whose father had opened India's bowling in two Tests against New Zealand in 1955–56, added six more wickets from another 22 overs toil in the second innings to gain his team a tense victory by 9 runs.

The world record for the most balls bowled and most runs conceded in any first-class match are held by C.S. Nayudu. Both records were set in the Ranji Trophy Final at Bombay on 4–8 March 1945. Representing Holkar, he bowled 152.5 six-ball overs (917 balls) of leg-breaks and googlies and conceded 428 runs as Bombay amassed scores of 462 and 764 (the second-highest second innings total in all first-class cricket). His full analyses were 64.5–10–153–6 and 88–15–275–5. Holkar replied with 360 and 492, Denis Compton, in India on wartime service, contributing 249 not out. A local businessman had promised Denis 100 rupees (about £7.50) for every run he scored over 100. Exhausted after his marathon innings in extreme heat and humidity, but elated by the handsome reward his score had earned, 'Compo' was dismayed to receive a message from his benefactor. It read simply: 'Very sorry, Mister Compton. I have been called away to Calcutta on very urgent business!'

WICKET-KEEPING RECORDS

The most dismissals by a wicket-keeper in a first-class innings in India is seven, the record being set by Sunil Benjamin when he held six catches and made one stumping for the Central Zone against the North in the final of the Duleep Trophy at the Brabourne Stadium, Bombay, in December 1973. This feat was emulated by Bob Taylor for England when he equalled the world Test match record by catching seven Indian batsmen at the Wankhede Stadium, Bombay, on the first day of the Golden Jubilee Test (15 February 1980). By holding another three catches in the second innings, Taylor set a new world Test record and a new first-class record for matches in India (*since equalled*).

Cricket Curiosities
B.K. ('Budhi') Kunderan, a wicket-keeper, opened India's batting and bowling against England at Edgbaston, Birmingham, in July 1967. With two of India's new-ball bowlers unavailable because of injury, Kunderan (4-0-13-0) was given his only bowl in first-class matches on that tour.

FIELDING RECORDS

The most catches taken in the field in a first-class innings in India is six by L.M.R. Deas for the Europeans against the Parsees in the Presidency Match at the Gymkhana Ground, Poona on 16 September 1898.

The Indian record for the most catches by a non-wicket-keeper in a first-class match is eight by F.G. Travers for the Europeans against the Parsees in a Bombay Quadrangular match on 3–5 December 1923.

THE BOMBAY PENTANGULAR

Until 1946 this annual tournament took pride of place in India's domestic fixture list. Originated in 1892 as the Presidency Match between the Europeans and the Parsees (the earliest Indian cricketers), the ultimate Pentangular Tournament was evolved by the addition of the Hindus (1907), the Mohammedans, or Muslims (1912), and The Rest (1937). Because of political agitation the tournament was abandoned as a major event after the 1945–46 season.

THE RANJI TROPHY

This championship was instituted in 1934 to commemorate the great Cambridge University, Sussex and England cricketer, 'Ranji' – Prince Kumar Shri Ranjitsinhji, the Jam Sahib of Nawanagar – who had died the previous year. Since 1946 it has been India's premier championship.

Between 1959 and 1973, Bombay established the world record for most consecutive national championship wins by winning the final in 15 successive seasons. Their record run was ended at Bangalore on 18 March 1974 when Karnataka defeated them in the semi-final by virtue of a first innings lead of 78 runs.

The 1982 final, played at the Feroz Shah Kotla Ground, Delhi, on 24–29 March between Delhi and Karnataka, was the most extraordinary match in the history of the Ranji Trophy. Delhi, confronted by the astronomical total of 705, overhauled their objective with two wickets to spare and thus won the championship on first innings after the contest had been allowed to continue into an extra (sixth) day. The match produced two world records: **the highest first innings aggregate (1412) in all first-class cricket, and the first time that a side scoring 700 had been led on first innings.**

RANJI TROPHY CHAMPIONS

1934–35 Bombay
1935–36 Bombay
1936–37 Nawanagar
1937–38 Hyderabad
1938–39 Bengal
1939–40 Maharashtra
1940–41 Maharashtra
1941–42 Bombay
1942–43 Baroda
1943–44 W. India States
1944–45 Bombay
1945–46 Holkar
1946–47 Baroda
1947–48 Holkar
1948–49 Bombay
1949–50 Baroda
1950–51 Holkar
1951–52 Bombay
1952–53 Holkar
1953–54 Bombay
1954–55 Madras
1955–56 Bombay
1956–57 Bombay
1957–58 Baroda
1958–59 Bombay
1959–60 Bombay
1960–61 Bombay
1961–62 Bombay
1962–63 Bombay
1963–64 Bombay
1964–65 Bombay
1965–66 Bombay
1966–67 Bombay
1967–68 Bombay
1968–69 Bombay
1969–70 Bombay
1970–71 Bombay
1971–72 Bombay
1972–73 Bombay
1973–74 Karnataka
1974–75 Bombay
1975–76 Bombay
1976–77 Bombay
1977–78 Karnataka
1978–79 Delhi
1979–80 Delhi
1980–81 Bombay
1981–82 Delhi
1982–83 Karnataka
1983–84 Bombay
1984–85 Bombay
1985–86 Delhi
1986–87 Hyderabad
1987–88 Tamil Nadu
1988–89 Delhi
1989–90 Bengal
1990–91 Haryana
1991–92 Delhi
1992–93 Punjab
1993–94 Bombay
1994–95 Bombay

THE DULEEP TROPHY

An inter-zonal tournament introduced in 1961 and named after Ranji's nephew, K.S. Duleepsinhji, who also played for Cambridge University, Sussex and England. Played early in the season on a knock-out basis, the Duleep Trophy frequently draws attention to new candidates for Test matches and tours overseas. In 1963–64 and 1988–89 the Trophy was shared when rain prevented a first innings decision.

DULEEP TROPHY CHAMPIONS

1961–62 West
1962–63 West
1963–64 South/West
1964–65 West
1965–66 South
1966–67 South
1967–68 South
1968–69 West
1969–70 West
1970–71 South
1971–72 Central
1962–73 West
1973–74 North
1974–75 South
1975–76 South
1976–77 West
1977–78 West
1978–79 North
1979–80 North
1980–81 West
1981–82 West
1982–83 North
1983–84 North
1984–85 South
1985–86 West
1986–87 South
1987–88 North
1988–89 North/West
1989–90 South
1990–91 North
1991–92 North
1992–93 North
1993–94 North
1994–95 North

First-Class Cricket in Pakistan

First-Class Cricket in Pakistan

First-class cricket was played in the various provinces of NW India and Bengal before 1947 when they became partitioned from India to form the two wings of Jinnah's Muslim state of Pakistan. The following cricket associations already existed: Northern India (renamed Punjab), Sind, and the North-West Frontier Province.

Although cricket was not immediately affected by partition and two players, Amir Elahi and Gul Mahomed, who were subsequently to represent Pakistan toured Australia with India in 1947–48, events soon combined to separate cricket as well. **The first first-class match in Pakistan after partition** was a drawn encounter between Punjab University and the Governor's XI staged at Lahore's Lawrence Gardens (Bagh-i-Jinnah) Ground on 6–8 February 1948. Maqsood Ahmed's 116 for the University was **the first hundred in Pakistan's first-class history after partition.**

The first Pakistan representative team to take the field drew with West Indies at Lahore on 26–29 November 1948. Three years later the MCC team interrupted their Test series in India to play four first-class matches and one minor game in Pakistan, and lost the second of two unofficial Tests. **Pakistan's first victory against a country of full Test status** was thus gained at Karachi on 2 December 1951.

Pakistan's first official overseas tour was to Ceylon where they won both the unofficial Test matches played at the Colombo Oval in March 1949.

The Board of Control for Cricket in Pakistan (BCCP) was formed on 1 May 1949. Sponsored by India and seconded by the MCC, Pakistan were admitted to full membership of the ICC (and thus awarded full Test status) on 28 July 1952. On 16 October of that year, Pakistan entered the official Test arena against India at Feroz Shah Kotla, Delhi. Although beaten in that match, they gained their first victory ten days later in the Second Test at Lucknow. At The Oval in August 1954, they became **the first country to win a Test match on their first tour of England.**

Although the Karachi Quadrangular Tournament was revived, it was not until 1953 that Pakistan's first national championship, the Qaid-e-Azam Trophy, was inaugurated.

TEAM RECORDS

The highest total in first-class cricket in Pakistan is 951 for 7 declared by Sind against Baluchistan at the National Stadium, Karachi, in a Qaid-e-Azam Trophy match on 18–20 February 1974. The innings, in reply to Baluchistan's 93, was dominated by the Sind captain, Aftab Baloch, who scored 428 in 584 minutes, hitting 25 fours. Sind's eventual margin of victory – an innings and 575 runs – is the sixth largest in all first-class cricket. Their total has been exceeded at first-class level only by Victoria, with scores of 1107 and 1059 in inter-state matches at Melbourne in the 1920s.

The most one-sided cricket match ever played was the Ayub Trophy fixture between Railways and Dera Ismail Khan at Lahore on 2–4 December 1964. After batting until lunch on the third day for 910 for 6 declared, Railways dismissed the visitors for 32 and 27 to win by an innings and 851 runs – **the largest margin of victory in all first-class cricket.** Pervez Akhtar contributed 337 not out to the Railways' total to establish **a world record for the highest maiden hundred in first-class cricket.** Dera Ismail Khan's second innings total of 27 and match aggregate of 59 are the lowest in first-class matches in Pakistan. Their two innings lasted only 28 overs in total and two different pairs of bowlers operated unchanged in the two innings.

BATTING RECORDS

The highest individual innings in all first-class cricket is 499 by Hanif Mohammad for Karachi against Bahawalpur at the Parsee Institute Ground, Karachi, on 8–11 January 1959. The match, a semi-final of the Qaid-e-Azam Trophy, was played on a coir matting pitch. After the visitors had been dismissed for 185, Hanif, aged 24 and the second of four brothers to represent his country in official Tests, opened the Karachi innings and scored 25 in 40 minutes before stumps. Next day he added another 230 runs in five hours. He batted on throughout the third day, overtook the previous world record score of 452 not out by Bradman, and, according to the scoreboard, had reached 496 with about two minutes of the session left. Off the last ball of the over he attempted a quick single to keep the strike and so complete his 500 off the final over. He was run out and returned to the pavilion to discover that the scoreboard was wrong and that he was only one run short of his unique target. Karachi, captained by Hanif's elder brother Wazir, who had also scored a century, declared at that total (772 for 7), and bowled out Bahawalpur for 108 to win by an innings and 479 runs. They went on to win the final against Services by 279 runs, Hanif scoring 130 in the first innings to total 712 runs in the tournament for an average of 178. His 499 occupied 635 minutes and included 64 fours.

Nowadays, the Parsee Institute Ground stages only minor youth matches, with grazing goats its only groundstaff.

The slowest century in all first-class cricket was scored in 557 minutes by Mudassar Nazar (114) for Pakistan in the First Test against England at the Gaddafi Stadium, Lahore, on 14–15 December 1977. Opening the innings in his second Test match, Mudassar scored 52 in 330 minutes on the first day. A minor riot interrupted his innings when he took his 99th run and confused the less mathematically adept spectators. With tea being taken, 45 minutes elapsed before his innings resumed and he took a further ten minutes to acquire the final single, reaching his hundred out of 306 for 3 in 9 hours 17 minutes.

Mudassar Nazar: slowest century in first-class cricket (Allsport)

When he was eventually caught off a hard return drive to the bowler, Mudassar had batted 591 minutes for 114 runs, a marathon which included 12 fours and 42 singles. His father, Nazar Mohammad, had opened the batting in Pakistan's first Test series, and, in the Second Test against India at Lucknow, had carried his bat through the innings and become **the first player to be on the field for an entire Test match.**

HIGHEST PARTNERSHIPS IN PAKISTAN FIRST-CLASS CRICKET

Wkt	Runs	Batsmen (scores)	Match	Venue	Season
1st	561	Waheed Mirza (324), Mansoor Akhtar (224*)	Karachi Whites v Quetta	Karachi	1976–77
2nd	426	Arshad Pervez (220), Mohsin Khan (220)	Habib Bank v Income Tax Dept.	Lahore	1977–78
3rd	456	Khalid Irtiza (290), Aslam Ali (236)	United Bank v Multan	Karachi	1975–76
4th	346	Zafar Altaf (268), Majid Khan (241)	Lahore Greens v Bahawalpur	Lahore	1965–66
5th	355	Altaf Shah (276), Tariq Bashir (196)	HBFC v Multan	Multan	1976–77
6th	353	Salahuddin (256), Zaheer Abbas (197)	Karachi v East Pakistan	Karachi	1968–69
7th	308	Waqar Hassan (189), Imtiaz Ahmed (209)	Pakistan v New Zealand	Lahore	1955–56
8th	249*	Shaukat Mirza (160*), Akram Raza (145*)	Habib Bank v PNSC	Lahore	1993–94
9th	207	Mahmood Hamid (202), Athar Laeeq (80)	Karachi Whites v Lahore	Karachi	1993–94
10th	196*	Nadim Yousuf (202*), Maqsood Kundi (109*)	MCB v National Bank	Lahore	1981–82

The partnership for the first wicket is a world first-class record.
HBFC – House Building Finance Corporation. MCB – Muslim Commercial Bank. PNSC – Pakistan National Shipping Corporation.

BOWLING RECORDS

The first Pakistani bowler to take all ten wickets in a first-class innings was Shahid Mahmood, a 30-year-old opening batsman and left-arm bowler of medium pace. Playing for Karachi Whites in a home Qaid-e-Azam Trophy match at the National Stadium against Khairpur on 6 September 1969, Shahid recorded a second innings analysis of 25–5–58–10 – still the most economical ten-wicket first-class analysis in Pakistan. Dismissed for 146, Khairpur lost by an innings and 56 runs in two days. In his only Test appearance, against England at Nottingham seven years earlier, Shahid had failed to take a wicket.

The youngest bowler to take all ten wickets in a first-class innings anywhere is Imran Adil. A right-arm fast-medium bowler, he was 18 years 345 days old when he took 10 for 92 for his birthplace, Bahawalpur, in a BCCP Patron's Trophy match against Faisalabad at the Iqbal Stadium, Faisalabad on 30–31 October 1989.

The best match analysis in first-class cricket in Pakistan is 15 for 76 by Fazal Mahmood for Punjab against Services in a semi-final of the Qaid-e-Azam Trophy at Lahore on 7–12 February 1957. He returned figures of 6 for 35 and 9 for 43 as Services (112 and 99) lost by an innings. Punjab went on to defeat Karachi in the final a month later. Now a senior police inspector, Fazal Mahmood is arguably Pakistan's greatest ever bowler. At a fast medium pace he could swing and cut the ball both ways off a nagging length, and could be virtually unplayable on matting or rain-affected turf pitches.

WICKET-KEEPING RECORDS

The world record for the most dismissals in any first-class innings is nine by Tahir Rashid for Habib Bank in a BCCP Patron's Trophy match against Pakistan Automobile Company at Gujranwala's Municipal Stadium on 28–29 November 1992. The 32-year-old Karachi-born wicket-keeper held nine catches and made one stumping in PACO's only innings.

FIELDING RECORDS

The most catches taken in the field in a first-class innings in Pakistan is six. The record was set by Gulfraz Khan in a Qaid-e-Azam Trophy match for Railways against the Muslim Commercial Bank at Sialkot in November 1981. His performance was equalled by Masood Anwar in a BCCP Patron's Trophy match for Rawalpindi against Lahore Division at the Pindi Club Ground in October 1983 during the course of his setting **the Pakistan first-class match record of eight catches in the field.**

TEN DISMISSALS IN A MATCH

	Ct	St	Match	Venue	Season
Taslim Arif	6	4	National Bank v Punjab	Lahore	1978–79
Arifuddin	9	1	United Bank v Karachi B	Karachi	1978–79
Kamal Najamuddin	9	1	Karachi v Lahore	Multan	1982–83
Azhar Abbas	7	3	Bahawalpur v Lahore Greens	Bahawalpur	1983–84
Anil Dalpat	8	2	Karachi v United Bank	Lahore	1985–86
Imran Zia	10	0	Bahawalpur v Faisalabad	Faisalabad	1989–90

QAID-E-AZAM TROPHY

Pakistan's premier national championship did not come into being until six years after Partition. It was named after Pakistan's first Governor-General, the Qaid-e-Azam ('Great Leader'), Mohammad Ali Jinnah (1876–1948). Head of the All-India Muslim League and the main creator of Pakistan, Jinnah was a great cricket enthusiast.

PIA – Pakistan International Airlines
ADBP – Agricultural Development Bank of Pakistan

HOLDERS

1953–54 Bahawalpur
1954–55 Karachi
1956–57 Punjab
1957–58 Bahawalpur
1958–59 Karachi
1959–60 Karachi
1961–62 Karachi B
1962–63 Karachi A
1963–64 Karachi Blues
1964–65 Karachi Blues
1966–67 Karachi
1968–69 Lahore
1969–70 PIA
1970–71 Karachi Blues
1972–73 Railways
1973–74 Railways
1974–75 Punjab A
1975–76 National Bank

1976–77 United Bank
1977–78 Habib Bank
1978–79 National Bank
1979–80 PIA
1980–81 United Bank
1981–82 National Bank
1982–83 United Bank
1983–84 National Bank
1984–85 United Bank
1985–86 Karachi
1986–87 National Bank
1987–88 PIA
1988–89 ADBP
1989–90 PIA
1990–91 Karachi Whites
1991–92 Karachi Whites
1992–93 Karachi
1993–94 Lahore
1994–95 Allied Bank

First-Class Cricket in Sri Lanka

First-Class Cricket in Sri Lanka

Cricket was introduced to Ceylon in 1832 by the Rev Brooke Bailey. Arriving from Cambridge as assistant master at the Colombo Academy (now the Royal College), he immediately added cricket coaching to his duties.

Ceylon's first cricket club, the Colombo Cricket Club, was formed in 1832. According to the *Colombo Journal* of 19 September 1832, the inaugural meeting, attended by between 40 and 50 members, framed rules and appointed a committee.

The first cricket match to be played in Ceylon was reported in the *Colombo Journal* of 3 November 1832. The Colombo CC suffered a ten-wicket defeat at the hands of a section of the British Garrison (the 97th Regiment), at the Galle Face Ground.

Until 1873 when the Colts CC was formed, units of the British Garrison provided the Colombo CC's sole opposition. From 1880 to 1912 George Vanderspar organized and promoted Ceylon's cricket to international level. A millionaire businessman who played for Somerset and MCC, he captained the Colombo CC and scored the Club's first century. His MCC connections enabled him to persuade touring teams to break their journeys to and from Australia with a match in Colombo. These whistle-stop tours continued until 1965. Vanderspar organized **the first tour by a Ceylon team overseas**, the Colombo CC visiting Calcutta in 1884–85.

The first overseas side to visit Ceylon was the All England team captained by the Hon I.F.W. Bligh on 13–14 October 1882. The tourists defeated a Colombo CC XVIII (all Englishmen) on first innings. Two days later, and 360 miles from Colombo, the tourists' ship *Pershawar* was rammed by a barque (*Glenroy*) and had to return to Ceylon for repairs and an inquiry. This allowed a second match to be played, Ivo Bligh's XI drawing with the Royal Dublin Fusiliers Officers. Both games were played on the Galle Face Ground at Colombo.

The first touring team to play first-class matches in Ceylon was the MCC in January and February 1927. Captained by A.E.R. Gilligan they played four games during an 18-week tour of the Indian sub-continent, during which they remained undefeated after 34 matches.

Ceylon's first centralized cricket administration was the Ceylon Cricket Association and was formed in 1922. The Ceylon Cricket Board of Control (formed 1948) merged with the Ceylon CA in 1965.

Sri Lanka's initial first-class tour was to England in 1975.

In 1988–89 the Lakspray Trophy tournament was accorded first-class status by the Board of Control for Cricket in Sri Lanka (BCCSL); prior to that season only matches involving first-class teams from overseas were considered first-class.

TEAM RECORDS

The highest total in first-class cricket in Sri Lanka is 549 for 8 wickets declared by the West Indians against Ceylon at the Colombo Oval (now the P. Saravanamuttu Stadium) on 22–23 January 1967. It included hundreds by Basil Butcher, Clive Lloyd and the captain, Gary Sobers.

The lowest total in first-class cricket in Sri Lanka is 31 by Kurunegala Youth against Sinhalese Sports Club in the 1993–94 Sara Trophy at the SSC Ground in Colombo.

BATTING RECORDS

The highest individual innings in Sri Lankan first-class cricket is 285 by Frank Worrell for a Commonwealth XI against Ceylon at the Colombo Oval on 16 February 1951. He batted only 274 minutes, hitting 5 sixes and 31 fours.

The highest innings by a Sri Lankan on home soil is 238 not out by Sri Lanka's current captain, Arjuna Ranatunga, for the Sinhalese Sports Club against Sebastianites Cricket and Athletic Club in Colombo during the 1992–93 Sara Trophy.

The first Sri Lankan batsman to score a hundred on first-class debut on home soil was M. Rodrigo. Opening Ceylon's second innings against the West Indians at the Colombo Oval on 20–21 February 1949, he carried his bat, contributing 135 not out towards a total of 318 in 382 minutes.

The first overseas batsman to score a hundred on

his first-class debut in Sri Lanka was Charles Barnett who made 116 in 125 minutes for the MCC against Ceylon at the Colombo Cricket Club Ground on 17 February 1934.

The first batsman to score a hundred in both innings of a first-class match in Sri Lanka was A.V. Mankad who made 105 and 100 not out for the Indians against the President's XI at Katugastota, Kandy, on 1–3 February 1974.

The highest first-class aggregate in a season is 1308 (average 62.28) by Aravinda de Silva for the Nondescripts and Sri Lanka in 1992–93.

The record for the most fifties in consecutive first-class innings is ten. Set by Ernest Tyldesley in 1926 and equalled by Don Bradman in 1947–48 and 1948, it was emulated in 1994–95 by Romesh Kaluwitharana for Galle and Western Province South.

Hashan Tillekeratne: record stand
(Allsport/Ben Radford)

HIGHEST PARTNERSHIPS IN SRI LANKAN FIRST-CLASS CRICKET

Wkt	Runs	Batsmen (scores)	Match	Venue	Season
1st	214	D. Ranatunga, A.A.W. Gunawardene	Sinhalese SC v Old Cambrians	Colombo	1989–90
2nd	289	W.A.M.P. Perera, T.P. Kodikara	Antonians v Rio SC	Colombo	1992–93
3rd	293	H.P. Tillekeratne, P.A. de Silva	President's XI v Sri Lanka U-23	Colombo	1992–93
4th	278	R.P.A.H. Wickramaratne, M.S. Atapattu	Sinhalese SC v Tamil Union	Colombo	1994–95
5th	301	F.M.M. Worrell, W.H.H. Sutcliffe	Commonwealth XI v Ceylon	Colombo	1950–51
6th	246 *	J.J. Crowe, R.J. Hadlee	New Zealand v Sri Lanka	Colombo	1986–87
7th	153	P.A. de Silva, A.G.D. Wickremasinghe	Nondescripts v Sinhalese SC	Colombo	1993–94
8th	160	P.B. Dassanayake, S. Silva	Sri Lanka U-23 v Sinhalese SC	Colombo	1992–93
9th	153	R. Wickramaratne, S. Munaweera	Colts v Singha SC	Colombo	1989–90
10th	118	A.W. Ekanayake, D. Amarasinghe	Kurunegala Youth v Antonians	Colombo	1991–92

BOWLING RECORDS

The best innings analysis in Sri Lankan first-class cricket is 10 for 41 in 19.2 overs by G.P. (Pramodya) Wickremasinghe in a Sara Trophy home match for Sinhalese Sports Club against Kalutara Physical Culture Club at Maitland Place, Colombo on 15 November 1991. Bowling right-arm fast-medium he skittled the visitors for 82 and recorded the only instance of a Sri Lankan bowler taking all ten wickets in any first-class match.

The best match analysis in Sri Lankan first-class cricket is 15 for 43 by Derek Underwood for J. Lister's International XI against the Ceylon President's XI at the Colombo Oval on 5–7 March 1968. A thunderstorm followed by blazing sun produced conditions ideally suited to the spin and swerve of the Kent and England left-hander. The home side were dismissed for 42 and 98, Underwood's innings analyses being 11.3–6–10–8 and 26.1–13–33–7.

The best match analysis by a Sri Lankan in first-class cricket is 15 for 91 by M.B. Halangoda in a

Lakspray Trophy match for Sinhalese SC against Singha SC on 2–4 February 1990. Bowling left-arm medium-fast, he returned innings figures of 8 for 64 and 7 for 27 at Colombo's Sinhalese Sports Club.

WICKET-KEEPING RECORDS

The most dismissals in an innings in Sri Lankan first-class cricket is six, the record being set by K.V. Bhandarkar for Holkar against Ceylon at the Colombo Oval on 17 April 1948. This record has been equalled on five occasions, most notably by L.R. (Lucky) Fernando, when he set a domestic first-class record, so far unequalled, by making ten dismissals in a match. Keeping for Moratuwa Sports Club in a Lakspray Trophy home match against Panadura SC on 26–28 January 1990, he held four catches in the first innings and six in the second.

S.A.R. (Amal) Silva set a world record by making 18 dismissals in consecutive Test matches (nine in each) for Sri Lanka against India in Colombo in August and September 1985. In the second match he also scored 111.

Cricket Curiosities
Sri Lanka's three Wettimuny brothers –
Sunil, Sidath and Mithra – had the
distinction of each opening the batting and
captaining their school, Ananda College,
and Colombo's premier cricket club, the
Sinhalese Sports Club. All three went on to
open the innings for their country in
representative matches

LAKSPRAY TROPHY

Sri Lanka's first domestic first-class competition was instituted in 1988–89 when the final rounds of Colombo's club championship were accorded that status, the champions being awarded the Lakspray Trophy.

HOLDERS

1988–89	Nondescripts
	Sinhalese SC
1989–90	Sinhalese SC

P. SARAVANAMUTTU ('SARA') TROPHY

In 1990 new sponsors, J and B, replaced the major club award with the Sara Trophy named after one of Ceylon's most eminent cricket administrators and benefactors.

HOLDERS

1990–91	Sinhalese SC
1991–92	Colts
1992–93	Sinhalese SC
1993–94	Nondescripts
1994–95	Sinhalese SC
	Bloomfield

SINGER TROPHY

An inter-provincial tournament was instituted for the Singer Trophy in 1989 to encourage the game's development throughout the country.

HOLDERS

1989–90	Western Province
1990–91	Western Province City
1991–92	Western Province North
1992–93	not held
1993–94	Western Province City
1994–95	Western Province City

First-Class Cricket in Zimbabwe

First-Class Cricket in Zimbabwe

Even though Zimbabwe is the newest of the ICC's full member countries, having been accorded Test match status on 8 July 1992, its cricket history is closely entwined with that of South Africa. It was the Hertfordshire empire-builder and diamond-mining entrepreneur Cecil Rhodes who, as prime minister of the Cape Colony, secured British extension in the territory that was to bear his name. Cricket was introduced there by employees of his chartered company. **The first cricket match to be played in Rhodesia** was between the Police and Civilians at Fort Salisbury in 1891, the Rhodesian Cricket Union being formed seven years later.

Although Rhodesia first competed in South Africa's national tournament for the Currie Cup in March 1905 (their **initial first-class match** being against Transvaal at Johannesburg), they did not reappear until 1929–30, and their sparse population prevented them from making a serious impact at cricket's higher levels until after the Second World War. They were withdrawn from the Currie Cup by the newly independent Zimbabwe government in 1980, appearing as 'Zimbabwe-Rhodesia' in their final season.

Touring teams visiting South Africa usually included Rhodesia on their itinerary, the country's **first home first-class match** being against H.D.G. Leveson-Gower's XI at Bulawayo in 1909–10.

It was not until 1993–94 that Zimbabwe's domestic matches were accorded first-class status, four teams (Mashonaland, Mashonaland Country Districts, Mashonaland U-24 and Matabeleland) competing for the Logan Cup.

LOGAN CUP WINNERS

1993–94	Mashonaland U-24
1994–95	Mashonaland

TEAM RECORDS

The highest total in first-class cricket in Zimbabwe is 600 for 6 wickets declared by the Sri Lankans against Mashonaland Country Districts at Harare in 1994–95.

David Houghton: Test record score for Zimbabwe (Allsport/Mike Hewitt)

The lowest total in first-class cricket in Zimbabwe is 56 by Zimbabwe against a Leicestershire XI at Salisbury on 8 March 1981.

BATTING RECORDS

The highest individual innings in Zimbabwean first-class cricket and Zimbabwe's record score at Test level is 266 by David Houghton in the Second Test against Sri Lanka at Queens Sports Club, Bulawayo on 20–21 October 1994. He batted for 11 hours 15 minutes, the longest innings played in Zimbabwe, faced 541 balls and hit 3 sixes and 35 fours.

The highest first-class aggregate in a season is 983 (average 57.82) by Grant Flower in 1994–95. His four hundreds included 201 not out in the First Test against Pakistan at Harare Sports Club, an innings which formed the backbone of Zimbabwe's record Test match total of 544 for 4 wickets declared and during which he shared with Andy Flower in the record partnership by brothers at Test level: 269 for the fourth wicket in 83 overs. Zimbabwe went on to gain their first Test victory in only their eleventh Test. Sadly, their heroic feats, including eight exceptional catches, were not televised as the Zimbabwe Cricket Union could not afford the fees levied by the national TV network to cover the series!

HIGHEST PARTNERSHIPS IN ZIMBABWEAN/RHODESIAN FIRST-CLASS CRICKET

Wkt	Runs	Batsmen (scores)	Match	Venue	Season
1st	261	D.J. McGlew, T.L. Goddard	Natal v Rhodesia	Bulawayo	1958–59
2nd	317*	R.G. Twose, Asif Din	Warwickshire v Mashonaland XI	Harare	1993–94
3rd	299	S. Ranatunga, P.A. de Silva	Sri Lankans v Mashonaland Country Districts	Harare	1994–95
4th	301	T.E. Bailey, P.B.H. May	MCC v Rhodesia	Salisbury	1956–57
5th	233*	G.W. Flower, G.J. Whittall	Zimbabwe v Pakistan	Harare	1994–95
6th	217*	H.P. Tillekeratne, A.G.D. Wickremasinghe	Sri Lanka B v Zimbabwe	Harare	1987–88
7th	177*	R.Benaud, A.K. Davidson	Australians v Rhodesia	Salisbury	1957–58
8th	175	I.P. Butchart, P.A. Strang	Mashonaland Country Districts v Matabeleland	Harare	1994–95
9th	268	J.B. Commins, N. Boje	South Africa A v Mashonaland	Harare	1994–95
10th	81	M. Prabhakar, R.R. Kulkarni	Young Indians v Zimbabwe	Harare	1983–84

BOWLING RECORDS

The best innings analysis in Zimbabwean first-class cricket is 9 for 71 by Mike Procter against Transvaal at Queens Ground, Bulawayo on 30 October 1972. Captaining Rhodesia, he claimed the first of his wickets during six overs with the new ball before bowling his side to victory in a 30-over spell of off-breaks.

First-Class Career Records

All records are complete to the end of the 1995 English season (18 September). Dates underlined denote the first half of an overseas season, ie 1971 means 1971–72.

The last column shows the number of seasons in which each batsman scored 1000 or more runs. J.B. Hobbs scored 1000 runs in each of 24 seasons in Britain and on two tours overseas.

Key to the less obvious team abbreviations:

CU   Cambridge University
EP   Eastern Province
G   Guyana
GW   Griqualand West
LI   Leeward Islands
N   Natal
ND   Northern Districts
NSW   New South Wales
NT   Northern Transvaal
OFS   Orange Free State
OU   Oxford University
PIA   Pakistan International Airlines
Q   Queensland
R   Rhodesia
SA   South Australia
T   Transvaal
WA   Western Australia
WP   Western Province

30 000 RUNS IN FIRST-CLASS MATCHES

		Career	I	NO	HS	Runs	Average	100	1000
J.B. Hobbs	Surrey	1905–1934	1315	106	316*	61 237	50.65	197	24+2
F.E. Woolley	Kent	1906–1938	1532	85	305*	58 969	40.75	145	28
E.H. Hendren	Middlesex	1907–1938	1300	166	301*	57 611	50.80	170	21+4
C.P. Mead	Hampshire	1905–1936	1340	185	280*	55 061	47.67	153	27
W.G. Grace	Gloucestershire	1865–1908	1493	105	344	54 896	39.55	126	28
W.R. Hammond	Gloucestershire	1920–1951	1005	104	336*	50 551	56.10	167	17+5
H. Sutcliffe	Yorkshire	1919–1945	1088	123	313	50 138	51.95	149	21+3
G. Boycott	Yorkshire/NT	1962–1986	1014	162	261*	48 426	56.83	151	23+3
T.W. Graveney	Glos/Worcs/Q	1948–<u>1971</u>	1223	159	258	47 793	44.91	122	20+2
T.W. Hayward	Surrey	1893–1914	1138	96	315*	43 551	41.79	104	20
D.L. Amiss	Warwickshire	1960–1987	1139	126	262*	43 423	42.86	102	23+1
M.C. Cowdrey	Kent/OU	1950–1976	1130	134	307	42 719	42.89	107	21+6
G.A. Gooch	Essex/WP	1973–1995	941	73	333	42 528	48.99	120	19+1
A. Sandham	Surrey	1911–<u>1937</u>	1000	79	325	41 284	44.82	107	18+2
L. Hutton	Yorkshire	1934–1960	814	91	364	40 140	55.51	129	12+5
M.J.K. Smith	Leics/OU/Warks	1951–1975	1091	139	204	39 832	41.84	69	19+1
W. Rhodes	Yorkshire/Patiala	1898–1930	1528	237	267*	39 802	30.83	58	20+1

		Career	I	NO	HS	Runs	Average	100	1000
J.H. Edrich	Surrey	1956–1978	979	104	310*	39 790	45.47	103	19+2
R.E.S. Wyatt	Warwicks/Worcs	1923–1957	1141	157	232	39 405	40.04	85	17+1
D.C.S. Compton	Middx/Holkar	1936–1964	839	88	300	38 942	51.85	123	14+3
G.E. Tyldesley	Lancashire	1909–1936	961	106	256*	38 874	45.46	102	18+1
J.T. Tyldesley	Lancashire	1895–1923	994	62	295*	37 897	40.66	86	19
K.W.R. Fletcher	Essex	1962–1988	1167	170	228*	37 665	37.77	63	20
C.G. Greenidge	Hants/Barbados	1970–1992	889	75	273*	37 354	45.88	92	15+2
J.W. Hearne	Middlesex	1909–1936	1025	116	285*	37 252	40.98	96	19
L.E.G. Ames	Kent	1926–1951	951	95	295	37 248	43.51	102	17
D. Kenyon	Worcestershire	1946–1967	1159	59	259	37 002	33.63	74	19
W.J. Edrich	Middlesex	1934–1958	964	92	267*	36 965	42.39	86	15
J.M. Parks	Sussex/Somerset	1949–1976	1227	172	205*	36 673	34.76	51	20
D. Denton	Yorkshire	1894–1920	1163	70	221	36 479	33.37	69	21
G.H. Hirst	Yorkshire	1891–1929	1215	151	341	36 323	34.13	60	19
I.V.A. Richards	Ll/Som/Q/Glam	1971–1993	796	63	322	36 212	49.40	114	14+3
A. Jones	Glam/WA/NT/N	1957–1983	1168	72	204*	36 049	32.89	56	23
W.G. Quaife	Warks/GW	1894–1928	1203	185	255*	36 012	35.37	72	24
R.E. Marshall	Barbados/Hants	1945–1972	1053	59	228*	35 725	35.94	68	18
G. Gunn	Nottinghamshire	1902–1932	1061	82	220	35 208	35.96	62	20
D.B. Close	Yorks/Somerset	1949–1986	1225	173	198	34 994	33.26	52	20
Zaheer Abbas	Karachi/PIA/Glos	1965–1986	768	92	274	34 843	51.54	108	11+6
J.G. Langridge	Sussex	1928–1955	984	66	250*	34 380	37.45	76	17
G.M. Turner	Otago/Worcs/ND	1964–1982	792	101	311*	34 346	49.70	103	15+3
C. Washbrook	Lancashire	1933–1964	906	107	251*	34 101	42.67	76	17+3
M. Leyland	Yorkshire/Patiala	1920–1948	932	101	263	33 660	40.50	80	17
H.T.W. Hardinge	Kent	1902–1933	1021	103	263*	33 519	36.51	75	18
M.W. Gatting	Middlesex	1975–1995	778	118	258	33 456	50.69	89	17+1
R. Abel	Surrey	1881–1904	1007	73	357*	33 124	35.46	74	14
A.I. Kallicharran	G/Warks/Q/T	1966–1990	834	86	243*	32 650	43.64	87	12+1
A.J. Lamb	WP/N'hants/OFS	1972–1995	772	108	294	32 502	48.94	89	13
C.A. Milton	Gloucestershire	1948–1974	1078	125	170	32 150	33.73	56	16
J.D.B. Robertson	Middlesex	1937–1959	897	46	331*	31 914	37.50	67	14+1
J. Hardstaff, jr	Notts/Auckland	1930–1955	812	94	266	31 847	44.35	83	13+1
J. Langridge	Sussex	1924–1953	1058	157	167	31 716	35.20	42	20
K.F. Barrington	Surrey	1953–1968	831	136	256	31 714	45.63	76	12+3
C.H. Lloyd	Guyana/Lancs	1963–1986	730	96	242*	31 232	49.26	79	10+4
Mushtaq Mohammad	Karachi/PIA/Northants	1956–1985	843	104	303*	31 091	42.07	72	12+3
C.B. Fry	OU/Sussex/Hants	1892–1921	658	43	258*	30 886	50.22	94	12
D. Brookes	Northamptonshire	1934–1959	925	70	257	30 874	36.10	71	17
P. Holmes	Yorkshire	1913–1935	810	84	315*	30 573	42.11	67	14+1
R.T. Simpson	Sind/Notts	1944–1963	852	55	259	30 546	38.32	64	13+1
K.G. Suttle	Sussex	1949–1971	1064	92	204*	30 225	31.09	49	17
L.G. Berry	Leicestershire	1924–1951	1056	57	232	30 225	30.25	45	18

D.G. Bradman holds the record for the highest career average in first-class cricket with 95.14 runs per innings. K.S. Ranjitsinhji achieved the highest average by any batsman whose career was based in England. Their full details:

		Career	I	NO	HS	Runs	Average	100	1000
D.G. Bradman	NSW/SA	1927–1948	338	43	452*	28 067	95.14	117	4+12
K.S. Ranjitsinhji	CU/Sussex	1893–1920	500	62	285*	24 692	56.37	72	11+1

100 HUNDREDS IN FIRST-CLASS MATCHES

		Career	Innings	100	Innings per 100
J.B. Hobbs	Surrey	1905–1934	1315	197	6.6
E.H. Hendren	Middlesex	1907–1938	1300	170	7.6
W.R. Hammond	Gloucestershire	1920–1951	1005	167	6.0
C.P. Mead	Hampshire	1905–1936	1340	153	8.7
G. Boycott	Yorkshire/NT	1962–1986	1014	151	6.7
H. Sutcliffe	Yorkshire	1919–1945	1088	149	7.3
F.E. Woolley	Kent	1906–1938	1532	145	10.5
L. Hutton	Yorkshire	1934–1960	814	129	6.3
W.G. Grace	Gloucestershire	1865–1908	1493	126	11.8
D.C.S. Compton	Middlesex/Holkar	1936–1964	839	123	6.8
T.W. Graveney	Glos/Worcs/Queensland	1948–1971	1223	122	10.0
G.A. Gooch	Essex/WP	1973–1995	941	120	7.8
D.G. Bradman	NSW/South Australia	1927–1948	338	117	2.8
I.V.A. Richards	Leewards/Som/Q/Glam	1971–1993	796	114	6.9
Zaheer Abbas	Karachi/PIA/Glos	1965–1986	768	108	7.1
A. Sandham	Surrey	1911–1937	1000	107	9.3
M.C. Cowdrey	Kent/OU	1950–1976	1130	107	10.5
T.W. Hayward	Surrey	1893–1914	1138	104	10.9
G.M. Turner	Otago/Worcestershire	1964–1982	792	103	7.6
J.H. Edrich	Surrey	1956–1978	979	103	9.5
L.E.G. Ames	Kent	1926–1951	951	102	9.3
G.E. Tyldesley	Lancashire	1909–1936	961	102	9.4
D.L. Amiss	Warwickshire	1960–1987	1139	102	11.1

2000 WICKETS IN FIRST-CLASS MATCHES

		Career	Runs	Wickets	Average	100W Season
W. Rhodes	Yorkshire/Patiala	1898–1930	69 993	4187	16.71	23
A.P. Freeman	Kent	1914–1936	69 577	3776	18.42	17
C.W.L. Parker	Gloucestershire	1903–1935	63 817	3278	19.46	16
J.T. Hearne	Middlesex	1888–1923	54 352	3061	17.75	15
T.W.J. Goddard	Gloucestershire	1922–1952	59 116	2979	19.84	16
W.G. Grace	Gloucestershire	1865–1908	51 545	2876	17.92	10
A.S. Kennedy	Hampshire	1907–1936	61 034	2874	21.23	15
D. Shackleton	Hampshire	1948–1969	53 303	2857	18.65	20
G.A.R. Lock	Surrey/Leics/WA	1946–1970	54 709	2844	19.23	14
F.J. Titmus	Middx/Surrey/OFS	1949–1982	63 313	2830	22.37	16
M.W. Tate	Sussex	1912–1937	50 571	2784	18.16	14 †
G.H. Hirst	Yorkshire	1891–1929	51 282	2739	18.72	15
C. Blythe	Kent	1899–1914	42 136	2506	16.81	14
D.L. Underwood	Kent	1963–1987	49 993	2465	20.28	10
W.E. Astill	Leicestershire	1906–1939	57 783	2431	23.76	9
J.C. White	Somerset	1909–1937	43 759	2356	18.57	14
W.E. Hollies	Warwickshire	1932–1957	48 656	2323	20.94	14
F.S. Trueman	Yorkshire	1949–1969	42 154	2304	18.29	12
J.B. Statham	Lancashire	1950–1968	36 999	2260	16.36	13
R.T.D. Perks	Worcestershire	1930–1955	53 770	2233	24.07	16

		Career	Runs	Wickets	Average	100W Season
J. Briggs	Lancashire	1879–1900	35 431	**2221**	15.95	12
D.J. Shepherd	Glamorgan	1950–1972	47 302	**2218**	21.32	12
E.G. Dennett	Gloucestershire	1903–1926	42 571	**2147**	19.82	12
T. Richardson	Surrey/Somerset	1892–1905	38 794	**2104**	18.43	10
T.E. Bailey	Essex/CU	1945–1967	48 170	**2082**	23.13	9
R. Illingworth	Yorkshire/Leics	1951–1983	42 023	**2072**	20.28	10
F.E. Woolley	Kent	1906–1938	41 066	**2068**	19.85	8
N. Gifford	Worcs/Warwicks	1960–1988	48 731	**2068**	23.56	4
G. Geary	Leicestershire	1912–1938	41 339	**2063**	20.03	11
D.V.P. Wright	Kent	1932–1957	49 307	**2056**	23.98	10
J.A. Newman	Hampshire/Canterbury	1906–1930	51 111	**2032**	25.15	9
A. Shaw	Notts/Sussex	1864–1897	24 580	**2028** ††	12.12	9
S. Haigh	Yorkshire	1895–1913	32 091	**2012**	15.94	11

† Including 116 wickets on MCC tour of India and Ceylon in 1926–1927.
†† Including one wicket for which no analysis is available.

1000 WICKET-KEEPING DISMISSALS

		Career	Dismissals	Ct	St
R.W. Taylor	Derbyshire	1960–1988	**1649**	1473	176
J.T. Murray	Middlesex	1952–1975	**1527**	1270	257
H. Strudwick	Surrey	1902–1927	**1497**	1242	255
A.P.E. Knott	Kent/Tasmania	1964–1985	**1344**	1211	133
F.H. Huish	Kent	1895–1914	**1310**	933	377
B. Taylor	Essex	1949–1973	**1294**	1083	211
D. Hunter	Yorkshire	1889–1909	**1253**	906	347
H.R. Butt	Sussex	1890–1912	**1228**	953	275
J.H. Board	Glos/Hawke's Bay	1891–1914	**1207**	852	355
H. Elliott	Derbyshire	1920–1947	**1206**	904	302
J.M. Parks	Sussex/Somerset	1949–1976	**1181**	1088	93
R. Booth	Yorkshire/Worcs	1951–1970	**1126**	948	178
L.E.G. Ames	Kent	1926–1951	**1121**	703	418
D.L. Bairstow	Yorkshire/GW	1970–1990	**1099**	961	138
G. Duckworth	Lancashire	1923–1947	**1096**	753	343
H.W. Stephenson	Somerset	1948–1964	**1082**	748	334
J.G. Binks	Yorkshire	1955–1975	**1071**	895	176
T.G. Evans	Kent	1939–1969	**1066**	816	250
A. Long	Surrey/Sussex	1960–1980	**1046**	922	124
G.O. Dawkes	Leics/Derbyshire	1937–1961	**1043**	895	148
R.W. Tolchard	Leicestershire	1965–1983	**1037**	912	125
W.L. Cornford	Sussex	1921–1947	**1017**	675	342

Catches taken in the field are included.

500 CATCHES BY NON-WICKET-KEEPERS

		Career	Catches
F.E. Woolley	Kent	1906–1938	1018
W.G. Grace	Gloucestershire	1865–1908	887
G.A.R. Lock	Surrey/Leics/WA	1946–1970	830
W.R. Hammond	Gloucestershire	1920–1951	819
D.B. Close	Yorkshire/Somerset	1949–1986	813
J.G. Langridge	Sussex	1928–1955	784
W. Rhodes	Yorkshire/Patiala	1898–1930	764
C.A. Milton	Gloucestershire	1948–1974	758
E.H. Hendren	Middlesex	1907–1938	754
P.M. Walker	Glamorgan/Transvaal/WP	1956–1972	697
J. Tunnicliffe	Yorkshire	1891–1907	695
J. Seymour	Kent	1900–1926	675
C.P. Mead	Hampshire	1905–1936	671
K.W.R. Fletcher	Essex	1962–1988	644
M.C. Cowdrey	Kent/OU	1950–1976	638
M.J. Stewart	Surrey	1954–1972	634
P.J. Sainsbury	Hampshire	1954–1976	617
P.J. Sharpe	Yorkshire/Derbyshire	1956–1976	617
K.J. Grieves	NSW/Lancashire	1945–1964	610
E.G. Hayes	Surrey/Leics	1896–1926	609
G.H. Hirst	Yorkshire	1891–1929	604
G.R.J. Roope	Surrey/GW	1964–1986	602
P.G.H. Fender	Sussex/Surrey	1910–1936	600
A.S.M. Oakman	Sussex	1947–1968	594
M.J.K. Smith	Leics/OU/Warwicks	1951–1975	593
R. Abel	Surrey	1881–1904	586
A.O. Jones	CU/Nottinghamshire	1892–1914	577
D.C. Morgan	Derbyshire	1950–1969	572
P.H. Parfitt	Middlesex	1956–1974	564
G.R. Cox	Sussex	1895–1928	551
T.W. Graveney	Glos/Worcs/Q	1948–1971	550
J.V. Wilson	Yorkshire	1946–1963	548
D.S. Steele	Northants/Derbyshire	1963–1984	546
L.C. Braund	Surrey/Somerset	1896–1920	545
A.E. Relf	Sussex/Auckland	1900–1921	537
A.S. Kennedy	Hampshire	1907–1936	530
W.J. Edrich	Middlesex	1934–1958	529
G.A. Gooch	Essex/WP	1973–1995	525
C.T. Radley	Middlesex	1964–1987	517
C.G. Greenidge	Hampshire/Barbados	1970–1992	516
K.F. Barrington	Surrey	1953–1968	515
D.B. Carr	Derbyshire/OU	1945–1968	500

Catches taken during occasional wicket-keeping appearances are included.

10 000 RUNS AND 1000 WICKETS
IN FIRST-CLASS MATCHES

		Career	Runs	Wickets	Doubles
Arnold, E.G.	Worcestershire	1899–1913	15 853	1069	4
Astill, W.E.	Leicestershire	1906–1939	22 731	2431	9
Bailey, T.E.	Essex/OU	1945–1967	28 641	2082	8
Birkenshaw, J.	Yorkshire/Leics/Worcs	1958–1981	12 780	1073	–
Botham, I.T.	Somerset/Worcs/Q/Durham	1974–1993	19 399	1172	–
Braund, L.C.	Surrey/Somerset	1896–1920	17 801	1114	3
Briggs, J.	Lancashire	1879–1900	14 092	2221	–
Brown, A.S.	Gloucestershire	1953–1976	12 851	1230	–
Brown, F.R.	CU/Surrey/Northants	1930–1961	13 325	1221	2
Carrick, P.	Yorkshire/EP/NT	1970–1993	10 300	1081	–
Cartwright, T.W.	Warwicks/Somerset/Glamorgan	1952–1977	13 710	1536	1
Close, D.B.	Yorkshire/Somerset	1949–1986	34 994	1171	2
Cox, G.R.	Sussex	1895–1928	14 643	1843	–
Douglas, J.W.H.T.	Essex	1901–1930	24 531	1893	5
Eastman, L.C.	Essex/Otago	1920–1939	13 385	1006	–
Emburey, J.E.	Middlesex/WP	1973–1995	11 782	1577	–
Fender, P.G.H.	Sussex/Surrey	1910–1936	19 034	1894	6
Flowers, W.	Nottinghamshire	1877–1896	12 891	1188	1
Geary, G.	Leicestershire	1912–1938	13 504	2063	–
Giffen, G.	South Australia	1877–1903	11 758	1023	3
Grace, W.G.	Gloucestershire	1865–1908	54 896	2876	8
Gunn, J.R.	Nottinghamshire	1896–1932	24 557	1242	4
Hadlee, R.J.	Canterbury/Notts	1971–1990	12 052	1490	1
Haig, N.E.	Middlesex	1912–1936	15 220	1117	3
Haigh, S.	Yorkshire	1895–1913	11 715	2012	1
Hearne, A.	Kent	1884–1910	16 346	1160	–
Hearne, J.W.	Middlesex	1909–1936	37 252	1839	5
Hirst, G.H.	Yorkshire	1891–1929	36 323	2739	14
Howorth, R.	Worcestershire	1933–1951	11 479	1345	3
Illingworth, R.	Yorkshire/Leicestershire	1951–1983	24 134	2072	6
Imran Khan	Lahore/Worcs/OU/PIA/Sussex/NSW	1969–1991	17 771	1287	–
Intikhab Alam	Karachi/PIA/Surrey/Sind/Punjab	1957–1982	14 331	1571	–
Jenkins, R.O.	Worcestershire	1938–1958	10 073	1309	2
Jupp, V.W.C.	Sussex/Northamptonshire	1909–1938	23 296	1658	10
Kennedy, A.S.	Hampshire	1907–1936	16 586	2874	5
King, J.H.	Leicestershire	1895–1925	25 122	1204	1
Knight, B.R.	Essex/Leicestershire	1955–1969	13 336	1089	4
Langridge, J.	Sussex	1924–1953	31 716	1530	6
Llewellyn, C.B.	Natal/Hampshire	1894–1912	11 425	1013	3
Lock, G.A.R.	Surrey/Leics/W. Australia	1946–1970	10 342	2844	–
Lockwood, W.H.	Nottinghamshire/Surrey	1886–1904	10 673	1376	2
M.D. Marshall	Barbados/Hampshire/Natal	1977–1994	10 829	1637	–
Morgan, D.C.	Derbyshire	1950–1969	18 356	1248	–
Mortimore, J.B.	Gloucestershire	1950–1975	15 891	1807	3
Newman, J.A.	Hampshire/Canterbury	1906–1930	15 333	2032	5
Nichols, M.S.	Essex	1924–1939	17 827	1833	8
Peel, R.	Yorkshire	1882–1899	12 135	1752	1
Procter, M.J.	Natal/WP/R/Glos/Natal	1965–1988	21 936	1417	–
Relf, A.E.	Sussex/Auckland	1900–1921	22 238	1897	8
Rhodes, W.	Yorkshire/Patiala	1898–1930	39 802	4187	16
Robson, E.	Somerset	1895–1923	12 620	1147	–

Sainsbury, P.J.	Hampshire	1954–1976	20 176	1316	–
Shepherd, J.N.	Barbados/Kent/R/Glos	1964–1985	13 353	1157	–
Sinfield, R.A.	Gloucestershire	1921–1939	15 674	1173	2
Smith, R.	Essex	1934–1956	12 042	1350	3
Smith, T.P.B.	Essex	1929–1952	10 161	1697	1
Sobers, G. St A.	Barbados/SA/Notts	1952–1974	28 315	1043	–
Tarrant, F.A.	Victoria/Middlesex/Patiala	1898–1936	17 952	1512	8
Tate, M.W.	Sussex	1912–1937	21 717	2784	8
Thompson, G.J.	Northamptonshire/Auckland	1897–1922	12 018	1591	2
Titmus, F.J.	Middlesex/Surrey/OFS	1949–1982	21 588	2830	8
Townsend, L.F.	Derbyshire/Auckland	1922–1939	19 555	1088	3
Tribe, G.E.	Victoria/Northants	1945–1959	10 177	1378	7
Trott, A.E.	Victoria/Middlesex/Hawke's Bay	1892–1911	10 696	1674	2
Wainwright, E.	Yorkshire	1888–1902	12 485	1062	1
Wellard, A.W.	Somerset	1927–1950	12 515	1614	3
Wensley, A.F.	Sussex/Auckland/Nawanagar	1922–1947	10 849	1142	1
White, J.C.	Somerset	1909–1937	12 202	2356	2
Woods, S.M.J.	CU/Somerset	1886–1910	15 345	1040	–
Woolley, F.E.	Kent	1906–1938	58 969	2068	8

10 000 RUNS AND 1000 WICKET-KEEPING DISMISSALS

		Career	Runs	Dismissals	W-K Doubles
L.E.G. Ames	Kent	1926–1951	37 248	1121	3
D.L. Bairstow	Yorkshire/GW	1970–1990	13 961	1099	–
J.H. Board	Gloucestershire/Hawke's Bay	1891–1914	15 674	1207	–
R. Booth	Yorkshire/Worcs	1951–1970	10 138	1126	–
G.O. Dawkes	Leics/Derbyshire	1937–1961	11 411	1043	–
T.G. Evans	Kent	1939–1969	14 882	1066	–
A.P.E. Knott	Kent/Tasmania	1964–1985	18 105	1344	–
J.T. Murray	Middlesex	1952–1975	18 872	1527	1
J.M. Parks	Sussex/Somerset	1949–1976	36 673	1181	–
H.W. Stephenson	Somerset	1948–1964	13 195	1082	–
B. Taylor	Essex	1949–1973	19 091	1294	–
R.W. Taylor	Derbyshire	1960–1988	12 065	1649	–
R.W. Tolchard	Leicestershire	1965–1983	15 288	1037	–

10 000 RUNS AND 1000 CATCHES

		Career	Runs	Catches
F.E. Woolley	Kent	1906–1938	58 969	1018

Woolley's career aggregates also include 2068 first-class wickets.

Women's Cricket

Women's Cricket

FIRST LADIES

The first account of a women's match was published in the *Reading Mercury* on 26 July 1745:

'The greatest cricket-match that ever was played in the South part of England was on Friday, the 26th of last month, on Gosden Common, near Guildford, in Surrey, between eleven maids of Bramley and eleven maids of Hambleton, dressed all in white. The Bramley maids had blue ribbons and the Hambleton maids red ribbons on their heads. The Bramley girls got 119 notches and the Hambleton girls 127. There was of both sexes the greatest number that ever was seen on such an occasion. The girls bowled, batted, ran and catched as well as most men could do in that game.'

Village cricket between women's teams had been popular in many parts of Surrey and Sussex before that first report.

The first time that women were invited to play on a major ground was on 13 July 1747 when the 'maids' of Westdean, Chilgrove and Charlton were 'bidden' to play a match on the famous Honourable Artillery Ground in London.

From these inter-village contests, women's cricket spread to the top of the social scale. In 1777 the *Morning Post* reported a match

'played in private between the Countess of Derby and some other Ladies of Quality and Fashion, at the Oaks, in Surrey, the rural and enchanting retreat of her ladyship'.

'The Woman of the Match' award seems to have been given to Elizabeth Ann Burrell, fourth daughter of a notable White Conduit Club player, who

'got more notches in the first and second innings than any lady in the game',

and was then aged 20 and extremely attractive. Her prize was the 8th Duke of Hamilton who married her before the next cricket season.

Not all women's cricket was elegant. The most disgraceful behaviour by female cricketers was reported in the *Nottingham Review* of 4 October 1833:

'Last week, at Sileby feast, the women so far forgot themselves as to enter upon a game of cricket, and by their deportment as well as frequent applications to the tankard, they rendered themselves objects such as no husband, brother,

parent, or lover could contemplate with any degree of satisfaction.'

The first woman technically to assist the development of cricket was Christina Willes, later Mrs Hodges. It is generally accepted that she originated round-arm bowling (*c* 1807) when she practised with her brother John in the barn of their home at Tonford, near Canterbury. Her full skirt of the period made the legitimate bowling style of the times impossible. John, who was to become a squire and sports patron, found round-arm bowling difficult to play, adopted it himself, was the first to be no-balled for employing it in a major match (see 'First Notches – Bowling'), and had the satisfaction of seeing the style made legal six years later in 1828. It was said that

'Willes, his sister and his dog (a retriever?) could beat any eleven in England'.

The first woman to be included in the 'Births and Deaths of Cricketers' section of *Wisden Cricketers' Almanack* was Martha Grace (née Pocock):

'Grace, Mrs H.M. (mother of W.G., E.M. and G.F.) b July 18, 1812, d July 25, 1884'.

Martha's husband, Dr Henry Mills Grace, was a Somerset man who in 1831 moved to Downend, a village four miles from Bristol, and took over a large general practice. A tremendous cricket enthusiast, he established the Mangotsfield Cricket Club for cricketers in the neighbouring villages, and prepared a cricket pitch for his seven children on the lawn of Downend House. Martha became as keen on the game as her husband and used to coach her sons. She drove her fourth son, William Gilbert – aged nearly six – in her pony-carriage to watch his first game of cricket when William Clarke's All-England Eleven came to Bristol on 22–24 June 1854 to play 22 of West Gloucestershire. The match was arranged by her husband who captained the home side. 'W.G.' wrote in his *Cricketing Reminiscences and Personal Recollections*:

'I was with my mother, who sat in her pony-carriage all day. I don't remember much about the cricket, but I recollect that some of the England team played in top hats. My mother was very enthusiastic, and watched every ball. She preserved cuttings of the newspaper reports of this and most other matches, and took great care of the score books. I have several of her scrap-books, with the cuttings pasted in, and

very useful I find them, because in those days "Wisden's Annual" was not in existence, and no proper record was kept.'

Two years later Martha Grace mentioned to George Parr that 'W.G.' would do better than his brother, 'E.M.', because his back play was superior. She attended all the matches she could, watched all the play and often criticized vociferously. Once, after 'W.G.' returned at the end of his innings, she rebuked him: 'Willie, Willie, haven't I told you over and over again how to play that ball?'

The first women's cricket club, White Heather, was founded at Nun Appelton, Yorkshire, in the summer of 1887 by eight ladies, the majority of aristocratic birth and independent means. The name was derived from the favourite badge of the founders, who adopted colours of pink, white and green for the same reason.

The club's most celebrated cricketer was Lucy Ridsdale, elder daughter of the Assay Master at the Royal Mint. She married Stanley Baldwin, Prime Minister three times between 1923 and 1937 and a fine batsman who averaged 62 in 1892.

The White Heather Club ceased to function as a playing club after the 1950 season. **The world's oldest surviving women's cricket club** is the Redoubtables WCC; founded in 1921 it is now based in Cheam, Surrey.

In 1890 the English Cricket and Athletic Association Limited organized two teams of women cricketers under the title of **'The Original English Lady Cricketers'**. The two teams, the Red XI and the Blue XI, played each other in exhibition matches on many county grounds around England and were the first to play at Headingley, Leeds. The OELC players were specially selected and coached, bowled overarm, and were forbidden to use their real names. Their uniform consisted of a flannel blouse and skirt, adorned round the hem and collar with striped bands of blue (or red) and white braid. A large blue (or red) bow kept in place the sailor collar, and they wore their colours on sashes around their waists. Caps perched on Victorian hair-styles completed their dress. The OELC was disbanded after two seasons.

The first tour by a women's cricket team took place in 1926 when a scratch team played on college grounds in Cheltenham and Malvern.

Following that successful first tour a number of its members called a meeting on 4 October 1926 when **the Women's Cricket Association was formed**. Its aims were simply to enable any woman or girl wishing to play cricket to do so, and to play the game with strict order and decorum. The first uniform regulation stipulated that 'WCA teams must play in white or cream. Hats and knickers must be white. Dresses and tunics must not be shorter than touching the ground when kneeling. Sleeveless dresses and transparent stockings are not permitted.'

Other countries followed England's example and official administrations for women's cricket were formed in Australia (1931), New Zealand (1933), Holland (1934), South Africa and Rhodesia (1952), Jamaica (1966), Trinidad and Tobago (1967), India (1973), Barbados (1973), Grenada (1974), Leinster (1979), Caribbean Women's Cricket Federation (1979), Scotland (1980), Ulster (1982), the Irish Women's Cricket Union (1984) and Canada (1994).

In 1958 the International Women's Cricket Council (IWCC) was formed to determine tour schedules between member countries.

The first overseas tour by a women's cricket team left Tilbury on the *SS Cathay* on 19 October 1934 bound for Australia and New Zealand. The 15 English players, captained by Betty Archdale, had been selected from those available after trial matches at Old Trafford and Northampton. **The first women's match involving an overseas team** took place on 24 and 26 November 1934 at Perth between Western Australia and England and was drawn. Molly Hide scored **the first century for a touring women's team**.

The first women's Test match was played between Australia and England at Brisbane on 28–31 December 1934, England winning by nine wickets after Myrtle Maclagan (off-breaks) had exploited a sticky wicket to record the remarkable analysis of 17–11–10–7. It remained the Test record until 1958.

The first Test century by a woman was scored in the Second Test at Sydney on 7 January 1935 by Myrtle Maclagan who, opening the innings, made 119 for England on the second day.

Some fifty years after the event she wrote: 'I have so often realized how lucky I was to make the first century in a Test match – that will always stand.' The first woman to score 1000 runs and take 50 wickets in Test cricket, she represented Surrey and England until 1951, and the Army until 1963 when she was 52.

The first women's cricket tour to England was made by Australia in 1937. They defeated England by 31 runs at the County Ground, Northampton on 12–15 June in **the first women's Test played in England**. The tourists were allowed scant opportunity for social licence during the tour as the rules laid down by the Australian WCA ordained that:

No member shall drink, smoke or gamble while on tour.

No girl may be accompanied by her husband, a relation or a friend.

Writing articles on cricket during the tour is strictly forbidden.

While on board ship, no girl shall visit the top deck of the liner after dinner.

Members of the team must retire to bed by 10pm during the voyage.

Members will do physical drill on deck at 7.15am daily except on Sundays.

The team will participate in all deck games.

The first women's cricket World Cup competition was held in England in 1973 and won by the host country who were captained by Rachael Heyhoe Flint.

The first women's cricket magazine was first published in England in May 1930, price 6d. *Women's Cricket* was founded by **Marjorie Pollard** who had been a member of the first women's cricket tour in 1926. A hockey international who, in 1935, had been described as one of that game's greatest exponents of all time, she became an institution in herself. In 1929 the WCA decided to publish its own paper and Marjorie Pollard had volunteered to produce and edit it. She remained its editor until 1949 when she handed over to Netta Rheinberg and Nancy Joy. As a player Marjorie Pollard was 'a mighty hitter, fine fielder and a resourceful captain. No year went by between 1929 and 1936 when she did not excel at one or other facet of the game.' (Netta Rheinberg in *Fair Play, the Story of Women's Cricket*.) Apart from being **the first public relations and publicity officer for women's cricket**, she was its **first reporter, first broadcaster** and **first commentator**. In 1965 she was awarded the OBE for services to sport.

Netta Rheinberg edited *Women's Cricket* until it failed to win its battle against inflation in 1967 and was *The Cricketer*'s women's cricket correspondent from 1959 to 1970. A former Middlesex captain, she managed the 1948–49 and 1957–58 tours of Australasia, playing in the First Test of the earlier tour. Women's cricket correspondent to *Wisden* from 1959 to 1988 and the **Cricket Society's first female vice-chairman** (1975 to 1988), she was awarded the MBE for services to women's cricket in 1984.

The first female to join the ACU was Doris Coysh (née Turner) in November 1959 and she was also **the first female umpire to pass the ACU examination.**

The first female chairman of the ACU was Sheila Hill (Kent) in March 1989.

Rachael Heyhoe, who added her husband's name when she married Derrick Flint in 1971, captained England from 1966 until 1977 and never suffered a defeat. A former England hockey international (goalkeeper) and county squash player, she has been an outstanding public relations and publicity officer for women's cricket, succeeding Netta Rheinberg as *The Cricketer*'s correspondent in

June 1971. The first to score 500 runs in Women's World Cup matches, she was captain of the England team in the WCA Golden Jubilee Match, on the first appearance of women's teams at Lord's on 4 August 1976 when England beat Australia by eight wickets in a 60-overs match. Commentator, broadcaster, after-dinner speaker (she was honoured with the Guild of Toastmasters' Best After-Dinner Speaker Award in 1973), and organizer of charity cricket matches, she was awarded the MBE in 1973 for services to women's cricket.

WOMEN'S TEST MATCH RECORDS

TEAM RECORDS

The highest innings total is 525 by Australia against India at Ahmedabad on 4 February 1984.

The highest innings total in a Test in England is 426 for 9 wickets declared by India at Blackpool on 3–4 July 1986.

The lowest innings total is 35 by England against Australia on a rain-affected pitch at St Kilda, Melbourne on 22 February 1958. This was in reply to Australia's total of 38.

The lowest innings total in a Test in England is 63 by New Zealand at Worcester on 5 July 1954.

BATTING RECORDS

The highest individual innings in women's Test cricket is 193 by Denise Annetts in 381 minutes for Australia against England at Collingham on 22–23 August 1987. She shared in **the first triple century partnership (309) in women's Tests,** her third-wicket partner, Lindsay Reeler (110*), scoring **the slowest women's Test century** in 440 minutes.

The highest score for England (and the highest in a three-day Test) is 189 by E.A. 'Betty' Snowball for England against New Zealand at Christchurch on 16 February 1935 in 222 minutes, having reached her hundred in 115 minutes.

The only instance of the same pair recording hundred opening partnerships in both innings of a women's Test was achieved by Enid Bakewell and Lynne Thomas for England against Australia on 3–5 July 1976 when they put on 116 and 164 at Edgbaston. Their second innings stand remains **the highest first-wicket partnership for England.**

The highest aggregate of runs in official Tests is 1594, average 45.54, with four centuries, in 22 matches by Rachael Heyhoe Flint for England between December 1960 and July 1979. She also hit **the first six in women's Tests** – over long-on against Australia at The Oval on 23 July 1963 – and recorded England's highest individual score in a home Test: 179 against Australia at The Oval on 27–28 July 1976, when an epic innings, lasting 521 minutes and including 30 fours, earned England a famous draw.

BOWLING RECORDS

The best innings analysis in women's Test cricket is 7 for 6 by Mary Duggan when she captained England against Australia at St Kilda, Melbourne, on 22 February 1958.

The best match analysis is 11 for 16 by Betty Wilson for Australia in the same match. No play was possible on the first day and both teams were dismissed cheaply on a 'sticky' pitch on the second day: Australia 38 (Mary Duggan 7 for 6), England 35 (Betty Wilson 7 for 7 including **the first hat-trick in women's Test cricket**). They are the two lowest totals and the two best analyses in women's Test matches. In the second innings Betty Wilson scored 100 and Australia declared at 202 for 9. England were 76 for 8 when the game ended. Betty Wilson's analysis of 4 for 9 not only gave her the match bowling record, it also enabled her to become **the first cricketer to complete the match double of 100 runs and ten wickets in a Test match.** The first instance in men's Test cricket occurred on 14 December 1960. In 1985 she became **the first woman cricketer to be awarded a place in Australia's 'Sports Hall of Fame'.**

The first English cricketer to achieve the Test match double of a century and ten wickets was Enid Bakewell. At Edgbaston on 1–3 July 1979 she carried England to victory by 24 runs in the Third Test against West Indies, scoring 68 and 112 not out, in addition to taking 3 for 14 and 7 for 61. Seven months later, Ian Botham recorded England's first match double in men's Test cricket during the Golden Jubilee Test against India in Bombay.

The best match analysis in a women's Test in England is 11 for 63 by Julia Greenwood against West Indies at Canterbury on 16–18 June 1979 in the first Test match involving a West Indies team.

The most wickets in a Test career is 77, average 13.49, in 17 matches by Mary Duggan for England between 1949 and 1963.

Denise Annetts (Australia): highest innings in women's Test cricket (Allsport/John Gichigi)

WICKET-KEEPING RECORDS

The most dismissals in a Test innings is eight (6 caught, 2 stumped) by Lisa Nye for England against New Zealand at Pukekura Park, New Plymouth on 12–15 February 1992.

The most dismissals in a Test match is nine (8 caught, 1 stumped) by Christina Matthews for Australia against India at St Peter's College, Adelaide on 2–5 February 1991. Matthews holds **the record for most dismissals in a Test career** with 58 (46 catches, 12 stumpings) in 20 matches.

SUMMARY OF OFFICIAL TEST MATCH RESULTS

ENGLAND v AUSTRALIA

Season	Venue	Played	England	Australia	Drawn
1934–35	Australia	3	2	–	1
1937	England	3	1	1	1
1948–49	Australia	3	–	1	2
1951	England	3	1	1	1
1957–58	Australia	3	–	–	3
1963	England	3	1	–	2
1968–69	Australia	3	–	–	3
1976	England	3	–	–	3
1984–85	Australia	5	1	2	2
1987	England	3	–	1	2
1991–92	Australia	1	–	1	–
		33	6	7	20

ENGLAND v NEW ZEALAND

Season	Venue	Played	England	N Zealand	Drawn
1934–35	New Zealand	1	1	–	–
1948–49	New Zealand	1	1	–	–
1954	England	3	1	–	2
1957–58	New Zealand	2	–	–	2
1966	England	3	–	–	3
1968–69	New Zealand	3	2	–	1
1984	England	3	–	–	3
1991–92	New Zealand	3	1	–	2
		19	6	–	13

ENGLAND v SOUTH AFRICA

Season	Venue	Played	England	S Africa	Drawn
1960–61	South Africa	4	1	–	3

ENGLAND v WEST INDIES

Season	Venue	Played	England	W Indies	Drawn
1979	England	3	2	–	1

ENGLAND v INDIA

Season	Venue	Played	England	India	Drawn
1986	England	3	–	–	3

AUSTRALIA v NEW ZEALAND

Season	Venue	Played	Australia	N Zealand	Drawn
1947–48	New Zealand	1	1	–	–
1956–57	Australia	1	1	–	–
1960–61	New Zealand	1	–	–	1
1971–72	Australia	1	–	1	–
1974–75	New Zealand	1	–	–	1
1978–79	Australia	3	1	–	2
1989–90	New Zealand	3	1	–	2
1994–95	New Zealand	1	–	–	1
		12	4	1	7

AUSTRALIA v WEST INDIES

Season	Venue	Played	Australia	W Indies	Drawn
1975–76	West Indies	2	–	–	2

AUSTRALIA v INDIA

Season	Venue	Played	Australia	India	Drawn
1976–77	Australia	1	1	–	–
1983–84	India	4	–	–	4
1990–91	Australia	3	2	–	1
		8	3	–	5

NEW ZEALAND v SOUTH AFRICA

Season	Venue	Played	N Zealand	S Africa	Drawn
1971–72	South Africa	3	1	–	2

NEW ZEALAND v INDIA

Season	Venue	Played	N Zealand	India	Drawn
1976–77	New Zealand	1	–	–	1
1984–85	India	3	–	–	3
1994–95	New Zealand	1	-	-	1
		5	–	–	5

WOMEN'S CRICKET RECORDS IN OTHER MATCHES

The highest innings total in any women's match is 567 by Tarana against Rockley at Rockley in New South Wales, Australia, in October 1896.

The record total in England is 410 for 2 declared by the South against the East at Oakham School, Rutland, on 29 May 1982.

The record individual innings in women's cricket is 224 not out in 135 minutes by Mabel Bryant for the Visitors against the Residents at Eastbourne, Sussex, in August 1901.

The highest score in a Test trial match was recorded by Jan Southgate when she made 201 not out for the South against the East at Oakham School, Rutland, on 29 May 1982. She shared an unbroken third-wicket partnership of 246 with Jackie Court (105 not out).

There have been two recorded instances of bowlers taking all ten wickets in women's cricket without conceding a run. The first to do so was Rubina Humphries, aged 15, for Dalton Ladies against Woodfield Sports Club at Huddersfield on 26 June 1931; she also scored all her side's runs. Her 10 for 0 feat was equalled in July 1962 by Rosemary White for Wallington Ladies against Beaconsfield Ladies.

The first tour double in women's cricket was achieved for England by Enid Bakewell (née Turton) on the 1968–69 tour of Australia and New Zealand. In 20 matches (eleven in Australia and nine in New Zealand) she scored 1031 runs (average 39.65) and, bowling slow left-arm, took 118 wickets (average 9.77). Playing against a New South Wales XI at Manly, she took a hat-trick, all her victims falling to catches by June Moorhouse at silly mid-off.

WOMEN'S WORLD CUP COMPETITIONS

The first Women's World Cup competition was staged in England in June and July 1973 and was the brainchild of Jack Hayward, an English millionaire based in the Bahamas who was a generous patron of women's cricket.

Subsequent competitions have been staged in India (January 1978), New Zealand (January and February 1982), Australia (November and December 1988) and England (July and August 1993).

The highest individual score in World Cup matches is 143 not out by Lindsay Reeler for Australia against Holland in Perth on 29 November 1988. The highest World Cup score for England is 138 not out by Janette Brittin against the International XI at Hamilton, New Zealand, on 14 January 1982. During the 1993 Final, Brittin (1007) became the first to score 1000 runs in World Cup matches.

1973 IN ENGLAND (60 overs)

Final table	P	W	L	NR	Points
ENGLAND	6	5	1	0	20
Australia	6	4	1	1	17
International XI	6	3	2	1	13
New Zealand	6	3	2	1	13
Trinidad & Tobago	6	2	4	0	8
Jamaica	6	1	4	1	5
Young England	6	1	5	0	4

1978 IN INDIA (50 overs)

Final table	P	W	L	Points
AUSTRALIA	3	3	0	12
England	3	2	1	8
New Zealand	3	1	2	4
India	3	0	3	0

1982 IN NEW ZEALAND (60 overs)

Qualifying matches

Results table	P	W	T	L	Points
AUSTRALIA	12	11	1	0	46
ENGLAND	12	7	2	3	32
New Zealand	12	6	1	5	26
India	12	4	0	8	16
International XI	12	0	0	12	0

FINAL

7 February: **AUSTRALIA** beat England by 3 wickets at Lancaster Park, Christchurch. England 151–5 (60 overs), Australia 152–7 (59 overs).

1988 IN AUSTRALIA (6o overs)

Qualifying matches

Results table	P	W	L	Points
AUSTRALIA	8	7	1	28
ENGLAND	8	6	2	24
New Zealand	8	5	3	20
Ireland	8	2	6	8
Holland	8	0	8	0

FINAL

18 December: **AUSTRALIA** beat England by 8 wickets at Melbourne Cricket Ground. England 127–7 (60 overs), Australia 129–2 (44.5 overs).

1993 IN ENGLAND (6o overs)

Qualifying matches

Results table	P	W	L	Points
NEW ZEALAND	7	7	0	28
ENGLAND	7	6	1	24
Australia	7	5	2	20
India	7	4	3	16
West Indies	7	2	5	8
Ireland	7	2	5	8
Denmark	7	1	6	4
Holland	7	1	6	4

FINAL

1 August: **ENGLAND** beat New Zealand by 67 runs at Lord's, London. England 195–5 (60 overs), New Zealand 128 (55.1 overs).

England captain Karen Smithies (right) and player of the match Jo Chamberlain celebrate victory over New Zealand in the 1993 World Cup final (Popperfoto)

Limited-Overs
Cricket

Limited-Overs Cricket

The most far-reaching innovation in professional cricket in the last hundred years has been limited overs one-day cricket.

The reason for its invention was purely financial. Attendances at the only inter-county competition in Britain, the County Championship, had fallen dramatically since the halcyon days immediately after the Hitler War. From two million in 1950 the total attendance at county matches dropped to 700 000 in 1963, the season when the first one-day county competition was introduced. An MCC committee had been set up in 1956 to examine the decline in attendances and the general tempo of the game. It was this committee, under the chairmanship of H.S. Altham, which proposed a one-day knock-out tournament.

The revolutionary concept was certainly not palatable to many administrators either at Lord's or around the counties, but the desperate financial position of county cricket dictated urgent action.

cricket' were bowled at Grace Road, Leicester, by Les Jackson to Maurice Hallam, and at Trent Bridge, Nottingham, by John Cotton to Mick Norman, at 11am on 2 May 1962.

The first 50 in limited-overs cricket was scored by the Leicestershire opener, Maurice Hallam. His score of 86 on that first historic morning remained the highest in one-day county cricket until Peter Marner scored **the first limited-overs century**: 121 for Lancashire against Leicestershire at Manchester in the preliminary round of the Gillette Cup on 1 May 1963. Hallam scored the second hundred on the following day. Ironically he had won the toss and elected to field.

The first wicket in limited-overs county cricket was taken by Nottinghamshire's opening bowler, John Cotton. His victim was Mick Norman, then playing for Northamptonshire, who registered **the first duck**. He was caught by wicket-keeper Geoff Millman who thereby made **the first catch**.

THE MIDLANDS KNOCK-OUT CUP

In 1962 a pilot scheme, sponsored by Leicestershire at the instigation of their secretary, Michael Turner, and featuring four counties, was held at Leicester and Nottingham in May. Each innings was restricted to 65 overs and no bowler could deliver more than 15 of them. Three matches were played. Leicestershire beat Derbyshire to reach the final against Northamptonshire who had beaten Nottinghamshire by 31 runs. In the final no limit was placed on the number of overs permitted to each bowler. This led to slow bowlers having scant say in the proceedings and was swiftly remedied when the rules of the knock-out cup proper were drafted. Northamptonshire defeated Leicestershire on their Grace Road Ground to become the first (and last) holders of the Midlands Knock-Out Cup.

Limited-overs cricket had been born. Traditionalists were alarmed – many still are. Sir Neville Cardus wanted it called 'Snicket' or 'Slogget' – anything but Cricket. The first balls in 'instant

THE KNOCK-OUT CUP

GILLETTE CUP/NATWEST TROPHY

The Knock-Out Competition proper (*Wisden Cricketers' Almanack* declined to call it the Gillette Cup in its review of that first season) began with a preliminary match between Lancashire and Leicestershire at Old Trafford, Manchester, on 1 May 1963. Rain held up the start of the new competition for three hours, thus ensuring it was the first one-day match to involve overtime. **The first Man of the Match award** in the Gillette Cup (or in any national competition) was won by Peter Marner who scored 121 and took 3 for 49 in his side's 101 runs victory. Lancashire did not re-engage him after the next season and he moved to Leicestershire.

Lancashire reached the semi-finals only to contribute to **the earliest finish** in these contests. Bowled out by Worcestershire for 59 in 95 minutes they lost by ten wickets after just 2 hours 10 minutes of play. That early closing time of 2.20pm was emulated at Westcliff-on-Sea in 1972 when Essex disposed of Middlesex with equal brevity.

The first Lord's Cup Final was held on Saturday, 7 September 1963 on a day of cloud and drizzle, but one which offered much excitement to a capacity crowd of over 25 000. Sussex elected to bat on a soft pitch and were all out for 168 in 60.2 overs. England wicket-keeper Jim Parks, whose son Bobby is now Hampshire's occupant of that post, contributed 57 – **the first half-century in a cup final**. The next highest score was 34. Norman Gifford took 4 for 33 in 15 overs of left-arm spin for Worcestershire and was judged the **first Man of the Match in a Lord's final. The first cup final adjudicators** were Herbert Sutcliffe, Frank Woolley and H.S. Altham (absent ill). When Sutcliffe and Woolley disagreed, the Duke of Norfolk and S.C. Griffith were asked to judge. They also disagreed and the ultimate judgment was made by Gordon Ross who had conceived the idea of a match award for these one-day games. Worcestershire made a valiant effort to acquire 2.5 runs per over as the light deteriorated. When Ted Dexter brought back his fast bowlers four wickets fell for five runs and, at 133 for 9, 36 runs were needed from the last pair. A belligerent innings from Roy Booth (33 not out) caused Dexter to position every available fielder on the boundary and he had taken the total to 154 when his partner was run out, leaving Sussex **the first holders of the Gillette Cup.**

In all subsequent years the length of each side's innings has been restricted to 60 overs, with 12 being the current personal limit for each bowler. The top five minor counties in the previous season's table were first included in 1964. Since 1983 the competition, sponsored from 1981 by the National Westminster Bank and played for the NatWest Trophy, has included the top 13 minor counties as well as Ireland and Scotland – 32 teams in all. The promotion of Durham to first-class status (1992) and the inclusion of Holland (1995) has reduced the minor county entrants to 11. Apart from a manic experiment in 1982 which involved a 10am start, the only major changes in the oldest limited-overs competition have involved its sponsor and restrictions on field-placing. The latter involve a minimum of six players, including bowler and wicket-keeper, being within a specific area (bounded by two semi-circles centred on each middle stump and with a radius of 30 yards, and joined by a parallel line on each side of the pitch), at the instant of delivery. Under this regulation Alvin Kallicharran recorded **the highest score in any limited-overs match in Britain:** 206 for Warwickshire against Oxfordshire at Edgbaston in 1984.

HIGHEST TOTAL IN A KNOCK-OUT CUP FINAL

322–5	Warwickshire v Sussex	1993

LOWEST TOTAL IN A KNOCK-OUT CUP FINAL

118	Lancashire v Kent	1974

HUNDREDS IN KNOCK-OUT CUP FINALS

G. Boycott	146	Yorkshire v Surrey	1965
C.H. Lloyd	126	Lancashire v Warwickshire	1972
D.M. Smith	124	Sussex v Warwickshire	1993
I.V.A. Richards	117	Somerset v Northants	1979
G. Cook	111	Northants v Derbyshire	1981
B.R. Hardie	110	Essex v Notts	1985
Asif Din	104	Warwickshire v Sussex	1993

Geoffrey Boycott's innings of 146 is the highest in any Lord's Final.

FIVE WICKETS IN KNOCK-OUT CUP FINALS

J. Garner	6–29	Somerset v Northants	1979
P.A.J. DeFreitas	5–26	Lancashire v Northants	1990
R. Illingworth	5–29	Yorkshire v Surrey	1965
G.R. Dilley	5–29	Worcestershire v Middlesex	1988

Asif Din (Warwickshire) on the way to a fine century in the 1993 NatWest Trophy final (Allsport/Adrian Murrell)

GILLETTE CUP WINNERS

1963	SUSSEX (168) beat Worcestershire (154)	14 runs
1964	SUSSEX (131–2) beat Warwickshire (127)	8 wickets
1965	YORKSHIRE (317–4c) beat Surrey (142)	175 runs
1966	WARWICKSHIRE (159–5) beatWorcestershire (155–8c)	5 wickets
1967	KENT (193) beat Somerset (161)	32 runs
1968	WARWICKSHIRE (215–6) beat Sussex (214–7c)	4 wickets
1969	YORKSHIRE (219–8c) beat Derbyshire (150)	69 runs
1970	LANCASHIRE (185–4) beat Sussex (184–9c)	6 wickets
1971	LANCASHIRE (224–7c) beat Kent (200)	24 runs
1972	LANCASHIRE (235–6) beat Warwickshire (234–9c)	4 wickets
1973	GLOUCESTERSHIRE (248–8c) beat Sussex (208)	40 runs
1974	KENT (122–6) beat Lancashire (118)	4 wickets
1975	LANCASHIRE (182–3) beat Middlesex (180–8c)	7 wickets
1976	NORTHAMPTONSHIRE (199–6) Lancashire (195–7c)	4 wickets
1977	MIDDLESEX (178–5) beat Glamorgan (177–9c)	5 wickets
1978	SUSSEX (211–5) beat Somerset (207–7c)	5 wickets
1979	SOMERSET (269–8c) beat Northamptonshire (224)	45 runs
1980	MIDDLESEX (202–3) beat Surrey (201)	7 wickets

NATWEST TROPHY WINNERS

1981	DERBYSHIRE (235–6c) beat Northamptonshire (235–9c)	Tie*
1982	SURREY (159–1) beat Warwickshire (158)	9 wickets
1983	SOMERSET (193–9c) beat Kent (169)	24 runs
1984	MIDDLESEX (236–6) beat Kent (232–6c)	4 wickets
1985	ESSEX (280–2c) beat Nottinghamshire (279–5c)	1 run
1986	SUSSEX (243–3) beat Lancashire (242–8c)	7 wickets
1987	NOTTINGHAMSHIRE (231–7) beat Northamptonshire (228–3c)	3 wickets
1988	MIDDLESEX (162–7) beat Worcestershire (161–9c)	3 wickets
1989	WARWICKSHIRE (211–6) beat Middlesex (210–5c)	4 wickets
1990	LANCASHIRE (173–3) beat Northamptonshire (171)	7 wickets
1991	HAMPSHIRE (243–6) beat Surrey (240–5c)	4 wickets
1992	NORTHAMPTONSHIRE (211–2) beat Leicestershire (208–7c)	8 wickets
1993	WARWICKSHIRE (322–5) beat Sussex (321–6c)	5 wickets
1994	WORCESTERSHIRE (227–2) beat Warwickshire (223–9c)	8 wickets
1995	WARWICKSHIRE (203–6) beat Northamptonshire (200)	4 wickets

* Derbyshire won by virtue of losing fewer wickets, scoring the equalizing run off the last possible ball when Geoff Miller sprinted and dived to complete a leg-bye – probably the fastest 'extra' ever taken.

THE SUNDAY LEAGUE

JOHN PLAYER/REFUGE ASSURANCE/ AXA EQUITY & LAW LEAGUE

A second limited-overs competition was introduced in 1969 and it remains the only one-day county competition which cannot be extended into a second or third day in the case of inclement weather. It is also the only one in which bowlers have the distance of their run-ups restricted and the only one in which a tie stands as an acceptable result.

It came about largely because of the success of a private promotion sponsored by Rothmans. The Rothmans 'Cavaliers', comprising great players of the past and present from all cricketing countries, played against a different professional county side each Sunday afternoon, often in aid of that county's beneficiary. The matches were designed to last for two hours each innings and were an ideal package for BBC2 television. The popularity of these matches grew steadily each season. From their humble beginnings in 1962 when they played untelevised matches on village greens and at small clubs, through their early televised days in 1965 (total attendance 34 000; total money collected £4100), the Cavaliers had blossomed to such proportions in 1967 (total attendance 114 000; total money collected £13 500), that they had attracted a bigger audience during the season than either the county champions (Yorkshire – 83 000) or runners-up (Kent – 76 000).

After the 1967 season the counties decided to institute a Sunday League of their own and, in the following year, the newly-formed TCCB appointed their secretary, S.C. Griffith, to negotiate contracts with a sponsor and television. Rothmans' rival tobacco firm, John Player and Sons, won the scramble for sponsorship and the BBC won the broadcasting contract. Both had been considerably heartened by seeing the crowd at Edgbaston one June Sunday of 1968 when Tom Cartwright's benefit fund was swelled by the sum of £3295.

The Sunday League has become an accepted part of the English season. Each county plays its 16 opponents once in a 40-overs game, less if the weather reduces the time available, the minimum being the farcical 10-overs slog. It has attracted a considerable following of its own, although a private survey carried out during the competition's first eight seasons showed that only a small proportion of the Sunday League following also attended Championship or Test matches, and vice versa. No matter. Sunday cricket has brought much benefit to the TCCB's exchequer and given tremendous entertainment value. Sadly, apart from occasional satellite coverage, it has not been possible since 1981 to watch an entire match on television each summer Sunday afternoon. In the present format, cricket is slotted in with two or three other sports and sometimes omitted altogether. Possibly this change of coverage resulted from John Arlott's retirement from all commentary boxes after the 1980 season. He could always be relied upon for original and witty comments, even if very little action was worthy of description.

In 1982 Sussex established new records by winning 14 of their 16 matches and totalling 58 points. They lost to Worcestershire by three wickets with an over to spare and the other match was abandoned without a ball bowled.

Imperial Tobacco ended their sponsorship after the 1986 season and were succeeded by Refuge Assurance (1987–1991), TCCB (1992) and AXA Equity & Law Insurance (1993 to date).

The competition has been limited to 40 overs per innings, apart from in 1993 when it was experimentally extended to 50.

SUNDAY LEAGUE CHAMPIONS

1969	Lancashire
1970	Lancashire
1971	Worcestershire
1972	Kent
1973	Kent
1974	Leicestershire
1975	Hampshire
1976	Kent
1977	Leicestershire
1978	Hampshire
1979	Somerset
1980	Warwickshire
1981	Essex
1982	Sussex
1983	Yorkshire
1984	Essex
1985	Essex
1986	Hampshire
1987	Worcestershire
1988	Worcestershire
1989	Lancashire
1990	Derbyshire
1991	Nottinghamshire
1992	Middlesex
1993	Glamorgan
1994	Warwickshire
1995	Kent

Dermot Reeve (left) and Tim Munton celebrate Warwickshire's Sunday League success in 1994 (Allsport/Clive Mason)

THE LEAGUE CUP

BENSON AND HEDGES CUP

Britain's third county limited-overs competition was introduced in 1972. The 17 first-class counties, supplemented by two select minor counties sides and Cambridge University, were divided into four regions of five teams. Each played the other four once and the top two qualified for the knock-out stage of the competition, which culminated in a July final at Lord's. The playing conditions were exactly the same as for the (then) Gillette Cup, except that each innings was limited to 55 overs and each individual bowler to eleven overs.

The competition has undergone only superficial changes, whereby the counties have been shuffled around in their mini-leagues or groups and the three extra sides have at times included Oxford University, a full Minor Counties XI, Scotland and Ireland. Since 1980 the three 'extra' teams have been Scotland, Combined Universities and Minor Counties. From 1987 cricketers from all universities, not just Cambridge and Oxford, were eligible for the combined eleven. Durham were admitted in 1992, one group being increased to six teams to accommodate them.

For 1993 and 1994, the group rounds were abandoned in favour of a straight knock-out tournament. They were restored in 1995.

The restriction on field-placing was introduced to all limited-overs cricket in 1982 following a trial in the Benson and Hedges Cup in 1981. It stated: 'At the instant of delivery, a minimum of four fieldsmen (plus the bowler and wicket-keeper) must be within an area bounded by two semi-circles centred on each middle stump (each with a radius of 30 yards) and joined by a parallel line on each side of the pitch. In the event of an infringement, the square-leg umpire shall call "No Ball".'

It immediately found favour with players and administrators. Ultra-defensive field-placings, involving nine or even ten men around the boundary in the closing stages of an innings, were no longer possible. Undefended spaces in the outfield prompted intriguing tactical battles between the batsmen and the opposition captain and bowlers.

BENSON AND HEDGES CUP WINNERS

1972	LEICESTERSHIRE (140–5) beat Yorkshire (136–9c)	5 wickets
1973	KENT (225–7c) beat Worcestershire (186)	39 runs
1974	SURREY (170) beat Leicestershire (143)	27 runs
1975	LEICESTERSHIRE (150–5) beat Middlesex (146)	5 wickets
1976	KENT (236–7c) beat Worcestershire (193)	43 runs
1977	GLOUCESTERSHIRE (237–6c) beat Kent (173)	64 runs
1978	KENT (148–4) Derbyshire (147)	6 wickets
1979	ESSEX (290–6c) beat Surrey (255)	35 runs
1980	NORTHAMPTONSHIRE (209) beat Essex (203–8c)	6 runs
1981	SOMERSET (197–3) beat Surrey (194–8c)	7 wickets
1982	SOMERSET (132–1) beat Nottinghamshire (130)	9 wickets
1983	MIDDLESEX (196–8c) beat Essex (192)	4 runs
1984	LANCASHIRE (140–4) beat Warwickshire (139)	6 wickets
1985	LEICESTERSHIRE (215–5) beat Essex (213–8c)	5 wickets
1986	MIDDLESEX (199–7c) beat Kent (197–8c)	2 runs
1987	YORKSHIRE (244–6c) beat Northamptonshire (244–7c)	Tied†
1988	HAMPSHIRE (118–3) beat Derbyshire (117)	7 wickets
1989	NOTTINGHAMSHIRE (244–7) beat Essex (243–7c)	3 wickets
1990	LANCASHIRE (241–8c) beat Worcestershire (172)	69 runs
1991	WORCESTERSHIRE (236–8c) beat Lancashire (171)	65 runs
1992	HAMPSHIRE (253–5c) beat Kent (212)	41 runs
1993	DERBYSHIRE (252–6c) beat Lancashire (246–7c)	6 runs
1994	WARWICKSHIRE (172–4) beat Worcestershire (170–9c)	6 wickets
1995	LANCASHIRE (274–7c) beat Kent (239)	35 runs

† Yorkshire won by losing fewer wickets in a tied match.

Hampshire skipper Mark Nicholas (far left) celebrates with his team after victory in the 1992 Benson & Hedges Cup final
(Allsport/Adrian Murrell)

HUNDREDS IN LEAGUE CUP FINALS

I.V.A. Richards	132*	Somerset v Surrey	1981
G.A. Gooch	120	Essex v Surrey	1979
P.A. de Silva	112	Kent v Lancashire	1995

FIVE WICKETS IN LEAGUE CUP FINALS

| S.T. Jefferies | 5–13 | Hampshire v Derbys | 1988 |
| J. Garner | 5–14 | Somerset v Surrey | 1981 |

HAT-TRICK IN LEAGUE CUP FINALS

| K. Higgs | 4–10 | Leics v Surrey | 1974 |

HIGHEST TOTAL IN LEAGUE CUP FINALS

| 290–6 | Essex v Surrey | 1979 |

LOWEST TOTAL IN LEAGUE CUP FINALS

| 117 | Derbyshire v Hampshire | 1988 |

NO CUP FINAL APPEARANCES

Three counties – Glamorgan, Durham and Sussex – have yet to reach the League Cup final.

RECORDS FOR THE THREE NATIONAL LIMITED-OVERS COMPETITIONS

	NAT WEST TROPHY	BENSON & HEDGES CUP	AXA, EQUITY & LAW LEAGUE
Innings overs limit	60 overs	55 overs	40 overs
Season instituted	1963 (Gillette Cup)	1972	1969 (John Player Lge)
Highest total	413–4 (60 overs) Somerset v Devon, Torquay 1990	388–7 (55 overs) Essex v Scotland, Chelmsford 1992	375–4 (40 overs) Surrey v Yorkshire, Scarborough 1995
Highest total batting second	350 (59.5 overs) Surrey v Worcestershire, The Oval 1994	318–5 (54.3 overs) Lancashire v Leicestershire, Manchester, 1995	317–6 (46 overs) Surrey v Notts The Oval 1993
Lowest total	39 (26.4 overs) Ireland v Sussex, Hove 1985	50 (27.2 overs) Hampshire v Yorkshire, Leeds 1991	23 (19.4 overs) Middlesex v Yorkshire, Leeds 1974
Highest individual score	206 A.I. Kallicharran, Warwicks v Oxfordshire, Birmingham 1984	198* G.A. Gooch, Essex v Sussex, Hove 1982	176 G.A. Gooch, Essex v Glamorgan, Southend 1983
Highest partnership	309* (3rd wkt) T.S. Curtis, T.M. Moody, Worcestershire v Surrey, The Oval 1994	285* (2nd wkt) C.G. Greenidge, D.R. Turner, Hampshire v Minor Counties (South), Amersham 1973	273 (2nd wkt) G.A.Gooch, K.S.McEwan Essex v Notts, Nottingham 1983
Best bowling analysis	8–21 M.A. Holding, Derbyshire v Sussex, Hove 1988	7–12 W.W. Daniel, Middlesex v Minor Counties (East), Ipswich 1978	8–26 K.D. Boyce, Essex v Lancashire, Manchester 1971
Wicket-keeping – most dismissals (match)	7 (7ct) A.J. Stewart, Surrey v Glamorgan, Swansea 1994	8 (8ct) D.J.S. Taylor, Somerset v Combined Universities, Taunton 1982	7 (6ct, 1st) R.W. Taylor, Derbyshire v Lancashire, Manchester 1975
Fielding – most catches (match)	4 A.S. Brown, Gloucestershire v Middlesex, 1963 4 G. Cook, Northamptonshire v Glamorgan, 1972 4 C.G. Greenidge, Hampshire v Cheshire, 1981 4 D.C. Jackson, Durham v Northamptonshire, 1984 4 T.S. Smith, Hertfordshire v Somerset, 1984 4 H. Morris, Glamorgan v Scotland, 1988 4 C.C. Lewis, Nottinghamshire v Worcestershire, 1992	5 V.J. Marks, Combined Universities v Kent, Oxford 1976	5 J.M. Rice, Hampshire v Warwickshire, Southampton 1978

LIMITED-OVERS INTERNATIONALS

The first one-day international was a hastily-arranged affair, played to appease the disappointed public on the final scheduled day of a rain-aborted Test match between Australia and England at Melbourne on 5 January 1971. By coincidence, the match not only took place on the very ground where Test cricket had begun 94 years earlier, but also resulted in an Australian victory against England. More significantly it attracted 46 000 spectators, produced receipts of $33 000, and began a revolu-tion in international cricket.

The first international man of the match was John Edrich, the Surrey and England opening batsman who scored 82 – **the first fifty in a one-day international.**

The first adjudicator was Charles Elliott, the former Derbyshire batsman and Test umpire who was in Australia on a Churchill Fellowship.

The first ball in these matches was bowled by Graham McKenzie to Geoffrey Boycott. **The first bowler to take a wicket** at this level was Jeff Thomson, who had Boycott caught by Bill Lawry.

When Australia toured England the following year, three limited-overs internationals replaced the extra (Sixth) Test previously agreed by the respective Boards.

The first century in limited-overs internationals was scored by Dennis Amiss for England against Australia at Old Trafford on 24 August 1972.

The first bowler to take five wickets in a one-day international was Dennis Lillee – for Australia against Pakistan at Headingley on 7 June 1975 in the first World Cup.

In Australia, the influence of television magnate Kerry Packer produced the dramatic advent of floodlit cricket, with such attendant innovations as white balls, black sightscreens, and coloured clothing. Skilful marketing of this instant formula produced a headlong proliferation of tournaments. The 1984–85 season saw the quite staggering total of 31 limited-overs internationals being staged in Australia during a period of just nine weeks.

Robin Smith during his unbeaten 167 for England against Australia in 1993 (Popperfoto)

RECORDS FOR ALL LIMITED-OVERS INTERNATIONALS (1970–71 to 1995)

Highest Total	363–7	England	v Pakistan	Nottingham	1992
Highest Total Batting Second	313–7	Sri Lanka	v Zimbabwe	New Plymouth	1991–92
Lowest Total	43	Pakistan	v West Indies	Cape Town	1992–93
Highest Aggregate	626	Pakistan (338–5)	v Sri Lanka (288–9)	Swansea	1983
Lowest Aggregate	88	Pakistan (43)	v West Indies (45–3)	Cape Town	1992–93

Highest Individual Score for each full ICC Member

189*	I.V.A Richards	**West Indies** v England	Manchester	1984
175*	Kapil Dev	**India** v Zimbabwe	Tunbridge Wells	1983
171*	G.M. Turner	**New Zealand** v East Africa	Birmingham	1975
169*	D.J. Callaghan	**South Africa** v New Zealand	Verwoerdburg	1994–95
167*	R.A. Smith	**England** v Australia	Birmingham	1993
145	D.M. Jones	**Australia** v England	Brisbane	1990–91
142	D.L. Houghton	**Zimbabwe** v New Zealand	Hyderabad (India)	1987–88
140	S.T. Jayasuriya	**Sri Lanka** v New Zealand	Bloemfontein	1994–95
137*	Inzamam-ul-Haq	**Pakistan** v New Zealand	Sharjah	1993–94

Highest Partnerships for each Wicket (* unbroken)

1st	212	G.R. Marsh/D.C. Boon	Australia v India	Jaipur	1986–87
2nd	263	Aamir Sohail/Inzamam-ul-Haq	Pakistan v New Zealand	Sharjah	1993–94
3rd	224*	D.M. Jones/A.R. Border	Australia v Sri Lanka	Adelaide	1984–85
4th	173	D.M. Jones/S.R. Waugh	Australia v Pakistan	Perth	1986–87
5th	152	I.V.A. Richards/C.H. Lloyd	West Indies v Sri Lanka	Brisbane	1984–85
6th	154	R.B. Richardson/P.J.L. Dujon	West Indies v Pakistan	Sharjah	1991–92
7th	115	P.J.L. Dujon/M.D. Marshall	West Indies v Pakistan	Gujranwala	1986–87
8th	119	P.R. Reiffel/S.K. Warne	Australia v South Africa	Port Elizabeth	1993–94
9th	126*	Kapil Dev/S.M.H. Kirmani	India v Zimbabwe	Tunbridge Wells	1983
10th	106*	I.V.A. Richards/M.A. Holding	West Indies v England	Manchester	1984

Best Bowling Analysis for each Full ICC Member

7–37	Aqib Javed	**Pakistan** v India	Sharjah	1991–92
7–51	W.W. Davis	**West Indies** v Australia	Leeds	1983
6–12	A. Kumble	**India** v West Indies	Calcutta	1993–94
6–14	G.J. Gilmour	**Australia** v England	Leeds	1975
6–29	S.T. Jayasuriya	**Sri Lanka** v England	Moratuwa	1992–93
5–20	V.J. Marks	**England** v New Zealand	Wellington	1983–84
5–22	M.N. Hart	**New Zealand** v West Indies	Margao	1994–95
5–29	A.A. Donald	**South Africa** v India	Calcutta	1991–92
4–21	E.A. Brandes	**Zimbabwe** v England	Albury	1991–92

Hat-Tricks

Jalaluddin	Pakistan v Australia	Hyderabad	1982–83
B.A. Reid	Australia v New Zealand	Sydney	1985–86
C. Sharma	India v New Zealand	Nagpur	1987–88
Wasim Akram	Pakistan v West Indies	Sharjah	1989–90
Wasim Akram	Pakistan v Australia	Sharjah	1989–90
Kapil Dev	India v Sri Lanka	Calcutta	1990–91
Aqib Javed	Pakistan v India	Sharjah	1991–92
D.K. Morrison	New Zealand v India	Napier	1993–94

Wicket-keeping – Most Dismissals in an Innings

5   R.W. Marsh (*Australia*), R.G. de Alwis (*Sri Lanka*), S.M.H. Kirmani (*India*), S. Viswanath (*India*), K.S. More (*India*), H.P. Tillekeratne (*Sri Lanka*), N.R. Mongia (*India*), A.C. Parore (*New Zealand*), D.J. Richardson (*South Africa*), Moin Khan (*Pakistan*), R.S. Kaluwitharana (*Sri Lanka*).

Fielding – Most Catches in an Innings

5 J.N. Rhodes South Africa v West Indies Bombay 1993–94

Allan Donald: top analysis for South Africa in limited-overs internationals
(Allsport/Graham Chadwick)

LIMITED-OVERS INTERNATIONALS RESULTS SUMMARY

1970–71 to 1995 inclusive

	M	Won by													Tied	NR
		E	A	SA	WI	NZ	I	P	SL	Z	B	C	EA	UAE		
England																
Australia	57	26	29	–	–	–	–	–	–	–	–	–	–	–	1	1
South Africa	4	4	–	0	–	–	–	–	–	–	–	–	–	–	–	–
West Indies	51	22	–	–	27	–	–	–	–	–	–	–	–	–	–	2
New Zealand	41	21	–	–	–	17	–	–	–	–	–	–	–	–	–	3
India	29	16	–	–	–	–	13	–	–	–	–	–	–	–	–	–
Pakistan	36	23	–	–	–	–	–	12	–	–	–	–	–	–	–	1
Sri Lanka	11	8	–	–	–	–	–	–	3	–	–	–	–	–	–	–
Zimbabwe	3	1	–	–	–	–	–	–	–	2	–	–	–	–	–	–
Canada	1	1	–	–	–	–	–	–	–	–	–	0	–	–	–	–
East Africa	1	1	–	–	–	–	–	–	–	–	–	–	0	–	–	–
Australia																
South Africa	20	–	12	8	–	–	–	–	–	–	–	–	–	–	–	–
West Indies	74	–	27	–	45	–	–	–	–	–	–	–	–	–	1	1
New Zealand	62	–	43	–	–	17	–	–	–	–	–	–	–	–	–	2
India	43	–	24	–	–	–	16	–	–	–	–	–	–	–	–	3
Pakistan	42	–	21	–	–	–	–	18	–	–	–	–	–	–	1	2
Sri Lanka	26	–	18	–	–	–	–	–	6	–	–	–	–	–	–	2
Zimbabwe	7	–	6	–	–	–	–	–	–	1	–	–	–	–	–	–
Bangladesh	1	–	1	–	–	–	–	–	–	–	0	–	–	–	–	–
Canada	1	–	1	–	–	–	–	–	–	–	–	0	–	–	–	–
South Africa																
West Indies	8	–	–	4	4	–	–	–	–	–	–	–	–	–	–	–
N Zealand	7	–	–	3	–	4	–	–	–	–	–	–	–	–	–	–
India	14	–	–	8	–	–	6	–	–	–	–	–	–	–	–	–
Pakistan	11	–	–	4	–	–	–	7	–	–	–	–	–	–	–	–
Sri Lanka	7	–	–	3	–	–	–	–	3	–	–	–	–	–	–	1
Zimbabwe	2	–	–	1	–	–	–	–	–	0	–	–	–	–	–	1
West Indies																
New Zealand	19	–	–	–	15	2	–	–	–	–	–	–	–	–	–	2
India	50	–	–	–	32	–	17	–	–	–	–	–	–	–	1	–
Pakistan	73	–	–	–	50	–	–	21	–	–	–	–	–	–	2	–
Sri Lanka	19	–	–	–	16	–	–	–	2	–	–	–	–	–	–	1
Zimbabwe	4	–	–	–	4	–	–	–	–	0	–	–	–	–	–	–
New Zealand																
India	36	–	–	–	–	16	20	–	–	–	–	–	–	–	–	–
Pakistan	36	–	–	–	–	14	–	20	–	–	–	–	–	–	1	1
Sri Lanka	32	–	–	–	–	22	–	–	8	–	–	–	–	–	–	2
Zimbabwe	5	–	–	–	–	5	–	–	–	0	–	–	–	–	–	–
Bangladesh	1	–	–	–	–	1	–	–	–	–	0	–	–	–	–	–
East Africa	1	–	–	–	–	1	–	–	–	–	–	–	0	–	–	–
India																
Pakistan	41	–	–	–	–	–	12	27	–	–	–	–	–	–	–	2
Sri Lanka	37	–	–	–	–	–	24	–	11	–	–	–	–	–	–	2
Zimbabwe	10	–	–	–	–	–	9	–	–	0	–	–	–	–	1	–
Bangladesh	3	–	–	–	–	–	3	–	–	–	0	–	–	–	–	–
East Africa	1	–	–	–	–	–	1	–	–	–	–	–	0	–	–	–
U A Emirates	1	–	–	–	–	–	1	–	–	–	–	–	0	–	–	–

Pakistan

Sri Lanka	49	–	–	–	–	–	–	38	10	–	–	–	–	–	–	1
Zimbabwe	9	–	–	–	–	–	–	7	–	1	–	–	–	–	1	–
Bangladesh	3	–	–	–	–	–	–	3	–	–	0	–	–	–	–	–
Canada	1	–	–	–	–	–	–	1	–	–	–	0	–	–	–	–
U A Emirates	1	–	–	–	–	–	–	1	–	–	–	–	–	0	–	–
Sri Lanka																
Zimbabwe	6	–	–	–	–	–	–	5	1	–	–	–	–	–	–	–
Bangladesh	4	–	–	–	–	–	–	4	–	0	–	–	–	–	–	–
	1001	123	182	31	193	99	122	155	52	5	0	0	0	0	9	30

LEAGUE TABLE OF ALL LIMITED-OVERS INTERNATIONALS

1970–71 to 1995 inclusive

	Matches	Won	Lost	Tied	No Result	% Won (exc NR)
West Indies	298	193	95	4	6	66.09
Australia	333	182	137	3	11	56.52
England	234	123	103	1	7	54.18
Pakistan	302	155	135	5	7	52.54
India	265	122	134	2	7	47.28
South Africa	73	31	40	–	2	43.66
New Zealand	240	99	130	1	10	43.04
Sri Lanka	191	52	130	–	9	28.57
Zimbabwe	46	5	38	2	1	11.11
United Arab Emirates	2	–	2	–	–	–
Canada	3	–	3	–	–	–
East Africa	3	–	3	–	–	–
Bangladesh	12	–	12	–	–	–

THE WORLD CUP

Sponsored by Prudential Assurance, this competition was first held in 1975. It was the first attempt at organizing a world cup for cricket since the rain-ruined Triangular Test Match Tournament of 1912. Blessed by the ultimate in fine weather – not a minute of play was lost during 15 matches spread over as many days – and culminating in a rousing final played before a packed and sun-drenched Lord's on the longest day of the year, the inaugural tournament was an unqualified success. That final, which entertained from 11am until 8.43pm, not only made a repeat competition mandatory (subsequently they have been staged at four-year intervals) but it also marked the acceptance of one-day limited-overs cricket at international level by players, spectators and, most importantly, cricket's administrators.

Prudential sponsored similar World Cup tournaments in 1979 and 1983, the latter producing one of cricket's most sensational giant-killing epics when a rank outsider, India, defeated the firm favourites, West Indies, in another enthralling final.

The 1987 competition, sponsored by Reliance Industrial, a Bombay textile company, was held simultaneously in India and Pakistan in October and

November. The semi-finals were played at Lahore and Bombay, with Eden Gardens, Calcutta, having the honour of staging the final.

The first two tournaments involved just 15 matches apiece, while the third and fourth each featured 27 games. The fifth World Cup, sponsored by Benson and Hedges expanded this tally to 39, with Australia staging 25 matches and New Zealand 14. It was the first to employ coloured clothing and a white ball, with ten of the Australian matches (including the Sydney semi-final and Melbourne final) played under floodlights. England became the first team to lose three finals.

The first three tournaments, all in Britain, featured 60 overs matches, the latter two have involved games of 50 overs per side, a format which became mandatory for all limited-overs internationals from September 1995.

WORLD CUP RECORDS 1975 to 1991–92

Highest total	360–4	West Indies v Sri Lanka	Karachi	1987–88
Highest total batting second	313–7	Sri Lanka v Zimbabwe	New Plymouth	1991–92
Lowest total	45	Canada v England	Manchester	1979
Highest match aggregate	626	Pakistan v Sri Lanka	Swansea	1983
Lowest match aggregate	91	Canada (45) v England (46–1)	Manchester	1979
Biggest victories	10 wickets	India beat East Africa	Leeds	1975
	10 wickets	West Indies beat Zimbabwe	Birmingham	1983
	10 wickets	West Indies beat Pakistan	Melbourne	1991–92
	202 runs	England beat India	Lord's	1975
Narrowest victories	1 wicket	West Indies beat Pakistan	Birmingham	1975
	1 wicket	Pakistan beat West Indies (last ball)	Lahore	1987–88
	1 run	Australia beat India	Madras	1987–88
	1 run	Australia beat India	Brisbane	1991–92
Highest individual score	181	I.V.A. Richards, W. Indies v SL	Karachi	1987–88
Hundred before lunch		A. Turner (101), Australia v SL	The Oval	1975

Highest partnership for each wicket

Wkt	Runs				
1st	182	R.B. McCosker, A. Turner	Australia v Sri Lanka	The Oval	1975
2nd	176	D.L. Amiss, K.W.R. Fletcher	England v India	Lord's	1975
3rd	195 *	C.G. Greenidge, H.A. Gomes	West Indies v Zimbabwe	Worcester	1983
4th	149	R.B. Kanhai, C.H. Lloyd	West Indies v Australia	Lord's	1975
5th	145 *	A. Flower, A.C. Waller	Zimbabwe v Sri Lanka	New Plymouth	1991–92
6th	144	Imran Khan, Shahid Mahboob	Pakistan v Sri Lanka	Leeds	1983
7th	75 *	D.A.G. Fletcher, I.P. Butchart	Zimbabwe v Australia	Nottingham	1983
8th	117	D.L. Houghton, I.P. Butchart	Zimbabwe v New Zealand	Hyderabad (India)	1987–88
9th	126 *	Kapil Dev, S.M.H. Kirmani	India v Zimbabwe	Tunbridge Wells	1983
10th	71	A.M.E. Roberts, J. Garner	West Indies v India	Manchester	1983

Best bowling	7–51	W.W. Davis, West Indies v Australia	Leeds	1983
Hat–trick		C. Sharma, India v New Zealand	Nagpur	1987–88
Most economical bowling	12–8–6–1	B.S. Bedi, India v East Africa	Leeds	1975
Most expensive bowling	12–1–105–2	M.C. Snedden, New Zealand v England	The Oval	1983
Wicket-keeping – most dismissals	5	S.M.H. Kirmani, India v Zimbabwe	Leicester	1983
Fielding – most catches	3	C.H. Lloyd, West Indies v Sri Lanka	Manchester	1975
	3	D.A. Reeve, England v Pakistan	Adelaide	1991–92
	3	Ijaz Ahmed (sr), Pakistan v Australia	Perth	1991–92
	3	A.R. Border, Australia v Zimbabwe	Hobart	1991–92

WORLD CUP FINALS

1975	WEST INDIES (291–8) beat Australia (274) by 17 runs	Lord's
1979	WEST INDIES (286–9) beat England (194) by 92 runs	Lord's
1983	INDIA (183) beat West Indies (140) by 43 runs	Lord's
1987–88	AUSTRALIA (253–5) beat England (246–8) by 7 runs	Calcutta
1991–92	PAKISTAN (249–6) beat England (227) by 22 runs	Melbourne

Javed Miandad leads the Pakistan charge in the 1992 World Cup final against England
(Popperfoto)

WORLD CUP RESULTS SUMMARY

	Played	Won	Lost	No Result
England	34	23	10	1
West Indies	32	22	9	1
Australia	30	17	13	0
Pakistan	31	17	13	1
New Zealand	29	16	13	0
India	29	14	14	1
South Africa	9	5	4	0
Sri Lanka	26	4	20	2
Zimbabwe	20	2	18	0
Canada	3	0	3	0
East Africa	3	0	3	0

Minor Cricket

Minor Cricket

In theory all cricket matches which are not termed 'First-Class' have to be classified under the heading of 'Minor Cricket'. If we accept that modern first-class cricket began in 1864 when over-arm bowling was legalized, then technically all cricket before that year was 'minor'. That certainly was not the case. In 1981 the Association of Cricket Statisticians published *A Guide to Important Cricket Matches Played in the British Isles 1709–1863*, which effectively begins with the first county match on record: Kent v Surrey at Dartford Brent on 29 June 1709. Although there are records of more than 700 'important' matches being played in the 18th century, playing conditions were so far removed from the modern game that it would be absurd to include them in records of first-class cricket. A much stronger case can be made for including all Great Matches played since 1815 when the end of the Napoleonic Wars heralded the rebirth of matches involving England, MCC and the county organizations of the day.

'Minor Cricket' is a general classification for the game at school, college, university (apart from Oxbridge), village and town club, military services, diocesan and minor county levels. It can encompass any match which does not warrant the status of first-class, great or important.

The sheer volume of minor cricket has made this area of the game a minefield for historians and statisticians. In many cases records were either not kept or have been destroyed. In listing the most important records for Minor Cricket, there can be no claim that, at some time somewhere in the world, they have not been equalled or surpassed. They are the best performances that are on record.

Cricket Curiosities

Playing for Alexandra Park 3rd XI against Hanwell 3rd XI on 23 August 1986, Ken Hudson (born 4 June 1908) shared a brief lastwicket partnership with Dean King (b 20 July 1973). Their age difference of 65 years 46 days is believed to constitute a partnership record - certainly at Hanwell on a Saturday.

BATTING RECORDS AND OUTSTANDING PERFORMANCES

The highest individual innings in all cricket is 628 not out by Arthur Edward Jeune Collins, who was then a 13-year-old schoolboy at Clifton College in Bristol. Playing in a Junior house match for Clarke's (now Poole's) House against North Town, he batted for 6 hours 50 minutes spread over 5 afternoons on 22, 23, 26, 27, 28 June 1899. Opening the innings, he carried his bat throughout a total of 836 all out and hit 1 six, 4 fives, 31 fours, 33 threes, 146 twos and 87 singles. The scorer gave his total as '628 – plus or minus 20, shall we say'. Collins completed the match double by taking seven wickets in the first innings and another four in the second as his house romped home by an innings and 688 runs.

Born in India in 1885, Collins was in the Clifton XI of 1901 and 1902. Joining the Army, he was gazetted Second Lieutenant in 1904 and promoted to Lieutenant in 1907. In 1912 he scored 58 and 36 at Lord's for the Royal Engineers against the Royal Artillery. A year later he was killed in action in Flanders.

G.V.W. (Gerald) Lukehurst (Kent 2nd XI), scored **six consecutive not out hundreds** for Gore Court CC and F. Day's XI between 3 July and 20 July 1955, when aged 37.

Greg Beacroft scored 268 (29 sixes and 11 fours) in 92 minutes for Yass Wallaroos against Williamsdale at Canberra, Australia, on 21 January 1979, the day after his 21st birthday.

The fastest recorded double century came off only 58 balls – many of which went over a cliff on the Channel Island of Alderney on 19 June 1983. Playing for Alderney against Sun Alliance, David Whatmore scored 210 off 61 balls, including 25 sixes and 12 fours. His first hundred was made off 33 balls and his second off only 25.

The fastest recorded hundred in terms of balls received against genuine bowling was scored off 20 balls by Lindsay Martin on 19 Dec 1987. Playing for Rosewater against Warradale, he hit 13 sixes, 5 fours and 2 singles.

V.F.S. (Vivian) Crawford of Surrey, scored a

century in 19 minutes at Cane Hill, Surrey on 16 September 1899 when he was 20 years old.

S.K. ('Shunter') Coen of Western Province, Orange Free State, Griqualand West and South Africa (two Tests against England in 1927–28) scored **50 runs in 7 minutes** for Gezira against the RAF in 1942. Then in his 40th year, he made all his runs in boundaries – 11 fours and a six.

Lt (later Lt-Col) Philip Mitford ran **eleven runs from one scoring stroke**, without the aid of overthrows, when playing in a Governor's Cup match in Malta on 28 May 1903.

In 1923 two naval cadets scored **174 runs in 33 minutes,** an average of over five runs per minute. K.A. Sellar (later Cdr 'Monkey' Sellar, DSO, DSC, RN) and L.K.A. Block (later Judge Block, DSC) were playing for the Royal Naval College, Dartmouth against Seale Hayne Agricultural College.

The most sixes hit off successive balls on record is nine. C.I.J. ('Jim') Smith of Wiltshire, Middlesex and England, achieved this feat in 1935 while playing for a Middlesex XI against Harrow and District at Rayners Lane, Harrow. That season 'Big Jim' hit 50 in 14 minutes against Kent at The Mote, Maidstone, and he was to reduce that time by 3 minutes against Gloucestershire in 1938. A renowned hitter, he frequently peppered the area between the Old Tavern and 'Q' Stand at Lord's, including blows that reached St John's Wood Road.

Smith's feat was equalled in Cairo, Egypt, in 1942–43 by A.D. (Dudley) Nourse, the backbone of both Natal and South African batting for two decades. Playing for a South African XI against the Military Police, his nine consecutive six-hits included six in one over.

Major (later Brigadier) W.M.E. (Michael) White scored **two separate hundreds on the same day** (23 July 1949) for Aldershot Services against the MCC at the Officers' Club Ground, Aldershot. After bowling unchanged throughout the MCC first innings and taking 4 for 85 in 41 overs, White had scored one run at the end of the first day's play. His innings of 112 (3 sixes and 24 fours) enabled the Services side to recover from 123 for 7 to 283 all out – a first innings lead of one run. His second century of the day carried his side to a six-wicket victory against the clock. After reaching three figures in 90 minutes, White took his score to 120 not out, and won the match with two successive boundaries. Two years earlier Mike White had marked his county debut for Northamptonshire by taking three wickets in six balls on two occasions, one in each Somerset innings.

The world record for most runs in one over of genuine bowling is 62. This extraordinary feat was achieved in a Queensland country match in 1968–69. H. Morley struck 9 sixes and 2 fours off an over from R. Grubb which included four no-balls.

The most runs all-run and without the benefit of overthrows off one ball is 17 by Garry Chapman at Windsor Reserve, Victoria, Australia on 13 Oct 1990. Playing for Banyule against Macleod, he pulled the ball to mid-wicket where it disappeared into grass some 10 inches (25 cm) high.

The world record partnership for any wicket is 664 for the third wicket. This was achieved in India during a Harris Shield match at Sassanian Ground, Bombay on 23–25 February 1988 when Vinod Kambli (349 not out) and Sachin Tendulkar (326 not out) shared an unbroken stand for Sharadashram Vidyamandir against St Xavier's High School.

The longest recorded time in which a batsman has failed to score is 100 minutes. Playing for the Gentlemen of Leicestershire against the Free Foresters at Oakham, Rutland, on 19 August 1963, Ian Balfour was marooned on five for his record period. He emerged from his hibernation to score another 34 runs.

BOWLING RECORDS AND OUTSTANDING PERFORMANCES

The feat of taking all 20 wickets in a match is not unique. **The first recorded instance of a bowler taking all ten wickets twice in the same match and bowling all his victims** occurred in 1881–82 in a minor match at Bendemeer, New South Wales, when F.R. 'The Demon' Spofforth, whose cut and swerve at fast-medium pace had bowled Australia to victory at The Oval in 1882 and brought about 'The Ashes', returned match figures of 20 wickets for 48 runs.

This feat was emulated by J. Bryant (Erskine v Deaf Mutes in Melbourne on 15 and 22 October 1887) and by Albert Rimmer (Linwood School v Cathedral Grammar School at Canterbury, New Zealand, in December 1925).

The only recorded instance of a bowler taking all ten wickets, all bowled, for no runs was achieved by Jennings Tune on 6 May 1922. He completed this dream rout in just five overs at Cliffe, Yorkshire, while playing for Cliffe against Eastrington in the Howden and District League.

In an inter-divisional Ships' Shield match at Purfleet, Essex, on 17 May 1924, J.W. Brockley, aged

17, took all ten wickets, clean bowled, for two runs in eleven balls, including a triple hat-trick.

Schoolboy Paul Hugo took nine wickets with nine consecutive balls in South Africa in February 1931. He was playing for Smithfield School against Aliwal North. His feat was equalled in New Zealand in December 1967 by Stephen Fleming, for Marlborough College 'A' XI against Bohally Intermediate at Blenheim.

The oldest man on record to complete a hat-trick is Lionel Deamer when he was aged 74 years 330 days. He achieved this remarkable feat on 6 July 1979 for Lloyds Bank (Midlands) CC against Earlswood CC, finishing with the impressive analysis of five wickets for 14 runs.

Maurice Hanes of Bedworth 2nd XI bowled 17 overs, 5 balls (107 consecutive balls) without conceding a run against A.P. Leamington 2nd XI at Bedworth, Warwickshire, on 16 June 1979. H. Hopkinson of Mildmay CC, London, took 99 wickets for 147 runs in 1910 – an average of only 1.48 runs per wicket.

WICKET-KEEPING AND FIELDING RECORDS

The only wicket-keeper on record to have dismissed an entire side is Welihinda Badalge Bennett on 1 March 1953. The 20-year-old Sri Lankan was a student at Mahinda College for whom he was playing when he stumped six and caught four of the Galle CC team on the Esplanade ground at Galle.

The highest number of recorded catches in a match is 14. Stephen Lane, a 13-year-old schoolboy, held seven catches in the field in each innings while playing for St Patrick's College, Silverstream, against St Bernard's College, Lower Hutt, in Wellington, New Zealand.

Cricket Curiosities

Cawood won a York Senior League match against Dringhouses in 1979 without once hitting the ball. Having dismissed their opponents for just 2 runs in the space of 39 balls, Cawood completed an emphatic victory when the first ball of their innings produced four byes.

MINOR COUNTIES CRICKET

The Minor Counties Cricket Association was formed in 1895 and it immediately instituted the Minor Counties Championship, with seven counties competing in that first season: Bedfordshire, Durham, Hertfordshire, Norfolk, Oxfordshire, Staffordshire and Worcestershire. The foundation dates of those clubs currently competing in the Championship are:

Bedfordshire	3 November 1899
Berkshire	17 March 1895
Buckinghamshire	15 January 1891
Cambridgeshire	6 June 1891
Cheshire	29 September 1908
Cornwall	12 November 1894
Cumberland	10 April 1948
Devon	26 November 1899
Dorset	5 February 1896
Herefordshire	9 January 1991
Hertfordshire	8 March 1876
Lincolnshire	28 September 1906
Norfolk	14 October 1876
Northumberland	December 1895
Oxfordshire	14 December 1921
Shropshire	28 June 1956
Staffordshire	24 November 1871
Suffolk	August 1932
Wiltshire	January 1893

Wales Minor Counties entered the Championship in 1988.

MINOR COUNTIES CHAMPIONS

The record number of titles is nine by Staffordshire. **The most successive titles** is three by Worcestershire 1896–98 and by Staffordshire 1991–93.

THE MINOR COUNTIES CHAMPIONS

1895	Norfolk
	Durham
	Worcestershire
1896	Worcestershire
1897	Worcestershire
1898	Worcestershire
1899	Northamptonshire
	Buckinghamshire
1900	Glamorgan
	Durham
	Northamptonshire

1901	Durham
1902	Wiltshire
1903	Northamptonshire
1904	Northamptonshire
1905	Norfolk
1906	Staffordshire
1907	Lancashire II
1908	Staffordshire
1909	Wiltshire
1910	Norfolk
1911	Staffordshire
1912	In abeyance
1913	Norfolk
1920	Staffordshire
1921	Staffordshire
1922	Buckinghamshire
1923	Buckinghamshire
1924	Berkshire
1925	Buckinghamshire
1926	Durham
1927	Staffordshire
1928	Berkshire
1929	Oxfordshire
1930	Durham
1931	Leicestershire II
1932	Buckinghamshire
1933	Undecided
1934	Lancashire II
1935	Middlesex II
1936	Hertfordshire
1937	Lancashire II
1938	Buckinghamshire
1939	Surrey II
1946	Suffolk
1947	Yorkshire II
1948	Lancashire II
1949	Lancashire II
1950	Surrey II
1951	Kent II
1952	Buckinghamshire
1953	Berkshire
1954	Surrey II

1955	Surrey II
1956	Kent II
1957	Yorkshire II
1958	Yorkshire II
1959	Warwickshire II
1960	Lancashire II
1961	Somerset II
1962	Warwickshire II
1963	Cambridgeshire
1964	Lancashire II
1965	Somerset II
1966	Lincolnshire
1967	Cheshire
1968	Yorkshire II
1969	Buckinghamshire
1970	Bedfordshire
1971	Yorkshire II
1972	Bedfordshire
1973	Shropshire
1974	Oxfordshire
1975	Hertfordshire
1976	Durham
1977	Suffolk
1978	Devon
1979	Suffolk
1980	Durham
1981	Durham
1982	Oxfordshire
1983	Hertfordshire
1984	Durham
1985	Cheshire
1986	Cumberland
1987	Buckinghamshire
1988	Cheshire
1989	Oxfordshire
1990	Hertfordshire
1991	Staffordshire
1992	Staffordshire
1993	Staffordshire
1994	Devon
1995	Devon

MINOR COUNTIES CHAMPIONSHIP RECORDS

Highest Total	621		Surrey II v Devon	The Oval	1928
Lowest Total	14		Cheshire v Staffordshire	Stoke	1909
Highest Score	282	E. Garnett	Berkshire v Wiltshire	Reading	1908
Most Runs - Season	1212	A.F. Brazier	Surrey II		1949
Record Partnership	388*	T.H. Clark & A.F. Brazier	Surrey II v Sussex II	The Oval	1949
Best Bowling					
- Innings	10-11	S. Turner	Cambridgeshire v Cumberland	Penrith	1987
- Match	18-100	N.W. Harding	Kent II v Wiltshire	Swindon	1937
Most Wickets					
- Season	119	S.F. Barnes	Staffordshire		1906

GLOSSARY

All-Rounder: a player who is worth his place either as a batsman or as a bowler. Can also refer to a batsman/wicket-keeper.

Amateur: the status of first-class cricketers who did not receive a salary or match fee but who were permitted 'out-of-pocket expenses'. This distinction from the professional was abolished by the Advisory County Cricket Committee meeting at Lord's on 26 November 1962, a decision later ratified by the MCC. The status still exists in minor cricket where clubs engage professionals.

Analysis: usually refers to bowling statistics for an innings or match, but can also describe a bowler's figures for the season or even his entire career. Innings analyses appear as 19.4–16–10–10 – but not often! That one, 19 overs and 4 balls – 16 maidens – 10 runs – 10 wickets, was achieved by Hedley Verity, Yorkshire's left-arm spin bowler, against Nottinghamshire at Leeds in 1932 and remains the record analysis in all first-class cricket.

Appeal: a call by a player to an umpire for a decision on any matter concerning play; usually refers to a call of 'How's that?' by a member of the fielding side which encompasses all ten ways of dismissing a batsman: bowled, caught, stumped, leg before wicket, hit wicket, run out, hit the ball twice, handled the ball, obstructing the field, and timed out.

Ashes: a trophy, housed in the Memorial Gallery at Lord's, which consists of a small urn supposedly containing the ashes of a bail burnt by some ladies in Sydney, and which was presented to the Hon Ivo Bligh after he had led his English team to a 2–1 victory against W.L. Murdoch's Australians in 1882–1883. The Ashes are normally at stake during Test matches between England and Australia. The trophy was conceived as a result of a mock obituary notice published in *The Sporting Times* after Australia had beaten England in England for the first time (29 August 1882). A note at the foot of this famous obituary announced that 'The body will be cremated and the ashes taken to Australia'. Bligh, who became the eighth Earl of Darnley, retained the urn and its embroidered velvet bag until his death in 1927, when it was bequeathed to the MCC. 'The

Ashes' remain at Lord's even when 'held' by Australia.

Average (Batting): the mean number of runs per completed innings over a period (ie season, tour, Test series, or career) achieved by a batsman; calculated by dividing his aggregate by the number of his innings discounting any in which he was 'not out' or 'retired hurt/ill'.

Average (Bowling): the mean cost of each wicket in terms of runs over a period (as above) achieved by a bowler; calculated by dividing the number of runs conceded (now including wides and no-balls) by the number of wickets taken.

Averages: comparative tables of batting and bowling averages.

Away-Swinger: a bowling delivery which moves in the air from leg to off (right to left as the bowler sees it). Also termed an 'out-swinger'.

Back up, to: in fielding, to prevent overthrows by standing behind the wicket-keeper or another fielder to stop the ball on its return if he misses it, or to support a fielder's throw from a long distance; in batting, the action of the non-striker in moving down the pitch immediately the ball is bowled in order to be ready for a run.

Backward Point: an offside fielding position between Point and the Slip area now usually referred to as 'Gully'.

Bails: two pieces of wood, each 4⅜ inches long, which are placed end to end on top of the stumps and which must not project more than ½ inch above them. The umpires may dispense with them during extremely windy conditions.

Ball: made of stitched leather dyed red with an interior of cork layers each bound with twine; for major cricket its circumference must not measure less than 8¹³⁄₁₆ inches nor more than 9 inches, and its weight, when new, must not be less than 5½ ounces nor more than 5¾ ounces. Other specifications are permitted for lower grade balls and for women's and junior cricket.

Bat: its blade (striking part) must be made of wood – normally willow – and must not exceed 4¼ inches in width; and may be covered with material for protection, strengthening or repair provided that it does not exceed 1/16 inch in thickness; the overall length of the bat (top of handle to bottom of blade) must not exceed 38 inches.

Beamer: a fast, head-high full pitch which is now categorically forbidden under Law 42 (Unfair Play).

Benefit: awarded by the first-class counties to players usually about ten seasons after winning their 1st XI caps. During the calendar year of their benefit, players are allowed to raise unlimited sums from subscriptions and lotteries and are usually awarded the profits of one home county match of their choosing.

Block: the mark or hole made by the batsman with the toe of his bat in the popping crease when taking guard. Also refers to totally defensive batting where the ball is merely stopped with the bat.

Blue: awarded for appearing for Cambridge or Oxford in a University Match.

Bosie: Australia's term for the googly – derived from the name of its originator, B.J.T. Bosanquet.

Bouncer: a fast short-pitched ball which is aimed to reach the batsman at shoulder height or above. An umpire has the power to prevent a bowler intimidating a batsman by bowling bouncers under the provisions of Law 42 (Unfair Play).

Boundary: the limit of the playing area on all sides which is usually marked by a rope, a white line or a fence; current playing conditions for first-class matches exhort the Ground Authority to provide the largest playing area possible, subject to no boundary exceeding a distance of 90 yards from the centre of the pitch or being closer than 50 yards. Also refers to a hit which sends the ball beyond the playing area; four runs are awarded if it touches the ground within the playing area first and six if it does not.

Bowl, to: to propel the ball fairly at the striking batsman's wicket.

Bowled: method of dismissal whereby the bowler bowls down the striker's wicket, even if the ball touches that batsman's bat or person first.

Bowling Crease: the whitewash painted line, 8 feet 8 inches in length, which extends equidistantly on either side of the stumps at each end of the pitch. Under the old no-ball law the bowler had to have part of one foot behind the bowling crease at the moment of delivery but, under the present front-foot law, it is now the popping crease which must not be overstepped.

Box: a light shield for protecting the genitals and worn by batsmen, wicket-keepers and some fielders occupying close positions. Also the old term for the fielding position which is now called 'Gully'.

Break: a ball's deviation from the straight on pitching.

Break-back: a fast off-break which is usually produced by the bowler cutting his fingers across the seam.

Bump Ball: a ball which rebounds directly from the striker's bat to the ground before being 'caught' by a fielder; to the distant spectator a 'bump ball' is usually impossible to distinguish from a genuine catch.

Bumper: a fast short-pitched ball (see 'Bouncer').

Bye: a run scored from a ball (other than a no ball or a wide) which passes the striker without touching his bat or his body.

Call: a batsman's summons to his partner to run. Also the umpire's act of announcing a no-ball, wide or dead ball.

Cap: cricketers' formal headgear. In English first-class cricket, a capped player is one who has been awarded his county 1st XI cap.

Carry One's Bat, to: the act of an opening batsman who remains at the wicket throughout his side's completed innings and is still not out at the fall of the tenth wicket. Batsmen who retire and resume their innings cannot qualify for this epithet.

Castle: colloquial term for the wicket.

Caught: method of dismissal whereby the striker has touched the ball with his bat, or his hand or glove (below the wrist) while holding the bat, and it is subsequently held by a fielder before it touches the ground.

Century: colloquial term for 100 runs.

Change Bowler: one brought on to bowl after the opening pair.

Chinaman: the left-arm bowler's off-break to the right-handed batsman.

Chop: a form of late cut, executed by bringing the bat down sharply on a ball on the off-side just as it passes the batsman, designed to steer the ball through the slip area.

Chucker: a bowler who infringes Law 24 (2) Note (a) by throwing the ball instead of bowling it.

Close Field: the fielding positions which are close to the striker such as the slips, gully, silly point, silly mid-off, silly mid-on, short-legs, and leg slip.

Closure: declaration.

Cow Shot: a rustic unorthodox stroke played across the line of the ball with a near-horizontal bat and which aims to send the ball on the leg-side.

Cradle: an apparatus made of slatted wood fixed to a concave metal frame on to which players throw the ball with a low trajectory to practise slip catching.

Creases: lines of whitewash painted on the pitch at either end and according to Law 9. They define the bowler's permitted area of delivery and also the limits within which the batsman cannot be stumped or run out. There are three types of crease at each end; the Bowling Crease, the Popping Crease and the Return Crease.

Creeper: a ball which shoots along the ground; also termed a 'shooter' or 'sneak'.

Cross-batted: a stroke made with an arc of the bat that is not perpendicular to the pitch and which is consequently aimed across the line of the ball.

Crumbling Pitch: one which is dry and disintegrating.

Cut: a stroke played with a horizontal bat at a short-pitched ball on the off-side (see 'Late Cut' and 'Square Cut').

Cutter: a batsman who cuts. Also a ball which, bowled at medium pace or above, is made to deviate off the ground on pitching.

Dead Ball: the ball becomes dead under Law 23 (1) when:
(a) It is finally settled in the hands of the wicket-keeper or the bowler.
(b) It reaches or pitches over the boundary.

(c) A batsman is out.
(d) Whether played or not, it lodges in the clothing or equipment of a batsman or the clothing of an umpire.
(e) A ball lodges in a protective helmet worn by a member of the fielding side.
(f) A penalty is awarded under Law 20 (Lost Ball) or Law 41 (1) (Fielding the Ball).
(g) The umpire calls 'over' or 'time'.
The ball ceases to be dead when the bowler starts his run-up or bowling action.

Declaration: the closing of an innings by the batting side's captain when he still has wickets standing. Declarations were not allowed until 1889 and then on the last day only. Not until 1951 were they permitted on the first day and then only as an experiment which was not incorporated into the Laws proper until 1957.

Deep: the playing area or field near the boundary which can also be described as the 'country'.

Defence: the batsman's technique in stopping the ball.

Delivery: the act of bowling the ball or the ball bowled.

Donkey Drop: a ball bowled high into the air by a slow bowler.

Drag, to: to drag the back foot when bowling. Also to drag the ball into the wicket (play on) when batting. Also to impart back-spin on the ball when bowling.

Draw: a match which ends without a clear result. Also the name of a batting stroke (no longer played intentionally) where the batsman lifted his front leg and deflected the ball underneath it.

Drive: a stroke aimed at the pitch of the ball with a perpendicular arc of the bat.

Driver: a batsman who specializes in the drive.

Duck: a score of 0.

Extras: runs added to the side's total but which are not credited to the batsman or debited to the bowler. Extras (known in Australia as 'sundries') comprise byes, leg-byes, wides and no-balls.

Field: the playing area. Can also refer to a fielder or the positioning of the fielders.

Fine: at a narrow angle to the wicket; the opposite of square.

Finger-Spin: one method of making the ball turn.

First-Class: the highest grade of match apart from Test cricket. Officially defined (by the then Imperial Cricket Conference) for the first time in 1947 as 'a match of three or more days' duration between two sides of eleven players officially adjudged first-class'. The status of teams is decided by the governing cricket body of the country concerned. A player who appears in a match deemed to be first-class becomes a 'first-class cricketer'.

Flight: the trajectory of the ball. Slow bowlers try to deceive the batsman with subtle variations of flight so that he misjudges the pitch of the ball.

Flipper: a ball bowled by leg-break bowlers which hurries off the pitch like a top-spinner. It is delivered from a special grip involving only the tips of the first and third fingers of the right hand and is flipped out of the hand from underneath the wrist.

Fly Slip: a slightly unusual fielding position about halfway between the slips and the boundary.

Follow-On: the side which bats first and leads by 200 runs in a match of five days or more, by 150 runs in a three or four-day match, by 100 runs in a two-day match, or by 75 runs in a one-day game, has the option of requiring the other side to 'follow their innings'; ie to bat again out of turn.

Follow-Through: the path of a bowler after the act of delivering the ball.

Forward Stroke: a stroke played by advancing the front foot (left foot if the batsman is right-handed) down the wicket to play the ball as close as possible to the place where it pitches.

Full Toss (or Full Pitch): a ball that reaches the batsman without bouncing.

Gardening: the act of repairing or flattening with the bat that part of a damp pitch which has become damaged by the ball's contact.

Gate: the sum of admission money taken at the gate or turnstiles. Also the space left between a batsman's feet and his bat if he does not move to the pitch of the ball correctly.

Gentlemen: the amateur or unpaid cricketers, as distinct from the Players or professionals. The distinction was abolished from English first-class cricket after the 1962 season.

Glance: a deflection of the ball off the face of the bat, usually to fine-leg.

Go Away, to: term for a ball leaving the batsman either in the air or on pitching.

Googly: an off-break bowled with a leg-break action or a left-arm bowler's leg-break delivered with a 'Chinaman' action.

Go With the Arm, to: term for a ball that follows the course of the bowler's arm either in the air or on pitching. A right-arm bowler can thus make his 'arm ball' leave the right-handed batsman; ie make it move from leg to off.

Greasy: a pitch or outfield affected by rain or over-watering.

Green-Top: a pitch that is well grassed. As it is likely to retain overnight moisture early in the day's play, it will obviously favour the faster bowlers.

Ground-Fielding: stopping the ball hit along or via the ground, as opposed to catching.

Groundsman: the person who tends the pitches and playing area. In Australia the term is 'curator'.

Ground-Staff: junior members of the playing staff of a county (or the MCC) who assist with the maintenance of the ground and with bowling in the nets, as well as being coached.

Grub: a ball bowled under-arm along the ground. Also called a 'sneak'.

Guard: given to the batsman on coming in by the umpire at the bowler's end so that he knows the position of his bat and feet in relation to the stumps he is guarding. He will ask for middle, middle-and-leg (or two legs), or leg stump and make his block (mark the ground where his bat rests) accordingly.

Gully: a close catching position on the offside between the slips and point.

Half-Cock: a defensive stroke which is neither forward nor back made when the batsman has misjudged the length of the ball and cannot adjust his feet in time.

Half-Volley: a ball that is overpitched, enabling the

batsman to hit it off the front foot an instant after it has bounced.

Handled the Ball: either batsman (not necessarily the striker) can be out if he touches the ball with his hands while it is in play – unless he has the permission of the fielding side. The wicket is not credited to the bowler.

Harrow Bat: a size of bat smaller than normal and suitable for a teenager.

Hat-trick: the feat of taking three wickets with three consecutive balls within the same match – it can be spread over two overs or even from the first innings into the second. Three wickets with three legitimate balls but with a no-ball interrupting the sequence does not count as a hat-trick. The term evolved from the custom of presenting the bowler with a top hat for achieving this feat. The first recorded instance occurred on 8 September 1858 at the Hyde Park Ground in Sheffield when H.H. Stephenson, playing for the All-England Eleven, took three wickets in three balls in the second innings and was presented with a white hat.

Hit the Ball Twice: the batsman is out if he hits the ball twice except for the sole purpose of defending his wicket. The dismissal is not credited to the bowler.

Hit Wicket: a batsman is out if, while the ball is in play, he breaks his wicket with any part of his person, dress or bat, at any time when playing the ball or in setting off for his first run. He is not out if he breaks his wicket while trying to avoid being run out or stumped. The dismissal is credited to the bowler.

Hook: the stroke made off the back foot by which a short ball is hit to leg with a cross bat.

How's That?: the standard form of appeal.

Inswinger: a ball which moves in flight from off to leg.

King Pair: short for a 'king pair of spectacles'. If, in a two-innings match, a batsman is out first ball for nought in both innings, he has 'bagged a king pair'.

Lap: a modern term for a cross-batted stroke, somewhere between a sweep and a pull, which hits the ball towards mid-wicket.

Late Cut: a wristy stroke played late and with a

horizontal bat to a short ball outside the off stump and which hits it downwards and past the slips.

Leg Before Wicket (lbw): a method of dismissal credited to the bowler and defined under Law 36 as follows:
(a) **Striker Attempting to Play the Ball** The striker shall be out LBW if he first intercepts with any part of his person, dress or equipment a fair ball which would have hit the wicket and which has not previously touched his bat or a hand holding the bat, provided that:
(i) the ball pitched in a straight line between wicket and wicket or on the off-side of the striker's wicket, or in the case of a ball intercepted full pitch would have pitched in a straight line between wicket and wicket; and
(ii) the point of impact is in a straight line between wicket and wicket, even if above the level of the bails.
(b) **Striker Making No Attempt to Play the Ball** The striker shall be out LBW even if the ball is intercepted outside the line of the off stump if, in the opinion of the umpire, he has made no genuine attempt to play the ball with his bat, but has intercepted the ball with some part of his person and if the circumstances set out in (a) above apply.

Leg Break: a ball that turns from leg to off on pitching.

Leg-Bye: a run obtained from a ball that has been unintentionally deflected by the batsman with any part of his person other than his hand or hands holding the bat, but has not touched the bat. Leg-byes are recorded as extras and are not debited to the bowler's analysis. A leg-bye scored off a no-ball is recorded as a no-ball.

Leg-Cutter: a fast leg-break bowled by cutting the fingers across the seam of the ball.

Leg-Side: the side of the pitch and field behind the batsman as he adopts his stance at the crease, ie the side containing his legs.

Leg-Theory: a method of bowling concentrated on the leg stump and the pads with an array of fielders in catching positions on the leg-side (the 'leg-trap').

Leg-Trap: a crescent of fielders in close catching positions on the leg-side in support of inswing, off-spin or leg-theory bowling.

Length: one of the basics of good bowling. A good-length ball is one which pitches at such a distance from the batsman that he is uncertain whether to play forward or back.

Light: one of three constantly varying factors affecting play (along with weather and the state of the pitch). Under the present Law 3 the umpires are sole judges of the fitness of the light for play without appeal from the batting side. Their decision can be overruled if both captains want play to continue.

Lob: a ball bowled or returned by a fielder under-arm.

Long Field: the area of the field in front of the bowler's end sightscreen where long-off and long-on patrol.

Long Handle: taken by an aggressive batsman intent on hitting out. The term derives from the batsman's grip; by moving his hands to the top of the handle he can increase the arc of his swing.

Long Hop: a short-pitched ball easily punished off the back foot on either side of the wicket.

Long-Leg: fielding position on or near the boundary behind the wicket on the leg-side – a very deep fine-leg.

Long-Off, Long-On: fielding positions on or near the boundary on either side of the sightscreen at the bowler's end.

Long-Stop: obsolete fielding position behind the wicket-keeper. It was once a vital position demanding a specialist fieldsman as wicket-keeping gloves were unknown until *c* 1820. The first wicket-keeper to dispense with a long-stop was Harry Phillips who kept wicket for Sussex from 1868 until 1891.

Lost Ball: an archaic provision, presumably retained for minor cricket, whereby, if the ball in play cannot be found or recovered, any fielder may call 'lost ball' when six runs shall be added to the score, or as many as have already been completed.

Maiden: an over from which no runs are scored by the batsmen. A maiden over must not include any no-balls or wides; since 1985 the penalty runs incurred by such deliveries have been debited to the bowler's analysis.

Match: a contest of two innings per side, except in one-day and limited-overs games.

Matting: an alternative to grass as a surface for the pitch. Can be made of jute (fibre from the bark of an East Indian plant), coir (coconut fibre), or of various synthetic substances. The base on which it is laid is vitally important and can vary from grass to concrete.

Meat: of the bat – the middle of the blade at its thickest point.

Middle: the 'square' on which the pitches are prepared.

Mow: cross-batted hit to leg.

Nets: a 'hollow' rectangle of string netting within which players practise on prepared pitches away from the main square or on synthetic pitches at indoor schools.

New Ball: either captain can demand a new ball at the start of each innings. Under the present Law 5, national governing bodies are left to determine the availability of a second new ball in matches of three or more days' duration, but stipulate a minimum of 75 overs. In Test matches in England the captain has the option of taking a new ball after 85 overs have been bowled with the old one. In all other first-class matches, including the County Championship, the number of overs is 100. Under ICC regulations effective from September 1995, a new ball will be available after 80 overs in all Test matches.

Night-Watchman: a lower-order batsman sent in to play out time when a wicket falls shortly before close of play, and to prevent a better batsman risking his wicket.

No-Ball: an illegal delivery. For a ball to be legitimate, it must be bowled and not thrown, the bowler's back foot must land within and not touching the return crease and its forward extension, and some part of his front foot (grounded or raised) must be behind the popping crease. In addition, the bowler must notify the batsman of any change in his mode of delivery; ie from over to round the wicket, under-arm to over-arm, right-arm to left-arm.

No-balls are also called for certain infringements by fielders and the wicket-keeper. A penalty of one run is awarded if no runs are made otherwise. Since 1985 such penalty runs have been debited to bowlers' individual analyses. Byes or leg-byes scored off a no-ball are recorded as no-balls. A batsman can be out off a no-ball in four ways: run out, handling the ball, hitting the ball twice, and obstructing the field. An extra ball must be bowled for every no-ball called so that each completed over contains six legal deliveries. Experimental regulations, introduced in Australia in 1989–90 and in Britain in 1993, applying only to domestic state and county competitions respectively, have awarded a penalty of two runs in addition to any scored from each no-ball (thus a no-ball hit for six adds eight runs to the total – six to the batsman and two to extras).

Not Out: to not lose one's wicket. 'Not out' innings are excluded when calculating batting averages. Also an umpire's negative reply to an appeal.

Obstructing the Field: either batsman can be out if he wilfully obstructs the fielding side by word or action. If the non-striker is responsible for an act of wilful obstruction which prevents a catch from being taken, it is the striker who is out. The dismissal is not credited to the bowler.

Off-Break: a ball that turns from off to leg on pitching.

Off-Cutter: a fast off-break bowled by cutting the fingers across the seam of the ball.

Off-Drive: a drive, usually made off the front foot, which hits the ball between cover and mid-off.

Off-Side: the side of the pitch and field in front of the batsman as he adopts his stance at the crease, opposite the side where his legs are.

On-Drive: a drive, usually made off the front foot, which hits the ball between mid-wicket and midon.

Out-Cricket: the collective effort of the fielding team.

Out-Field: the outer part of the playing area away from the table or square.

Out of His Ground: the batsman must have some part of his bat in his hand or of his person grounded behind the line of the popping crease; on the line is out.

Outswinger: a ball which moves in flight from leg to off.

Over: the period of play, or total of balls bowled, between one changing of ends and the next. Six-ball overs have been in operation universally in first-class cricket since the 1979–80 season, although Law 22 does provide for either six or eight.

Over the Wicket: the method of bowling where the operative arm is close to or over the stumps, ie to a right-handed batsman, a right-arm bowler bowls from the off-side and a left-arm bowler delivers from the leg-side.

Overthrow: a throw-in by a fielder which is not gathered at the stumps and which enables the batsmen to take a further run or more. Runs thus taken are termed overthrows but, unless they are extras, they are credited to the striker and debited to the bowler's analysis.

Pad-Play: the act of deliberately stopping balls with the pads.

Pair: a pair of spectacles – two scores of nought in the same match.

Pitch: the specially prepared area, 5 feet in width and 22 yards (one agricultural chain) long, between the two sets of stumps.

Play: the action of the game. Also the umpire's call to begin.

Played On: term meaning to deflect the ball into the stumps with the bat. It is recorded as 'bowled'.

Plumb: a true pitch, perfect for batting. Also it can describe an lbw decision that is so obviously out (to all observers except the victim), that the batsman should have 'walked' without waiting for an appeal.

Point: a close fielding position square with the wicket on the offside 'at the point of the bat'.

Pop: a ball which lifts sharply off the pitch is said to pop.

Popping Crease: the line across the pitch marking the forward limit of the batsman's safe ground. Painted in whitewash 4 feet in front of the stumps, it is now the line which controls the bowler's front foot.

Professional: a player employed to coach and/or play by clubs and schools. Before amateur status was abolished in English cricket at the end of the 1962 season it described a paid player.

Pull: a forceful stroke off the front foot made with a vertical bat across the line of a ball pitching on or outside the off stump, and sending the ball between mid-on and mid-wicket.

Put In, to: to ask the opposition to bat first: ie to elect to field on winning the toss.

Quickie: colloquial term for a fast bowler.

Quick Wicket: a hard pitch from which the ball bounces quickly.

Reach: the distance which a batsman can stretch forward to reach the pitch of a ball.

Retire Hurt or Ill: a batsman may retire, ie end his innings voluntarily, at any time. If his action is the result of injury or illness, it is regarded as 'not out' and he may resume his innings at the fall of a wicket or the retirement of another batsman. If he leaves the field or retires for any other reason, it is recorded as 'Retired, out' and he can only resume his innings with the consent of the opposing captain.

Return: a throw back to the stumps at either end after the ball has been fielded.

Return Creases: the lines at each end of the bowling crease, parallel with a line between the two sets of stumps and 4 feet 4 inches from the middle stump's centre. They are marked to at least 4 feet behind the wicket but are considered to be unlimited in length. Since the introduction of the front foot no-ball law, the return crease has been extended to join the popping crease and so complete the rectangle.

Round the Wicket: the method of bowling where the operative arm is the one farther from the stumps, ie to a right-handed batsman, a right-arm bowler bowls from the leg-side and a left-arm one delivers from the off-side.

Rubber: a set of Test matches between the same two countries and played during one season. Also termed a series.

Run: the unit of scoring.

Runner: the member of the batting side allowed to run for a batsman who, during the match, is incapacitated by illness or injury. If possible, he should have already batted in that innings and, if the injured batsman is wearing gloves and pads, he must be similarly equipped.

Run Out: a method of dismissal not credited to the bowler. Either batsman can be Run Out if in running he is out of his ground and the wicket is broken by the fielding side. The batsman nearest to the broken wicket is the one dismissed if they are in the act of running. If a batsman remains in or returns to his ground and the other batsman joins him there, the latter is out if his wicket is broken. If a batsman is run out, only that run being attempted is not scored. The one exception involves an injured batsman ignoring his runner and being run out himself, when no runs are scored.

Run the Ball Away: to cause it to move away from the batsman towards the slips.

Run-Up: a bowler's approach to his delivery stride.

Score Book: the volume of printed forms on which the match is recorded.

Score Card: a printed card giving the teams and allowing space for innings and bowling details to be recorded. A document seldom available outside Britain.

Scorer: person who records the details of the match.

Scratch Team: a privately collected side with no bond of common membership.

Seam: the stitching around the circumference of the ball that fastens together its leather segments. It plays an important part in bowling techniques.

Seam Bowler or Seamer: any bowler of medium pace or faster who makes the ball deviate by pitching it on its seam rather than using cut or fingerspin.

Selector: in England, one of a committee appointed annually by the Test and County Cricket Board (TCCB) to choose England teams for that season's Test matches. For choosing tours overseas, the selectors are usually joined by the tour captain and manager, and by the chairman of the TCCB Cricket Committee.

Session: one of three periods of play separated by lunch and tea intervals.

Shooter: a ball that does not rise off the ground after pitching.

Short-Leg: a close catching position on the leg-side, defined more precisely by its relationship to the batsman's wicket; ie forward, square or backward.

Short Run: when either batsman fails to make good his ground at one end when running two or more runs, the umpire calls and signals 'one short', and the run is not counted. Also a quickly taken single for a short hit.

Shoulder Arms: used to describe a batsman's action when he holds the bat aloft and allows an off-side ball to pass without playing a stroke.

Sight-Screen: the screen, usually white and mobile, sited beyond the boundary behind the bowler to give the batsman the clearest possible view of the ball. For Test matches in England the TCCB has ruled that ground authorities must provide sight-screens at both ends. For night cricket which uses a white ball, the screens have to be black.

Silly: close; ie silly mid-on is synonymous with forward short leg.

Single: one run.

Skier: steepling hit.

Slip: fielding position on the offside and adjacent to the wicketkeeper. First slip is next to the 'keeper and any others are numbered outwards towards gully.

Square-Cut: a stroke made off the back foot with a horizontal bat to a short ball outside the off stump, and which despatches it just backward of point.

Sticky Wicket: a rain-affected pitch which has begun to dry out under the sun's heat, forming a hard crust over soft, wet soil. This allows the ball to bite, turn and lift sharply. Also termed a 'glue pot'.

Stone-Waller: an extremely defensive batsman who is more concerned with safeguarding his wicket than with scoring runs.

Stumps: normally of ash. Three stumps (off, middle and leg) form the wicket when surmounted by two bails.

Stumped: a batsman is out if, in receiving a ball that is not a no-ball but which may be a wide, he is out of his ground and the wicket is put down by the wicket-keeper without the intervention of another fielder. If this happens when he is not attempting a run, he is out stumped and the dismissal is credited to the bowler.

Substitute: a substitute player may field for any member of the side who, during that particular match, is incapacitated by illness or injury. The consent of the opposing captain must be obtained for the use of a substitute if any player is prevented from fielding for any other reason. The opposing captain cannot object to any particular player acting as substitute, nor, under the 1980 code, to where he shall field apart from keeping wicket. A player may bat, bowl or field even though a substitute has acted for him. Any catches or stumpings made by a substitute are recorded as 'ct/st sub', although

current books containing the full scores of Test matches do add the substitute's name in brackets. A substitute is not permitted to bat or bowl unless he is replacing a player called from a County Championship match to stand by for England's Test team. The first instance of this regulation being invoked occurred on 29 July 1982 when David Brown, the former England fast bowler who was Cricket Manager of Warwickshire, substituted for Gladstone Small in the match against Lancashire at Southport, bowled 13 overs and took a wicket before making way for the player England had not needed after all.

Sweep: a stroke played off the front foot from the crouch position with a horizontal bat usually to a ball pitched on or outside the leg stump. Denis Compton was the master and main perpetrator of the sweep and a large proportion of his runs were scored behind the wicket on the leg-side from it.

Swerve: old term for swing – lateral movement of the ball in the air.

Tail: those players who are not selected for their batting ability and who occupy the lower places in the batting order.

Team: a match is played between two sides or teams of eleven players each, one of whom is captain.

Testimonial: awarded by counties to players and, occasionally, officials, who have given long service. Unlike a Benefit, it does not include the proceeds of a county match.

Test Match: a contest of two innings per side and usually of five days' duration between two full members of the International Cricket Conference.

Tie: a match which ends with an equal aggregate of runs scored by both sides and with the side batting last having completed its innings.

Top-Spin: spin which causes the ball to gain pace after bouncing but not to deviate laterally. It is an additional weapon in the leg-break bowler's armoury.

Toss: a coin is tossed by the home captain and his opposite number calls 'heads' or 'tails'. The winner has choice of innings.

Tour: sequence of away matches played by one team without returning home. The term is usually reserved for the fixed itinerary of a team travelling abroad.

Track: colloquial term for the pitch.

Twelfth Man: the emergency (substitute) fielder and drinks waiter.

Umpire's Signals: these are laid down in Law 3 of the 1980 code and must be acknowledged by an official scorer before the game can proceed:
Boundary: by waving the arm from side to side.
Boundary 6: by raising both arms above the head.
Bye: by raising an open hand above the head.
Dead Ball: by crossing and recrossing the wrists below the waist.
Leg-Bye: by touching a raised knee with the hand.
No-Ball: by extending one arm horizontally.
Out: by raising the index finger above the head. If not out, the umpire shall call 'not out'.
Short run: by bending the arm upwards and by touching the nearer shoulder with the tips of the fingers.
Wide: by extending both arms horizontally.

Wicket: the three wooden stumps with two wooden bails on top that are pitched opposite and parallel to each other and 22 yards apart. Each wicket when set must be 9 inches wide with the tops of the stumps 28 inches above the ground. The bails are 4⅜ inches long and, when in position on top of the stumps, must not project more than ½ inch above them. In an extreme wind the umpires may decide to dispense with the bails. The term wicket is often, quite incorrectly, used to describe the pitch.

Wicket-keeper: the fielder who, protected by pads and gauntlets, fields behind the stumps at the batsman's end. Before the specialist position was introduced in the late 18th century, a fielder was placed in the deep behind the batsman (long-stop).

Wicket Maiden: an over in which no runs are scored by the batsmen but in which at least one wicket falls which has been credited to the bowler. It must not include any no-balls or wides.

Wide: a ball bowled so high over or so wide of the wicket that, in the opinion of the umpire, it passes out of the reach of the striker, standing in a normal guard position. It must be called and signalled by the bowler's umpire as soon as it passes the line of the striker's wicket. If no extras result from it, a penalty of one run is added to the score and another ball must be bowled to replace it in that over. Since 1985 such penalty runs have been debited to bowlers' individual analyses. Unlike no-balls, wides are not included in the total of balls received by the batsman as he cannot score off a wide. He can, however, be out to a wide in five ways: stumped, hit wicket, run out, handled the ball, or obstructing the field. If a batsman hits a ball called 'wide', the umpire must revoke his call.

Wrong-Un: another term for the googly – an off-break bowled with a leg-break action.

Yorker: a ball pitched well up so that, at the instant the bat on its downswing reaches the vertical, it passes underneath it. The term probably originated in Yorkshire because bowlers there were especially proficient at pitching balls on that length.

Index

Bold type denotes an illustration. (Group photographs are not included.)

Abbreviations used in the index:

Aus	Australia
CU	Cambridge University
E	England
EP	Eastern Province
GW	Griqualand West
I	India
NSW	New South Wales
NZ	New Zealand
Q	Queensland
OFS	Orange Free State
OU	Oxford University
P	Pakistan
SA	South Africa
SL	Sri Lanka;
T	Transvaal
Tas	Tasmania
V	Victoria
WA	Western Australia
WI	West Indies
WP	Western Province
Z	Zimbabwe

B

Chatfield, Ewen John MBE b 3 Jul 1950 (Wellington; NZ) 52

Chatterjee, Premanshu Mohan b 10 Aug 1927 (Bengal) 174

Chauhan, Chetandra Pratap Singh b 21 Jul 1947 (Maharashtra; Delhi; I) 142

Chitty, John 10

Chowdhury, Nirode Ranjan 1923-79 (Bengal; Bihar; I) 36

Clark, Edward Winchester 'Nobby' 1902-82 (Northants; E) 118

Clark, Thomas Henry 1924-81 (Surrey) 221

Clarke, William 1798-1856 (Notts; All-E) 17, 196

Clay, John Charles 1898-1973 (Glam; E) 104, 130

Clayton, Geoffrey b 3 Feb 1938 (Lancs; Somerset) 122

Clift, Patrick Bernard b 14 Jul 1953 (Rhodesia, Natal, Leics) 114

Close, Dennis Brian CBE b 24 Feb 1931 (Yorks; Somerset; E) 61, 88, 92, 189, 192, 193

Cobden, Frank Carroll 1849-1932 (CU) 135

Coe, Samuel 1873-1955 (Leics) 114

Coen, Stanley Keppel 'Shunter' 1902-67 (WP; OFS; GW; SA) 219

Collinge, Richard Owen b 2 Apr 1946 (C Dist; Wellington; N Dist; NZ) 35, 39, 52

Collins, Arthur Edward Jeune 1885-1913 (Clifton College) 218

Collins, Herbert Leslie 1889-1959 (NSW; Aus) 37

Collymore, Desmond John b 28 Jun 1956 (Windward Is) 161

Commins, John Brian b 19 Feb 1965 (WP; Boland; SA) 187

Compton, Denis Charles Scott CBE b 23 May 1918 (Middx; Holkar; E) 36, 40, 41, 67, 81, 83, 116, 122, 151, 152, 153, 174, 189, 190

Congdon, Bevan Ernest OBE b 11 Feb 1938 (C Dist; Wellington; Otago; Canterbury; NZ) 43

Coningham, Arthur 1863-1939 (Q; NSW; Aus) 49

Connolly, Alan Norman b 29 Jun 1939 (V; Middx; Aus) 52

Constantine, Sir Learie Nicholas MBE Baron Maravel and Nelson 1902-71 (Trinidad; WI) 92

Contractor, Nariman Jamshedji b 7 Mar 1934 (Gujarat; Railways; I) 59

Conway, Arthur Joseph 1885-1954 (Worcs) 106, 130

Cook, Cecil 'Sam' b 23 Aug 1921 (Glos; E) 88

Cook, Geoffrey b 9 Oct 1951 (Northants; EP; E) 205, 210

Cook, Geoffrey William b 9 Feb 1936 (CU; Kent) 135

Cook, Stephen James b 31 Jul 1953 (T; Somerset; SA) 77, 104, 122

Cooley, Bertram Clifford 1874-1935 (Natal) 153

Cooper, Bransby Beauchamp 1844-1914 (Middx; Kent; V; Aus) 23, 24

Cooper, Kevin Edwin b 27 Dec 1957 (Notts) 87

Copley, Sydney Herbert 1905-86 (Notts) 56

Copson, William Henry 1908-71 (Derbys; E) 85

Cork, Dominic Gerald b 7 Aug 1971 (Derbys; E) 50, 50

Cornford, Walter Latter 'Tich' 1900-64 (Sussex; E) 191

Corrall, Percy 1906-94 (Leics) 114

Cottam, Robert Michael Henry b 16 Oct 1944 (Hants; Northants; E) 108

Cotton, John b 7 Nov 1940 (Notts; Leics) 204

Court, Jacqueline b 1950 (Middx; E) 201

Cowdrey, Sir Michael Colin CBE b 24 Dec 1932 (OU; Kent; E) 32, 35, 39, 41, 45, 48, 49, 56, 60, **60**, 188, 190, 192

Cowper, Robert Maskew b 5 Oct 1940 (V; WA; Aus) 34, 67

Cox, George Reuben 1873-1949 (Sussex) 126, 192, 193

Coysh, Doris (née Turner) 1907-86 (Middx; South; E) 198

Craig, Ian Davis b 12 Jun 1935 (NSW; Aus) 141

Crawford, Vivian Frank Shergold 1879-1922 (Surrey; Leics) 218-9

Crawford, William Patrick Anthony b 3 Aug 1933 (NSW; Aus) 139

Crawley, Leonard George 1903-81 (CU; Essex; Worcs) 162

Crisp, Robert James DSO MC 1911-94 (Rhodesia; WP; Worcs; SA) 154

Croft, Colin Everton Hunte b 15 Mar 1953 (Guyana; Lancs; WI) 52

Crowe, Jeffrey John b 14 Sep 1958 (Auckland; S Aus; NZ) 168, 183

Crowe, Martin David MBE b 22 Sep 1962 (Auckland; C Dist; Somerset; Wellington; NZ) 34, 35, **36**, 39, 43, 56, 68, 166, 167

Crump, Brian Stanley b 25 Apr 1938 (Northants) 86

Dyer, Dennis Victor 1914-90 (Natal; SA) 49

Dymock, Geoffrey b 21 Jul 1945 (Q; Aus) 30, 48

Dyson, Jack b 8 Jul 1934 (Lancs) 73

E

Ealham, Alan George Ernest b 30 Aug 1944 (Kent) 90

East, David Edward b 27 Jul 1959 (Essex) 88, 102

East, Robert John b 31 Mar 1953 (OFS) 155

Eastman, Lawrence Charles 1897-1941 (Essex; Otago) 193

Edmonds, Philippe Henri b 8 Mar 1951 (CU: Middx; EP; E) 51

Edrich, John Hugh MBE b 21 Jun 1937 (Surrey; E) 39, 41, 189, 190, 211

Edrich, William John DFC 1916-86 (Middx; E) 81, 83, 116, 120, 134, 150, 189, 192

Edward II, King of England 1284-1327 9

Eggar, John Drennan 1916-83 (OU; Hants; Derbys) 98

Ekanayake, Ajith Wijeratne b 3 Oct 1965 (Kurungala Youth; NW Prov) 183

Elliott, Charles Standish b 24 Apr 1912 (Derbys) 98, 211

Elliott, Gideon 1828-69 (V) 146

Elliott, Harry 1891-1976 (Derbys; E) 98, 99, 191

Ellis, Mathew 1870-1940 (V) 140

Emburey, John Ernest b 20 Aug 1952 (Middx; WP; E) 51, 57, 70, 193

Emmett, Thomas 1841-1904 (Yorks; E) 23, 25

Endean, William Russell b 31 May 1924 (T; SA) 151, 152-3

English, Edward Apsey 1864-1966 (Hants) 93

Evans, Thomas Godfrey CBE b 18 Aug 1920 (Kent; E) 40, 54, 58, 141, 191, 194

Everett, Samuel Charles 1901-70 (NSW) 139

F

Fagg, Arthur Edward 1915-77 (Kent; E) 76

Fairbrother, Neil Harvey b 9 Sep 1963 (Lancs; T; E) 124

Farrimond, William 1903-79 (Lancs; E) 112

Faulkner, George Aubrey DSO; Major 1881-1930 (T; SA) 58

Fazal Mahmood b 18 Feb 1927 (N India; Punjab; Lahore; P) 29, 53, 70, 180

Fender, Percy George Herbert 1892-1985 (Sussex; Surrey; E) 78, 92, 192, 193

Ferguson, William Henry BEM 'Fergie' 1880-1957 (Australian scorer) 13, 78

Fernando, Lucky Rogers b 11 Sep 1970 (Moratuwa) 184

Ferris, John James 1867-1900 (NSW; S Aus; Aus; Glos; E) 62

Fielder, Arthur 1877-1949 (Kent; E) 28, 83, 134

Findlay, Thaddeus Michael b 19 Oct 1943 (Windward Is; WI) 163

Fingleton, John Henry Webb 1908-81 (NSW; Aus) 27, 33, 39, 143

Firth, Jack 1918-81 (Yorks; Leics) 114

Flavell, John Alfred b 15 May 1929 (Worcs; E) 130

Fleetwood-Smith, Leslie O'Brien 'Chuck' 1910-71 (V; Aus) 48, 86

Fleming, Stephen (Marlborough Coll, NZ) 220

Fletcher, Duncan Andrew Gwynne b 27 Sep 1948 (Rhodesia; Z) 215

Fletcher, Keith William Robert OBE b 20 May 1944 (Essex; E) 41, 60, 80, 102, **103**, 189, 192, 215

Flint, Derrick b 14 Jun 1924 (Warks) 198

Flower, Andrew b 28 Apr 1968 (Mashonaland; Z) 39, **40**, 54, 61, 187, 215

Flower, Grant William b 20 Dec 1970 (Mashonaland; Z) 39, 40, 61, 69, 187

Flowers, Wilfred 1856-1926 (Notts; E) 193

Foley, Cyril Pelham Lt Col 1868-1936 (CU; Middx) 72

Ford, Francis Gilbertstone Justice 1866-1940 (CU; Middx; E) 72

Fordham, Alan b 9 Nov 1964 (Northants) 74, 118

Foster, Neil Alan b 6 May 1962 (Essex; T; E) 87

Foster, Reginald Erskine 'Tip' 1878-1914 (OU; Worcs; E) 34, 36, 67, 153

Fowler, Graeme b 20 Apr 1957 (Lancs; Durham; E) 76, **76**, 80

Francis, MG (OFS) 152

Frank, Charles Newton 1891-1961 (T; SA) 37

Fraser, Angus Robert Charles b 8 Aug 1965 (Middx; E) 51

Fredericks, Roy Clifton b 11 Nov 1942 (Guyana; Glam; WI) 43

Greenwood, Julia b 1951 (Yorks; E) 199

Gregory, Charles William 1878-1910 (NSW) 141

Gregory, David William 1845-1919 (NSW; Aus) 22, 23, 24, **24**

Gregory, Edward James 'Ned' 1839-99 (NSW; Aus) 13, 23, 24

Gregory, John Morison 'Jack' 1895-1973 (NSW; Aus) 27, 37, 56, 89

Gregory, Robert James 1902-73 (Surrey) 104

Greig, Anthony William b 6 Oct 1946 (Border; EP; Sussex; E) 41, 51, 57

Grieves, Kenneth John 1925-92 (NSW; Lancs) 112, 192

Griffith, Mike Grenville b 25 Nov 1943 (CU; Sussex) 85, 126

Griffith, Stewart Cathie 'Billy' CBE, DFC 1914-93 (CU; Surrey; Sussex; E; Sec. MCC) 12, 205, 207

Grimmett, Clarence Victor 1891-1980 (Wellington; V; S Aus; Aus) 45, 46, 51, 54, 132, 145

Grout, Arthur Theodore Wallace 'Wally' 1927-68 (Q; Aus) 54, 88-9, 145

Grubb, R 219

Guillen, Simpson Clairmonte b 24 Sep 1924 (Trinidad; WI; Canterbury; NZ) 62

Gul Mahomed 1921-92 (N India; Muslims; Baroda; Hyderabad; Lahore; I; P) 62, 173, 178

Gulfraz Khan (Railways) 180

Gunawardene, Aruna Alwis Wijesiri b 31 Mar 1969 (Sinhalese SC) 183

Gunn, George 1879-1958 (Notts; E) 61, 77, 120, 189

Gunn, George Vernon 1905-57 (Notts) 77

Gunn, John Richard 1876-1963 (Notts; E) 193

Gunn, William 1858-1921 (Notts; E) 120

Gupte, Subhash Pandrinath 'Fergie' b 11 Dec 1929 (Bombay; Bengal; I) 53, 70, 174

Gurusinha, Asanka Pradeep b 16 Sep 1966 (Sinhalese SC; SL) 30, 39, 68

H

Hadlee, Sir Richard John MBE b 3 Jul 1951 (Canterbury; Notts; Tasmania; NZ) 43, 44, 45, **45**, 46, 47, 48, 52, 57, 61, 69, 70, 92, 183, 193

Hadow, Walter Henry 1849-98 (OU; Middx) 76

Hagan, David Andrew b 25 Jun 1966 (OU) 86

Haig, Nigel Esmé 1887-1966 (Middx; E) 193

Haigh, Schofield 1871-1921 (Yorks; E) 191, 193

Halangoda, Mahinda Bandula b 26 Apr 1961 (Sinhalese SC) 183-4

Hall, James William b 30 Mar 1968 (Sussex) 80

Hall, Wesley Winfield b 12 Sep 1937 (Barbados; Trinidad; Q; WI) 52

Hallam, Maurice Raymond b 10 Sep 1931 (Leics) 114, 204

Hallows, Charles 1895-1972 (Lancs; E) 83, 112

Hamence, Ronald Arthur b 25 Nov 1915 (S Aus; Aus) 74

Hammond, Walter Reginald 1903-65 (Glos; E) 27, 32, 34, 35, 38, 41, 56, 68, 83, 90, 91, 95, 106, 134, 147, 188, 190, 192

Hanes, Maurice (Bedworth CC) 220

Hanif Mohammad b 21 Dec 1934 (Bahawalpur; Karachi; PIA; P) 34, 35, 38, 44, 54, 68, 139, 161, 178-9

Harbottle, Michael Neale; Brig b 17 Feb 1917 (Army) 75-6

Hardie, Brian Ross b 14 Jan 1950 (Essex; Scotland) 205

Harding, Norman Walter 1916-47 (Kent) 221

Hardinge, Harold Thomas William 1886-1965 (Kent; E) 189

Hardstaff, Joseph jr 1911-90 (Notts; Services; Auckland; E) 26, 120, 189

Hargreave, Sam 1875-1929 (Warks) 128

Harman, George Frederick Uniake 1874-1975 (Dublin U) 93

Harman, William Ronayne 1869-1962 (Ireland) 93

Harris, Sir George Robert Canning 4th Baron GCSI GCIE CB 1851-1932 (OU; Kent; E) 30, 55, 93, 145

Harris, Leston Livingstone b 28 Jun 1967 (Leeward Is) 163

Harris, Michael John 'Pasty' b 25 May 1944 (Middx; Notts; EP; Wellington) 120

Harrison, George Pickering 'Shoey' 1862-1940 (Yorks) 88

Harrison, Leonard b 8 Jun 1922 (Hants) 108

Hart, Matthew Norman b 16 May 1972 (N Dist; NZ) 212

Hart, Ronald Terence b 7 Nov 1961 (C Dist; NZ) 167

I

J

Strang, Paul Andrew b 28 Jul 1970 (Mashonaland; Z) 187

Streak, Heath Hilton b 16 Mar 1974 (Matabeleland; Hants; Z) 46, 47, **47**, 49, 53, 70

Street, George Benjamin 1889-1924 (Sussex; E) 126

Strudwick, Herbert 1880-1970 (Surrey; E) 89, 95, 124, 191

Strydom, Jan Joubert b 8 Sep 1962 (OFS) 153

Studd, Charles Thomas 1860-1931 (CU; Middx; E) 92

Subba Row, Raman CBE b 29 Jan 1932 (CU; Surrey; Northants; E) 118

Sueter, Thomas 1749-1827 (Hambledon; Surrey; E) 12

Sunderam, Pradeep b 21 Mar 1960 (Rajasthan) 174

Sunnucks, Peter Regan b 22 Jun 1916 (Kent) 76

Surridge, Walter Stuart 1917-92 (Surrey) 90, 91, 94

Susskind, Manfred Julius 1891-1957 (Middx; CU; T; SA) 49

Sutcliffe, Bert b 17 Nov 1923 (Auckland; Otago; N Dist; NZ) 27, 68, 166, 167

Sutcliffe, Herbert 1894-1978 (Yorks; E) 29, 30, 32, 41, 81, 82, 83, 102, 132, 188, 190, 205

Sutcliffe, William Herbert Hobbs b 22 May 1960 (Yorks) 183

Sutherland, John Grey 'Jock' b 5 Nov 1945 (Wakutu CC) 169

Suttle, Kenneth George b 25 Aug 1928 (Sussex) 95, 189

Symonds, Andrew b 9 Jun 1975 (Q; Glos) **79**, 80, 167

T

Taber, Hedley Brian b 29 Apr 1940 (NSW; Aus) 145-6

Tahir Rashid b 21 Nov 1960 (Karachi; Habib Bank) 180

Tallon, Donald 1916-84 (Q; Aus) 145

Tariq Bashir (House Building Finance Corp) 179

Tarrant, Francis Alfred 1880-1951 (V; Middx; Patiala) 116, 194

Taslim Arif b 1 May 1954 (Karachi; Sind; Nat Bank; P) 55, 180

Tate, Maurice William 1895-1956 (Sussex; E) 27, 31, 49, 51, 57, 92, 118, 126, 190, 194

Tavaré, Christopher James b 27 Oct 1954 (OU; Kent; Somerset; E) 80, 110

Tayfield, Hugh Joseph 'Toey' 1929-94 (Natal; Rhodesia; SA) 46, 47, 48, 52, 69, 154

Taylor, Brian b 19 Jun 1932 (Essex) 102, 191, 194

Taylor, Bruce Richard b 12 Jul 1943 (Canterbury; Wellington; NZ) 52

Taylor, Derek John Somerset b 12 Nov 1942 (Surrey; Somerset; GW) 122, 210

Taylor, Herbert Wilfred MC 1889-1973 (Natal; T; WP; SA) 31

Taylor, John Morris 1895-1971 (NSW; Aus) 138

Taylor, Mark Anthony b 27 Oct 1964 (NSW; Aus) 30, 32, 42

Taylor, Neil Royston 21 Jul 1959 (Kent) 110

Taylor, Robert William MBE b 17 Jul 1941 (Derbys; E) 54, 55, 58, 95, 98, 99, 174, 191, 194, 210

Tendulkar, Sachin Ramesh b 24 Apr 1973 (Bombay; I) 36, 37, 37, 68, 219

Terry, Richard Benjamin (umpire) 23

Thomas, Lynne b 29 Sep 1939 (West; Glam; E) 198

Thompson, George Joseph 1877-1943 (Northants; Auckland; E) 194

Thomson, Jeffrey Robert b 16 Aug 1950 (NSW; Q; Middx; Aus) 51, 211

Thomson, Nathaniel Frampton Davis 1839-96 (NSW; Aus) 22, 23, 24

Thornton, Charles Inglis 1850-1929 (CU; Kent; Middx) 79

Thwaites, Colin Geoffrey b 23 Jan 1955 (V) 141

Tillekeratne, Hashan Prasantha b 14 Jul 1967 (Nondescripts; SL) 44, 55, 56, 183, **183**, 187, 212

Timms, Bryan Stanley Valentine b 17 Dec 1940 (Hants; Warks) 108

Titmus, Frederick John MBE b 24 Nov 1932 (Middx; Surrey; OFS; E) 51, 57, 116, 190, 194

Tolchard, Roger William b 15 Jun 1946 (Leics; E) 114, 191, 194

Toogood, Giles John b 19 Nov 1961 (OU) 135

Townsend, Charles Lucas 1876-1958 (Glos; E) 85, 89

Townsend, Leslie Fletcher 1903-93 (Derbys; Auckland; E) 194

Traicos, Athanasios John b 17 May 1947 (Rhodesia; Mashonaland; Z) 61, 62

Travers, F. G. (Europeans) 174

Tribe, George Edward b 4 Oct 1920 (V; Northants; Aus) 118, 194

Trott, Albert Edwin 1873-1914 (V; Aus; Middx; Hawke's Bay; E) 62, 69, 85, 92, 156, 194

Walkley, Edgar Allen b 1878 (S Aus) 143

Wall, Thomas Welbourn 'Tim' 1904-81 (S Aus; Aus) 144

Waller, Andrew Christopher b 25 Sep 1959 (Mashonaland; Z) 215

Walsh, Courtney Andrew b 30 Oct 1962 (Jamaica; Glos; WI) 28, 46, 52, 69, 89

Walsh, John Edward 1912-1980 (NSW; Leics) 114

Walters, Kevin Douglas MBE (NSW; Aus) 35, 42, 142, 143

Waqar Hassan b 12 Sep 1932 (Services; Karachi; P) 179

Waqar Younis b 16 Nov 1971 (Multan; Utd Bank; Surrey; P) 48, 53, **53**, 69, 70, 87

Ward, Albert 1865-1939 (Yorks; Lancs; E) 39

Ward, David Mark b 10 Feb 1961 (Surrey) 110

Ward, William 1787-1849 (Surrey; Hants) 11

Wardle, John Henry 1923-85 (Yorks; E) 27, 51

Warne, Shane Keith b 13 Sep 1969 (V; Aus) **28**, 51, 69, 212

Warren, Arnold 1875-1951 (Derbys; E) 83

Warren, Russell John b 10 Sep 1971 (Northants) 74

Warton, Robert Gardner, Major (Essex; WP) 150, 156

Washbrook, Cyril CBE b 6 Dec 1914 (Lancs; E) 189

Wasim Akram b 3 Jun 1966 (PACO; Lahore; PIA; Lancs; P) 53, 57, 212

Wasim Bari b 23 Mar 1948 (Karachi; PIA; Sind; P) 54, 55, 59, 168

Wasim Hasan Raja b 3 Jul 1952 (Lahore; Sargodha; Universities; PIA; Punjab; Nat Bank; P) 70

Wass, Thomas George 1873-1953 (Notts) 120

Wassan, Atul Satish b 23 Mar 1968 (Delhi; I) 40

Watson, Frank Bramley 1898-1976 (Lancs) 112, 162

Watson, William b 7 Mar 1920 (Yorks; Leics; E) 114

Watson-Smith, Raymond b 20 Feb 1940 (Border) 152

Watt, Leslie b 17 Sep 1924 (Otago; NZ) 167

Waugh, Mark Edward b 2 Jun 1965 (NSW; Essex; Aus) 42, 143, **143**, 144

Waugh, Stephen Rodger b 2 Jun 1965 (NSW; Somerset; Aus) 42, 143, **143**, 144, 212

Wazir Mohammad b 22 Dec 1929 (Bahawalpur; Karachi; P) 179

Webb, Rupert Thomas b 11 Jul 1922 (Sussex; T) 126

Webbe, Alexander Josiah 1855-1941 (OU; Middx; E) 73

Webster, Dr Rudi Valentine b 10 Jun 1939 (Warks; Scotland; Barbados; Otago) 86

Weekes, Sir Everton de Courcy OBE b 26 Feb 1925 (Barbados; WI) 32, 35, 43

Wellard, Arthur William 1902-80 (Somerset; E) 122, 194

Wells, John 1759-1835 (Hambledon; Hants; E) 13

Wensley, Albert Frederick 1898-1970 (Sussex; Auckland; Nawanagar) 194

Wessels, Kepler Christoffel b 14 Sep 1957 (OFS; Sussex; WP; N Transvaal; Q; EP; Aus; SA) **20**, 62, **62**

Wettimuny, Mithra de Silva b 11 Jun 1951 (SL) 184

Wettimuny, Sidath b 12 Aug 1956 (SL) 184

Wettimuny, Sunil b 2 Feb 1949 (SL) 184

Wharton, Alan b 1923-93 (Lancs; Leics; E) 73

Whatmore, David Michael Roberets b 6 Apr 1949 (Alderney) 218

Wheatley, John 1860-1962 (Canterbury) 93

White, Cyril de Lacey 1909-87 (Border) 155

White, John Cornish 'Farmer' 1891-1961 (Somerset; E) 122, 190, 194

White, Rosemary b 22 Jan 1938 (Surrey) 201

White, Thomas 'Shock' or 'Daddy' 1740-1831 (Surrey) 11

White, William Michael Eastwood, Brigadier CBE b 22 May 1913 (CU; Northants) 219

Whitehead, Harry 1874-1944 (Leics) 130

Whittall, Guy James b 5 Sep 1972 (Matabeleland; Z) 187

Whysall, William Wilfrid 'Dodger' 1887-1930 (Notts; E) 120

Wickham, Archdale Palmer, Rev Preb 1855-1935 (OU; Somerset) 90

Wickham, FJ (T) 154

Wiener, Julien Mark b 1 May 1955 (V; Aus) 143

Wickremaratne, Rupanath (Colts CC) 183

Wickremaratne, Ranasinghe Pattikirikoralalage Aruna Hemantha b 21 Feb 1971 (Sinhalese SC; W Prov City) 183

Y

Z